Practical RichFaces

Second Edition

Max Katz
Ilya Shaikovsky

Apress®

Practical RichFaces, Second Edition

ISBN-13 (pbk): 978-1-4302-3449-4

ISBN-13 (electronic): 978-1-4302-3450-0

President and Publisher: Paul Manning
Lead Editor: Steve Anglin
Technical Reviewer: Jason Lee
Editorial Board: Clay Andres, Steve Anglin, Mark Beckner, Ewan Buckingham, Gary Cornell, Jonathan Gennick, Jonathan Hassell, Michelle Lowman, James Markham, Matthew Moodie, Duncan Parkes, Jeffrey Pepper, Frank Pohlmann, Douglas Pundick, Ben Renow-Clarke, Dominic Shakeshaft, Matt Wade, Tom Welsh
Coordinating Editor: Jessica Belanger
Copy Editor: Kimberly Burton
Compositor: Mary Sudul
Indexer: SPi Global
Cover Designer: Anna Ishchenko

Distributed to the book trade worldwide by Springer Science+Business Media, LLC., 233 Spring Street, 6th Floor, New York, NY 10013. Phone 1-800-SPRINGER, fax (201) 348-4505, e-mail orders-ny@springer-sbm.com, or visit www.springeronline.com.

For information on translations, please e-mail rights@apress.com, or visit www.apress.com.

Apress and friends of ED books may be purchased in bulk for academic, corporate, or promotional use. eBook versions and licenses are also available for most titles. For more information, reference our Special Bulk Sales–eBook Licensing web page at www.apress.com/bulk-sales.

The source code for this book is available to readers at www.apress.com. You will need to answer questions pertaining to this book in order to successfully download the code.

To Victoria and Evelyn
—Max

I dedicate this book to my wife, Zoya, and our son, Nikita,
who are my inspiration in everything I do
—Ilya

Contents at a Glance

Contents

About the Authors

■ **Max Katz** is a senior systems engineer and lead RIA (Rich Internet Application) strategist at Exadel, a software development company. He is a well-known speaker appearing at many conferences, webinars, and JUG (Java Users Groups) meetings.

Max leads Exadel's RIA and mobile strategy. Part of this role is working as the developer advocate for Tiggr Mobile Apps Builder (gotiggr.com), a cloud-based application for building mobile web and native apps for any device. In addition, Max leads Exadel's open-source projects (exadel.org), such as Fiji, Flamingo, and JavaFX Plug-in for Eclipse.

Max has been involved with RichFaces since its inception, publishing numerous articles, providing consulting and training, and authoring the first edition of *Practical RichFaces* (Apress, 2008). Max also co-authored the DZone RichFaces 3 Refcard and the DZone RichFaces 4 Refcard. You can find Max's writings about RIA and mobile technologies on his blog, mkblog.exadel.com, and you can find his thoughts about these topics and others on Twitter at @maxkatz.

Max has a BS in computer science from the University of California, Davis, and an MBA from Golden Gate University.

■ **Ilya Shaikovsky** is a product engineer at Exadel. He has worked on the popular RichFaces project since its inception.

As part of the RichFaces project, Ilya gathered new component requirements, built new custom components, and developed RichFaces demo applications. He also acted as a community liaison and helped answer customers' and users' questions. In addition, Ilya has led a number of large enterprise development projects that used RichFaces, solving many performance and scalability problems along the way. He also led the Exadel Fiji project, a rich JSF library for wrapping Flash and JavaFX as JSF components. Prior to the RichFaces project, Ilya worked on the Exadel Studio product line, now part of JBoss Developer Studio and JBoss Tools.

Ilya has produced a wide variety of information on RichFaces. He acted as a reviewer on the first edition of *Practical RichFaces* and wrote a chapter in it. He also co-authored the DZone RichFaces 3 Refcard and the DZone RichFaces 4 Refcard. In addition to this, he is the author of two RichFaces-related blogs: in.relation.to/Bloggers/Ilya and www.jroller.com/a4j/. You can follow Ilya on Twitter at @ilya_shaikovsky.

Ilya has a master's degree in computer science from Belarusian State University in the Republic of Belarus.

About the Technical Reviewer

 **Jason Lee** is a senior member of the technical staff for Oracle, where he works on the GlassFish project on the Administration Console and RESTful Administration interface teams. He has more than 14 years of professional experience, ranging from Java AWT desktop applications to enterprise web applications, in a variety of languages and frameworks. Jason has been involved with JavaServer Faces since 2005, both as a committer on Mojarra, the JSF reference implementation, as well as being a member of the JSF 2.0 Expert Group. He is active in the Oklahoma City Java Users Group, both as a speaker and former president. He blogs about various technologies at `http://blogs.steeplesoft.com`. Jason lives in Oklahoma with his wife, two sons, and one Boxer.

Acknowledgments

We are very fortunate to know some very smart people who helped us make this book so much better. We want to thank Maksim Turchyn, Eugenia Sergueeva, Philip Daineko, Andrii Kokov, and Anton Udovichenko (all from Exadel) for providing initial technical review.

We would like to extend a very big thank you to Willhelm Lehman, Ileana Lehman, Jay Balunas, Bernard Labno, Adrian Mitev, Whesley Hales, Brian Leathem, Daniel Hinojosa, Lukas Frync, Pavol Pitonak, Demetrio Filocamo, Prabhat Jha, Gleb Galkin, Anton Belevich, and Maksim Kashynski, whose amazing technical reviews made the book so much better.

We want to extend a special thank you to Jason Lee for his technical expertise and for patiently reviewing all our code examples.

We want to give a special thank you to Charles Cowens for always being there to edit our materials, provide writing advice, and trying to make our English "sound better."

We want to extend a special thank you to Pavel Yaschenko, your strong expertise in HTML, JavaScript, and CSS helped us tremendously.

We want to extend a special thank you to Alexander Smirnov, the original creator of RichFaces, for his technical review and for always being willing to answer any RichFaces questions. His "small personal" project in 2005 became the most popular JSF framework today.

We want to extend a very special thank you to Nick Belaevski for his technical review and, more importantly, for always being ready to help with any RichFaces questions and provide advice. Thank you for your tremendous contribution to RichFaces.

We want to thank everyone at Apress for all their guidance and support, especially Jessica Belanger for not giving up on us.

Lastly, we want to thank everyone at Exadel for supporting us through this endeavor.

Introduction

We have been involved with JSF and RichFaces for many years now, including teaching JSF and RichFaces courses for many years. From our experience, we have come to realize that many developers are using RichFaces and JSF without understanding the full potential of the technology. Without this understanding, developers can't fully utilize the framework.

Of course, after a bit of trial and error, almost everyone gets their application to work in some form. However, developers often don't understand why their particular application works. And, more importantly, developers get frustrated and grow to dislike the technology. That's an important reason we wrote this second edition of Practical RichFaces—to raise the level of understanding in the developer community so this frustration can be avoided and so that RichFaces and JSF can be appreciated for the great technologies they are.

This book is entirely based on the new and improved JSF 2 and covers the new and greatly improved RichFaces 4. We cover all the most important concepts, features, tags, and components available in RichFaces that you need to know—all in one place. While the book doesn't try to cover every single attribute for every single component, that's not really necessary. However, with the solid understanding of core concepts, features, and tags that you will get from this book, we guarantee you will be able to use any RichFaces component.

Who Should Read This Book

The book is for anyone with a basic knowledge of JSF who wants to learn how to build Ajax-based applications with RichFaces. If you are completely new to JSF, we recommend picking up a book on JSF 2. Even if you have been using RichFaces 4 (or RichFaces 3), this book will fill in many of the gaps. We are sure you will say at least once in the course of reading this book, "I didn't know that was possible with RichFaces!" or "I didn't know I could do that!"

CHAPTER 1

The Basics

Welcome to *Practical RichFaces*, second edition. In your hands (or on your computer/phone/tablet), you've got everything you need to start developing cool and rich Ajax applications with JSF and RichFaces. In this first chapter, we will give you a short overview of JavaServer Faces (JSF), as RichFaces is a framework for JSF. Although we do assume that you have some knowledge of JSF, don't worry—even if you are just starting, we made sure the material and all the examples in this book are very easy to understand. Once we cover JSF, we will discuss RichFaces: its features and the history behind it, how it got started and where it is today. Lastly, we will share two stories to help you keep an open mind when using JSF, as well as some tips on working with a server-side framework. The stories are from our personal experiences and should help you become a better JSF and RichFaces developer.

Tell Me About RichFaces First!

You bought this book to learn about RichFaces, so we are going to squeeze in this short section so you don't have to wait. We will then do quick overview of JSF, and go back to telling you more about RichFaces in more detail. You probably think of RichFaces as a rich component library (and that's fine). But, is it also much more. Rich components are just one of the main features that RichFaces offers. RichFaces is a rich framework for JSF and offers rich and Ajax components in two tag libraries (a4j: and rich:), a Skins feature, a client-side validation extension based on JSR-303 Bean Validation, and CDK (Component Development Kit).

Of course you get many other features, which we will cover throughout the book, such as advanced rendering features, event handling options, and Ajax client queue optimization. The components are something you can "feel and touch," so let us give you a quick example of what kind of components RichFaces offers.

The a4j: tag library offers many core or foundation components, such as buttons and links with built-in Ajax support, Ajax polling, and Ajax status. At this stage, however, it's more interesting to look at examples of components from the rich: tag library. In Figure 1-1, you can see a rich tab panel and calendar components.

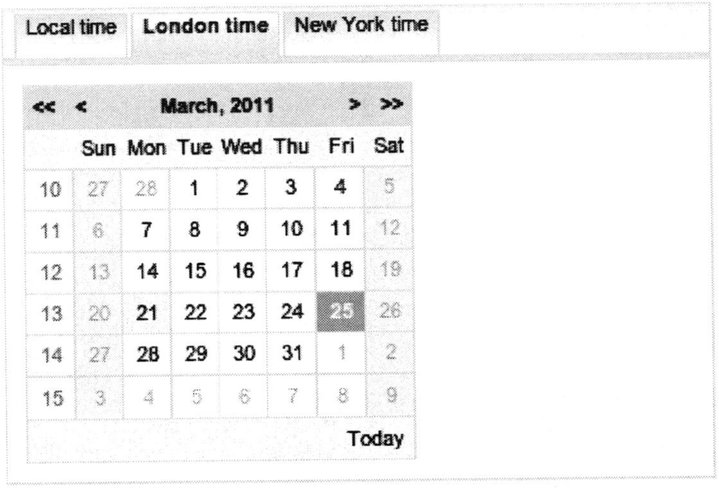

Figure 1-1. RichFaces tab panel and calendar (blueSky skin)

If you are reading an electronic version of this book, then Figure 1-1 will appear in light blue color. By changing just one parameter, we can render the page in the ruby skin, as shown in Figure 1-2. Another difference in Figure 1-2 is that it is also showing an optional control to select time. Each component offers a large number of customization options.

Figure 1-2. RichFaces tab panel and calendar with time selection (ruby skin)

The tabs can be switched via Ajax, as well as previous/next month in the calendar. Let's look at one more rich component, shown in Figure 1-3. It shows a rich inplace input component displayed three times. Inplace input renders initially as a label (first component); when clicked, it switches to an input (second component); and then back to a label when editing is done (third component).

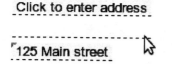

Figure 1-3. Rich inplace input component (shown in three modes)

We hope you now get an idea of what RichFaces can do. Trust us, it can do a whole lot more. We will now take a brief detour to tell you a little bit about JSF. Why? Well, RichFaces is a JSF frameworks, it is based entirely on JSF so it's important to know how the underlying framework works.

What is JSF?

Let's start with the simplest definition. JSF is just a framework for building web applications. To be a little bit more specific, we are building a browser-based or HTML application, no plug-ins involved. You are probably thinking, there are at least a couple dozen other frameworks that would fit this description. JSF has a number of features that makes it different than other frameworks. Let's review them.

JSF Application Is Built Out of UI Components

JSF is a Java framework for building browser-based user interfaces (UIs) out of reusable components. The emphasis in JSF is on UI components. When working with UI components, you won't deal with HTML markup directly because JSF and other rich components will provide all the necessary UI widgets to build the application. However, HTML tags still play an important role in the layout of the page. Within the components themselves, renderers (Java classes for generating HTML) are responsible for producing the appropriate markup. Because you are building web applications and the client is basically the browser, the markup needed is HTML (although it can be anything like WML, SGL, or even XML) so the components' renderers will generate the HTML markup that will be sent to the client (browser).

JSF Is a Standard

JSF is a part of the Java 6 (and 5) Enterprise Edition (Java EE) platform. This means that a bunch of companies and individuals got together and agreed on how the framework should work. The debate whether standards are good or bad is beyond the scope of this book but at least the framework was designed by more than just one entity.

JSF Has Two Main Versions

Today there are two JSF versions: version 1.2 is a part of the Java EE 5 platform and JSF 2 is a part of the Java EE 6 platform.

JSF Has Two Main Implementations

Because JSF is a specification, today there are two main implementations. The first is Mojarra, a reference implementation from Oracle. The other is MyFaces from Apache. A great place to learn more about JSF is JavaServerFaces.org (`www.javaserverfaces.org`).

JSF Is Very Extendable

The extensibility feature is probably most responsible for making JSF a popular tool for building web applications. From the beginning, JSF was designed to be extended. Through standards, JSF allows you to extend the framework with new features and more advanced functionality. You are getting new functionality, but you are doing it in a standard and accepted way. One area that benefits most from this is the rich UI component ecosystem, which includes RichFaces. This eco-system is not limited to UI components—custom converters, validators, view handlers, and other extensions are created as well.

The Most Important JSF Features

JSF offers a long list of features. However, since this is not a dedicated JSF book, we will briefly cover the three most important features: user interface components, events, and the new Ajax functionality in JSF 2. If you feel you need to review your JSF skills, we recommend the following two books: *Core JavaServer Faces, Third Edition* by David Geary and Cay Horstmann (Prentice Hall, 2010) and *JavaServer Faces 2.0, The Complete Reference* by Ed Burns and Chris Schalk (McGraw-Hill, 2009).

■ **Tip**   Two really great places to start learning JSF are `http://javaserverfaces.org` and `http://jsfcentral.com`.

User Interface Components

UI components are the main feature of the JSF framework. JSF ships with about 30 ready-to-use user interface components. Usually referred to as standard components, they provide basic user interface widgets for input, output, commands (buttons and links), labels, and layout, as well as simple controls to display tabular data. A number of utility components such as loading styles, scripts, and HTML page sections (head, body) are available as well.

All JSF web applications are built out of components. A JSF UI component is a server-side Java object capable of processing input, firing actions, and rendering content. Component hierarchy is what JSF deals with. And tags are used for building that component tree. A JSF component can be as simple as an input field or as sophisticated as a tabbed panel or tree. For example, the following tag represents an input component:

```
<h:inputText value="#{order.amount}"/>
```

This is an input component that is bound (connected) to some Java object. You would place this tag on a JSF page instead of directly writing HTML code. The component behind the tag knows how to generate all the necessary and correct HTML, CSS, and JavaScript. Tags represent the server-side UI components and are used to build the JSF component tree shown in Figure 1-4.

Component Rendering

The JSF framework separates a component from the way it is presented (encoding) and the way input is processed (decoding). The appearance of the component can be easily varied for the type of display device available (for example, a mobile phone). For this book, you'll work only with the HTML rendering kit that JSF provides out of the box.

The following list demonstrates some of the features renderers provide:

- Rendering can be done by the component itself or delegated to a special renderer class.
- Rendering markup such as WML and XML, in addition to HTML.
- Standard JSF components come with an HTML 4.0.1 rendering kit.

Figure 1-4 shows how all this fits together.

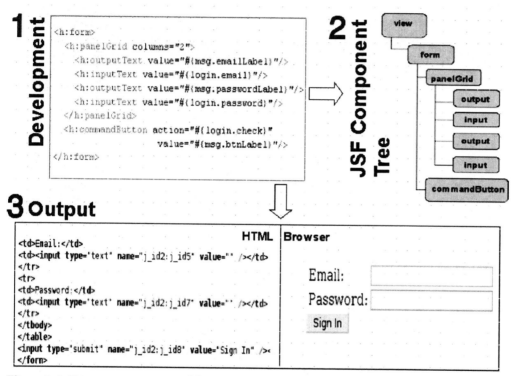

Figure 1-4. Tags represent server-side components. Server-side components render markup (HTML) at the end of the JSF request.

Let's walk through the numbered parts of this figure.

1. This is a JSF page that consists of JSF tags. When the page is processed by JSF, these tags create JSF UI components (Java classes) shown in the second part of the figure.

2. This is the JSF UI component tree that represents the components defined on the JSF page. The component tree goes through a sophisticated life cycle where various things happen, such as conversion and validation. At the end, JSF will ask each component renderer to render markup.

3. The panel on the left is the generated HTML code and the panel on the right shows what users see in the browser. This is just the standard HTML 4.0.1 version.

As you can see, usually you won't be working with HTML markup directly. You will simply use components that render the entire necessary markup.

A note on rendering other markup languages. In the early days of JSF, the idea that components can render different markup based on client device was an interesting one. At that time, the mobile devices available usually worked with markup languages such as XML or WML. Today the situation is very different. Most modern mobiles devices, such as smart phones and tablets, come with powerful browsers supporting all the latest HTML, JavaScript, and CSS features. In some cases, the browser on a mobile device is better than the one on a PC. This means that generation markup other than HTML is no longer as important or has simply faded with the availability of mobile phones and other devices that support HTML.

This doesn't mean that renderers no longer play an important role. Even though HTML is now supported on various devices, renderers still play a role in regards to the kind of markup (HTML) that is generated. With the explosion of mobile devices, we now have to develop applications for a large number of different screen sizes. There is only so much "content" (or real estate) that can fit on a mobile phone with a 3.5-inch screen, or a tablet with a 7-inch screen, or even on a large laptop screen. This is exactly where renderers can help. Based on the device, screen size, and even screen resolution, the renderers can provide different markup.

Events

JSF takes you beyond the request/response paradigm and provides a powerful event-based model. The UI components that you use to build the user interface are sending events (when activated or clicked) to the server (browser events such as click are mapped to server-side component events). Listeners then process the events. For example, clicking a button (which is a UI component) is an event that is processed by an appropriate listener. (The JSF event-based model offers an approach to UI development similar to other user interface frameworks such as Swing and Flex.)

For instance, in the *#{simpleBean.save}* expression defined in an action attribute, *save* is a method inside *simpleBean* bean. It is usually referred to as a JSF action and will be invoked when the button is clicked:

```
<h:commandButton value="Submit" action="#{simpleBean.save}"/>
```

Before we continue, you need to be familiar with the JSF life-cycle phases shown in Figure 1-5 and need to understand what each phase does. We will be using this same diagram to show RichFaces concepts. Make sure you understand what each phase does and what happens to the flow in case of a conversion/validation error or when using the immediate="true" attribute. Understanding the life cycle can also help with debugging your JSF applications with phase listeners. You will be using a phase listener later in this book. In case you need to brush up on JSF phases, this article at Javabeat (www.javabeat.net/articles/54-request-processing-lifecycle-phases-in-jsf-1.html) is a good place to do that.

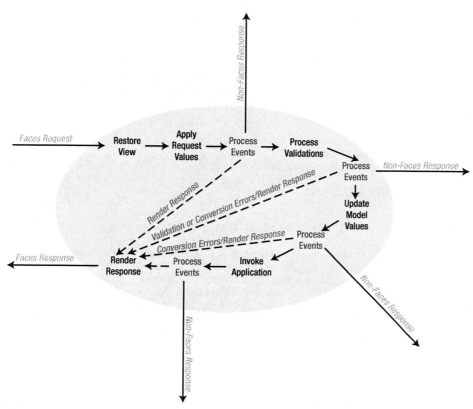

Figure 1-5. JSF life cycle

Ajax

When JSF 1.x was developed, it didn't have any Ajax features simply because Ajax didn't exist as we know it today. Luckily in 2006 RichFaces came along and made it very easy to add Ajax functionality to existing or new JSF applications. For example, if you had a standard input text component like the following:

```
<h:inputText value="#{order.amount}"/>
```

To send an Ajax request based on some event was very easy with RichFaces. All you had to do is add the `<a4j:support>` tag, specify the event to fire the Ajax request, and specify which components to re-render, as follows:

```
<h:inputText value="#{order.amount}">
    <a4j:support event="onkeyup" reRender="id1"/>
</h:inputText/>
<h:outputText value="#{order.total}" id="id1"/>
```

When JSF EG (Expert Group) started working on JSF version 2, they introduced basic Ajax support into the specification. The Ajax behavior `<f:ajax>` in JSF 2 is closely based on the popular RichFaces 3 `<a4j:support>` tag. Taking the above example, adding Ajax support in JSF 2 is done like this:

```
<h:inputText value="#{order.amount}">
  <f:ajax event="keyup" render="id1"/>
</h:inputText/>
<h:outputText value="#{order.total}" id="id1"/>
```

This example looks very similar to the RichFaces 3 example. The obvious changes are the new behavior (<f:ajax>), the event is specified without the *on*-part and instead of reRender, the *render* attribute is used. However, the core Ajax concepts are very similar. In addition to using <f:ajax> behavior, it's also possible to send an Ajax request in a programmatic way, as follows:

```
<h:form id="form">
  <h:commandButton id="button" value="Update"
    onclick="jsf.ajax.request(this,event, {render:'form:out'});  ↵
    return false;" />
  <h:output Text value="#{timeBean.now}" id="out"/>
</h:form>
```

Even though basic, Ajax is now part of the JSF 2 standard. We will cover more <f:ajax> features later in the book.

Before we tell you more about RichFaces, we must ask: why would you use JSF? Well, the shortest answer is that (after a short learning curve) JSF simplifies development. The basic purpose of any framework is to simplify development by hiding the tasks that are common to any application. JSF does exactly that. You don't have to worry anymore about how to get data from the request or how to define navigation or convert values. JSF provides all this and more out of the box. If all the plumbing is covered by the framework, that leaves you more time to work on the actual application. Finally, a JSF component approach makes it the perfect technology to be used with Ajax.

An Overview of RichFaces

If you are wondering why we need RichFaces if there is now Ajax functionality in JSF 2, it's because the Ajax functionality in JSF 2 is very basic. You only get <f:ajax> behavior. That's not enough to build real rich enterprise Ajax applications. That's exactly why you need RichFaces, a rich framework for JSF. It consists of the following parts:

- Rich and Ajax components divided into two tag libraries (a4j:, rich:)

- Skins

- Client-side and object validation extension for Bean Validation (JSR 303)

- CDK (Component Development Kit)

Besides these main parts, RichFaces extends the standard JSF 2 Ajax request queue, and adds various rendering optimization attributes that we will cover in this book. A RichFaces application can also be deployed in the cloud, to places such as GAE (Google Apps Engine), Amazon EC2, and CloudBees, and OpenShift. RichFaces not only extends JSF, it makes JSF richer. In fact, you can't use RichFaces without JSF. You use RichFaces with either the Mojarra JSF (Oracle RI) implementation or the MyFaces implementation. RichFaces simply provides ready-to-use Ajax components (and other features) to enable building Ajax-based applications. Another way to look at it as extra JSF components beyond what standard JSF provides. These components provide all the necessary JavaScript, so you almost never have to work with JavaScript directly.

> ■ **Note** Whenever we mention RichFaces, we always refer to RichFaces version 4. RichFaces 3.x is based on JSF 1.2. RichFaces 3.3.3 supports JSF 1.2 and has very basic support for JSF 2. This version was introduced for projects that needed to be deployed on a Java EE 6 application server, which shipped with JSF 2 when RichFaces 4 wasn't yet available. Everything in this book is based on RichFaces 4 version. Client-side validation is only available starting with RichFaces 4.

Table 1-1 summarizes JSF and RichFaces version compatibility.

Table 1-1. *JSF and RichFaces Compatibility Matrix*

	JSF 1.1	JSF 1.2	JSF 2
RichFaces 3.1.x	X		
RichFaces 3.3.2		X	
RichFaces 3.3.3		X	X (basic support)
RichFaces 4			X

RichFaces's Component Tag Libraries

RichFaces components are divided into two tag libraries: one tag library is called a4j:, and the other is called rich:. The a4j: tag library provides page-level Ajax support and other utility tags. It basically provides foundation-like controls where you decide how to send a request, what to send to the server, and what to update. This approach gives you a lot of power and flexibility. The rich: tag library provides rich UI components. Rich components are anything beyond what the standard HTML tags provide; for example, a tab panel. There is no standard JSF nor HTML tag for a tab panel, so RichFaces provides one that makes it a rich component (beyond out-of-the-box HTML). Many rich components also have built-in Ajax support. These components fire an Ajax request and do partial page updates automatically. And most of them support pluggable and customizable Ajax behavior using a4j: tags.

RichFaces Skins

Another major feature is skins. Any number of skins (defined via a property file) can be created with different color schemes. When a particular skin is set, component renderers will refer to that skin and generate colors and styles based on that skin. This means you can easily change the look and feel of the whole application by simply switching to a different skin. Skins can be customized, created, and overwritten on a CSS level. We have dedicated Chapter 12 to this topic.

RichFaces Client-side Validation

JSF comes with a number of out-of-the-box validators and JSF 2 now also supports Bean Validation (JSR 303). RichFaces 4 takes validation a step further and adds client-side validation based on Bean

Validation. It is now possible to perform validation on the client according to JSR-303 definitions. It means that basic client-side validation no longer requires creating and plugging custom JavaScript validators to components; it just synchronizes them for different layers at the framework level.

Also, with RichFaces you will be able to achieve that validation across the whole application following the DRY (http://en.wikipedia.org/wiki/Don%27t_repeat_yourself) principle. In case validating on the client is not possible, Ajax fallback (server-side) support is available. Besides, RichFaces provides so-called Object Validation that allows validating server-side Entities in the whole, even if some properties are not present in current view. Client-side validation is covered in Chapter 11.

RichFaces' Component Development Kit

Another part of the framework is the Component Development Kit (CDK). The CDK includes various Maven archetypes, a code generation facility, descriptors and tests generation facility, and a templating facility that allows the creation of renderer classes using only page code. These features enable a component developer to avoid the routine process of component creation. The CDK greatly simplifies and speeds up rich component development with built-in Ajax support. This edition of the book now includes CDK coverage. CDK is covered in Chapter 13.

Using RichFaces with CDI and Dependency Injection

Contexts and Dependency Injection, or CDI (JSR 299), and Dependency Injection for Java (JSR 330) are both part of the Java EE 6 platform. Both provide services and components to make it simpler to develop enterprise Java applications. Although JSF 2 now provides a simpler way to configure beans with annotations, using CDI beans instead of JSF beans gives a lot more flexibility and power to the developer by providing a unified programming model. JSF 2 works with CDI Beans out of the box. As RichFaces 4 is based on JSF 2, CDI can be used with any RichFaces 4 components as well. So that we don't introduce another layer (which is really outside the scope of this book), examples in this book will use standard JSF beans. In all examples, JSF beans can be easily replaced with CDI beans.

RichFaces: A Historical Perspective

If you search for RichFaces, eventually you will see a reference to Ajax4jsf. This section provides a brief history of Ajax4jsf and how it became part of RichFaces. Ajax4jsf has its roots in RichFaces. The Ajax4jsf framework was created and designed by Alexander Smirnov. In early 2005, he was looking to add a "hot" new technology along with the associated experience to his résumé. Roughly at the same time, Jesse James Garrett was establishing the concept of Ajax. Meanwhile, JSF was starting to pick up steam. Alexander figured, why not just merge the two so it would be easy to have Ajax functionality within a JSF application?

He started the project on SourceForge.net, called it Telamon (taken from the Shakespearean play, *Antony and Cleopatra*), and Ajax4jsf was born. In the fall of that same year, Smirnov joined Exadel, a software engineering company, and continued to develop the framework. Smirnov's goal was to create a tool that was easy to use, would add client-side richness to pure server-side JSF technology, and could be used with any existing JSF component libraries.

The first version of what would become Ajax4jsf was released in March 2006. It wasn't quite a stand-alone thing yet. Rather, it was part of a product called Exadel RichFaces. Later in the same year, RichFaces was split off, and the Ajax4jsf framework was born.

While RichFaces provided out-of-the-box components, or what's called a component-centric Ajax approach (components that do everything you need), Ajax4jsf provided what's called page-wide Ajax support. You as a developer specify what parts of the page should be processed on the server after client-side user actions, and also what parts should be rendered back (rendering is happening on the server and partial DOM updating is happening on the client) after processing. Ajax4jsf became an open source project hosted on Java.net, while RichFaces became a commercial JSF component library. Ajax4jsf became a very popular project because it arrived at the right time (just when people were starting to add Ajax to their applications), but more importantly, because it was very easy to use.

If you had a button such as

```
<h:commandButton value="Submit" action="#{bean.save}"/>
```

and wanted to add Ajax capability, all you had to do was change the namespace and add a *reRender* attribute (RichFaces 3 code), as follows:

```
<a4j:commandButton value="Submit" action="#{bean.save}" reRender="id1, id2"/>
```

And if you had an input field and wanted to add Ajax capability to it, then all you had to do next was add a `<a4:support>` tag inside, as follows:

```
<h:inputText value="#{order.amount}">
  <a4j:support event="onkeyup" reRender="id1, id2"/>
</h:inputText/>
```

Fast-forward to March 2007. JBoss and Exadel forged a partnership where Ajax4jsf and RichFaces would be under the JBoss umbrella and called JBoss Ajax4jsf and JBoss RichFaces. RichFaces would also be open source and free. In September 2007, JBoss and Exadel decided to recombine Ajax4jsf and RichFaces under the RichFaces name. This made sense because both libraries were free and open source. Having just one product solved many version and compatibility issues that existed before, such as figuring out which version of Ajax4jsf works with which version of RichFaces.

Although today you will still see an `a4j:` namespace used, the product is now called RichFaces.

Before we end this chapter, we would like to offer some advice from our personal experience that will help you become a better JSF and RichFaces developer.

Understanding That JSF Application Is Running on the Server

Based on our experience teaching JSF, it is sometimes difficult for people who are new to JSF to grasp the idea behind the JSF component tree and how it relates to what they see in the browser. It's important to keep in mind that JSF is a server-side framework (thus the name JavaServer Faces). This means the application is running on the server. This also means that any event processing will be done on the server. Now, how does this all fit with what you see in the browser? The browser is basically a user-readable view of the tree. It's just a mirror image of the tree, but in a format (the browser) you can understand. When building a JSF application, it might help to think you are always working with the JSF component tree. Anything you change or invoke is always on the component tree, and the browser is just a client for displaying pages.

You might be wondering, but what about Ajax? In the context of JSF, when using rich components, they will render all the necessary JavaScript to send an Ajax request from the browser to the server. When the request is done, JSF will render some components from the component tree and send that response back to the browser. Upon receiving the response, JavaScript in the browser will do a DOM update (or partial page update). Even though we now have rich components, Ajax JSF requests are still sent to the server. To give you a little head start, there are also what's called client-side events. These events happen on the browser, such as expanding or collapsing a panel. In such case no request is sent to the server. We will cover them in more detail later in the book.

When Starting with JSF, Keep an Open Mind

It's not difficult to find forums, blog posts, and other resources from people who are just starting with JSF and are dissatisfied with the framework. You must remember that most people who are starting with JSF are coming from JSP, Struts, or a similar homegrown framework. When they start evaluating JSF, they bring the same style and development approach to JSF that they used with JSP and Struts. This is where all the problems start.

You can't take that approach and use it with JSF. It provides a whole different paradigm to web development—as we've explained. The user interface is developed from UI components; it's very different from what people are used to doing with JSP and Struts. So when someone tries to do simple things in a "JSP way" in JSF, they fail and get frustrated. He might say, "But I could do this in JSP in about five minutes." Of course, he or she probably could, but JSP is not really doing anything more than mixing Java and HTML. JSP provides so little abstraction that you can do basically anything—even if in most cases it isn't done correctly, the key is that it was still accomplished one way or another.

This approach doesn't work anymore in JSF. Before you become dissatisfied with JSF, it's important to spend at least some time learning the framework and understanding how it works before actually evaluating it for a project. Put your JSP or Struts approach aside for a second, and learn how to build web applications using UI components. We promise that you will have much more success with JSF this way.

Summary

This chapter briefly introduced JSF, Ajax, and RichFaces. The goal was to give you a general picture of how all these technologies fit together. In Chapter 2, you'll install the tools you'll use in this book, and then you will jump into using one of the first RichFaces tags, <a4j:ajax>.

CHAPTER 2

Getting Started

In this chapter we are going to get our hands dirty. We will set up our working environment so that you can try all the examples. As JSF 2 now has Ajax functionality built-in, we will cover that first and then move on to RichFaces and start showing you how RichFaces extends that functionality.

Setting Up

RichFaces can be used in any container that is JSF 2 compatible. This means all servers compliant with the Java EE 6 specification (JBoss AS6/7, Glassfish 3) and all major servlet containers (Tomcat, Jetty, and Resin).

Adding RichFaces to an Existing JSF 2 Project

Not to tie you to any specific IDE (integrated development environment), but we will use Apache Maven to set up a project. Since RichFaces is built on top of JSF 2, its installation is as easy as adding a few JARs to your project. Configure your repositories following the Maven Getting Started Guide located on the JBoss Community web site at http://community.jboss.org/wiki/MavenGettingStarted-Users. Then, simply add Listing 2-1 to your projects pom.xml. Complete Maven guide can be found at: http://www.sonatype.com/books/mvnref-book/reference.

Listing 2-1. Add this to your projects pom.xml

```
<dependencyManagement>
  <dependencies>
    <dependency>
      <groupId>org.richfaces</groupId>
      <artifactId>richfaces-bom</artifactId>
      <version>${richfaces.version}</version>
      <scope>import</scope>
      <type>pom</type>
    </dependency>
  </dependencies>
</dependencyManagement>
…
<dependency>
  <groupId>org.richfaces.ui</groupId>
  <artifactId>richfaces-components-ui</artifactId>
```

```
</dependency>
<dependency>
  <groupId>org.richfaces.core</groupId>
  <artifactId>richfaces-core-impl</artifactId>
</dependency>
```

For other build systems, such as Ant, just add the following JARs to your projects `WEB-INF/lib` directory:

- `richfaces-core-api-<ver>.jar`
- `richfaces-core-impl-<ver>.jar`
- `richfaces-components-api-<ver>.jar`
- `richfaces-components-ui-<ver>.jar`
- `sac-1.3.jar`
- `cssparser-0.9.5.jar`
- `google-guava-r08.jar`

▓ **Note** Version of `sac-x.x.jar` and `cssparster-x.x.x.jar` are the most current as of writing of this book. Please check the JBoss Community RichFaces web site at `www.jboss.org/richfaces` for the latest versions.

Optional Dependencies

There are a number of optional JAR files (dependencies) you may want to add to a RichFaces project depending on your deployment or features you want to use. The optional JAR files are for client-side validation when using Apache Tomcat, caching, and using Component Development Kit annotations.

Validation Dependencies

If you are deploying to Apache Tomcat and will be using client-side validation, then the following JARs are also needed:

- `validation-api.jar`
- `hibernate-validator.jar`
- `slf4j-api.jar`
- `slf4j-jdk14.jar`

Listing 2-2 shows the Maven dependency that should be used.

Listing 2-2. *The Maven dependency that should be used*

```
<dependency>
    <groupId>org.hibernate</groupId>
    <artifactId>hibernate-validator</artifactId>
    <version>4.1.0.Final</version>
</dependency>
```

▨ **Note** validation-api will be brought in transitively with hibernate-validator.

If deploying to a Java EE 6 server, then these libraries are not needed with the application because they are included in the server. It's still a good idea to include the dependency, but change the scope to provided in order to use during the application build.

Caching Dependencies

For optimal performance it's recommended to add one of the following caching frameworks to the application classpath: Ehcache, JBoss Cache, or OSCache. When you create a new RichFaces project with the RichFaces Maven archetype, Ehcache dependency is present in the pom.xml file, as shown in Listing 2-3.

Listing 2-3. Create a new RichFaces project with the RichFaces Maven archetype

```
<dependency>
    <groupId>net.sf.ehcache</groupId>
    <artifactId>ehcache</artifactId>
</dependency>
```

CDK (Component Development Kit) Annotations Dependencies

Listing 2-4 shows compile time dependency. It is only needed if you are creating or accessing RichFaces components instances in your application actions or listeners in order to define CDK annotations.

Listing 2-4. Shows compile time dependency

```
<dependency>
    <groupId>org.richfaces.cdk</groupId>
    <artifactId>annotations</artifactId>
    <scope>provided</scope>
</dependency>
```

Creating a New Project with RichFaces

The RichFaces project also contains several Maven archetypes to quickly create projects (including one for a Google App Engine targeted project).

Listing 2-5 shows a simple project generation where groupId defines the package for Java classes (for example, managed beans) and artifactId defines the name for the project.

Listing 2-5. Shows a simple project generation

```
mvn archetype:generate
  -DarchetypeGroupId=org.richfaces.archetypes
  -DarchetypeArtifactId=richfaces-archetype-simpleapp
  -DarchetypeVersion=<version>
  -DgroupId=<groupId>
  -DartifactId=<artifactId>
```

Listing 2-6 shows actual code for generating a RichFaces project.

Listing 2-6. Generating a RichFaces project

```
mvn archetype:generate \
  -DarchetypeGroupId=org.richfaces.archetypes \
  -DarchetypeArtifactId=richfaces-archetype-simpleapp \
  -DarchetypeVersion=4.0.0.Final \
  -DgroupId=org.richfaces.book  \
  -DartifactId=richfaces4-start
```

Listing 2-7 shows a standard Maven project structure.

Listing 2-7. The standard Maven project structure

```
richfaces4-start
    /src
    /target
    pom.xml
    readme.txt
```

The project comes with a simple one-page application. Let's deploy and run the project to make sure everything works. If you open the readme.txt file, you will see the commands to build the application for either a Tomcat or a JBoss 6 server.

▓ **Tip** If you want to try the latest snapshot version, change the version to 4.0.1-SNAPSHOT or 4.1.0-SNAPSHOT.

The Tomcat command is as follows:

```
mvn clean package
```

The following is a Tomcat and JBoss 6 command:

```
mvn clean package -P release
```

As you can see, creating a new RichFaces 4 project is very simple and you can easily open it in any IDE that supports importing a Maven-based project. Even though it's possible to use plain Eclipse (we recommend Eclipse for Java EE Developer) there is one IDE that has the best RichFaces 4 support out there, and that's JBoss Tools or JBoss Developer Studio.

JBoss Tools is an open source and free set of plug-ins for Eclipse, which provides wizards, advanced source and visual tools for building JSF 2 and RichFaces 4 applications. Additional features include Seam, CDI, JPA, and Hibernate tools. You can download JBoss Tools from www.jboss.org/tools. As of writing of this book, you would want to download JBoss Tools version 3.2 for Eclipse 3.6 (or the latest version 3.3 for Eclipse 3.7).

You will also find instructions on how to install JBoss Tools. It's rather simple: you will need to download the latest supported Eclipse for Java EE developers and then point to the JBoss Tools plug-ins URL in the Eclipse Install Software screen. Finally, you will need a servlet container such as Tomcat to deploy the application. We recommend Tomcat 7.

If you would rather install everything from one file (Eclipse, JBoss Tools), then you can choose JBoss Developer Studio. You can download JBoss Developer Studio from www.jboss.com/products/devstudio/.

Once you set up Eclipse or Eclipse with JBoss Tools, there are two ways to import the Maven project into Eclipse. One method is to execute the following command inside the project root folder:

```
mvn eclipse:eclipse -Dwtpversion=2.0
```

This command makes it possible to import the project into Eclipse by adding Eclipse project configuration files such as .project and .classpath. Once you run this command in Eclipse, select File/Import/General/Existing Project into Workspace and point to the project root directory.

An alternative method is by installing the M2Eclipse (http://m2eclipse.sonatype.org/) plug-in, which helps with working with Maven-based projects in Eclipse. If you install the optional Integration with Web Tools Project (WTP) M2Eclipse extension, it will allow you to easily deploy to a Tomcat server. Once installed, select File/Import/Maven/Existing Maven Projects and point to project root.

░ **Tip**   If Eclipse is not your cup of tea, NetBeans and IntelliJ are excellent IDEs and both have first class Maven support.

Configuring RichFaces

There is nothing you actually need to do to configure RichFaces. If you look inside the web.xml file in the generated project, you will see no mention of a RichFaces filter. Starting with RichFaces 4, you don't need to register a filter in the web.xml file. If RichFaces JARs are present in the project, RichFaces will be used.

Configuring a Skin

The only feature you might want to configure is a RichFaces skin. Skins are covered in detail in Chapter 13, but to use any of the out-of-the-box skins, just set the context parameter shown in Listing 2-8.

Listing 2-8. Setting RichFaces skin in web.xml file

```
<context-param>
    <param-name>org.richfaces.skin</param-name>
    <param-value>ruby</param-value>
</context-param>
```

ruby is one of the built-in skins. You can choose any skin from the following list:

- DEFAULT
- plain
- emeraldTown
- blueSky
- wine
- japanCherry
- ruby
- classic

- deepMarine
- NULL

Ajax in JSF 2

JSF 2 comes with basic Ajax functionality built in. If you have used RichFaces 3, then you will see that JSF 2 Ajax was greatly inspired by the popular RichFaces <a4j:support> tag. You will see that the concepts are the same, with a few things changed, such as attribute names. If you are new to RichFaces, don't worry, in this chapter we will cover everything from the beginning.

Ajax in JSF 2 comes in a form <f:ajax> behavior. Notice that we call it a behavior instead of a component. A behavior is a new concept in JSF 2. A behavior in JSF 2 is a client-side behavior (functionality) that is added to a component. Let's see how to use the standard Ajax functionality in JSF 2 before we get to RichFaces.

When working with Ajax in the context of JSF, you need to keep three things in mind: First, how to send an Ajax request; second, what to process on the server (partial view processing); and third, what to render (partial view rendering).

Sending an Ajax Request

Sending an Ajax request is pretty straight forward: you really just have one option and that's using <f:ajax> behavior. This behavior is always attached to another UI component on a page; it's never used by itself. Listing 2-9 shows an example.

Listing 2-9. *Sending an Ajax Request*

```
<h:inputText value="#{bean.text}">
    <f:ajax />
</h:inputText>
```

That's pretty simple, right? We just added the ability to fire an Ajax request when the value inside the input field changes. The Ajax request is fired from the client (browser) and always on some browser event, such as click, change, and so forth. To be more precise, it can be any event supported by the parent UI component. Components represent HTML elements in the browser, so it's all the events that are supported by that particular HTML element.

The managed bean is shown in Listing 2-10.

Listing 2-10. *Managed bean*

```
@ManagedBean
@RequestScoped
public class Bean {

    private String text;

    // getter and setter
}
```

You probably noticed that we didn't actually specify the event, but said that the Ajax request would be fired when the value in the input field changes. The reason the Ajax request would fire on value change is because the default valuechange event is used. Every UI component in JSF 2 has a standard event on which the Ajax request would be fired if one is not explicitly specified. For example, with `<h:commandButton>` the default event is action.

When we want to fire an Ajax request on an event other than the default, or when we just want to make the code more readable by showing the event, then the event attribute is used. It is described in Table 2-1.

Table 2-1. Event attribute

Attribute	Description
event	String on which event an Ajax request will be fired. If not specified, a default behavior based on a parent component will be applied. The default event is action for ActionSource (for example, button) components and valueChange for EditableValueHolder components (for example, input). action and valueChange are actual String values that can be an applied event attribute.

If we wanted to specify the change event in our example, which is also the default event, it would look like in Listing 2-11 and work exactly the same way.

Listing 2-11. Specify the change event

```
<h:inputText value="#{bean.text}">
    <f:ajax event="change"/>
</h:inputText>
```

Or we could use a different event, as shown in Listing 2-12.

Listing 2-12. Changing the default event

```
<h:inputText value="#{bean.text}">
    <f:ajax event="keyup"/>
</h:inputText>
```

░ **Note** If you are familiar with RichFaces 3, you specify the event with on [eventName], for example onchange. In JSF 2 and RichFaces 4, you only specify the actual action: keyup.

If we were using a button, it would look like in Listing 2-13.

Listing 2-13. Example button

```
<h:commandButton value="Save">
    <f:ajax/>
</h:commandButton>
```

We are not specifying the event, as it will default to click. If we wanted to specify a different event, we would use the event attribute shown in Listing 2-14.

Listing 2-14. Event attribute

```
<h:commandButton value="Save">
    <f:ajax event="mouseover"/>
</h:commandButton>
```

Now that we covered the basics of firing an Ajax request, let's add a very important part: partial view rendering.

Partial View Rendering

Now that we know how to fire an Ajax request, we also would like to do a partial page update or partial view rendering.

■ **Note** From now on, whenever we use <f:ajax> tag, we will specify the event even if it's the default event. We believe it makes the code more readable and easier to understand.

As we are in the context of JSF, we can specify which component or components we would like to update or render via the render attribute described in Table 2-2.

Table 2-2. render attribute

Attribute	Description
render	Determines ids of components to be rendered.

Updating our example would look like Listing 2-15.

Listing 2-15. Updating the example

```
<h:form>
    <h:panelGrid>
        <h:inputText value="#{bean.text}" >
            <f:ajax event="keyup" render="text"/>
        </h:inputText>
        <h:outputText id="text" value="#{bean.text}" />
    </h:panelGrid>
</h:form>
```

On every keyup, an Ajax request will be fired to the server. The request will go through the standard JSF life cycle, but instead of rendering the entire view, we are only going to render the <h:outputText> component with text id.

▓ **Note** In RichFaces 3, the attribute to specify what to re-render is called `reRender`. In JSF 2 it is called `render`. As RichFaces 4 is based on JSF 2, it uses `render` in all components. You could also define ids using absolute addressing, such as when updating a component with the same "text" id placed in other form. For example, `render=":form2:text"`.

In the earlier example, we set `render` to one component. We can also decide to render more than one component. In this case, we would just list the ids of all components, space separated, as follows:

```
<f:ajax event="keyup" render="id1 id2 id3"/>
```

In case you don't want to list every single component, it's possible to render just the parent container, such as `<h:panelGrid>`. In this case, all its children components will also be rendered, as shown in Listing 2-16.

Listing 2-16. Rendering all components inside a panel

```
<h:commandButton value="Save">
    <f:ajax event="click" render="out"/>
</h:commandButton>
…
<h:panelGrid id="out">
    <h:outputText />
    <h:outputText />
</h:panelGrid>
```

In addition to the component id, *render* can also be set to a number of predefined values, as shown in Table 2-3.

Table 2-3. Render attribute predefined values

Value	Description
@all	Render all the components in a view.
@none	Render no components in view (this is also the default value if render is not specified).
@this	Render only the component that fired the Ajax request.
@form	Render all components inside the form.
id	One or more ids of components to be rendered.
EL	EL expression that resolves to ids from a Collection of strings.

Before we move on to partial view processing, there is one more thing we want to tell you. You will hear people use the terms *partial page update* and *partial view rendering* interchangeably. That's absolutely fine, but it's worth pointing out how they relate in the context of JSF.

In JSF, the view is rendered on the server. When we add Ajax, the view is still rendered on the server—we just don't need to render everything. We render specified components and thus we refer to it as partial view rendering. When the rendered response (after an Ajax request) is sent to the browser, that's where the partial page update happens in the browser. There is a JavaScript library that takes the response and does the DOM (Document Object Model) update. It's fine to use a partial page update or partial view rendering—as long as you understand that the markup is rendered on the server and the actual page update happens in the browser.

Partial View Processing

Without Ajax, when a page (form) is submitted, the entire form is processed on the server. When we say *processed on the server*, we refer to input or action components that go through the JSF life cycle; in particular, phases such as Apply Request Values, Process Validation, Update Model, and Invoke Application.

Again, without Ajax it's simple. The entire form or all the components within the form are processed. When working with Ajax, the situation is different. We might want only a particular component to be processed and not process all other components; for example, if we only want to validate one component and don't need to validate anything else. In such case, we need to be able to select which component is processed.

Deciding what to process is done via the execute attribute, described in Table 2-4.

Table 2-4. Execute attribute

Attribute	Description
execute	Determines ids of components to be processed on server.

The execute attribute can have different values, as shown in Table 2-5.

Table 2-5. Execute attribute values

Attribute	Description
@all	Process all components in the view.
@none	Process no components in the view.
@this	Process only this component, the component that triggered the Ajax request (default).
@form	Process all components within this form (from which Ajax request was fired).
ids	Implicit ids of components to be processed, space separated.
EL	Process ids resolved form Collection of strings.

Notice that default value is @this, which means that the component firing the Ajax request will be processed by default. Listing 2-17 shows an example.

Listing 2-17. Example

```
<h:commandButton value="Click">
  <f:ajax render="id"/>
</h:commandButton>
```

This is equivalent to Listing 2-18.

Listing 2-18. *Another example*

```
<h:commandButton value="Click">
  <f:ajax execute="@this" render="id"/>
</h:commandButton>
```

Everything is good if we only want to process (execute) the button. But what happens if we have something like Listing 2-19?

Listing 2-19. Example code

```
<h:form>
    <h:panelGrid columns="2">
        <h:outputText value="Text:" />
        <h:inputText value="#{bean.text}" />

        <h:outputText value="Echo:" />
        <h:outputText id="text" value="#{bean.text}" />

        <h:outputText value="Count:" />
        <h:outputText id="count" value="#{bean.count}" />
    </h:panelGrid>
    <h:commandButton value="Submit">
        <f:ajax render="text count" listener="#{bean.countListener}" />
    </h:commandButton>
</h:form>
```

The managed bean is shown in Listing 2-20.

Listing 2-20. *Managed bean*

```
@ManagedBean
@RequestScoped
public class Bean {

    private String text;
    private Integer count;

    public void countListener(AjaxBehaviorEvent event) {
        count = text.length();
    }
}
```

Everything appears to be fine, but when you run it you will get an error. Do you see where the problem is? We attached Ajax behavior to a button, using the default value for execute, which is @this.

When the button is clicked, only that button is processed; the input fields are not processed and inside the listener you will get an exception (NullPointerException as the text property is null).

This code example introduced another <f:ajax> behavior attribute, listener, which is described in Table 2-6.

Table 2-6. listener attribute

Attribute	Description
listener	Listener method to invoke during Ajax request.

Notice that the listener takes one argument of a type AjaxBehaviorEvent, as shown in Listing 2-21.

Listing 2-21. The listener takes one argument of a type AjaxBehaviorEvent

```
import javax.faces.event.AjaxBehaviorEvent;

public void listenerName(AjaxBehaviorEvent event) {
    ...
}
```

■ **Note** The entire form is still submitted to the server. But only the button is processed (executed) on the server. If you have been using RichFaces 3, then this is something you will run into immediately because the entire form was processed by default.

There are a number of ways to fix the problem. First, we can list the ids we want to process in the execute attribute, as shown in Listing 2-22.

Listing 2-22. Listed ids we want to process in the execute attribute

```
<h:form>
    <h:panelGrid columns="2">
        <h:outputText value="Text:" />
        <h:inputText id="inputText" value="#{bean.text}" />

        <h:outputText value="Echo:" />
        <h:outputText id="text" value="#{bean.text}" />

        <h:outputText value="Count:" />
        <h:outputText id="count" value="#{bean.count}" />
    </h:panelGrid>
    <h:commandButton value="Submit">
        <f:ajax render="text count" listener="#{bean.countListener}"
            execute="inputText"/>
    </h:commandButton>
</h:form>
```

▨ **Note** Even though we don't list a button in the `execute` list, the button is processed automatically because it's the control that's being activated.

Instead of listing the ids, another option is to use the predefined value @form to process the entire form, as shown in Listing 2-23.

Listing 2-23. Option to use the predefined value @form

```
<h:form>
    <h:panelGrid columns="2">
        <h:outputText value="Text:" />
        <h:inputText id="inputText" value="#{bean.text}" />

        <h:outputText value="Echo:" />
        <h:outputText id="text" value="#{bean.text}" />

        <h:outputText value="Count:" />
        <h:outputText id="count" value="#{bean.count}" />
    </h:panelGrid>
    <h:commandButton value="Submit">
        <f:ajax render="text count" listener="#{bean.countListener}"
            execute="@form"/>
    </h:commandButton>
</h:form>
```

You are probably wondering at this point, where is the RichFaces coverage? Well, we wanted to make sure that you are familiar with basic Ajax features in JSF 2 first, as everything in RichFaces 4 is based on the core JSF 2 functionality.

Now that we have covered the basics, we can start learning how RichFaces upgrades and makes more powerful this basic feature set. If you feel that you need a little more JSF 2 coverage, we recommend the following two books: *Core JavaServer Faces (Third Edition)* by David Geary and Cay Horstmann (Prentice Hall, 2010), and *JavaServer Faces 2.0: The Complete Reference* by Ed Burns and Chris Schalk (McGraw-Hill, 2009).

RichFaces <a4j:ajax>

The first thing we should tell you is that the good old and popular `a4j:support` has been retired. Instead, there is now the new and shiny `<a4j:ajax>` tag. Why the change? RichFaces 4 is based on JSF 2 and in order to show that RichFaces simply extends the core functionality, the tag follows the same naming convention, and so is now called `<a4j:ajax>`.

At this point you are probably wondering what's the difference between the standard `<f:ajax>` and `<a4j:ajax>` tag. First of all, `<a4j:ajax>` is 100-percent based on `<f:ajax>` behavior functionality.

Listing 2-24 shows one of the examples used in this chapter.

Listing 2-24. Example

```
<h:inputText value="#{bean.text}">
   <f:ajax event="change"/>
</h:inputText>
```

We can rewrite as shown in Listing 2-25.

Listing 2-25. Rewrite of Listing 2-24

```
<h:inputText value="#{bean.text}">
   <a4j:ajax event="change"/>
</h:inputText>
```

And it's going to work exactly the same way. In other words, anywhere you see <f:ajax>, it can be replaced with <a4j:ajax>, and everything will work exactly the same way. What else do you get besides a name change? Table 2-7 summarizes the extras you get when using the <a4j:ajax> tag.

Table 2-7. Extra features with <a4j:ajax> behavior

Attribute	<f:ajax>	<a4j:ajax>
event	Event on which to fire Ajax request. Works the same in JSF 2 and RichFaces.	
execute	@all	@all
	@this	@this
	@form	@form
	@none	@none
	id	ids
	EL	EL (different behavior, ids are resolved in current request) @region (when a4j:region is used) Covered in Chapter 3
render	@all	@all
	@this	@this
	@form	@form
	@none	@none
	id	ids (can be comma separated)
	EL	EL (different behavior, ids are resolved in current request)
listener	Listener to be invoked during Ajax request. Works the same in JSF 2 and RichFaces.	
onevent	Name of JavaScript function to handle UI events. Works the same in JSF 2 and RichFaces.	

Attribute	<f:ajax>	<a4j:ajax>
onerror	Name of JavaScript function to handle error event. Works the same in JSF 2 and RichFaces.	
immediate	If true, events will be processed during Apply Request Values phase. Otherwise, during Invoke Application phase. Works the same in JSF 2 and RichFaces.	
disabled	If true, Ajax behavior will not be rendered. Works the same in JSF 2 and RichFaces.	
onbegin	n/a	JavaScript to execute before Ajax request.
onbeforedomupdate	n/a	JavaScript to execute after response comes back but before DOM update.
oncomplete	n/a	JavaScript to execute after DOM update.
bypassUpdates	n/a	Skips Update Model and Invoke Application phases, useful for form validation.
limitRender	n/a	Skips all a4j:outputPanel ajaxRendered="true" areas. Only renders what is set in current render attribute. Covered in Chapter 3.
status	n/a	Name of status to display during Ajax request. Covered in Chapter 3.

Let's now explore each feature or upgrade in more detail.

render Attribute Options

As you have seen, the render attribute works the same way except for a few differences when using id or EL, as shown in Table 2-8.

Table 2-8. render attribute

Attribute	Description
render	@all @this @form @none id (can be comma separated—RichFaces-only feature) EL (different behavior, ids are resolved in current request—RichFaces-only feature)

In standard JSF 2, it's possible to list any number of ids in render, each separated by a space, as shown in Listing 2-26.

Listing 2-26. List any number of ids, each separated by a space

```
<h:inputText value="#{bean.text}">
   <f:ajax event="change" render="id1 id2 id3 idX"/>
</h:inputText>
```

When using <a4j:ajax>, in addition to a space, it's also possible to separate with a comma (,) as shown in Listing 2-27.

Listing 2-27. Example of separating ids with a comma instead of just a space

```
<h:inputText value="#{bean.text}">
   <f:ajax event="change" render="id1, id2, id3, idN"/>
</h:inputText>
```

We believe using a comma is a little easier and more familiar for those who used <a4j:support> with RichFaces 3, but it's really up to you.

The second difference is more important. Next, we'll use an example to show how it works in JSF 2.

Dynamic render

To show how a dynamic render works in JSF 2, we'll create a sample page to look like Figure 2-1.

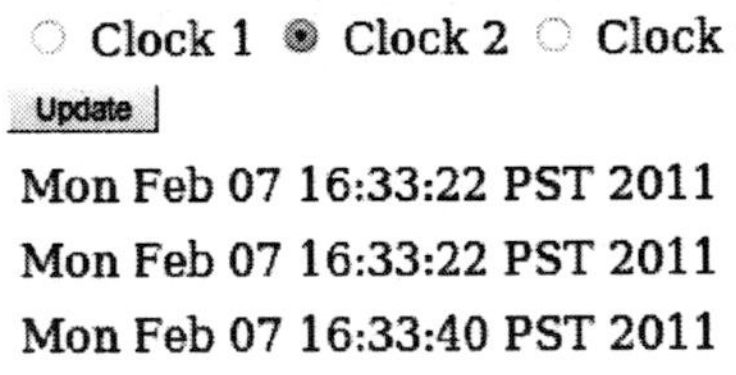

Figure 2-1. Dynamic render with three clocks

Instead of hard coding the component to render, we are going to select which component we would like to update. Now, being able to set the render attribute to an EL is supported by JSF 2; however, it works slightly different when using RichFaces.

Listing 2-28 shows the JSF page.

Listing 2-28. Shows the JSF page

```
<h:form id="form">
   <h:panelGrid>
      <h:selectOneRadio value="#{bean.selection}">
         <f:selectItem itemValue="clock1" itemLabel="Clock 1" />
         <f:selectItem itemValue="clock2" itemLabel="Clock 2" />
         <f:selectItem itemValue="clock3" itemLabel="Clock 3" />
      </h:selectOneRadio>
      <h:commandButton id="updateButton" value="Update">
         <f:ajax event="click" execute="@form" listener="#{bean.selectComponents}"
                 render="#{bean.renderComponents}" />
      </h:commandButton>
   </h:panelGrid>
   <h:panelGrid cellspacing="6">
      <h:outputText id="clock1" value="#{bean.clock1}" />
```

```
        <h:outputText id="clock2" value="#{bean.clock2}" />
        <h:outputText id="clock3" value="#{bean.clock3}" />
    </h:panelGrid>
</h:form>
```

Listing 2-29 shows the managed bean.

Listing 2-29. *Shows the managed bean*

```java
import java.util.ArrayList;
import java.util.Date;
import java.util.List;

import javax.annotation.PostConstruct;
import javax.faces.bean.ManagedBean;
import javax.faces.context.FacesContext;
import javax.faces.event.AjaxBehaviorEvent;

@ManagedBean
@RequestScoped
public class Bean {

    private String selection;
    private List <String> renderComponents;

    @PostConstruct
    public void init (){
        renderComponents = new ArrayList <String>();
        renderComponents.add("updateButton");
    }
    public void selectComponents (AjaxBehaviorEvent event){
        renderComponents.add(selection);
    }
    public List<String> getRenderComponents() {
        return renderComponents;
    }
    public String getSelection() {
        return selection;
    }
    public void setSelection(String selection) {
        this.selection = selection;
    }
    public Date getClock1() {
        return new Date();
    }
    public Date getClock2() {
        return new Date();
    }
    public Date getClock3() {
        return new Date();
    }
}
```

Select Clock 2 and press update. Nothing happens. Now go ahead and select Clock 3. Click update. Clock 2 got updated. That's not a bug, that's how JSF 2 works with render bound to an EL.

Let's take it step by step, as follows:

1. Page is rendered for the first time

2. Select any clock, let's say Clock 1. Click submit.

3. The value of Clock1 is sent to the server. At this point we would expect component Clock1 to be rendered (but, it will only happen on next request).

4. During rendering, #{bean.renderComponents} is resolved and the Clock1 id is rendered into the page.

5. When we next select Clock 3, for example, and fire the request, the Clock1 id that was rendered into the page will now be rendered.

As you can see, when using EL in render, there is a one request delay when rendering the components. What this means is that components (ids) to be rendered need to come from the browser. In order for the desired component id to be updated at each request, we need to render the actual button—so that #{bean.renderComponents} will be resolved and a new value will be rendered. This is accomplished by the following init() method:

```
renderComponents.add("updateButton");
```

To solve this problem, we can work directly with JSF's PartialViewContext class. This class holds the ids to be rendered; and if we add the id programmatically, then the render will happen at the right time. The updated selectComponents method will look like Listing 2-30.

Listing 2-30. The updated selectComponents method

```
public void selectComponents (AjaxBehaviorEvent event){
    UIComponent button = event.getComponent();
    UIOutput output = (UIOutput)button.findComponent(selection);
    FacesContext.getCurrentInstance().getPartialViewContext().getRenderIds().
        add(output.getClientId());
}
```

We first get a reference to the button component that fired the Ajax request. We then use findComponent(id) method to find the output component that we want to render. On the last line, we get the output component client id and add the components to be rendered.

This allows us to include the component id to be rendered in the current request, instead of being one request behind as we saw before. With this change, we can also update the init() method shown in Listing 2-31.

Listing 2-31. Update the init() method

```
@PostConstruct
public void init (){
    renderComponents = new ArrayList <String>();
}
```

We can take out render="#{bean.renderComponents}" because it's no longer used. The button will look as shown in Listing 2-32.

Listing 2-32. Displays how the button will look after you take out render="#{bean.renderComponents}"

```
<h:commandButton id="updateButton" value="Update">
    <f:ajax event="click" execute="@form" listener="#{bean.selectComponents}"/>
</h:commandButton>
```

This approach works, but we believe it should be simpler. We believe it would have been simpler if we could continue using render="#{bean.renderComponents}" and having the ids resolved in the same request. That's possible if we use the RichFaces <a4j:ajax> behavior.

▩ **Tip**   JSF 2 just passes all the parameters from the client side to the server. RichFaces 4 also evaluates the parameters on the server side.

Dynamic render with RichFaces

When using RichFaces <a4j:ajax> and render="#{bean.renderComponents}", the component ids to be rendered are resolved in the current request. To go back to our original example, just switch to using <a4j:ajax> and everything will work. Listing 2-33 shows the JSF page again.

Listing 2-33. Shows the JSF page

```
<h:form id="form">
    <h:panelGrid>
        <h:selectOneRadio value="#{bean.selection}">
            <f:selectItem itemValue="clock1" itemLabel="Clock 1" />
            <f:selectItem itemValue="clock2" itemLabel="Clock 2" />
            <f:selectItem itemValue="clock3" itemLabel="Clock 3" />
        </h:selectOneRadio>
        <h:commandButton id="updateButton" value="Update">
        <a4j:ajax event="click" execute="@form"
            listener="#{bean.selectComponents}"
              render="#{bean.renderComponents}"/>
        </h:commandButton>
    </h:panelGrid>
    <h:panelGrid cellspacing="6">
        <h:outputText id="clock1" value="#{bean.clock1}" />
        <h:outputText id="clock2" value="#{bean.clock2}" />
        <h:outputText id="clock3" value="#{bean.clock3}" />
    </h:panelGrid>
</h:form>
```

All we did is change the behavior name from <f:ajax> to <a4j:ajax>.
Listing 2-34 shows the managed bean.

Listing 2-34. Shows the managed bean

```
@ManagedBean
@RequestScoped
public class Bean {

    private String selection;
    private List <String> renderComponents;

    @PostConstruct
    public void init (){
        renderComponents = new ArrayList <String>();
```

```
    }
    public void selectComponents (AjaxBehaviorEvent event){
        renderComponents.add(selection);
    }
    public List<String> getRenderComponents() {
        return renderComponents;
    }
    public String getSelection() {
        return selection;
    }
    public void setSelection(String selection) {
        this.selection = selection;
    }
    public Date getClock1() {
        return new Date();
    }
    public Date getClock2() {
        return new Date();
    }
    public Date getClock3() {
        return new Date();
    }
}
```

Notice that we no longer need to add the button to the list of components to be rendered. Running the application, everything is now updated as you would expect.

Simplicity is just one of the advantages to using <a4j:ajax> and the render attribute bound to EL. One more advantage is that evaluating the ids on the server instead of getting them client side is more secure, as anyone could send a request with ids using <f:ajax>. If this happens with <a4j:ajax>, these ids will simply be ignored.

■ **Note** The same functionality is available on other RichFaces tags, such as <a4j:commandButton>, <a4j:commandLink>, <a4j:poll>, and <a4j:jsFunction>. We will cover this in Chapter 3. We used the listener attribute on either <f:ajax> or <a4j:ajax> behaviors. If you have an action or an actionListener set on the button or link, those will be invoked in a standard way.

---

execute Attribute Options

The same way it's possible to bind the render attribute to EL or decide which components to render in runtime, it's also possible to decide which components to execute in runtime or bind the execute attribute to EL. For example:

```
<f:ajax event="blur" execute="#{bean.executeComponents}" render="out"/>
```

When using just JSF 2, execute works in similar fashion to render in regards to when the ids are resolved. As with render, the ids in execute are resolved but then rendered to the page and only used on the next request. When using RichFaces a4j:ajax behavior instead of f:ajax, then ids are resolved and those components are executed in the current request.

```
<a4j:ajax event="blur" execute="#{bean.executeComponents}" render="out"/>
```

While determining which components to render at runtime is common, determining which components to execute is rarely used, if at all. But, it's important to understand the difference in when ids are resolved and when they are used when using JSF 2 `<f:ajax>` and RichFaces `<a4j:ajax>` behaviors.

RichFaces offers one more option for deciding what to execute with its `<a4j:region>` tag. This tag will be covered in Chapter 3.

bypassUpdates Attribute

Validation is obviously a very common task in any Web application. When only validating form inputs, it's usually not necessary to go through all the JSF life cycle phases, in particular Update Model and Invoke Application phases. In this section you will learn how to skip these two phases when validating form fields to optimize the JSF request. Let's start with a very simple example that looks like Figure 2-2.

Name:

Age:

Register

Figure 2-2. *A simple registration form.*

Figure 2-3 shows how it looks when an error has occurred.

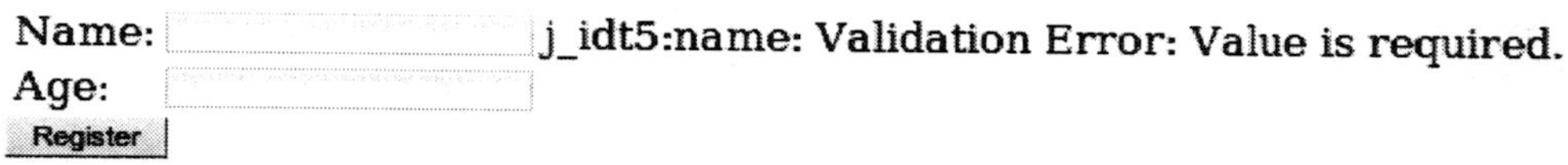

Name: j_idt5:name: Validation Error: Value is required.

Age:

Register

Figure 2-3. *A simple registration with an error message*

Listing 2-35 shows the `register.xhtml` page.

Listing 2-35. *Shows the register.xhtml page*

```
<h:form>
   <h:panelGrid columns="3">
      <h:outputText value="Name:" />
      <h:inputText id="name" value="#{bean2.name}">
         <f:validateRequired/>
         <f:validateLength minimum="3"/>
         <a4j:ajax event="blur" render="errorName"/>
      </h:inputText>
      <h:message id="errorName" for="name"/>

      <h:outputText value="Age:" />
      <h:inputText id="age" value="#{bean2.age}">
         <f:validateRequired/>
         <f:validateLongRange minimum="0"/>
         <a4j:ajax event="blur" render="errorAge"/>
      </h:inputText>
      <h:message id="errorAge" for="age"/>
   </h:panelGrid>
   <h:commandButton value="Register" action="result"/>
</h:form>
```

Listing 2-36 shows the `result.xhtml` page.

Listing 2-36. Shows the result.xhtml page

```
<h:panelGrid>
      <h:outputText value="#{bean2.name}, #{bean2.age}" />
</h:panelGrid>
```

Listing 2-37 shows the managed bean.

Listing 2-37. Shows the managed bean

```
@ManagedBean
@RequestScoped
public class Bean2 {
    private String name;
    private Integer age;

    // getters and setters
}
```

This is a very simple registration form with Ajax-based validation. In other words, when we blur the field (tab out or click outside), an Ajax request is fired. We start going through JSF phases. If there is a validation error, after Process Validations, we go to Render Response. If there is no validation error, then we finish all the phases, going through Update Model and Invoke Application. To see this in action, let's create a phase listener that will print a message to the console as we pass each phase.

In case you need to review the JSF phases, they are shown in Figure 2-4.

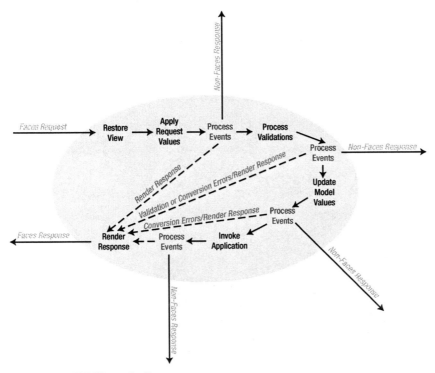

Figure 2-4. JSF life cycle diagram

JSF fires what are called phase events before and after each phase. We can write a listener to listen to these events and output a message to the log. The phase listener can be used for anything else, such as injecting a custom functionality between phases.

The phase listener is shown in Listing 2-38.

Listing 2-38. The phase listener

```
import javax.faces.event.PhaseEvent;
import javax.faces.event.PhaseId;
import javax.faces.event.PhaseListener;

public class PhaseTracker implements PhaseListener {

    public void afterPhase(PhaseEvent event) {
        event.getFacesContext().getExternalContext().log("AFTER
            "+event.getPhaseId());
    }
    public void beforePhase(PhaseEvent event) {
        event.getFacesContext().getExternalContext().log("BEFORE
            "+event.getPhaseId());
    }
    public PhaseId getPhaseId() {
        return PhaseId.ANY_PHASE;
    }
}
```

The methods beforePhase and afterPhase are very simple. All we do is print a message to the log. getPhaseId() returns the phase id for which to call this particular listener. We would like the listener to be invoked for each phase, so we return PhaseId.ANY_PHASE. It's possible to return a particular phase such as PhaseId.INVOKE_APPLICATION or it's also possible to return two or more phases.

The final step is to register this phase listener in a JSF configuration file (faces-config.xml), as shown in Listing 2-39.

Listing 2-39. Register the phase listener in a JSF configuration file

```
<lifecycle>
  <phase-listener>org.richfaces..book.PhaseTracker</phase-listener>
</lifecycle>
```

There is no annotation yet for phase listeners in JSF 2.

When you load the page, place the mouse cursor inside the name field, but then click somewhere else. You should see the console shown in Listing 2-40.

Listing 2-40. Displayed console

```
INFO: BEFORE RESTORE_VIEW 1
Feb 8, 2011 2:39:49 PM org.apache.catalina.core.ApplicationContext log
INFO: AFTER RESTORE_VIEW 1
Feb 8, 2011 2:39:49 PM org.apache.catalina.core.ApplicationContext log
INFO: BEFORE APPLY_REQUEST_VALUES 2
Feb 8, 2011 2:39:49 PM org.apache.catalina.core.ApplicationContext log
INFO: AFTER APPLY_REQUEST_VALUES 2
Feb 8, 2011 2:39:49 PM org.apache.catalina.core.ApplicationContext log
```

```
INFO: BEFORE PROCESS_VALIDATIONS 3
Feb 8, 2011 2:39:49 PM org.apache.catalina.core.ApplicationContext log
INFO: AFTER PROCESS_VALIDATIONS 3
Feb 8, 2011 2:39:49 PM org.apache.catalina.core.ApplicationContext log
INFO: BEFORE RENDER_RESPONSE 6
Feb 8, 2011 2:39:49 PM org.apache.catalina.core.ApplicationContext log
INFO: AFTER RENDER_RESPONSE 6
```

We arrived at Phase 3, validation failed and we jumped to Phase 6. So far it all makes sense. Now enter a valid value either for name or age. You should now see the console shown in Listing 2-41.

Listing 2-41. *After entering a valid value, you will see the following console*

```
INFO: BEFORE RESTORE_VIEW 1
Feb 8, 2011 2:41:23 PM org.apache.catalina.core.ApplicationContext log
INFO: AFTER RESTORE_VIEW 1
Feb 8, 2011 2:41:23 PM org.apache.catalina.core.ApplicationContext log
INFO: BEFORE APPLY_REQUEST_VALUES 2
Feb 8, 2011 2:41:23 PM org.apache.catalina.core.ApplicationContext log
INFO: AFTER APPLY_REQUEST_VALUES 2
Feb 8, 2011 2:41:23 PM org.apache.catalina.core.ApplicationContext log
INFO: BEFORE PROCESS_VALIDATIONS 3
Feb 8, 2011 2:41:23 PM org.apache.catalina.core.ApplicationContext log
INFO: AFTER PROCESS_VALIDATIONS 3
Feb 8, 2011 2:41:23 PM org.apache.catalina.core.ApplicationContext log
INFO: BEFORE UPDATE_MODEL_VALUES 4
Feb 8, 2011 2:41:23 PM org.apache.catalina.core.ApplicationContext log
INFO: AFTER UPDATE_MODEL_VALUES 4
Feb 8, 2011 2:41:23 PM org.apache.catalina.core.ApplicationContext log
INFO: BEFORE INVOKE_APPLICATION 5
Feb 8, 2011 2:41:23 PM org.apache.catalina.core.ApplicationContext log
INFO: AFTER INVOKE_APPLICATION 5
Feb 8, 2011 2:41:23 PM org.apache.catalina.core.ApplicationContext log
INFO: BEFORE RENDER_RESPONSE 6
Feb 8, 2011 2:41:23 PM org.apache.catalina.core.ApplicationContext log
INFO: AFTER RENDER_RESPONSE 6
```

As validation didn't fail, we competed all the phases. The next question is: do we need to go through all the phases when we are only validating? Probably not. When only validating, it's enough to reach Phase 3 (Process Validations), and even if the input is correct we can jump to the Render Response phase. Why invoke the Update Model and Invoke Application phases when we actually don't need to? Let's make our request quicker.

When the Register button is clicked, we don't want to go through all the phases, we want to skip Update Model and Invoke Application phases. How do we achieve that? That's where the *bypassUpdates* attribute is going to help us and described in Table 2-9.

Table 2-9. *bypassUpdates attribute*

Attribute	Description
bypassUpdates	Skips Update Model and Invoke Application phases, useful for form validation.

Listing 2-42 shows updating the JSF page and setting bypassUpdates="true".

Listing 2-42. Updating the JSF page

```
<h:form>
    <h:panelGrid columns="3">
        <h:outputText value="Name:" />
        <h:inputText id="name" value="#{bean2.name}">
            <f:validateRequired/>
            <f:validateLength minimum="3"/>
            <a4j:ajax event="blur" render="errorName" bypassUpdates="true"/>
        </h:inputText>
        <h:message id="errorName" for="name"/>

        <h:outputText value="Age:" />
        <h:inputText id="age" value="#{bean2.age}">
            <f:validateRequired/>
            <f:validateLongRange minimum="0"/>
            <a4j:ajax event="blur" render="errorAge" bypassUpdates="true"/>
        </h:inputText>
        <h:message id="errorAge" for="age"/>
    </h:panelGrid>
    <h:commandButton value="Register" action="result"/>
</h:form>
```

Running the page again and entering invalid values causes validation to fail; and from the Process Validations phase we jump to Render Response, as before. But, when we enter a valid value, we get the same behavior because we set *bypassUpdates="true"*. For example, entering 'Joe' in the name field and then clicking outside the field should allow you to see it in the console shown in Listing 2-43.

Listing 2-43. Example of the console after entering the name field

```
INFO: AFTER RESTORE_VIEW 1
Feb 8, 2011 3:01:28 PM org.apache.catalina.core.ApplicationContext log
INFO: BEFORE APPLY_REQUEST_VALUES 2
Feb 8, 2011 3:01:28 PM org.apache.catalina.core.ApplicationContext log
INFO: AFTER APPLY_REQUEST_VALUES 2
Feb 8, 2011 3:01:28 PM org.apache.catalina.core.ApplicationContext log
INFO: BEFORE PROCESS_VALIDATIONS 3
Feb 8, 2011 3:01:28 PM org.apache.catalina.core.ApplicationContext log
INFO: AFTER PROCESS_VALIDATIONS 3
Feb 8, 2011 3:01:28 PM org.apache.catalina.core.ApplicationContext log
INFO: BEFORE RENDER_RESPONSE 6
Feb 8, 2011 3:01:28 PM org.apache.catalina.core.ApplicationContext log
INFO: AFTER RENDER_RESPONSE 6
```

Once we reach the Process Validation phase, the component is validated and we go directly to the Render Response phase. Again, there is no need to continue with the other phases because they will be invoked when the Register button is clicked. So to summarize, bypassUpdates is useful when doing Ajax-based validation.

JavaScript Interactions or Callback Events

Firing an Ajax request doesn't require writing any JavaScript code. Using <f:ajax> or the more advanced <a4j:ajax> makes it possible to fire an Ajax request from any component. However, there might be a situation where you might want to call or inject a custom JavaScript function before or after the Ajax request completes. JSF 2 provides two callback events, onevent and onerror, which allow you to invoke a custom JavaScript during the Ajax request. They are described in Table 2-10.

Table 2-10. Standard Ajax request callback events

Attribute	Description
onevent	Name of JavaScript function to handle UI events.
onerror	Name of JavaScript function to handle error events.

onevent consists of three sub-events, described in Table 2-11.

Table 2-11. onevent Sub-Events Descriptions

Event name	Description
begin	Occurs just before the Ajax request is fired.
complete	Occurs right after the Ajax response completes but before the DOM update.
success	Occurs after DOM update. In case of an error, this event will be replaced by the *onerror* function call.

Let's start with a simple example. The application looks like Figure 2-5.

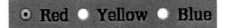

Figure 2-5. A simple form with different colors

Listing 2-44 shows the JSF page.

Listing 2-44. Shows the JSF page

```
<h:form>
    <h:panelGrid id="panel" style="background-color: #{bean3.color}">
        <h:selectOneRadio value="#{bean3.color}">
            <f:selectItem itemValue="red" itemLabel="Red" />
            <f:selectItem itemValue="yellow" itemLabel="Yellow" />
            <f:selectItem itemValue="blue" itemLabel="Blue" />
            <f:ajax event="click" render="panel" />
        </h:selectOneRadio>
    </h:panelGrid>
</h:form>
```

Listing 2-45 shows the managed bean.

Listing 2-45. Shows the managed bean

```
@ManagedBean
@RequestScoped
public class Bean3 {
    private String color;

    // getter and setter
}
```

Let's see how we can use the *onevent* callback to add custom JavaScript to be called during the Ajax request. Keep in mind these are client-side (browser) events. First, we need to create the JavaScript function. We can place Listing 2-46 right after the <body> tag in the JSF page.

Listing 2-46. Creating a JavaScript function

```
<script>
function ajaxRequestListener (event){
    if (event.status == 'begin'){
        if(!confirm('Are you sure you want change the color?' + '
            ('+event.status+')')) {
                form.reset();
                return false;
        }
    }
    else if (event.status == 'complete'){
        alert('Just before DOM update' + ' ('+event.status+')');
    }
    else if (event.status == 'success'){
        alert('Color changed. We told you so.' + ' ('+event.status+')');
    }
}

</script>
```

Because the ajaxRequestListener JavaScript function will be called three times, at *begin*, *complete* and *success* points, the function has three if-statements to handle each event separately. The only thing we are left to do is add the callback function to <f:ajax> behavior, as shown in Listing 2-47.

Listing 2-47. Adding a callback function to <f:ajax> behavior

```
<h:form>
    <h:panelGrid id="panel" style="background-color: #{bean3.color}">
        <h:selectOneRadio value="#{bean3.color}">
            <f:selectItem itemValue="red" itemLabel="Red" />
            <f:selectItem itemValue="yellow" itemLabel="Yellow" />
            <f:selectItem itemValue="blue" itemLabel="Blue" />
            <f:ajax event="click" render="panel" onevent="ajaxRequestListener"/>
        </h:selectOneRadio>
    </h:panelGrid>
</h:form>
```

Figure 2-6 shows running the application and selecting a new color.

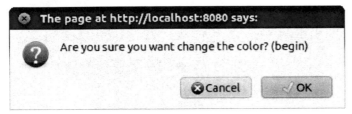

Figure 2-6. Selecting Blue color, begin sub-event

Figure 2-7 shows the complete sub-event alert dialog.

Figure 2-7. Selecting Blue color, complete sub-event

Figure 2-8 shows the success sub-event alert dialog.

Figure 2-8. Selecting Blue color, success sub-event

Let's now add the *onerror* callback function. Listing 2-48 shows the JavaScript function.

Listing 2-48. Shows the JavaScript function

```
function ajaxErrorListener (event){
    alert ('Status: '+event.status + "\nHTTP error: "+event.description );
}
```

We also need to set onerror attribute in <f:ajax> tag. Listing 2-49 shows the updated <f:ajax> tag.

Listing 2-49. Setting the onerror attribute in <f:ajax> behavior

```
<f:ajax event="click" render="panel" onevent="ajaxRequest"
    onerror="ajaxErrorListener"/>
```

To see how this works, load the page, stop the server, and then click to change the color. You will first see begin and complete messages. begin is shown because an Ajax request is fired. complete is shown because the response completed, but with an error. At this point, the onerror callback function is called and you will see the message shown in Figure 2-9.

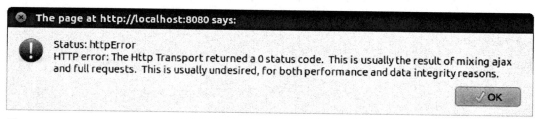

Figure 2-9. onerror callback event

RichFaces makes working with callback functions simpler. *onevent* actually consists of three sub-events (begin, complete, success) and if you are interested in just one of them, you would need to check for that event, otherwise the same function will be called for all three. RichFaces makes it easier by making available three attributes on the <a4j:ajax> behavior: onbegin, onbeforedomupdate, and oncomplete. Each of these attributes is mapped to a different event, as described in Table 2-12.

Table 2-12. RichFaces callback events

<a4j:ajax> attribute	JSF 2 event mapping	Description
onbegin	begin	JavaScript to execute before Ajax request.
onbeforedomupdate	complete	JavaScript to execute after response comes back but before DOM update.
oncomplete	success	JavaScript to execute after DOM update.

Listing 2-50 shows updating the example to use <a4j:ajax> with these attributes.

Listing 2-50. Updating the example to use <a4j:ajax>

```
<h:form>
    <h:panelGrid id="panel" style="background-color: #{bean3.color}">
        <h:selectOneRadio value="#{bean3.color}">
            <f:selectItem itemValue="red" itemLabel="Red" />
            <f:selectItem itemValue="yellow" itemLabel="Yellow" />
            <f:selectItem itemValue="blue" itemLabel="Blue" />
                <a4j:ajax render="panel"
```

```
            onbegin="if(!confirm('Are you sure you want change the
                color'))
        {form.reset(); return false;};"
        oncomplete="alert('Color changed. We told you so.')"
        onbeforedomupdate="alert('Just before DOM update')" />
    </h:selectOneRadio>
  </h:panelGrid>
</h:form>
```

Each event is exposed as a separate attribute, which makes it easier to use. You no longer need to define a function and check for each event. Do keep in mind that these attributes are only available on the RichFaces <a4j:ajax> behavior.

Summary

In this chapter we showed you how to set up a RichFaces project using Maven and covered how to use JSF 2 standard <f:ajax> behavior. We then showed you how RichFaces <a4j:ajax> behavior upgrades the standard <f:ajax> with extra features and attributes.

Chapter 3 will continue coverage of how RichFaces upgrades and extends standard Ajax functionality with tags such as <a4j:commandButton>, <a4j:commandLink>, <a4j:poll>, <a4j:jsFunction>, and <a4j:region> tags among the few. Keep in mind that all the features and attributes we covered in this chapter are also available on the tags we just listed. We will also cover advanced client queue customization and features that RichFaces provides on top of standard JSF 2 queue.

a4j:* Tags, Features and Concepts

In previous chapters we covered the RichFaces <a4j:ajax> tag, which extends and upgrades the standard *<f:ajax>* tags with more features and options. In this chapter we are going to continue covering a4j:* library tags, features, and concepts. We will cover additional tags that fire an Ajax request, such as *<a4j:poll>*, *<a4j:jsFunction>*, advanced rendering options using the *<a4j:outputPanel>* component, advanced execute options, and numerous upgrades to the standard Ajax client queue.

Sending an Ajax Request

In this section you will learn how to use three new RichFaces components to send an Ajax request: <a4j:commandButton> (and <a4j:commandLink>) is a button with built-in Ajax behavior; <a4j:jsFunction> allows you to send an Ajax request from any HTML event or JavaScript function; and <a4j:poll> enables you to periodically send an Ajax request.

Using <a4j:commandButton> and <a4j:commandLink>

Adding Ajax behavior to a JSF button or link is not very difficult and looks as shown in Listing 3-1 when using a button.

Listing 3-1. Adding Ajax behavior to a JSF button

```
<h:form>
...
    <h:commandButton value="Send">
      <f:ajax event="click" render="out"/>
    </h:commandButton>
</h:form>
```

And using a link instead of a button, it is virtually identical, as shown in Listing 3-2.

Listing 3-2. Using a link instead of a button

```
<h:form>
...
    <h:commandLink value="Send">
      <f:ajax event="click" render="out"/>
    </h:commandLink>
```

```
      <h:outputText id="out"/>
</h:form>
```

In both examples, when a button is clicked an Ajax request will be fired and a component with id out will be rendered. In most cases you have a number of input fields and then a button to submit them, as shown in Listing 3-3.

Listing 3-3. Shows that you have a number of input fields and then a button to submit them

```
<h:form>
   <h:panelGrid columns="2">
      <h:outputText value="Name:"/>
      <h:inputText value="#{bean.name}"/>
      <h:outputText value="Echo:"/>
      <h:outputText id="echo" value="#{bean.name}"/>
      <h:outputText value="Count:"/>
      <h:outputText id="count" value="#{bean.count}"/>
   </h:panelGrid>
   <h:commandButton value="Submit" action="#{bean.countAction}">
      <f:ajax event="click" render="echo count"/>
   </h:commandButton>
</h:form>
```

The managed bean code is shown in Listing 3-4.

Listing 3-4. The managed bean code

```
@ManagedBean
@RequestScoped

public class Bean {

   private String name;
   private Integer count;

   public void countAction (){
      count = name.length();
   }
   // getters and setters
}
```

When you run the above example, it's not going to work because we forgot to modify the execute attribute on the <f:ajax> behavior. If you remember from Chapter 2, the default execute value for <f:ajax> is @this. @this means only this (current) component will be executed and the input components will not. To fix it, we have to add execute attribute as shown in Listing 3-5.

Listing 3-5. Adding execute attribute

```
<h:form>
   <h:panelGrid columns="2">
      <h:outputText value="Name:"/>
      <h:inputText value="#{bean.name}"/>
      <h:outputText value="Echo:"/>
      <h:outputText id="echo" value="#{bean.name}"/>
```

```
        <h:outputText value="Count:"/>
        <h:outputText id="count" value="#{bean.count}"/>
    </h:panelGrid>
    <h:commandButton value="Submit" action="#{bean.countAction}">
        <f:ajax event="click" execute="@form" render="echo count"/>
    </h:commandButton>
</h:form>
```

■ **Tip**   The default value for execute in `<f:ajax>` behavior is `@this`. Also, we recommend always setting the event attribute, even if using a default value, to reduce errors and make the code more readable.

RichFaces makes it easier to use a button or link with Ajax support by providing button and link components with built-in Ajax: `<a4j:commandButton>` and `<a4j:commandLink>`. Listing 3-6 shows an example we saw earlier.

Listing 3-6. Example

```
<h:form>
...
    <h:commandButton value="Send">
        <f:ajax event="click" render="out"/>
    </h:commandButton>
</h:form>
```

When using the RichFaces `<a4j:commandButton>`, the example would look like Listing 3-7.

Listing 3-7. Example when using the RichFaces `<a4j:commandButton>`

```
<h:form>
...
    <a4j:commandButton value="Send" render="out"/>
</h:form>
```

We went from three to just one line of code. It looks simpler and cleaner. There is one more difference we need to tell you about. Let's rewrite this example using the `<a4j:commandButton>`, as shown in Listing 3-8.

Listing 3-8. Example using the `<a4j:commandButton>`

```
<h:form>
    <h:panelGrid columns="2">
        <h:outputText value="Name:"/>
        <h:inputText value="#{bean.name}"/>
        <h:outputText value="Echo:"/>
        <h:outputText id="echo" value="#{bean.name}"/>
        <h:outputText value="Count:"/>
        <h:outputText id="count" value="#{bean.count}"/>
    </h:panelGrid>
    <a4j:commandButton value="Submit" render="echo count" action="#{bean.countAction}"/>
</h:form>
```

If you run the example in Listing 3-8, it will work as expected and notice that we didn't have to specify the execute attribute. Because it is so common when using a button to also execute input fields inside the form, the execute in the `<a4j:commandButton>` (and `<a4j:commandLink>`) is set by default to `@form`. You can always overwrite the default value by using either a predefined value such as `@all`, ids, or EL, as shown in Table 3-1. We also don't need to set the event attribute. `<a4j:commandButton>` uses the `click` event by default.

■ **Tip**   The `<a4j:commandButton>` and `<a4j:commandLink>` execute is set to `@form`.

Table 3-1. Important `<a4j:commandButton>` and `<a4j:commandLink>` Ajax attributes

Event	Value
execute	*@all* *@this* *@form* (default value) *@none* ids EL expression bound to List, Set or just String with id's (id's are resolved in current request) *@region* (when a4j:region is used)
render	*@all* *@this* *@form* *@none* ids (can be comma separated) EL expression bound to List, Set or just String with ids (ids are resolved in current request)

The following Ajax attributes are available to use with `<a4j:commandButton>` and `<a4j:commandLink>` tags: onbegin, onbeforedomupdate, oncomplete, bypassUpdates, limitRender, data, and status.

■ **Note**   `<a4j:commandLink>` works exactly the same as `<a4j:commandButton>`, but instead of a button it will render a link.

Ajax Request from any Event or JavaScript Function Using `<a4j:jsFunction>`

So far we covered two ways to fire an Ajax request: first using a `<a4j:ajax>` behavior, and next using either `<a4j:commandButton>` or `<a4j:commandLink>`. `<a4j:ajax>` (and `<f:ajax>` on which it's based) is a behavior and is always attached based on some event to another UI component, such as a button, select, and so forth. It's never used by itself. `<a4j:commandButton>` is a button with built-in Ajax behavior and `<a4j:commandLink>` is a link with built-in Ajax behavior. All provide a specific functionality. But let's say we would like to fire an Ajax request from an HTML tag, not a JSF component. We can't use `<a4j:ajax>`—

it's a behavior and has to be attached to another JSF component. This is where <a4j:jsFunction> is useful. It allows you to fire an Ajax request from any JavaScript event or function.

To see how <a4j:jsFunction> works, let's take an example we saw in the previous section, as shown in Listing 3-9.

Listing 3-9. Shows how <a4j:jsFunction> works

```
<h:form>
    <h:panelGrid columns="2">
        <h:outputText value="Name:" />
        <h:inputText value="#{bean.name}" />
        <h:outputText value="Echo:" />
        <h:outputText id="echo" value="#{bean.name}" />
        <h:outputText value="Count:" />
        <h:outputText id="count" value="#{bean.count}" />
    </h:panelGrid>
    <a4j:commandButton value="Submit" render="echo, count"
        action="#{bean.countAction}" />
</h:form>
```

Instead of using <a4j:commandButton>, let's use <a4j:jsFunction> to fire an Ajax request, as shown in Listing 3-10.

Listing 3-10. Using <a4j:jsFunction> to fire an Ajax request

```
<h:form>
    <h:panelGrid columns="2">
        <h:outputText value="Name:" />
        <h:inputText value="#{bean.name}" />
        <h:outputText value="Echo:" />
        <h:outputText id="echo" value="#{bean.name}" />
        <h:outputText value="Count:" />
        <h:outputText id="count" value="#{bean.count}" />
    </h:panelGrid>
    <input type="button" value="Submit" onclick="sendAjaxRequest();"/>

    <a4j:jsFunction name="sendAjaxRequest" execute="@form"
        action="#{bean.countAction}" render="echo, count"/>
</h:form>
```

The execute attribute of <a4j:function> is set to @this according to the JSF default value, so there we explicitly changed it to @form to have all the inputs processed.

Listing 3-10 shows the changes we made. First, we replaced <a4j:commandButton> with a regular HTML button; next, we defined <a4j:jsFunction>. Notice that the button also has a click event that calls a sendAjaxRequest() JavaScript function. This function is defined by <a4j:jsFuction> and it's just a standard JavaScript function. If we look at the rendered code, the function we are calling looks like Listing 3-11.

Listing 3-11. This function is defined by <a4j:jsFuction>

```
<script type="text/javascript">
    sendAjaxRequest=function(){RichFaces.ajax("j_idt5:j_idt11",null, {"incId":"1"} )};
</script>
```

Without `<a4j:jsFunction>` we would have to type something similar by hand. `<a4j:jsFunction>` looks just like any other control that fires an Ajax request: there is an execute attribute, there is an action attribute, and there is a render attribute. Everything we learned about these attributes applies here as well. What you get is the ability to fire a standard Ajax request from any HTML tag, based on any event that tag supports.

▪ **Tip**   The `<a4j:jsFunction>` execute attribute default value is `@this`.

In Listing 3-11 we called `sendAjaxRequest()` directly from the click event. We can as easily invoke `sendAjaxRequest()` from another JavaScript function, which would allow us to invoke any other logic before firing the request, as shown in Listing 3-12 (changes are in bold).

Listing 3-12. Shows how to easily invoke sendAjaxRequest() from another JavaScript function

```
<h:form>
    <h:panelGrid columns="2">
        <h:outputText value="Name:" />
        <h:inputText value="#{bean.name}" />
        <h:outputText value="Echo:" />
        <h:outputText id="echo" value="#{bean.name}" />
        <h:outputText value="Count:" />
        <h:outputText id="count" value="#{bean.count}" />
    </h:panelGrid>
    <input type="button" value="Submit" onclick="doAjax();"/>
    <a4j:jsFunction name="sendAjaxRequest" execute="@form"
        action="#{bean.countAction}"  render="echo, count"/>
    <script>
        function doAjax () {
            // do something here
            sendAjaxRequest();
            }
    </script>
</h:form>
```

There is one more case where `<a4j:jsFunction>` is very useful. You may call the function to get values from the server, serialize them, and pass to the client using the data attribute. You can then use the data received in some client-side function. An example is shown in Listing 3-13, where the data received from the server is shown in an alert window with an oncomplete event.

Listing 3-13. The data received from the server is shown in an alert window

```
<h:form>
    <input type="button" value="Update" onclick="updateName('Joe');"/>
    <a4j:jsFunction name="updateName" render="showname"
        data="#{jsFunctionNameBean.greeting}" oncomplete="alert(event.data)">
        <a4j:param name="param1" assignTo="#{jsFunctionNameBean.name}"/>
    </a4j:jsFunction>
    <h:outputText id="showname" value="#{jsFunctionNameBean.greeting}"/>
</h:form>
```

The managed bean is shown in Listing 3-14.

Listing 3-14. The managed bean

```
@ManagedBean (name="jsFunctionNameBean")
@RequestScoped
public class JSFunctionNameBean {

    private String name; // setter and getter

    public String getGreeting () {
        return "Hello "+this.name;
    }
}
```

In this example, the value of #{jsFunctionNameBean.greeting} property gets serialized after the name is set on the server-side, it is then passed back to the client and displayed using JavaScript alert. In a real application you may want to bring any additional data from the server and call some real post-processing JavaScript handlers function. This is very useful if you need to pass some inputs to the server, get a result back, and then process the result with the oncomplete script.

In the next section we will see how to pass parameters to the JavaScript function created with <a4j:jsFunction> and, in turn, send them to the server. Then, we will see an alternative way to send an Ajax request from any HTML event or JavaScript script using a standard JSF programmatic Ajax approach.

Passing Parameters with <a4j:param>

Let's look at another example where an Ajax request is not fired directly from a JSF component, but from an HTML tag when a mouse is placed over the name of a drink, as shown in Figure 3-1.

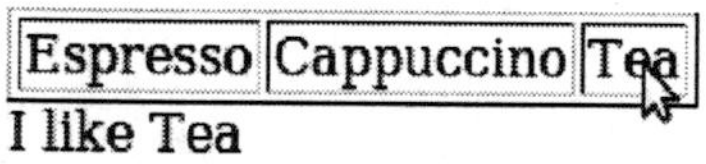

| Espresso | Cappuccino | Tea |

I like Tea

Figure 3-1. Using <a4j:jsFunction> with <a4j:param>

Listing 3-15 shows the JSF code.

Listing 3-15. The JSF code

```
<table border="1">
    <tr>
        <td onmouseover="setdrink('Espresso')"
            onmouseout="setdrink('')">Espresso</td>
        <td onmouseover="setdrink('Cappuccino')"
            onmouseout="setdrink('')">Cappuccino</td>
        <td onmouseover="setdrink('Tea')"
            onmouseout="setdrink('')">Tea</td>
    </tr>
</table>
<h:outputText id="drink" value="I like #{jsFunctionDrinkBean.drink}" />

<h:form>
```

```
    <a4j:jsFunction name="setdrink" execute="@form" render="drink">
        <a4j:param name="param1" assignTo="#{jsFunctionDrinkBean.drink}" />
    </a4j:jsFunction>
</h:form>
```

The managed bean code is shown in Listing 3-16.

Listing 3-16. The managed bean code

```
@ManagedBean (name="jsFunctionDrinkBean")
@RequestScoped
public class JSFunctionDrinkBean {

    private String drink;
    // setter and getter
}
```

We no longer fire a request from a JSF component; the Ajax request is fired from HTML tag when we place the mouse over the table row (onmouseover event) and is also fired when we move the mouse out (onmouseout event). When one of these events occurs, a call to setdrink(..) is made. setdrink is a JavaScript function defined by <a4j:jsFuction>, which in turn fired the Ajax request and could also do partial page rendering.

You will notice one difference from the previous example; our JavaScript function defined by <a4j:jsFunction> takes a parameter, either the name of the drink or an empty string. We somehow have to pass it to the bean, set it to the drink attribute, and then render it. This is done via the <a4j:param> tag. Parameters will be passed in the same order as defined inside the <a4j:jsFunction> tag.

The <a4j:param> is very similar to the standard <f:param>, but with one major and very helpful difference. When using <f:param>, the value is added to the request and then has to be retrieved from the request with this link of code. Listing 3-17 shows a very simple example using <f:param>.

Listing 3-17. Using the <f:param> value to the request

```
<a4j:commandButton>
    <f:param name="firstName" value="Tammy"/>
</a4j:commandButton>
```

To get the value inside the bean, we can use something like the following:

```
String value = FacesContext.getCurrentInstance().getExternalContext()
    .getRequestParameterMap().get("firstName");
```

Going back to <a4j:param>, it adds a parameter to the request in the same fashion, but also does the assignment automatically. In other words, it will set the value into the bean property, assuming it has a setter method. It's just an upgraded version of <f:param> where you don't have to do anything to get the value. Listing 3-18 shows an example using <a4j:param>.

Listing 3-18. Using <a4j:param> instead of <f:param>

```
<a4j:commandButton>
    <a4j:param name="firstName" value="Tammy" assignTo="#{paramBean.firstName}"/>
</a4j:commandButton>
```

The firstName property, with getter and setter needs present inside the managed bean, is shown in Listing 3-19.

Listing 3-19. The managed bean

```
@ManagedBean
@RequestScoped
public class ParamBean {

    private String firstName;

    public String getFirstName() {
        return firstName;
    }
    public void setFirstName(String firstName) {
        this.firstName = firstName;
    }
}
```

When defining a JavaScript function with `<a4j:jsFunction>`, which takes a parameter, then `<a4j:param>` is used to define and assign the parameter to a bean property. In case you need to pass more than one parameter, you can include as many `<a4j:param>` tags as you need, as shown in Listing 3-20.

Listing 3-20. Including as many `<a4j:param>` tags as you need

```
<a4j:jsFunction>
    <a4j:param name="param1" assignTo="#{someBean.value1}" />
    <a4j:param name="param2" assignTo="#{someBean.value2}" />
    <a4j:param name="param3" assignTo="#{someBean.value3}" />
</a4j:jsFunction>
```

The name has to be in the form of `param1`, `param2`, and `param3`.

We've shown how to pass parameters from the server side back and forth (as parameters encoded from server-side EL expressions or just string constants). But it's actually possible to pass pure client-side parameters. This means you can pass a result of a JavaScript function or JavaScript expression using `<a4j:param>` when the noEscape attribute is set to true. Listing 3-21 shows such example.

Listing 3-21. Passing a result of a JavaScript function or JavaScript expression using `<a4j:param>`

```
<a4j:commandButton value="Set position" >
    <a4j:param noEscape="true" value="(jQuery(window).width()/2)-250"
assignTo="#{someBean.left}"/>
    <a4j:param noEscape="true" value="(jQuery(window).height()/2)-150"
assignTo="#{someBean.top}"/>
</a4j:commandButton>
```

▓ **Tip**   You can also use `<a4j:param>` with non-Ajax action components such as `<h:commandButton>`, and GET components such as `<h:button>`.

Programmatic Ajax in JSF 2

JSF 2 does offer a way to send an Ajax request programmatically from the client (available request parameters for sending Ajax request programmatically are listed in Table 3-2). In order to do it, we first need to load the JavaScript library shown in Listing 3-22. (When using the <f:ajax> behavior, or any RichFaces tag, JavaScript libraries are loaded automatically.)

Listing 3-22. Loading the JavaScript library

```
<h:head>
    <h:outputScript name="jsf.js" library="javax.faces"/>
<h:/head>
```

Firing an Ajax request would look like Listing 3-23.

Listing 3-23. Firing an Ajax request

```
<h:form id="form">
   <h:panelGrid>
      <h:commandButton id="button" value="Update"
         onclick="jsf.ajax.request(this,event, {render:'form:out'}); return false;" />
      <h:outputText value="#{manualAjax.now}" id="out" />
   </h:panelGrid>
</h:form>
```

Table 3-2. Request Parameters for Sending Ajax Request Programmatically

Parameter	Description
this	DOM element that triggers this Ajax request
event	JavaScript event object
render	The same value when using <f:ajax> and defaults to @this
execute	The same value when using <f:ajax> and defaults to @none

▦ **Note** render has to point to a client id, not a component id.

Listing 3-24 shows another example using <h:inputText>.

Listing 3-24. Example using <h:inputText>

```
<h:form id="form2">
   <h:panelGrid>
      <h:inputText value="#{manualAjax.text}"
         onkeyup="jsf.ajax.request(this, event, {render:'form2:out'});
```

```
            return false;" />
        <h:outputText value="#{manualAjax.text}" id="out" />
    </h:panelGrid>
</h:form>
```

We believe it's simpler to use `<a4j:jsFuction>` because you don't have to manually write any JavaScript code and you get all the extra features and functionality that are also available in `a4j:ajax` behavior.

The following Ajax attributes are available to use with `<a4j:jsFunction>`: onbegin, onbeforedomupdate, oncomplete, bypassUpdates, and limitRender, data, and status.

`<a4j:jsFunction>` might look like a very simplistic tag. Although it's simple to use, it's actually very powerful. Like any JSF component that exposes client events (almost all components do), `<a4j:jsFunction>` can be used with those events to fire an Ajax request. Take any HTML tag and `<a4j:jsFunction>` can be used to fire an Ajax request based on some tag event. In theory, anywhere `<a4j:ajax>` is used, `<a4j:jsFunction>` can replace it because when the markup is rendered, the JavaScript that `<a4:ajax>` renders is very similar to what `<a4j:jsFunction>` renders. You can look at `<a4j:jsFuction>` as a lower level or foundation tag for all Ajax firing tags and behaviors.

Polling with <a4j:poll>

`<a4j:poll>` works in an almost identical fashion to all the other action components we have discussed, but instead of having to click or type something to send a request, the component will periodically send (poll) an Ajax request to the server. You can easily specify which components to update via the render attribute and which action or actionListener to invoke. All the core Ajax concepts we covered so far apply to this component as well. Let's walk through an example where you see the server time running. You will also be able to stop and start the clock.

When the page is loaded, the application will look as shown in Figure 3-2.

| Start Clock | Stop Clock | **Wed Mar 23 13:41:11 PDT 2011**

Figure 3-2. *Using <a4j:poll>*

When the page is loaded for the first time, the clock is off. You can then use the buttons to start or stop the clock. Before we start, it's important to keep in mind that the default value for execute is @this when using the `<a4j:poll>` component.

Listing 3-25 shows the JSF page.

Listing 3-25. *Shows the JSF page*

```
<h:form>
    <a4j:poll id="poll" interval="500" enabled="#{clockBean.enabled}"
        render="clock" />
    <h:panelGrid columns="2">
        <h:panelGrid columns="2">
            <a4j:commandButton value="Start Clock"
                action="#{clockBean.startClock}"
                render="poll" />
            <a4j:commandButton value="Stop Clock"
                action="#{clockBean.stopClock}"
                render="poll" />
        </h:panelGrid>
        <h:outputText id="clock" value="#{clockBean.now}" />
```

```
            </h:panelGrid>
    </h:form>
```

It has a couple of important attributes: interval defines how often a request will be sent to the server (in milliseconds), and enabled determines whether the component will send a request depending on whether it's set to true or false. You need to be able to stop or start the polling when some condition happens.

When the page is loaded for the first time, enabled is evaluated to false, and thus the poll is disabled. When the Start Clock button is clicked, the startClock method will set enabled to true, which enables the polling. <a4j:poll> polls the server every 500 milliseconds (half a second) and updates the component that displays the time. When the Stop Clock button is clicked, enabled is set to false, which disables the polling.

Whenever you enable or disable the component in runtime, you need to render the component. This is needed so the new value for enabled is read and the JavaScript is updated in the browser to either start or stop polling.

Also notice we place <a4j:poll> inside the same form as the buttons. Placing <a4j:poll> inside the same form is fine because by default its execute is set to @this. Even if we had other input component inside the form, they would be sent to the server but they wouldn't be processed on the server. You could place <a4j:poll> inside its own form and submit less data to the server. Our example is rather simple, and although <a4j:poll> can be placed in the same form, the concept can be applied to a larger application.

Listing 3-26 shows the managed bean.

Listing 3-26. The managed bean

```
@ManagedBean
@RequestScoped
public class ClockBean {

    private boolean enabled; // getter and setter

    public java.util.Date getNow() {
        return new java.util.Date();
    }
    public void stopClock() {
        enabled = false;
    }
    public void startClock() {
        enabled = true;
    }
}
```

The following Ajax attributes are available to use with <a4j:poll>: onbegin, onbeforedomupdate, oncomplete, bypassUpdates, and limitRender, data, and status.

Advanced Partial View Rendering Options

In this section you are going to learn about advanced rendering features available in RichFaces. We will first cover the auto-rendered panel—whose content is automatically rendered on any Ajax request—and then show you how to limit rendering to only components shown in the current render attribute.

Auto-Rendered Areas with <a4j:outputPanel>

To render a component or a set of components, we use the render attribute. render attributes can take any of the following values: @all, @this, @form, @none, ids, and EL expressions bound to Set, List, or String with ids. RichFaces adds an important feature when using EL, the ids are resolved in the same request. We covered this feature in Chapter 2. One more thing you get with RichFaces is the ability to separate ids with a comma (versus just a space in JSF 2), as follows:

```
render="id1, id2, id3"
```

Using render with ids is definitely sufficient but can get rather complicated if there are some components that need to be rendered on every request. If we also assume that there are numerous components that send an Ajax request, we would need to specify components to be rendered on every such component or behavior. RichFaces solves this problem by making available a special <a4j:outputPanel> component, which when used, all components inside the panel are always rendered on any Ajax request without the need to point to the panel or the components inside via render.

Listing 3-27 shows an example using <a4j:outputPanel>. By itself, <a4j:outputPanel> is not much different than <h:panelGroup>. However, to make this panel and everything inside of it auto-rendered, we set a special ajaxRendered="true" attribute, as shown in Listing 3-27.

Listing 3-27. Setting a special ajaxRendered="true" attribute

```
<h:form>
    <a4j:commandButton value="Update time" />
    <a4j:outputPanel ajaxRendered="true">
      <h:outputText value="#{clockBean.now}" />
    </a4j:outputPanel>
</h:form>
```

Notice that <a4j:commandButton> doesn't have the render attribute, however time is still rendered because we use <4j:outputPanel ajaxRendered="true">, which again, marks the entire panel as an auto-rendered area.

Another common place where <a4j:outputPanel> is used is to wrap components is on a page that is not rendered on the initial page display, but rendered after the Ajax request. This is also a common problem some users run into when starting with JSF and Ajax. Let's take the Seven Wonders of the World example shown in Figure 3-3.

◉ Show ○ Hide

7 Wonders of The World

Name	Location
Chichen Itza	Mexico
Christ the Redeemer	Brazil
Colosseum	Italy
Great Wall of China	China
Machu Picchu	Peru
Petra	Jordan
Taj Mahal	India

Figure 3-3. Show or hide the Seven Wonders of the World list

There are two buttons at the top, to hide or show the table. When the page is rendered for the first time, the table is not rendered (hidden). Then, selecting Show should render the table.

The JSF page is shown in Listing 3-28.

Listing 3-28. Showing the JSF page

```
<h:form>
    <h:panelGrid>
        <h:selectOneRadio value="#{dynamicUpdateBean.display}">
            <f:selectItem itemLabel="Show" itemValue="true" />
            <f:selectItem itemLabel="Hide" itemValue="false" />
            <a4j:ajax execute="@this" render="wonderList" />
        </h:selectOneRadio>
    </h:panelGrid>

    <h:dataTable id="wonderList" value="#{wonderListBean.list}"
        var="wonder" rendered="#{dynamicUpdateBean.display}">
        <f:facet name="header">7 Wonders of The World</f:facet>
        <h:column>
            <f:facet name="header">Name</f:facet>
            <h:outputText value="#{wonder.name}" />
        </h:column>
        <h:column>
            <f:facet name="header">Location</f:facet>
            <h:outputText value="#{wonder.location}" />
        </h:column>
    </h:dataTable>
</h:form>
```

In Listing 3-28, #{dynamicUpdateBean.display} is set to false when the page is rendered for the first time, and thus the table is not displayed. When selecting the Show button, we use Ajax request to set #{dynamicUpdateBean.display} to true and then render the table. If you run this code, the table will not be shown. As we mentioned earlier, this is a common stumbling block for users who are starting to use JSF and Ajax. The root of the problem is that we tried to re-render a component not previously rendered in the page. Before we explain this problem, Listing 3-29 shows the Wonder class.

Listing 3-29. Shows the Wonder class

```
public class Wonder {

    private String name;
    private String location;

    public Wonder(String name, String location) {

        this.name = name;
        this.location = location;
    }
    // Getters and setters
}
```

Listing 3-30 shows the managed bean that holds the list of wonders.

Listing 3-30. The managed bean that holds the list of wonders

```java
@ManagedBean
@RequestScoped
public class WonderListBean {

    private ArrayList <Wonder> list;

    public ArrayList<Wonder> getList() {
        return list;
    }
    @PostConstruct
    public void init () {
        list = new ArrayList <Wonder>();
        list.add(new Wonder("Chichen Itza", "Mexico"));
        list.add(new Wonder("Christ the Redeemer", "Brazil"));
        list.add(new Wonder("Colosseum", "Italy"));
        list.add(new Wonder("Great Wall of China", "China"));
        list.add(new Wonder("Machu Picchu", "Peru"));
        list.add(new Wonder("Petra", "Jordan"));
        list.add(new Wonder("Taj Mahal", "India"));
    }
}
```

When the page was rendered for the first time, the table component wasn't rendered. In other words, no markup was sent to the browser. When we select Show, we send an Ajax request and set #{dynamicUpdateBean.display} to true. We also render the table (render="wonderList"). Table markup is sent to the browser. Now, the problem is that RichFaces doesn't know which browser DOM node to update with the table content simply because no such node existed before.

Ajax updates are done based on ids. When some markup is rendered and sent to the browser, it comes with an id. JavaScript is responsible for updating the DOM and will try to locate a node with exactly the same id. If such an id is found, then the new content will replace the old content in the DOM and we get an Ajax update. If such a node isn't found, as in our case, then the new content is simply ignored.

The solution is to create a placeholder for a table that is always rendered. Then, instead of updating (rendering) the table, we will render the placeholder. Anything inside the placeholder will always be updated without any problems. If we use <a4j:outputPanel>, we actually get two features at once. We first get a placeholder, but we also don't need to render the table anymore as <a4j:outputPanel ajaxRendered="true"> is an auto-rendered panel. Listing 3-31 shows this using <a4j:outputPanel>.

Listing 3-31. Using <a4j:outputPanel>

```xml
<h:form>
   <h:panelGrid>
      <h:selectOneRadio value="#{dynamicUpdateBean.display}">
         <f:selectItem itemLabel="Show" itemValue="true" />
         <f:selectItem itemLabel="Hide" itemValue="false" />
            <a4j:ajax execute="@this"/>
      </h:selectOneRadio>
   </h:panelGrid>
   <a4j:outputPanel ajaxRendered="true" layout="block">
      <h:dataTable id="wonderList" value="#{wonderListBean.list}"
         var="wonder" rendered="#{dynamicUpdateBean.display}">
         ...
```

```
        </h:dataTable>
    </a4j:outputPanel>
</h:form>
```

If you look at the page code, using the Firebug Firefox plug-in (http://getfirebug.com) for example, you will see that <a4j:outputPanel> renders a span HTML tag. If we didn't want to use an auto-rendered panel, then we can still use <a4j:outputPanel> with an id, but will have to render it as shown in Listing 3-32.

Listing 3-32. Using <a4j:outputPanel> with an id

```
<h:form>
    <h:panelGrid>
        <h:selectOneRadio value="#{dynamicUpdateBean.display}">
            <f:selectItem itemLabel="Show" itemValue="true" />
            <f:selectItem itemLabel="Hide" itemValue="false" />
            <a4j:ajax execute="@this" render="wonderPanel"/>
        </h:selectOneRadio>
    </h:panelGrid>
    <a4j:outputPanel id="wonderPanel" layout="block">
        <h:dataTable id="wonderList" value="#{wonderListBean.list}"
            var="wonder" rendered="#{dynamicUpdateBean.display}">
            ...
        </h:dataTable>
    </a4j:outputPanel>
</h:form>
```

Listing 3-33 replaces <a4j:outputPanel> with <h:panelGrid> as a placeholder and works exactly the same.

Listing 3-33. Replacing <a4j:outputPanel> with <h:panelGrid>

```
<h:form>
    <h:panelGrid>
        <h:selectOneRadio value="#{dynamicUpdateBean.display}">
            <f:selectItem itemLabel="Show" itemValue="true" />
            <f:selectItem itemLabel="Hide" itemValue="false" />
            <a4j:ajax execute="@this" render="wonderPanel"/>
        </h:selectOneRadio>
    </h:panelGrid>
    <h:panelGrid id="wonderPanel">
        <h:dataTable id="wonderList" value="#{wonderListBean.list}"
            var="wonder" rendered="#{dynamicUpdateBean.display}">
            ...
        </h:dataTable>
    </h:panelGrid>
</h:form>
```

There is one more feature worth mentioning. <a4j:outputPanel> can also be used for layout. It comes with a layout attribute that can be set to either block to render a <div> tag, inline to render a <span> tag (default). Listing 3-34 shows an example using the block value.

Listing 3-34. Shows an example using the block value

```
<a4j:outputPanel layout="block">
…
</a4j:outputPanel>
```

■ **Note** Similar to `<h:panelGroup>`, `<a4j:outputPanel>` can produce `<span>` or `<div>` elements according to the `layout` attribute. `<span>` is encoded by default. It's important to have it defined as a block when using block HTML elements, such as `<div>` and `<table>`, in order to have valid HTML encoded.

Using the limitRender Attribute to Turn off Auto-Rendered Panels

The auto-rendered panel is a good feature to have, as it makes it easier to mark parts of the page that should always be rendered. You no longer need to point to components with render. However, there might be a situation where a particular Ajax action on a page should not update the auto-rendered panels but be limited to only what is set in the current render. We are trying to see how to turn off auto-rendered panels in a specific case. We are going to use the page shown in Figure 3-4. 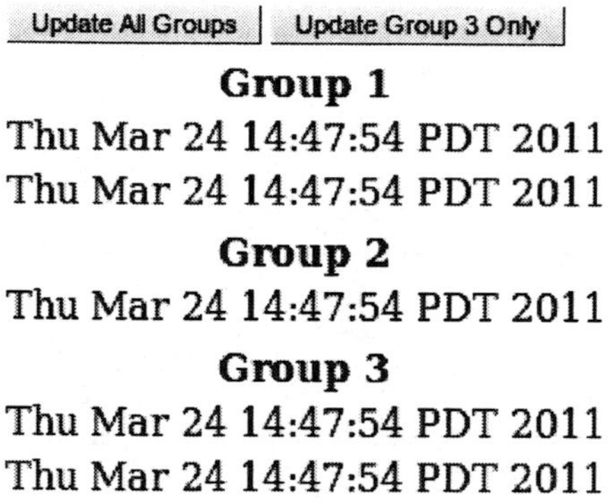

Update All Groups | Update Group 3 Only
Group 1
Thu Mar 24 14:47:54 PDT 2011
Thu Mar 24 14:47:54 PDT 2011
Group 2
Thu Mar 24 14:47:54 PDT 2011
Group 3
Thu Mar 24 14:47:54 PDT 2011
Thu Mar 24 14:47:54 PDT 2011

Figure 3-4. Turning off auto-rendered panels

The JSF page is shown in Listing 3-35.

Listing 3-35. The JSF page

```
<h:form>
    <h:panelGrid columns="2">
        <a4j:commandButton value="Update All Groups" render="group1, group2" />
        <a4j:commandButton value="Update Group 1 and 2 Only" render="group1, group2"
            limitRender="true" />
    </h:panelGrid>
    <h:panelGrid columns="1" id="group1">
        <f:facet name="header">Group 1</f:facet>
        <h:outputText value="#{timeBean.time1}" />
```

59

```
            <h:outputText value="#{timeBean.time2}" />
         </h:panelGrid>
         <h:panelGrid columns="1" id="group2">
            <f:facet name="header">Group 2</f:facet>
            <h:outputText value="#{timeBean.time3}" />
         </h:panelGrid>
         <a4j:outputPanel ajaxRendered="true" layout="block">
            <h:panelGrid id="group3">
               <f:facet name="header">Group 3</f:facet>
               <h:outputText value="#{timeBean.time4}" />
               <h:outputText value="#{timeBean.time5}" />
            </h:panelGrid>
         </a4j:outputPanel>
</h:form>
```

In Listing 3-5, when the Update All Groups button is clicked, all the clocks are rendered (updated). Group 1 and Group 2 are updated via ids, as the button has render="group1, group2". Group 3 is updated because it is inside an auto-rendered panel. If the second button is clicked (Update Groups 2 and 3 only), then only Group 1 and Group 2 are rendered. Group 3, which is inside the auto-rendered panel, is not updated. The reason it's not updated is because use limitRender="true" is in the second button. What this means is to limit rendering only to a component set in the current render attribute (in our case it's Group1 and Group2). Another way to look at it is we turned off all auto-rendered panels for this particular button. This is a handy feature and gives you further flexibility and control in customizing what to render.

Note limitRender="true" can also be used to turn off auto rendering of <rich:message> and <rich:messages> components.

Advanced Execute Options

In this section you are going to learn about a number of advanced execute options available in RichFaces. We will first learn about the RichFaces <a4j:region> tag, which allows you to define what to execute in a more declarative way and then learn how to skip phases in the JSF lifecycle when doing validation.

Defining Execute Regions with <a4j:region>

When sending an Ajax request it's always important to keep in mind what is going to be processed or executed on the server. As we know, when using <f:ajax> or <a4j:ajax> the execute attribute defaults to @this (other values execute can be set to are: @all, @form, @none, id's, EL expressions similar to used in render). When using RichFaces <a4j:poll> or <a4j:jsFunction>, the execute attribute also defaults to @this. But, when using <a4j:commandButton> or <a4j:commandLink>, the execute attribute sets to the @form value. Why did RichFaces change the default value? In the majority of cases, a button or link are used inside a form to perform a complete form submit. You will enter information and click a button or a link to submit. As you have just entered input, you need to process that input as well. If execute was set to the default value of @this, we would need to include every input component inside the form to be executed as well, or set execute to @form (or parent container id). Having the <a4j:commandButton> and <a4j:commandLink> execute attribute default to @form, makes development easier.

RichFaces adds another feature that makes marking what to execute simpler. RichFaces adds `<a4j:region>` and the @region keyword. Listing 3-36 shows a JSF that will not work, as `<a4j:ajax>` nested inside `<h:commandButton>` doesn't have the execute attribute set.

Listing 3-36. *Shows a JSF that will not work*

```
<h:form>
   <h:panelGrid>
      <h:selectOneMenu id="type" value="#{flowerRegionBean.type}">
         <f:selectItem itemValue="Roses" itemLabel="Roses" />
         <f:selectItem itemValue="Tulips" itemLabel="Tulips" />
         <f:selectItem itemValue="Irises" itemLabel="Irises" />
      </h:selectOneMenu>
      <h:selectOneMenu id="size" value="#{flowerRegionBean.size}">
         <f:selectItem itemValue="Small" itemLabel="Small" />
         <f:selectItem itemValue="Large" itemLabel="Large" />
         <f:selectItem itemValue="Extra Large" itemLabel="Extra Large" />
      </h:selectOneMenu>
      <h:selectOneMenu value="#{flowerRegionBean.vase}">
         <f:selectItem itemValue="Standard vase" itemLabel="Standard vase" />
         <f:selectItem itemValue="Premium vase" itemLabel="Premium vase" />
         <f:selectItem itemValue="No vase" itemLabel="No vase" />
      </h:selectOneMenu>
      <h:commandButton value="Buy Flowers!">
         <a4j:ajax event="click"/>
      </h:commandButton>
   </h:panelGrid>
   <a4j:outputPanel ajaxRendered="true" layout="block">
      <h:panelGrid>
         <h:outputText value="#{flowerRegionBean.type}" />
         <h:outputText value="#{flowerRegionBean.size}" />
         <h:outputText value="#{flowerRegionBean.vase}" />
      </h:panelGrid>
   </a4j:outputPanel>
</h:form>
```

The managed bean is shown in Listing 3-37.

Listing 3-37. *The managed bean*

```
@ManagedBean
@RequestScoped
public class FlowerRegionBean {

   private String type;
   private String size;
   private String vase;

   // getters and setters
}
```

To make this work, we would either have to list all input components in execute attribute or set an ID on the panel grid and point execute to it. The alternative approach, which is more declarative in nature, is to use `<a4j:region>`. Therefore, to make the example in Listing 3-37 work, all we need to do is wrap input components and the button inside `<a4j:region>`, as shown in Listing 3-38.

Listing 3-38. Wrap input components and the button inside `<a4j:region>`

```
<h:form>
    <a4j:region>
        <h:panelGrid>
            ...
            <h:commandButton value="Buy Flowers!">
                <a4j:ajax event="click" />
            </h:commandButton>
        </h:panelGrid>
    </a4j:region>
    <a4j:outputPanel ajaxRendered="true">
        <h:panelGrid>
            <h:outputText value="#{flowerRegionBean.type}" />
            <h:outputText value="#{flowerRegionBean.size}" />
            <h:outputText value="#{flowerRegionBean.vase}" />
        </h:panelGrid>
    </a4j:outputPanel>
</h:form>
```

This approach is more declarative, as you no longer need to specify which IDs to execute. Any Ajax request from within the region and all input components inside the region will be executed (unless other Ajax components or behaviors specify what components to execute explicitly, in which case they will override the region) . When using a region, you can also use the @region keyword, as follows:

```
<a4j:ajax event="click" execute="@region"/>
```

This indicates to execute everything inside the region and is optional. Even if we don't specify @region, as we did in our example, the region is executed by default.

Skipping Model Updates During Validation

Validating an input field only when the user tabs out or clicks elsewhere is a popular technique that can easily be done with Ajax using the blur event. Listing 3-39 shows an example.

Listing 3-39. Validating an input field with Ajax using the blur event

```
<h:form>
    <h:panelGrid columns="3">
        <h:outputText value="Name:" />
        <h:inputText id="name" value="#{bypassUpdatesBean.name}" >
            <a4j:ajax event="blur" render="nameMessage"/>
        </h:inputText>
        <h:message for="name" id="nameMessage"/>

        <h:outputText value="Email:" />
        <h:inputText id="email" value="#{bypassUpdatesBean.email}" >
            <a4j:ajax event="blur" render="emailMessage" />
        </h:inputText>
        <h:message for="email" id="emailMessage"/>
```

```
        <h:outputText value="Age:" />
        <h:inputText id="age" value="#{bypassUpdatesBean.age}" >
            <a4j:ajax event="blur" render="ageMessage" />
        </h:inputText>
        <h:message for="age" id="ageMessage"/>
    </h:panelGrid>
    <h:commandButton value="Submit" action="page2"/>
</h:form>
```

Each input field has an Ajax behavior attached to its `blur` event. After the input has been entered and the user clicks elsewhere or tabs out, an Ajax request will be sent. Validation constraints are defined using Bean Validation annotations inside the managed bean, as shown in Listing 3-40. Now, once the entire form has been filled and validated, there is button to submit in order to invoke the application logic to do something with the input, such as add a new record.

Listing 3-40. Validation constraints are defined using Bean Validation annotations inside the managed bean

```
@ManagedBean
@RequestScoped
public class BypassUpdatesBean {

    @Length (min=3, message="Name must be at least {min} characters long")
    private String name;

    @Email(message="Invalid email address")
    private String email;

    @Min(value=1, message="Age must be greater than 0")
    private Integer age;

    // Getters and setters
}
```

Let's look closely at what happens when a `blur` event occurs. When a `blur` event occurs, an Ajax request is sent to the server and the component's data is validated. If we look at what phases we pass when this request is sent, then we would see the following (also, at the end of this section, read how to create a phase tracker):

- Restore View
- Apply Request Values
- Process Validations
- Update Model Values
- Invoke Application
- Render Response

Now, is it really necessary to go through Update Model and Invoke Application phases when only validating? The answer is no. No action is called and when the submit button is clicked, we then go through all the phases as expected. So, when validating, we really just need to get to Process Validations and we can safely jump to Render Response from there. If validation fails, we will go to Render Response anyway, but we would like to go to Render Response even if the value is valid.

If you look closely at the JSF page is Listing 3-41, you will notice that each <a4j:ajax> has an extra attribute: bypassUpdates="true".

Listing 3-41. Notice that each <a4j:ajax> has an extra attribute: bypassUpdates="true"

```
<h:form>
    <h:panelGrid columns="3">
        <h:outputText value="Name:" />
        <h:inputText id="name" value="#{bypassUpdatesBean.name}" >
            <a4j:ajax event="blur" render="nameMessage" bypassUpdates="true"/>
        </h:inputText>
        <h:message for="name" id="nameMessage"/>

        <h:outputText value="Email:" />
        <h:inputText id="email" value="#{bypassUpdatesBean.email}" >
            <a4j:ajax event="blur" render="emailMessage" bypassUpdates="true"/>
        </h:inputText>
        <h:message for="email" id="emailMessage"/>

        <h:outputText value="Age:" />
        <h:inputText id="age" value="#{bypassUpdatesBean.age}" >
            <a4j:ajax event="blur" render="ageMessage" bypassUpdates="true"/>
        </h:inputText>
        <h:message for="age" id="ageMessage"/>
    </h:panelGrid>
    <h:commandButton value="Submit" action="page2"/>
</h:form>
```

This attribute does exactly what we want. It will take use to Process Validations and then jump to Render Response even if the value is valid. We will pass through the following phases:

- Restore View
- Apply Request Values
- Process Validations
- Render Response

■ **Tip** Use bypassUpdates to optimize the JSF lifecycle during form validation.

Creating a Phase Tracker

Listing 3-42 shows an example of a simple phase tracker. When registered in a JSF configuration file, it will output what JSF phases have passed during a JSF request.

Listing 3-42. An example of a simple phase tracker

```
package org.richfaces.book.utils.PhaseTracker
public class PhaseTracker implements javax.faces.event.PhaseListener{

    public void afterPhase(PhaseEvent e) {
```

```
      e.getFacesContext().getExternalContext().log("after "+e.getPhaseId());
    }
    public void beforePhase(PhaseEvent e) {
      e.getFacesContext().getExternalContext().log("before "+e.getPhaseId());
    }
    public PhaseId getPhaseId() {
      return PhaseId.ANY_PHASE;
    }
}
```

Listing 3-43 shows a phase tracker registration in a JSF configuration file.

Listing 3-43. *A phase tracker registration in a JSF configuration file (`faces-config.xml`)*

```
<lifecycle>
  <phase-listener>org.richfaces.book.utils.PhaseTracker</phase-listener>
</lifecycle>
```

While running with the phase tracker, Listing 3-44 shows the output when validation error occurs.

Listing 3-44. *Shows the output when validation error occurs*

```
Apr 5, 2011 4:24:33 PM org.apache.catalina.core.ApplicationContext log
INFO: before RESTORE_VIEW 1
Apr 5, 2011 4:24:33 PM org.apache.catalina.core.ApplicationContext log
INFO: after RESTORE_VIEW 1
Apr 5, 2011 4:24:33 PM org.apache.catalina.core.ApplicationContext log
INFO: before APPLY_REQUEST_VALUES 2
Apr 5, 2011 4:24:33 PM org.apache.catalina.core.ApplicationContext log
INFO: after APPLY_REQUEST_VALUES 2
Apr 5, 2011 4:24:33 PM org.apache.catalina.core.ApplicationContext log
INFO: before PROCESS_VALIDATIONS 3
Apr 5, 2011 4:24:33 PM org.apache.catalina.core.ApplicationContext log
INFO: after PROCESS_VALIDATIONS 3
Apr 5, 2011 4:24:33 PM org.apache.catalina.core.ApplicationContext log
INFO: before RENDER_RESPONSE 6
Apr 5, 2011 4:24:33 PM org.apache.catalina.core.ApplicationContext log
INFO: after RENDER_RESPONSE 6
```

Controlling Traffic with Client Queue

JSF 2 comes with a built-in Ajax client queue. There is nothing you need to do; the queue is there by default on every page. It's a page level queue and is used by all components. The standard queue provides basic functionality. It will automatically queue requests and ensure that the last Ajax request will finish before a new one is sent. Let's trace the events when using standard Ajax queue, as follows:

1. The button is clicked.

2. An Ajax request is sent to the server; let's call the request A1.

3. While request A1 is being executed, the same button or any other control is activated three times.

4. Three requests are now queued.

5. Once A1 request comes back, the first request in the queue is sent. Two are left in the queue.

6. Two requests are now queued.

RichFaces adds additional functionality on top of the standard JSF 2 queue, such as the following:

- Event combining from the same and different components
- Request delay
- Ignoring "stale" responses
- Defining named and unnamed (view, form) queues
- Overwriting queue settings by individual components

It's very important to note that the RichFaces queue doesn't replace an existing JSF 2 queue, it uses the same queue and only upgrades the queue with additional features and advanced functionality.

■ **Note** The Ajax client queue only work for Ajax requests. It is not used for regular (non-Ajax) requests.

Let's start with how a queue is defined. A queue is added with the <a4j:queue> tag and is configured in the following ways:

- View-level queue (unnamed). A queue is defined outside any forms. All components use the same queue settings.

- Form-level queue (unnamed). A queue is defined inside a form. All components inside the form use this queue setting. Overwrites queue settings defined at view-level queues.

- Queue is given a name (named). Any components that need to use this queue must reference the queue by its name. In this case, default queues (view and form) are ignored for controls that referenced it. Overwrites queue settings defined at view-level and form-level queues.

Listing 3-45 shows a view-level queue.

Listing 3-45. Shows a view-level queue

```
<a4j:queue/>
<h:form>
...
</h:form>
<h:form>
     ...
</h:form>
```

Listing 3-46 shows a form-level queue.

Listing 3-46. Shows a form-level queue

```
<h:form>
<a4j:queue/>
...
</h:form>
<h:form>
<a4j:queue/>
...
</h:form>
```

Listing 3-47 shows one view-level queue and one form-level queue. Components within form "form1" will use the queue inside the form. All other components, including inside form "form2", will use the view-level queue.

Listing 3-47. Shows one view-level queue and one form-level queue

```
<a4j:queue/>
<h:form id="form1">
<a4j:queue/>
...
</h:form>
<h:form id="form2">
...
</h:form>
```

Listing 3-48 shows a named queue. When using a named queue, components have to reference the queue via its name. This is done with a special tag called <a4j:attachQueue>.

Listing 3-48. Shows a named queue

```
<a4j:queue name="ajaxQueue" />
<h:form>
    <a4j:commandButton>
        <a4j:attachQueue name="ajaxQueue"/>
    </a4j:commandButton>
</h:form>
```

<a4j:attachQueue> provides the same attributes as <a4j:queue> does(described later). They should be used to redefine queue settings for specific components.

The <a4j:attachQueue> tag is also used to overwriting unnamed queue settings. In that case, the name attribute should be omitted.

░ **Tip** A queue defined with a name on a page will not be used by components that don't explicitly reference this named queue.

Let's review how the standard queue works and then show what extra features RichFaces adds to the queue. The standard JSF queue will queue all events and will not send the next request until the one executing on the server returns. That's pretty good functionality out-of-the-box, but you are still missing a number of features.

■ **Note** If you want to see how the standard JSF 2 queue works switch all Ajax requests to be sent with `<f:ajax>` behavior.

Combining Events from the Same Component

One of the features that RichFaces adds on top of the standard queue is the ability to combine events from the same component. If a particular button is clicked multiple times (while there is another request on the server), all events from this button will be "combined." In other words, when the request executing on the server completes, only one request will be sent to process multiple clicks done during that time. This is the behavior you usually want. If the same button is clicked seven times, you will want only one request to be sent.

Let's look at an example in Listing 3-49, which shows two buttons. Each button updates the time in its column, and when an Ajax request is sent, the appropriate status is shown in the upper-right corner of the browser.

Listing 3-49. *Shows two buttons*

```
<a4j:status name="action1Status" startText="Button A"
    startStyle="background-color: #ffA500;
    font-weight:bold;
    position: absolute;
    right: 5px;
    top: 1px;
    width: 140px;" />
<a4j:status name="action2Status" startText="Button B"
    startStyle="background-color: #FF0000;
    font-weight:bold;
    position: absolute;
    right: 5px;
    top: 1px;
    width: 120px;" />

<a4j:queue/>

<h:form>
    <h:panelGrid columns="2" border="1">
        <a4j:commandButton value="Button A" action="#{queueBean.action1}"
            render="now1" status="action1Status"/>
        <a4j:commandButton value="Button B" action="#{queueBean.action2}"
            render="now2" status="action2Status"/>
        <h:outputText id="now1" value="#{queueBean.now1}" />
        <h:outputText id="now2" value="#{queueBean.now2}" />
    </h:panelGrid>
</h:form>
```

The rendered page is shown in Figure 3-5.

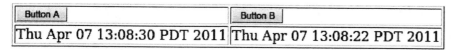

Figure 3-5. Using the RichFaces queue

The managed bean is rather simple and shown in Listing 3-50. One thing to point out, we put both actions to sleep to give us a more "real world" scenario.

Listing 3-50. The managed bean

```
@ManagedBean
@RequestScoped
public class QueueBean {

    public Date getNow1 (){
        return (new Date ());
    }
    public Date getNow2 (){
        return (new Date ());
    }
    public void action1 () {
        try {
            Thread.sleep (4000);
        } catch (InterruptedException e) {
            e.printStackTrace();
        }
    }
    public void action2 () {
        try {
            Thread.sleep (1000);
        } catch (InterruptedException e) {
            e.printStackTrace();
        }
    }
}
```

Now that we have the code down, let's examine how the queue works. Because it's a RichFaces application and we use RichFaces components, we get some extra features.

If you click Button A once, a request—let's call it A1—will be sent to the server and it will take 4 seconds for it to complete. If you click Button A again within the 4 seconds (A2), the new event will be queued and only be sent when request A1finishes executing on the server. This is nothing new, you get this functionality from the standard queue. Table 3-3 shows the sequence of events.

Table 3-3. Sequence of events

Event (control activated)	Client Queue	Server
A1	[empty]	A1 (being processed for 4 seconds)
A2	A2	A1

A2 will be fired only when request A1 completes.

Let's do something similar, but while request A1 is executing on the server, we will click the button multiple times. Because the same button is clicked, each new event or click will overwrite (or combine) with the currently queued event. No matter how many times you click the button, only one event will be sent to the server. This feature will prevent flooding the server with identical requests. The sequence of events is shown in Table 3-4.

Table 3-4. Sequence of events when the same button is clicked multiple times

Event (control activated)	Client Queue	Server
A1	[empty]	A1 (being processed for 4 seconds)
A2	A2	A1
A3	A3 (replaces A2)	A1
A4	A4 (replaces A3)	A1
A5	A5 (replaces A4)	A1
A6	A6 (replaces A5)	A1 (completed)
		A6

Once request A1 completes, request A6 will be sent and the client queue is now empty.

■ **Tip** Events from the same component are "combined" together.

There is also a second button. Let's trace the events when we mix clicking both buttons, shown in Table 3-5.

Table 3-5. Queue events with two buttons

Event (control activated)	Client Queue	Server
A1	[empty]	A1 (being processed for 4 seconds)
A2	A2	A1
A3	A3 (replaces A2)	A1
B1	B1A3 (queue front)	A1
B2	B2A3	A1

Event (control activated)	Client Queue	Server
A4	A4B2A3	A1
B3	B3A4B2A3	A1

Notice that something different happened here. As long as we were clicking Button A, those events were combined. Once we clicked Button B and the last event in the queue was from A, events no longer could be combined and that event was added to the queue. What this means is that events can be combined as long as the event just activated and the event last in queue are from the same component.

RichFaces queue features are there even though we didn't place the <a4j:queue> tag on the page. In fact, you get a queue on every page automatically. RichFaces provides this application-wide on all pages with the context parameter, as shown in Listing 3-51.

Listing 3-51. RichFaces provides this application-wide on all pages with the context parameter

```
<context-param>
    <param-name>org.richfaces.queue.global.enabled</param-name>
    <param-value>true</param-value>
</context-param>
```

When defining some of the queues we mentioned earlier—view-level, form-level and component mapped—all are just overwriting a queue with a bigger scope. If at some point you need to set any attributes on this global queue, the name of the queue is org.richfaces.queue.global, and setting attributes would look like the following:

```
<a4j:queue name="org.richfces.queue.global" requestDelay="2000">
```

Setting a Delay

You can set a delay on a queue by using the *requestDelay* attribute (set to 4 seconds in the following sample):

```
<a4j:queue requestDelay="4000">
```

This means that every request will be queued and delayed by 4 seconds before sending. Note that this is a view-level queue and so all the controls will be delayed by 4 seconds. Another way to look at a delay is that it is the time to wait for new requests to be fired from the same component and for this new event to replace the one that has been queued. Let's trace events with Table 3-6.

Table 3-6. Queue Events with Delay

Event (control activated)	Client Queue (4-sec. delay)	Server
A1	A1	
A2 (within 4 seconds)	A2 (replaces A1)	
A3 (within 4 seconds)	A3 (replaces A2)	
A4 (after 4 seconds)	A4	A3

For event A4 to be fired, two things need to happen: the previous request from the server has to finish and the A4 delay time has to pass.

We told you that each component can overwrite either view-level or form-level queue settings by using the `<a4j:attachQueue>` behavior. Right now our delay is view-level. For the second button, let's overwrite the delay and set it to 0, as shown in Listing 3-52.

Listing 3-52. Overwrite the delay and set it to 0

```
<a4j:commandButton value="Button B" action="#{queueBean.action2}" render="now2"
        status="action2Status">
    <a4j:attachQueue requestDelay="0"/>
</a4j:commandButton>
```

Button A will use the view-level queue and each event will be delayed 4 seconds. Button B will still use the view-level queue but overwrites the delay by setting it to 0.

In Table 3-6, we used only one component. Let's see what happens if we now use two buttons. Let's say we queued A1, and within the delay period of 4 seconds, we clicked Button B. What will happen is shown in Table 3-7: event A1 will fire immediately, without waiting for its delay period to pass.

If you didn't have this book, your first reaction might have been to think it's a bug. But, it's not a bug. The reason event A1 was sent without waiting for its delay to pass is because B1 cannot be combined with A1, and as there are no more events queued that can be combined with A1, A1 fires immediately. To reinforce, a delay could be used to wait for the same events (from the same component) to be combined.

Table 3-7. Queue with a Delay Used to Wait for Requests from the Same Components

Event (control activated)	Client Queue (4-sec. delay)	Server
A1	A1	
B1 (within 4 seconds)	B1	A1

Combining Events from Different Components

We showed that events from the same component (when queued) are combined. It's also possible to combine events from different components by placing them in the same request group using the *requestGroupingId* attribute. As this setting applies to individual components, we use the *`<a4j:attachQueue>`* tag to set that parameter, as shown in Listing 3-53.

Listing 3-53. Use the `<a4j:attachQueue>` tag to set that parameter

```
<a4j:commandButton value="Button A" action="#{queueBean.action1}"
 render="now1"
    status="action1Status">
    <a4j:attachQueue requestGroupingId="ajaxGroup" />
</a4j:commandButton>

<a4j:commandButton value="Button B" action="#{queueBean.action2}"
 render="now2"
    status="action2Status">
    <a4j:attachQueue requestGroupingId="ajaxGroup" requestDelay="0" />
</a4j:commandButton>
```

Once we update both buttons to belong to the same request group, let's trace the sequence in Table 3-8.

Table 3-8. Combining Queue Events

Event (control activated)	Client Queue (4-sec. delay)	Server
A1	A1	
A2 (within 4 seconds)	A2 (replaces A1)	
B1	Replaces A2, fires immediately as B1 has no delay	B1

Events A1 and A2 are combined because they are from the same component. When we queue the event, B1, it combines (or replaces) A2, as both buttons are now in the same request group id. Now, B1 fires immediately, as it doesn't have any delay. If we were to put a delay for 1 second (1000ms), for example, then B1 would replace A2 and fire after 1 second.

Ignoring "Stale" Responses

Let's review an example we saw earlier where a lowercase string is converted to an uppercase string. In the earlier example, we invoked the action after clicking a button. This example is slightly updated; we now invoke the action on the *keyup* event. The JSF page is shown in Listing 3-54.

Listing 3-54. The JSF page

```
<h:form>
    <a4j:status startText="Working..."
        startStyle="background-color: #ffA500;
        font-weight:bold;
        position: absolute;
        left: 520px;
        top: 1px;
        width: 100px;" />

    <a4j:queue requestDelay="500"/>
    <h:panelGrid>
        <h:panelGrid>
            <h:outputText value="Enter lower case text to convert to upper
                case:" />
            <h:inputText value="#{queueIgnoreOldBean.text}" >
                <a4j:ajax event="keyup" render="upper"
                    listener="#{queueIgnoreOldBean.upperCase}"/>
            </h:inputText>
        </h:panelGrid>
        <h:outputText id="upper" value="#{queueIgnoreOldBean.text}" />
    </h:panelGrid>
</h:form>
```

Notice that we put a delay of a half second before sending the Ajax request. This will allow us to "combine" events. Or in other words, wait for the user to enter more letters.

The managed bean is shown in Listing 3-55.

Listing 3-55. The manage bean

```
@ManagedBean
@RequestScoped
public class QueueIgnoreOldBean {
    private String text;

    // Getter and setter

    public void upperCase(AjaxBehaviorEvent event) {
        try {
            Thread.sleep(2500);
        } catch (InterruptedException e) {
            e.printStackTrace();
        }
        setText(text.toUpperCase());
    }
}
```

Let's say we type the word "dog." A request will be sent, it takes 2.5 seconds for the action to be executed, at which point we should see the word DOG rendered in the page. Let's repeat this again, but when the request is being executed on the server, quickly delete "dog" and type "cat."

The result that you will see is that first DOG will be rendered and then CAT will be rendered. Now the question is, does it make sense to render DOG if the user has changed the input to "cat?" The answer will depend, but in most cases there is no more need to show DOG because the user typed "cat." DOG is in this case is a "stale" response. Whether you want to render DOG or not is up to you. Luckily, RichFaces provides a queue feature that allows you to ignore "stale" responses. The RichFaces queue provides an ignoreDupResponse attribute that allows you to do just that. When set to true, it will ignore duplicate responses from the same component. What does duplicate mean? Duplicate means that if a request is currently being executed and another request from the same component (or components grouped by requestGroupingId) is queued, then it will ignore the original response or DOM update. It's important to understand that the request will execute on the server (we can't stop it there), only the DOM update will be dropped or ignored.

To ignore a "stale" response, we add the ignoreDupRepsonses attribute to the queue, as follows:

```
<a4j:queue requestDelay="500" ignoreDupResponses="true"/>
```

Let's run the page again. Enter "dog," and while the request is being executed (status is shown), quickly delete and type "cat." You should now see only CAT rendered. The original response (DOG) finished, but we decided to ignore this DOM update.

It's important to keep in mind that RichFaces provides a great number of advanced features, but it just upgrades the standard JSF 2 queue.

More a4j:* Tags and Features

This section will cover more a4j:* tags and features, such as how to show status during an Ajax request, how to display Ajax request/response logging information, and a simpler way to invoke action listeners.

Showing Ajax Status with <a4j:status>

Many web sites that use Ajax show an Ajax request status such as a moving animated image or a "Loading..." message at the top of the screen. Some block the entire page while the Ajax request is being executed. There are a number of reasons why it might make sense to show an Ajax request status. As there is no full page refresh, the user might not even be aware that a request is being executed. Showing the status indicates that something is happening—and perhaps the user won't click the button or link again. Well, as you probably know by now, there is no such thing as "perhaps" in web development. Another usage is to block the screen while the Ajax request is being executed in order to prevent the user from clicking any actions until the Ajax request is complete. Without debating this any further, it's up to you if you want to show the Ajax status. Our job is to show you how to use a <a4j:status> component in RichFaces. This component is used to show an Ajax request status.

The following are three ways define <a4j:status>:

- Status per view (page). Status is placed outside any form. Any component that fires an Ajax request on this page will activate this status.

- Status per form. Status is placed inside a form. Any component within that form that fires an Ajax request will activate this status (view status will not be activated).

- Named status. Status is given a name and components that fire an Ajax request must refer to that status by name. If no component references this status, the status will not be shown.

So, how do you define what the component shows? The simplest way is to use two attributes named startText and stopText. startText shows any text when the request is being executed on the server, and stopText is the text shown when there is no active Ajax request. A third attribute, errorText, is available to display text in case of server error.

The following three figures show Ajax at different steps. To keep the example simple but still demonstrate the full power of <a4j:status>, we are going to take and convert a string entered in uppercase.

Figure 3-6 shows the page after it was just loaded; however, stopText is already displayed because there is no active Ajax request.

Figure 3-6. *No active Ajax request; page just loaded*

■ **Tip** To avoid showing status when no Ajax request is active, simply don't set stopText property (or stop facet).

Figure 3-7 shows when there is an active request on the server.

Figure 3-7. *During active Ajax request*

Figure 3-8 shows after the request is done.

hello world   Convert Done

HELLO WORLD

Figure 3-8. After Ajax request is completed

The JSF page is shown in Listing 3-56.

Listing 3-56. The JSF page

```
<h:form>
   <h:panelGrid>
      <h:panelGrid columns="3">
         <h:inputText value="#{ajaxStatusBean.text}" />
         <a4j:commandButton value="Convert" action="#{ajaxStatusBean.upperCase}"
            render="upper"/>
         <a4j:status startText="Working..." stopText="Done" />
      </h:panelGrid>
      <h:outputText id="upper" value="#{ajaxStatusBean.text}" />
   </h:panelGrid>
</h:form>
```

In Listing 3-56, the status is placed inside the form, thus any other component activated inside this form will invoke (show) this status as well.

The managed bean is shown in Listing 3-57.

Listing 3-57. The manage bean

```
@ManagedBean
@RequestScoped
public class AjaxStatusBean {

   private String text;

   public void upperCase () {
      try {
         Thread.sleep (3000);
      } catch (InterruptedException e) {
         e.printStackTrace();
      }
      setText(text.toUpperCase());
   }
   public String getText() {
      return text;
   }
   public void setText(String text) {
      this.text = text;
   }
}
```

The bean is rather simple. The only thing you will notice is that we put the action to sleep for 3 seconds. Without this, the action is executed very fast and it's difficult to see the status. So, this is really only done to "mimic" a more realistic example.

Seeing the text "Done" is not something you would expect when the page first loads. It's perfectly fine not to use it at all and only define startText. When the page loads for the first time, nothing will be displayed and when Ajax is activated, startText content will be displayed.

```
<a4j:status startText="Working..."/>
```

You can also style the label shown with startStyle attribute (stopStyle also available), as follows:

```
<a4j:status startText="Working..." startStyle="background-color:#ffA500"/>
```

You are not limited to displaying the status next to the button or link; using the style attribute you can specify absolute positioning for the status. Let's move the status outside the form; this means that any component on the page will activate this status and that we are moving the status to display at the very top of the browser window, as shown in Figure 3-9.

Figure 3-9. *Using absolute positioning for Ajax status*

The code is shown in Listing 3-58.

Listing 3-58. *The code for the Ajax status*

```
<a4j:status id="ajaxStatus" startText="Working..."
        startStyle="background-color: #ffA500;
        font-weight:bold;
        position: absolute;
        left: 520px;
        top: 1px;
        width: 100px;" />
<h:form>
    <h:panelGrid>
        <h:panelGrid columns="3">
            <h:inputText value="#{ajaxStatusBean.text}" />
            <a4j:commandButton value="Convert"
                action="#{ajaxStatusBean.upperCase}"
                render="upper" />
        </h:panelGrid>
        <h:outputText id="upper" value="#{ajaxStatusBean.text}" />
    </h:panelGrid>
</h:form>
```

Right now any component will show this status. Let's update the page so that the status is shown only when we click the Convert button. We first need to give the status a name, as shown in Listing 3-59. Note that we are setting the name, not the id.

Listing 3-59. *Giving the status a name*

```
<a4j:status id="ajaxStatus" name="ajaxStatus" startText="Working..."
        startStyle="background-color: #ffA500;
```

```
    font-weight:bold;
    position: absolute;
    left: 520px;
    top: 1px;
    width: 100px;" />
```

Next we need to update `<a4j:commandButton>` to reference that status, using the status attribute as follows:

```
<a4j:commandButton value="Convert"
    action="#{ajaxStatusBean.upperCase}" render="upper"
    status="ajaxStatus"/>
```

The status will be shown only when this button is activated. No other component anywhere on the page will activate this status. Again, this is called a named status.

■ **Note**   Any RichFaces components that sends an Ajax request can show (activate) `<a4j:status>`. A named status will not be shown if no component references it by name.

So far so good, but you might have noticed that if we use the `startText` and `stopText` attribute then we are limited to displaying only text. It's possible to display rich content, other components for example, if we use facets defined on the `<a4j:status>` tag: start, stop, and error. You probably already guessed how they work—identical to `startText`, `stopText`, and `errorText`, but allow you to display any content inside them. Listing 3-60 shows an example using the `start` facet with an image.

Listing 3-60. An example using the start facet with an image

```
<h:form>
    <h:panelGrid>
        <h:panelGrid columns="3">
            <h:inputText value="#{ajaxStatusBean.text}" />
            <a4j:commandButton value="Convert" action="#{ajaxStatusBean.upperCase}"
                render="upper" />
            <a4j:status>
                <f:facet name="start">
                    <h:graphicImage value="/status/ajax-loader.gif" />
                </f:facet>
            </a4j:status>
        </h:panelGrid>
        <h:outputText id="upper" value="#{ajaxStatusBean.text}" />
    </h:panelGrid>
</h:form>
```

The result is shown in Figure 3-10.

Figure 3-10. Showing the Ajax status with an image

Showing a Popup During an Ajax Request

`<a4j:status>` comes with two events that can be used to invoke any JavaScript onstart and onstop events. Using `<a4j:status>` onstart and onstop events with the combination of the `<rich:popupPanel>` component, we can block the page during an Ajax request. This could be used so that the user won't click any other buttons or links on the page when an Ajax request is being executed.

Using the `<a4j:status>` API with `<rich:popupPanel>` is shown in Listing 3-61. With onstart, we show a popup panel, and with onstop, we hide the popup panel. `<rich:popupPanel>` can also be configured as a non-blocking popup. We will cover this component in Chapter 6.

Listing 3-61. Using the `<a4j:status>` API with `<rich:popupPanel>`

```
<h:form>
    <h:panelGrid>
        <h:panelGrid columns="3">
            <h:inputText value="#{ajaxStatusBean.text}" />
            <a4j:commandButton value="Convert"
                action="#{ajaxStatusBean.upperCase}"
                render="upper" />
            <a4j:status onstart="#{rich:component('statusPanel')}.show();"↵
                onstop="#{rich:component('statusPanel')}.hide();" />
        </h:panelGrid>
        <h:outputText id="upper" value="#{ajaxStatusBean.text}" />
    </h:panelGrid>
</h:form>

<rich:popupPanel id="statusPanel" header="Converting">
    <h:outputText value="Please wait.." />
</rich:popupPanel>
```

The result is shown in Figure 3-11.

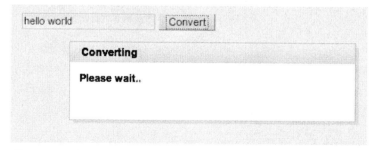

Figure 3-11. Popup panel is opened on Ajax request with `<a4j:status>` JavaScript API

`<a4j:status>` also comes with JavaScript API listed in Table 3-9.

Table 3-9. <a4j:status> JavaScript API

Method name	Description
start()	Switches status to the start state.
stop()	Switches status to the stop state.
error()	Switches status to the error state.

JavaScript API is useful when you need to utilize the same status for non-Ajax requests (by invoking start() on the <h:commandButton> click, for example), or to show it during any time-consuming JavaScript activities.

Displaying Logging and Debugging Information with <a4j:log>

<a4j:log> is a client-side utility for Ajax logging and debugging. It generates JavaScript that opens a debug window, logging client processing information such as requests, responses, and DOM changes.

To use it, just place <a4j:log/> tag on a page, as follows:

```
<a4j:log />
```

It shows output when an Ajax request is fired, so let's use it with a button with the current time, as shown in Listing 3-62.

Listing 3-62. A button with the current time

```
<h:form id="form">
   <h:panelGrid>
      <a4j:commandButton id="Update" value="Update" render="time"/>
      <h:outputText value="#{logBean.now}" id="time"/>
   </h:panelGrid>
   <a4j:log />
</h:form>
```

When the page is rendered and the button is clicked, you will see the output shown in Figure 3-12.

```
 Update
Fri Mar 11 14:02:26 PST 2011
 Clear   info  ▼
info [14:02:26.637]: Received 'begin' event from <input id=form:Update ...>
info [14:02:26.650]: Received 'beforedomupdate' event from <input id=form:Update ...>
info [14:02:26.655]: Listing content of response changes element:
Element update for id=form:time
<update id="form:time"><![CDATA[<span id="form:time">Fri Mar 11 14:02:26 PST 2011</span>]]></update>
Element update for id=javax.faces.ViewState
<update id="javax.faces.ViewState"><![CDATA[-1565513347267642006:3043818015224894739]]></update>
info [14:02:26.657]: Received 'success' event from <input id=form:Update ...>
info [14:02:26.658]: Received 'complete' event from <input id=form:Update ...>
```

Figure 3-12. Output from <a4j:log> component

Selecting the debug level and hitting the Update button will produce a more verbose output, as shown in Figure 3-13.

```
Update
Fri Mar 11 14:11:26 PST 2011
Clear  debug
debug[14:11:26.683]: New request added to queue. Queue requestGroupId changed to form:Update
debug[14:11:26.686]: Queue will wait 0ms before submit
debug[14:11:26.688]: richfaces.queue: will submit request NOW
info [14:11:26.692]: Received 'begin' event from <input id=form:Update ...>
info [14:11:26.779]: Received 'beforedomupdate' event from <input id=form:Update ...>
debug[14:11:26.782]: Server returned responseText: <?xml version='1.0' encoding='UTF-8'?> <partial-response>
<changes><update id="form:time"><![CDATA[<span id="form:time">Fri Mar 11 14:11:26 PST 2011</span>]]></update>
<update id="javax.faces.ViewState"><![CDATA[1014556862738387902:-3598009113069668963]]></update></changes>
</partial-response>
info [14:11:26.790]: Listing content of response changes element:
Element update for id=form:time
<update id="form:time"><![CDATA[<span id="form:time">Fri Mar 11 14:11:26 PST 2011</span>]]></update>
Element update for id=javax.faces.ViewState
<update id="javax.faces.ViewState"><![CDATA[1014556862738387902:-3598009113069668963]]></update>
debug[14:11:26.795]: richfaces.queue: ajax submit successfull
debug[14:11:26.797]: richfaces.queue: Nothing to submit
info [14:11:26.799]: Received 'success' event from <input id=form:Update ...>
info [14:11:26.800]: Received 'complete' event from <input id=form:Update ...>
```

Figure 3-13. Output from <a4j:log> component with debug level selected

In case there is an error, such as server not running, you might see output like Figure 3-14.

```
Update
Fri Mar 11 14:11:26 PST 2011
Clear  debug
debug[14:18:41.912]: New request added to queue. Queue requestGroupId changed to form:Update
debug[14:18:41.913]: Queue will wait 0ms before submit
debug[14:18:41.914]: richfaces.queue: will submit request NOW
info [14:18:41.918]: Received 'begin' event from <input id=form:Update ...>
info [14:18:41.923]: Received 'beforedomupdate' event from <input id=form:Update ...>
info [14:18:41.924]: Server returned responseText:
debug[14:18:41.926]: richfaces.queue: ajax submit error
debug[14:18:41.926]: richfaces.queue: Nothing to submit
error[14:18:41.927]: Received 'error@httpError' event from <input id=form:Update ...>
error[14:18:41.928]: [0] undefined: undefined
info [14:18:41.929]: Received 'complete' event from <input id=form:Update ...>
```

Figure 3-14. Output from <a4j:log> component when server error occurs

If you want to set a log level during development, then the level attribute can be used, as follows:

```
<a4j:log level="DEBUG"/>
```

The level attribute can be set to the following values:

- ERROR
- DEBUG
- INFO
- WARN
- ALL (the default setting, logs all data)

The default behavior is for the log to be rendered inside the page. As an alternative, the log can be opened in a popup window. To do that, set the mode attribute to popup, as follows:

```
<a4j:log mode="popup"/>
```

To open the popup, press Ctrl+Shift+L. To reconfigure the hot key combination, set the hotkey attribute to a new letter; for example hotkey="D" will open the popup when pressing Ctrl+Shift+D.

■ **Note** The log is automatically updated after each Ajax request. It does not need to be explicitly re-rendered.

Using <a4j:actionListener>

<a4j:actionListener> is a small upgrade over the standard <f:actionListener> in JSF. Using <a4j:actionListener>, it's possible to define a listener method inside a managed bean and reference it using a standard method-binding expression, as shown in Listing 3-63.

Listing 3-63. Defining a listener method inside a managed bean

```
<a4j:commandButton value="Update (a4j:actionListener)" render="out">
    <a4j:actionListener listener="#{actionListenerBean.listener}"/>
</a4j:commandButton>
```

Inside a managed bean, the listener would be defined like Listing 3-64.

Listing 3-64. Defining the listener inside the managed bean

```
public void listener (ActionEvent event){
  FacesContext.getCurrentInstance()
    .addMessage(null, new FacesMessage("a4j:actionListener - listener
      invoked at "+new Date()));
}
```

Defining the listener inside the managed bean would give you access to other bean properties and methods.

■ **Tip** Using the <a4j:actionListener> is a good way to add multiple listeners to a component.

As you probably know, there are two ways to define an action listener with a JSF standard <f:actionListener> tag. Both are a little more complicated than using the <a4j:actionListener> we just showed. The first one is using binding, as shown in Listing 3-65.

Listing 3-65. Define an action listener using binding

```
<a4j:commandButton value="Update (binding)" render="out">
    <f:actionListener binding="#{actionListenerBean.anotherListener}"/>
</a4j:commandButton>
```

Inside a managed bean, you need to define an inner anonymous class for this listener, as shown in Listing 3-66. In this case, you also get access to bean properties and methods from within the anonymous inner class.

Listing 3-66. Define an inner anonymous class for this listener

```
public ActionListener getAnotherListener () {
    return new ActionListener (){
        public void processAction (ActionEvent event){
            FacesContext.getCurrentInstance()
                .addMessage(null, new FacesMessage("binding - listener invoked at
                    "+new Date()));
        }
    };
}
```

The last option, and probably the least popular, is to implement in the interface. We will show it to you so that you can compare all three methods. Listing 3-67 shows the interface. Note that the class is not registered as a managed bean.

Listing 3-67. Shows the interface

```
public class YetAnotherListener  implements javax.faces.event.ActionListener{
    public void processAction(ActionEvent event) throws
        AbortProcessingException {
        FacesContext.getCurrentInstance()
            .addMessage(null, new FacesMessage("Interface - listener invoked
                at "+new Date()));
    }
}
```

Using this on a page is shown in Listing 3-68. Notice that we use the type attribute, which takes the full class name as a string, not a value expression. Using this approach you don't have access to properties from this page.

Listing 3-68. Use the type attribute which takes the full class name as a string

```
<a4j:commandButton value="Update (Interface)" render="out">
    <f:actionListener
        type="org.richfaces.book.actionlistener.YetAnotherListener"/>
</a4j:commandButton>
```

Now that you have seen all three approaches, using `<a4j:actionListener>` appears to be the most straightforward. You simply define a listener inside a managed bean and reference it via a standard method-binding expression.

▥ **Tip**   The `<a4j:actionListener>` tag supports all `<f:actionListener>` tag attributes and features.

Summary

This chapter covered some of the most important upgrades that RichFaces adds on top of standard JSF. In this chapter we showed you additional RichFaces components for sending an Ajax request, such as `<a4j:commandButton>`, `<a4j:commandLink>`, `<a4j:poll>`, and `<a4j:jsFunction>`. We then covered advanced rendering options such as using the `<a4j:outputPanel>` component and the `limitRender` attribute.

When deciding what part of the JSF view to execute, RichFaces adds another advanced option by providing the `<a4j:region>` component. RichFaces greatly upgrades the standard JSF queue with advanced features and flexible customization options. As we continue the RichFaces journey in the next chapter, we are going to introduce you to rich components or the rich:* tag library.

Getting Started
with Rich Components

Now that we have covered RichFaces foundation, a4j:* tags, advanced features, and customization, in this chapter we are going to get started with rich components or the rich:* tag library. We won't cover all the components here; we have other chapters for that. In this chapter, we will show you the concepts and common features that all rich components share. Some common features are using facets, components JavaScript API, and sending Ajax requests. Once you master these concepts, you will be able to use any rich component available today or introduced in a future RichFaces release.

Rich or Ajax Component?

If you're asking—should I use a rich or Ajax component?—it doesn't matter. It can be either one or even both as long as we understand what we are talking about. Let's take an example using the <rich:inplaceInput> component. The component renders as a label, as shown in Figure 4-1.

Click to edit

Figure 4-1. <rich:inplaceInput> in label state

When clicking on the label, the component switches to input, as shown in Figure 4-2.

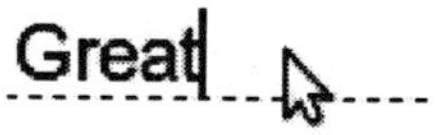

Great

Figure 4-2. <rich:inplaceInput> in input state

This component is rich because it provides a rich UI—or a rich way for entering input. But, at the same time, behind the scenes it's just a regular input field. Could this also be an Ajax component? Probably yes. However, it's important to understand that this component doesn't send an Ajax request automatically. In other words, when changing from label to input or input to label, no Ajax request will be sent. All the changes will only happen on the client (browser). An even better name for this would be a rich client component. Now, don't get discouraged, there is a way to send an Ajax request from this component and we will show it to you later.

So, there are components in RichFaces (rich:* tag library) that are rich client components, but they don't send an Ajax request. But, there are other rich client components that do send an Ajax request. One such example is the `<rich:tabPanel>` component. In other words, Ajax behavior (based on some event) is built into them.

Now that it's clearer what we're exactly dealing with, let's explore the common features and concepts that rich components share.

Rich Components Features

All rich components share a number of common features, as follows:

- Redefining parts of a component using facets
- Sending an Ajax request
- Using component client-side JavaScript API
- Emitting client-side events (client behavior can be attached to such events)
- Skins

■ **Note** Some rich components might not have all the features. To get the most up-to-date information, visit the RichFaces documentation page at `www.jboss.org/richfaces/docs`.

Chapter 13 of this book covers skins in depth. We don't cover the components of the other three items with the same depth. That's not the goal here. The goal is to show you the important concepts that all rich components share. But, again, the following chapters will cover various rich components in more detail.

Redefining Parts of a Component Using Facets

Let's start with the popular tab panel component, which is shown in Figure 4-3.

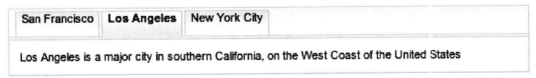

Figure 4-3. Rich tab panel

The JSF page code is shown in Listing 4-1.

Listing 4-1. The JSF page code

```
<h:form>
    <rich:tabPanel style="width:40%" switchType="ajax">
        <rich:tab header="San Francisco">
            <h:outputText value="San Francisco is a major city in northern California, on the↵
```

```
                West Coast of
                the United States" />
          </rich:tab>
          <rich:tab header="Los Angeles">
            <h:outputText value="Los Angeles is a major city in southern California, on the⏎
                West Coast of
                the United States" />
          </rich:tab>
          <rich:tab header="New York City">
            <h:outputText value="New York City is a major city on the East Coast of the United⏎
   States" />
          </rich:tab>
      </rich:tabPanel>
</h:form>
```

    `<rich:tabPanel>` is a container for one or more `<rich:tab>` components. You can place any content or components inside each tab. The header for each tab is defined by the header attribute. This is good, but what if you wanted to put an image of the city or the city flag next to the name? Using the header attribute, we can't really do it, as we are limited only to text.

    How can we do it? Luckily, the component (and many other rich components) provides facets so that we can redefine some parts of the component with any content; and in our case that would be the header. Using a facet called header, we can redefine each tab header with images, text, or really anything we want. We are no longer limited by text. Before we move on, notice that we also set the `switchType` attribute to `ajax`, which is also the default value. You can also set `switchType` to `client` or `server` switching modes.

    Let's add the city flag for each city to its header, as shown in Figure 4-4.

Figure 4-4. Rich tab panel with images in tab headers

    The updated JSF page is shown in Listing 4-2.

Listing 4-2. The updated JSF page

```
<h:form>
    <rich:tabPanel style="width:40%" switchType="ajax">
      <rich:tab>
          <f:facet name="header">
            <h:panelGrid columns="2">
                <h:outputText value="San Francisco" />
                <h:graphicImage value="/images/sf_flag.png" height="25" width="25" />
            </h:panelGrid>
          </f:facet>
          <h:outputText value="San Francisco is a major city in northern California, on the⏎
                West Coast of
                the United States" />
      </rich:tab>
      <rich:tab>
          <f:facet name="header">
```

```
            <h:panelGrid columns="2">
                <h:outputText value="Los Angeles" />
                <h:graphicImage value="/images/la_flag.png" height="25" width="25" />
            </h:panelGrid>
        </f:facet>
        <h:outputText value="Los Angeles is a major city in southern California, on the⏎
            West Coast of
            the United States" />
    </rich:tab>
    <rich:tab>
        <f:facet name="header">
            <h:panelGrid columns="2">
                <h:outputText value="New York City" />
                <h:graphicImage value="/images/nyc_flag.png" height="25" width="25" />
            </h:panelGrid>
        </f:facet>
        <h:outputText value="New York City is a major city on the East Coast of the United⏎
States" />
        </rich:tab>
    </rich:tabPanel>
</h:form>
```

If you look closely at Listing 4-2, we have added a facet named header. Inside the facet we placed the city name and city flag image. It's also important to mention that both the city name and the city flag image are inside a panel grid. The JSF facet can only have one child. If we want to include more than one component, we need to wrap them inside a container. We used <h:panelGrid>, we could have also used <h:panelGroup>. Using the header facet, we are able to define the header for each tab with any content; we are no longer limited to just text. In addition to the header facet, <rich:tab> panel provides other facets. The complete list of facets is shown in Table 4-1.

Table 4-1. *<rich:tab> Facets*

Facet Name	Description
header	Allows you to customize the header with any content.
headerActive	This facet is used when the tab is currently active.
headerInactive	This facet is used when the tab is not currently active.
headerDisabled	This facet is used when the tab is disabled.

How do you find which facets are available? The best place to learn this is the RichFaces components guide. You can find it by visiting www.jboss.org/richfaces/docs.

Many other RichFaces components offer various facets that allow you to redefine various parts of the component.

Sending an Ajax Request

Let's look at another important feature in rich components: sending an Ajax request. As we said before, there are components that have built-in Ajax behavior and there are components that are pure client-side. These components don't have built-in Ajax behavior, but we can easily add it. Let's use our tab example. `<rich:tab>` is one rich component that has built-in Ajax support.

The switching of tabs is by default done via Ajax, but can also be set to either client or server. When we select a new tab, an Ajax request is sent and the entire content of the new tab will be rendered. You don't have to do anything. Now, it's also possible to render content outside the tab. We will show it to you a little bit later.

The JSF page with the tab panel we used earlier is shown in Listing 4-3. The only difference is that we added a component that shows time.

Listing 4-3. The JSF page with the tab panel used earlier

```
<h:form>
    <rich:tabPanel style="width:40%" switchType="ajax">
        <rich:tab header="San Francisco">
            <h:outputText value="San Francisco is a major city in northern California, on the⏎
                West Coast of
                the United States" />
            <h:outputText value="#{timeBean.now}" />
        </rich:tab>
        <rich:tab header="Los Angeles">
            <h:outputText value="Los Angeles is a major city in southern California, on the⏎
                West Coast of
                the United States" />
            <h:outputText value="#{timeBean.now}" />
        </rich:tab>
        <rich:tab header="New York City">
            <h:outputText value="New York City is a major city on the East Coast of the United⏎
                States" />
            <h:outputText value="#{timeBean.now}" />
        </rich:tab>
    </rich:tabPanel>
</h:form>
```

Inside the managed bean, there is a single method, as shown in Listing 4-4.

Listing 4-4. Single method used inside the managed bean

```
public Date getNow (){
    return new Date();
}
```

Every time a tab is switched, the time component in the corresponding tab will be updated. Rendering content outside the tab panel is very simple: all we have to do is use the render attribute. Listing 4-5 shows a page where the time component is placed outside the tab panel. One other thing to notice is that each `<rich:tab>` now has the render attribute set to point to the component we want to update.

Listing 4-5. Shows a page where the time component is placed outside the tab panel

```
<h:form>
    <rich:tabPanel style="width:40%">
        <rich:tab header="San Francisco" render="time">
            <h:outputText value="San Francisco is a major city in northern California, on the↵
                West Coast of
                the United States" />
        </rich:tab>
        <rich:tab header="Los Angeles" render="time">
            <h:outputText value="Los Angeles is a major city in southern California, on the↵
                West Coast of
                the United States" />
        </rich:tab>
        <rich:tab header="New York City" render="time">
            <h:outputText value="New York City is a major city on the East Coast of the United↵
                States" />
        </rich:tab>
    </rich:tabPanel>
    <h:outputText value="#{timeBean.now}" id="time" />
</h:form>
```

As an alternative, instead of pointing via render, another option is to wrap any components to be updated inside `<a4j:outputPanel ajaxRendered="true">`. Also, keep in mind that all attributes we covered in previous chapters, such as limitRender and queue features, are available to use.

Tab panel is a rich component that has Ajax behavior built-in. Now let's look at the `<rich:inplaceInput>` component. It's a rich client component, but doesn't have built-in Ajax behavior.

When we place the component on a page, it provides a very rich way to enter any input, as follows:

```
<rich:inplaceInput value="#{inplaceInputBean.text}"
    defaultLabel="Click to edit" showControls="true"/>
```

Figure 4-5 shows the component activated on a page.

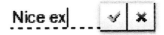

Figure 4-5. Inplace input component in input mode

The key thing to understand is that all the changes we make are happening only on the client; no Ajax request is sent to the server. Why? Well, it's a rich client component (with just regular input behind the scenes). How do you send an Ajax request? One way is to place a button or link inside the form, next to the component. Once a value has been entered into `<rich:inplaceInput>` component (and saved, the component changes to label), the button or link next to the component is clicked. This is not much different than using a standard input field.

Let's say we want to send an Ajax request when a new value is saved inside `<rich:inplaceInput>`. Turns out that this is very easy as well. All we need to do is add an Ajax behavior based on an event, as shown in Listing 4-6.

Listing 4-6. Add an Ajax behavior based on an event

```
<h:form>
    <h:panelGrid>
        <rich:inplaceInput value="#{inplaceInputBean.text}" defaultLabel="Click to edit"
            showControls="true">
            <a4j:ajax event="change" render="echo"/>
        </rich:inplaceInput>
        <h:outputText value="#{inplaceInputBean.text}" id="echo"/>
    </h:panelGrid>
</h:form>
```

Listing 4-6 shows a simple example where a value entered inside <rich:inplaceInput> and saved, will be displayed or echoed next to it. This is done by adding <a4j:ajax> behavior based on a change event. That's it. As you can see, even though <rich:inplaceInput> might be a new component to you, using it is very simple. We apply the same concepts we already know. This also means that any other rich component that defines any client event handlers, such as *onclick* or *onblur*, can have an Ajax behavior attached to it. This is a very powerful concept and gives you a lot of flexibility.

It's worth mentioning again: all other attributes, such as *limitRender*, *bypassUpdates*, queue optimization, and much more, are available to use in <a4j:ajax> as well.

How do you find which events are available on a component? The RichFaces components documentation at www.jboss.org/richfaces/docs will list all the client events available on a component.

Using Component Client-side JavaScript API

JSF is a server-side framework, which means that, in most cases, when we need to control a component such as change a value or property, we send a request to the server, make the change, and update the component on the client.

Let's again take our tab panel example to place three buttons or links outside the tab panel. Each button will be labeled with the city name. By clicking the button, the associated tab is selected. The page is shown in Figure 4-6.

Figure 4-6. Selecting tabs with components outside the tab panel

This is pretty easy to do. First we add a *name* attribute to each tab. Then we bind the *activeItem*, as follows, to a bean property that holds current tab name:

```
activeItem="#{cityBean.selectedTab}"
```

Next there would be an action (or actionListener) on each button. Inside each action we set an *activeItem* attribute based on the button clicked. Listing 4-7 shows the page code.

Listing 4-7. Shows the page code

```
<h:form>
    <a4j:commandButton value="San Francisco" action="#{cityBean.sfAction}" render="cities"/>
    <a4j:commandButton value="Los Angeles" action="#{cityBean.laAction}" render="cities"/>
    <a4j:commandButton value="New York City" action="#{cityBean.nycAction}" render="cities"/>
    <rich:tabPanel id="cities" style="width:40%" activeItem="#{cityBean.selectedTab}">
        <rich:tab header="San Francisco"  name="sf" >
            ...
        </rich:tab>
        <rich:tab header="Los Angeles" name="la">
            ...
        </rich:tab>
        <rich:tab header="New York City" name="nyc">
            ...
        </rich:tab>
    </rich:tabPanel>
</h:form>
```

Listing 4-8 shows the managed bean with actions.

Listing 4-8. Shows the managed bean with actions

```
@ManagedBean
@RequestScoped
public class CityBean {

    private String selectedTab="sf"; // getter and setter

    public void sfAction () {
        this.selectedTab="sf";
    }
    public void laAction () {
        this.selectedTab ="la";
    }
    public void nycAction () {
        this.selectedTab ="nyc";
    }
}
```

This is an easy way to switch tabs by sending an Ajax request to the server. Let's say we want to do the same thing, but instead using plain HTML buttons and without using any of our code to manage active tab from custom listeners. Many rich components provide client-side JavaScript API, which allows us to control the component entirely on the client. <rich:tabPanel> provides such API as well.

There are two things we need to know before using the API. First, we need to get a reference to the component in the browser. Second, we need to know what methods are available for us to call. To get a reference to the component, we are going to use a RichFaces built-in #{rich:component('id')} client function. As for the JavaScript API that is available, you will need to use the RichFaces components guide. But, for the next example, we will tell you the available JavaScript API.

Let's take the tab example and change the buttons to call the tab panel's JavaScript API to switch tabs. Listing 4-9 shows the JSF page with updated buttons.

Listing 4-9. Shows the JSF page with updated buttons

```
<h:form>
    <input type="button" value="San Francisco"
        onclick="#{rich:component('cities')}.switchToItem('sf')"/>
    <input type="button"  value="Los Angeles"
        onclick="#{rich:component('cities')}.switchToItem('la')"/>
    <input type="button"  value="New York City"
        onclick="#{rich:component('cities')}.switchToItem('nyc')"/>

    <rich:tabPanel id="cities" style="width:40%" >
        <rich:tab header="San Francisco" name="sf">
            <h:outputText value="San Francisco is a major city in northern California, on the↵
                West Coast of
                the United States" />
        </rich:tab>
        <rich:tab header="Los Angeles" name="la">
            <h:outputText value="Los Angeles is a major city in southern California, on the↵
                West Coast of
                the United States" />
        </rich:tab>
        <rich:tab header="New York City" name="nyc">
            <h:outputText  value="New York City is a major city on the East Coast of the United↵
                States" />
        </rich:tab>
    </rich:tabPanel>
</h:form>
```

There are a number of interesting things in Listing 4-9 The three buttons are just plain HTML buttons. This means they don't send an Ajax request. You probably noticed that every onclick attribute is set to an interesting expression. Those are the two things we needed to invoke client-side JavaScript API: one, a reference to the component, and two, a method name to invoke.

#{rich:component('id')} is a built-in RichFaces function that gives us a reference to a component's JavaScript property, which holds all the available functions. Once we have the reference, it's just a matter of calling the function we need. In our case the function name is switchToItem('itemName'), and we are passing the tab name we want to display.

You might have noticed that we still send an Ajax request to the server. The request is sent because the switchType attribute is set to ajax by default on the tab panel. Even though we switched to another tab via the component's JavaScript API, tab content is not available, and so it has to get it from the server. To make it client only, set switchType="client" and try running it again. You can place <a4j:log> on the page and you will see that no Ajax request is now sent.

Table 4-2 lists all the JavaScript API on the <rich:tabPanel> component.

Table 4-2. <rich:tabPanel> client-side JavaScript API

Method Name	Description
getItems()	Return an array of the tabs contained in the tab panel.
getItemsNames()	Return an array of the tab names contained in the tab panel.
switchToItem(itemName)	Switch to and display the item identified by the `itemName` string passed as a parameter. Can also be set to the following predefined names: @first, @last, @prev, @next

If we wanted to use switchToItem(itemName) and use the predefined names, you would add the code shown in Listing 4-10.

Listing 4-10. Using switchToItem(itemName) and the predefined names

```
<input type="button" value="First" onclick="#{rich:component('cities')}.switchToItem↵
('@first')"/>
<input type="button"  value="Next" onclick="#{rich:component('cities')}.switchToItem↵
('@next')"/>
<input type="button"  value="Prev" onclick="#{rich:component('cities')}.switchToItem↵
('@prev')"/>
<input type="button"  value="Last" onclick="#{rich:component('cities')}.switchToItem↵
('@last')"/>
```

Many other rich components provide client-side API. How do you find the available API? Again, visit the RichFaces components guide located at www.jboss.org/richfaces/docs. Every component that has API will be listed under the JavaScript API section.

This is a very powerful feature in RichFaces that adds a lot of flexibility to your application. You can control rich components entirely on the client.

Summary

In this chapter we covered the key concepts shared by rich components: using facets, sending an Ajax request from rich components, and using components client-side JavaScript API. These concepts are very important and will be the foundation for the rest of the chapters in this book. The next chapter will introduce you to rich input and selection components.

Rich Input and Select Components

Data input is one of the main functions of any web application. RichFaces provides various, easy-to-use rich components for entering input such as `<rich:inplaceSelect>`, `<rich:autocomplete>`, `<rich:calendar>`, and many more. As with all rich components, rich input components come with a skins feature, a rich JavaScript client API, and facets to make it easier for you to redefine component markup. All the rich input components and their powerful and flexible features will make it easy for you to create applications using RichFaces.

▧ **Note** Although some components provide out-of-the-box Ajax functionality, others, such as `<rich:toolbar>`, don't provide any Ajax functionality. Components like that just provide rich UI. All components in the `rich:` tag library can also be skinned. *Skins*, covered in more detail in Chapter 12, let you change the look and feel of the application easily and on the fly. We just wanted to mention this in case you were wondering why a component such as `<rich:toolbar>` is rich.

▧ **Note** When you run examples in other chapters and notice that your colors are different, don't be concerned. We are simply using a different skin for many of the screen shots in this book. This chapter uses the `blueSky` skin. Jump forward to Chapter 12 to discover the types of skins available. Pick any one you want, and set it in the `web.xml` file per the instructions in that chapter. Also keep in mind that if you have the printed book, then the screen shots will be black and white. If you have the eBook, then you will have color screen shots.

Getting Started

All the rich input components described in this chapter extend standard JSF inputs and selects with specific rich capabilities, customization, and features. This means that the UIInput (base class for input components) core functionality is available for every component. For example, as with standard JSF input components, all rich input-based components support the following features:

- Binding to the model using the value attribute
- Attaching converters and validators

- Ability to disable the input

- Customization of tab order for inputs on the page

All the inputs have a number of new features unified across most of the components, which will be shown throughout the chapter and include the following:

- *Default label support.* When the initial value is not specified, an optional label can be used to provide instructions to the user; for example, "Click to edit."

- *Many controls can be activated and used via keyboard.* It is also possible to disable or enable keyboard support.

■ **Note**   Most features described in this chapter are applicable to most input components, except one: the `<rich:fileUpload>` component. Although still an input, it is based on different foundation classes than other input components. We cover the `<rich:fileUpload>` component at the end of this chapter.

Using <rich:inplaceInput>

`<rich:inplaceInput>` is a rich extension to the standard input component; an example is shown in Figure 5-1.

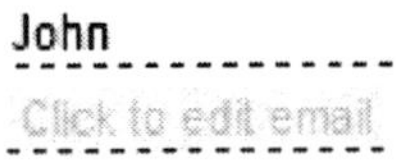

John
- - - - - - - - - - - - - -
Click to edit email
- - - - - - - - - - - - - -

Figure 5-1. <rich:inplaceInput> component

It's possible to click the label to have the component switch to an input field. Once the input is entered, the component switches back to label state. So, let's start with the simplest case, shown in Listing 5-1.

Listing 5-1. The simplest case.

```
<h:form>
    <h:panelGrid columns="1">
        <rich:inplaceInput value="#{inplaceInputBean.name}"
            defaultLabel="Click to edit name"/>
        <rich:inplaceInput value="#{inplaceInputBean.email}"
            defaultLabel="Click to edit email"/>
    </h:panelGrid>
</h:form>
```

The managed bean is shown in Listing 5-2.

Listing 5-2. The managed bean

```
@ManagedBean
@RequestScoped
public class InplaceInputBean {

    private String email;
    private String name;

    // Setter and getter methods
}
```

This is really not much different from using the standard input component. One extra attribute that we are using here is defaultLabel, which sets the label that you can click to start editing the value. Figure 5-2 shows what this code produces.

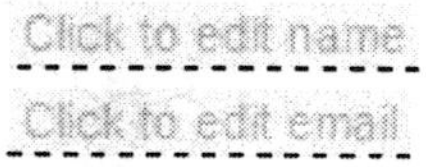

Figure 5-2. <rich:inplaceInput> with default labels

If the value to which the component is bound has an initial value, then that value will be displayed instead of the label.

Once the value has been changed, the change in value is indicated by a small red triangle in the top-left corner, as shown in Figure 5-3.

Figure 5-3. <rich:inplaceInput> with the value changed

To start editing, you click the label. When done editing, you click anywhere outside the component to save the input. This is important: keep in mind that nothing is sent to the server. In other words, no Ajax request is fired to the server. The value has changed only in the browser. This means it's a rich client-side component. You would click a button or a link to submit the page. Alternatively, it's possible to use <a4j:ajax> on component JavaScript events to send an Ajax request to the server (the events are shown later).

There is also an option to add controls to save or cancel the changes, as shown in Figure 5-4. To enable controls, set showControls="true".

Figure 5-4. <rich:inplaceInput> with controls to save or cancel the input

The component provides many event handlers attributes. One of the most common is the standard *onchange* event attribute, which is normally used to add some processing when the value is changed. You can use it to send an Ajax request to validate the new input. In Listing 5-3, we attached Ajax behavior to be fired on change event. Every edit and saving of the value causes the output to be updated with the entered string value.

Listing 5-3. Attaching Ajax behavior to be fired on change event

```
<h:form>
    <h:panelGrid columns="1">
        <rich:inplaceInput value="#{inplaceInputBean.name}"
            defaultLabel="Double click to edit name" editEvent="dblclick">
            <a4j:ajax event="change" render="out" />
        </rich:inplaceInput>
        <h:outputText value="#{inplaceInputBean.name}" id="out"/>
    </h:panelGrid>
</h:form>
```

Entering a new value into the component, and either blurring (tabbing out or clicking outside the component) or pressing the Enter key, causes an Ajax request with a new value to be sent to the server, updating the output component. Note that the editEvent attribute allows you to customize the event, which will cause the component to be switched to editable state. In our example, dblclick used.

Let's look at another feature. Whenever the control loses focus and the value has been changed, the new value gets applied. It looks similar to a spreadsheet functionality (you tab out and the new value gets set). However, in some cases any input change could be tied to an expensive server-side database call or a complex service invocation. In such cases, the user should confirm before the value is saved. saveOnBlur="false" could be used and will cause the component to cancel changes. It's useful when showControls="true".

```
<rich:inplaceInput value="#{inplaceInputBean.name}"
    saveOnBlur="false" showControls="true" defaultLabel="Click to edit name"/>
```

If the saveOnblur property is set to false, applying a new value is only possible by using the Enter key or clicking on the save UI control. Losing focus will reset the value to the previous value.

This covers the <rich:inplaceInput> component. Keep in mind again that all the standard conversion and validation rules apply here as well.

JavaScript API

The component provides the JavaScript functions shown in Table 5-1, which could be invoked on the client.

Table 5-1. <rich:inplaceInput> JavaScript API

Method Name	Description
getValue()	Used to get the current value of the component
setValue(newValue)	Used to set a new value to the component
isEditState()	Returns a flag that indicates if the component is currently being edited
save()	Performs storing the new value and switching to a simple label presentation
cancel()	Performs resetting the value to previous and switching to a simple label presentation

Listing 5-4 shows an example updating another <rich:inplaceInput> input component on the client.

Listing 5-4. Updating another <rich:inplaceInput> input component on the client

```
<h:panelGrid>
    <rich:inplaceInput defaultLabel="Enter your name" id="name"
        onchange="#{rich:component('nickname')}.
            setValue(#{rich:component('name')}.getValue());" />
    <rich:inplaceInput defaultLabel="Enter your nickname" id="nickname" />
</h:panelGrid>
```

With the code in Listing 5-4, the nickname input component will be set to a value entered in the name input component, when that value changes (on change event). Note that this assignment is done via the component JavaScript API and thus no event or Ajax request is fired to the server.

Using <rich:inplaceSelect>

<rich:inplaceSelect> is similar to <rich:inplaceInput>, but instead of allowing the user to enter the value, it shows a drop-down list from which a value can be selected, as shown in Figure 5-5.

Figure 5-5. <rich:inplaceInput> component

Figure 5-6 shows the component when activated.

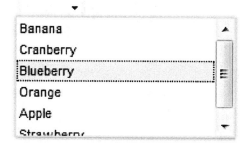

Figure 5-6. <rich:inplaceSelect> component activated

Listing 5-5 shows the JSF page code.

Listing 5-5. Shows the JSF page code

```
<rich:inplaceSelect value="#{inplaceSelectBean.fruit}"
    defaultLabel="Select fruit">
    <f:selectItem itemValue="1" itemLabel="Banana" />
    <f:selectItem itemValue="2" itemLabel="Cranberry" />
    <f:selectItem itemValue="3" itemLabel="Blueberry" />
    <f:selectItem itemValue="4" itemLabel="Orange" />
    <f:selectItem itemValue="5" itemLabel="Apple" />
```

```
    <f:selectItem itemValue="6" itemLabel="Strawberry" />
</rich:inplaceSelect>
```

The bean for the samples contains the single string property with getter and setter, so it's omitted. The same defaultLabel attribute (as in <rich:inplaceInput>) sets the label to be displayed if #{inplaceSelectBean.fruit} is initialized to one of the values; then that value will be displayed instead of the "Select fruit" label.

Creating the list of options is rather simple. You just use the standard <f:selectItem> or <f:selectItems> tag to build the list. The core of this component is based on the JSF standard UISelectOne class.

As with <rich:inplaceInput>, you can add controls to the component in order to either save or cancel the edited value by setting showControls="true" (see Figure 5-7).

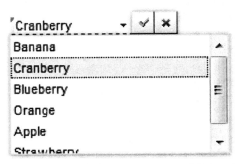

Figure 5-7. <rich:inplaceSelect> additional UI controls

Also similar to <rich:inplaceInput>, the components provide a set of client-side event handlers that could be processed on the client side or used to fire Ajax requests. Let's create a simple dependent select component using the Ajax requests fired on the *change* component event. The page is shown in Listing 5-6.

Listing 5-6. Creating a simple dependent select component using the Ajax request

```
<h:form>
    <h:panelGrid>
    <rich:inplaceSelect defaultLabel="Double click to select items type" ↵
        value="#{inplaceSelectBean2.currentType}"
        valueChangeListener="#{inplaceSelectBean2.valueChanged}" ↵
        editEvent="dblclick">
        <f:selectItems value="#{inplaceSelectBean2.firstList}" />
        <a4j:ajax event="change" render="second" execute="@this" />
        </rich:inplaceSelect>
        <a4j:outputPanel id="second" layout="block">
            <rich:inplaceSelect value="#{inplaceSelectBean2.currentType}" ↵
                defaultLabel="Click to select item"
                rendered="#{not empty inplaceSelectBean2.currentType}">
                <f:selectItems value="#{inplaceSelectBean2.secondList}" />
            </rich:inplaceSelect>
        </a4j:outputPanel>
        <h:panelGrid>
    </h:form>
```

A simple Java bean, which holds both of the select item lists and changes the second list when selection in the first list is changed, is shown in Listing 5-7.

Listing 5-7. *A simple Java bean*

```java
@ManagedBean
@RequestScoped
public class InplaceSelectBean2 {
    private static final String[] FRUITS = { "Banana", "Cranberry", "Blueberry", "Orange" };
    private static final String[] VEGETABLES = { "Potatoes", "Broccoli", ↵
        "Garlic", "Carrot" };
    private String currentItem = null;
    private String currentType = null;
    private List<SelectItem> firstList = new ArrayList<SelectItem>();
    private List<SelectItem> secondList = new ArrayList<SelectItem>();

    public InplaceSelectBean2() {
        SelectItem item = new SelectItem("fruits", "Fruits");
        firstList.add(item);
        item = new SelectItem("vegetables", "Vegetables");
        firstList.add(item);
        for (int i = 0; i < FRUITS.length; i++) {
            item = new SelectItem(FRUITS[i]);
        }
    }

    public void valueChanged(ValueChangeEvent event) {
        secondList.clear();
        if (null != event.getNewValue()) {
            String[] currentItems;
            if (((String) event.getNewValue()).equals("fruits")) {
                currentItems = FRUITS;
            } else {
                currentItems = VEGETABLES;
            }
            for (int i = 0; i < currentItems.length; i++) {
                SelectItem item = new SelectItem(currentItems[i]);
                secondList.add(item);
            }
        }
    }
    //Getters and setters
}
```

After the page renders you should see a single select, as shown in Figure 5-8.

Select fruit

Figure 5-8. *<rich:inplaceSelect> component*

After a value is selected, a second select will appear with the items based on the chosen type, as shown in Figure 5-9.

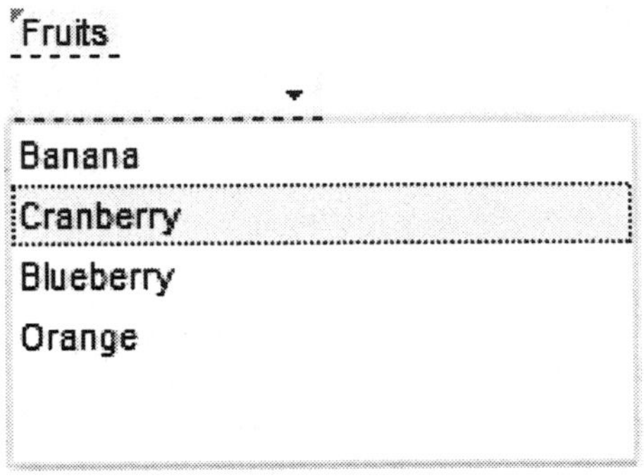

Figure 5-9. Dependent <rich:inplaceSelect> components

■ **Note** The editEvent attribute used in the sample works the same as <rich:inplaceInput>. You should dou-
ble-click to trigger switching to the edit state.

There are options that allow you to make a selection in a more careful fashion: saveOnSelect and
saveOnBlur. You already know about saveOnBlur from the <rich:inplaceInput> section, so let's look at
saveOnSelect. Normally as you could see trying a sample select saves value and getting to the saved state
right after the selection is made. If that attribute is set to false, the list will be closed on selection; but the
component will not save the value waiting for additional actions, like pressing enter, clicking the UI save
control, or blurring the component if the saveOnBlur has a true value.

JavaScript API

The component provides the same JavaScript API as <rich:inplaceInput>. Table 5-2 shows methods
that are only available on the <rich:inplaceSelect> component.

Table 5-2. <rich:inplaceSelect> JavaScript API

Method Name	Description
showPopup()	Performs opening the pop-up with items
hidePopup()	Closes the pop-up with items
setValue(newValue)	Sets the new value to component. As it's a select component, remember to pass the value to that method instead of a label

This covers the <rich:inplaceSelect> components available in the RichFaces 4 release.

Using <rich:autocomplete>

<rich:autocomplete> is an input component that provides suggestions during user input. For those who worked with RichFaces 3, this component is redesigned and combines the functionality of <rich:suggestionBox> and rich:comboBox components. Even though <rich:autocomplete> provides a rich input feature, under the hood it's just the basic input component.

The new <rich:autocomplete> component can be configured to work in the following four modes:

- *Ajax*. Every *keyup* triggers an Ajax request that updates the suggestions list and shows new results to the user.

- *Cached Ajax*. In this mode, the component requests data when the minimum number of characters is entered, but doesn't make additional requests if the prefix does not change. Further list filtering is performed completely on the client side until the prefix changes.

- *Client*. All the data is rendered to the client when the component is rendered. From then on, only client filtering is used for suggestions. No Ajax requests are fired to the server.

- *Lazy Client*. Similar to client mode, a complete list is fetched only after the component is activated and the minimum number of characters is entered. No additional Ajax requests are performed after that, even if the initial prefix changes. Client filtering is performed on further typing, as the component expects all the data loaded during a single Ajax request.

Let's review two completely new modes: cached Ajax and lazy client. These two work similarly but without additional optimization of requests count. Although we mentioned optimization, these two modes could be still useful in some cases. For example, where the list is really small and additional Ajax requests for data are unexpected, only the client mode should be used. Or if the suggestions fetching algorithm is complex and depends on every letter in user input, Ajax mode should be used.

Listing 5-8 shows an example of *<rich:autocompete>* using the lazy client mode.

***Listing 5-8.** An example of* <rich:autocompete> *using the lazy client mode*

```
<h:form>
    <rich:autocomplete autocompleteList="#{autocompleteBean.suggestions}" ↵
        mode="lazyClient"/>
</h:form>
```

Listing 5-9 shows the managed bean.

***Listing 5-9.** The managed bean*

```
@ManagedBean
@SessionScoped
public class AutocompleteBean {
    private List<String> suggestions = null;

    public AutocompleteBean() {
        suggestions = new ArrayList<String>();
        suggestions.add("Banana");
        suggestions.add("Cranberry");
        suggestions.add("Blueberry");
```

```
        suggestions.add("Orange");
        suggestions.add("Apple");
        suggestions.add("Strawberry");
    }
    //Getter and setter
}
```

Figure 5-10 shows what is rendered when the user starts typing.

Figure 5-10. *<rich:autocomplete> component*

The component fetches all the suggestions via Ajax when the first letter is entered, and assumes that the list will not be changed. All further filtering will be on the client. An Ajax request is sent to get all the data just once, the first time the component is activated, and no further requests will be sent. If we change the mode to client in Listing 5-8, the component will render all the data to the client on initial rendering and no Ajax requests will be sent at all. Any filtering will be done on the client.

The autocompleteList attribute is used to define data for the component. It points the component to a list of strings. In addition, the component provides one more way to define data: the autocompleteMethod attribute. It should be defined with a method that accepts a single string parameter and returns a list of suggestions. The parameter passed is the current value (prefix) from client input. Inside the method you can write any custom logic to return a list of suggestions based on the prefix passed from the client. But if you are using the autocompleteMethod for suggestions population instead of autocompleteList for client or lazy client mode, then you should not consider the prefix, as the component assumes that all the data will be loaded and thus will make no requests on prefix changes. Listing 5-10 shows how it works when using cachedAjax mode.

Listing 5-10. *Using cachedAjax mode*

```
<h:form>
    <rich:autocomplete autocompleteMethod="#{autocompleteBean.autocomplete}"
        mode="cachedAjax" tokens="," minChars="2" />
</h:form>
```

Listing 5-11 shows the method code from the managed bean (it uses the same suggestions list).

Listing 5-11. *Shows the method code from the managed bean*

```
public List<String> autocomplete(String prefix) {
    List<String> result = new ArrayList<String>();
    for (String suggestion : suggestions) {
        if (suggestion.startsWith(prefix)){
            result.add(suggestion);
        }
    }
    return result;
}
```

We should get almost the same results as from the previous example. However, there are two differences. Attribute minChars specifies the minimum number of characters entered before the component will ask the server side for suggestions (send an Ajax request). You will get the suggestions only after typing two or more letters. The tokens attribute is used and is set to a single comma (,) value. This attribute should be defined with some string and every character after that token string will become a separator between words. So, every character from that string (defined using token attribute) becomes a separator between different words. Figure 5-11 shows what happens when using a token followed by additional characters (prefix).

Figure 5-11. *<rich:autocomplete> using tokens*

Let's try to change mode from cachedAjax to just ajax. In such case you will see that the request will be sent on every keyup after two letters entered rather than being called only on prefix changes.

Now, let's review more attributes that affect the look and feel, as well as selection features. The component can render an additional button that will show all the suggestions even if the minChars condition hasn't been satisfied, as shown in Listing 5-12.

Listing 5-12. *Rendering an additional button that shows all the suggestions*

```
<h:form>
    <rich:autocomplete autocompleteList="#{autocompleteBean.suggestions}" ↵
        mode="lazyClient" showButton="true" selectFirst="true" />
</h:form>
```

The result is shown in Figure 5-12. Note the button on the right side of input (with the arrow pointing down). Also, notice that the first matching suggestion is shown inside the input and will be set into the input when you blur out. That's getting achieved by the selectFirst attribute set to true.

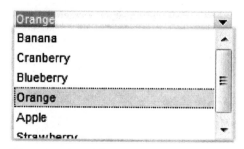

Figure 5-12. *<rich:autocomplete> with selectFirst="true"*

Another design-related attribute is autofill. If set to *true*, the component will insert the remaining part of the first matching suggestion, as shown in Figure 5-13. It will be inserted selected so further input will update it.

Figure 5-13. <rich:autocomplete> with autofill="true"

<rich:autocomplete> Client-side Filter Customization

You're able to return the suggestions from the server according to any custom filtering logic in *autocompleteMethod*. But, the same could be done on the client side when using client mode or just autocompleteList for fetching the data. All you have to define is the clientFilterFunction attribute, which should be set to a JavaScript function name that does the filtering. It should accept two parameters: prefix entered and suggestion string. It should return true in case the string matches the prefix, or false if not. The method will be called by the component for every available suggestion for the current prefix. The default filter function uses "startsWith" logic to filter results, but you can easily customize it to use anything else. For example, Listing 5-13 shows a JavaScript function that performs filtering using the "contains" rule for substring value.

Listing 5-13. Shows a JavaScript function that performs filtering

```
<script>
function customFilter(subString, value){
    if(subString.length>=1) {
        if(value.indexOf(subString)!=-1)
            return true;
        else
            return false;
    }
    return true;
};
</script>

<h:form>
    <rich:autocomplete autocompleteList="#{autocompleteBean.suggestions}" ↵
        mode="lazyClient" clientFilterFunction="customFilter"/>
</h:form>
```

Running the JavaScript custom filter function is shown in Figure 5-14. User-entered "be" appears as a substring in all three values shown in the list.

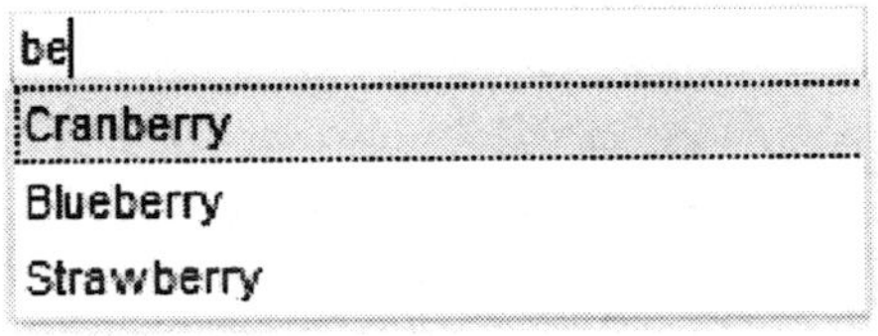

Figure 5-14. <rich:autocomplete> custom client filtering

As mentioned earlier, "contains" logic is now used for filtering instead of the default "startsWith."

Using Complex Markup in <rich:autocomplete> Pop-ups

The <rich:autocomplete> examples we have shown you so far used a simple list of strings in the pop-up as suggestions for user input. In general, you're free to use any custom objects for suggestions. In that case the component should be defined with the pop-up list representation and the property of the custom object, which should actually be inserted into the input when that object is selected.

Let's look at an example using custom objects and start with a managed bean, shown in Listing 5-14.

Listing 5-14. An example using custom objects

```
@ManagedBean
@SessionScoped
public class StatesSuggestionBean {

private List<State> statesList;

    private String state; // Getter and setter

    @PostConstruct
    public void init() {
        statesList = new ArrayList<State>();
        statesList.add(new State("Alabama", "Montgomery"));
        statesList.add(new State("Alaska", "Juneau"));
        statesList.add(new State("Arizona", "Phoenix"));
        statesList.add(new State("Arkansas", "Little Rock"));
        statesList.add(new State("California", "Sacramento"));
        statesList.add(new State("Colorado", "Denver"));
        statesList.add(new State("Connecticut", "Hartford"));
        statesList.add(new State("Delaware", "Dover"));
        statesList.add(new State("Florida", "Tallahassee"));
        statesList.add(new State("Georgia", "Atlanta"));
        statesList.add(new State("Hawaii", "Honolulu"));
        statesList.add(new State("Idaho", "Boise"));
        statesList.add(new State("Illinois", "Springfield"));
        statesList.add(new State("Indiana", "Indianapolis"));
        statesList.add(new State("Iowa", "Des Moines"));
        statesList.add(new State("Kansas", "Topeka"));
        statesList.add(new State("Kentucky", "Frankfort"));
        statesList.add(new State("Louisiana", "Baton Rouge"));
        statesList.add(new State("Maine", "Augusta"));
        statesList.add(new State("Maryland", "Annapolis"));
        statesList.add(new State("Massachusetts", "Boston"));
        statesList.add(new State("Michigan", "Lansing"));
        statesList.add(new State("Minnesota", "St. Paul"));
        statesList.add(new State("Mississippi", "Jackson"));
        statesList.add(new State("Missouri", "Jefferson City"));
        statesList.add(new State("Montana", "Helena"));
        statesList.add(new State("Nebraska", "Lincoln"));
        statesList.add(new State("Nevada", "Carson City"));
        statesList.add(new State("New Hampshire", "Concord"));
        statesList.add(new State("New Jersey", "Trenton"));
        statesList.add(new State("New Mexico", "Santa Fe"));
        statesList.add(new State("New York", "Albany"));
```

```
        statesList.add(new State("North Carolina", "Raleigh"));
        statesList.add(new State("North Dakota", "Bismarck"));
        statesList.add(new State("Ohio", "Columbus"));
        statesList.add(new State("Oklahoma", "Oklahoma City"));
        statesList.add(new State("Oregon", "Salem"));
        statesList.add(new State("Pennsylvania", "Harrisburg"));
        statesList.add(new State("Rhode Island", "Providence"));
        statesList.add(new State("South Carolina", "Columbia"));
        statesList.add(new State("South Dakota", "Pierre"));
        statesList.add(new State("Tennessee", "Nashville"));
        statesList.add(new State("Texas", "Austin"));
        statesList.add(new State("Utah", "Salt Lake City"));
        statesList.add(new State("Vermont", "Montpelier"));
        statesList.add(new State("Virginia", "Richmond"));
        statesList.add(new State("Washington", "Olympia"));
        statesList.add(new State("West Virginia", "Charleston"));
        statesList.add(new State("Wisconsin", "Madison"));
        statesList.add(new State("Wyoming", "Cheyenne"));
    }

    public List<State> getStatesList() {
        return statesList;
    }
}
```

Listing 5-15 shows the State class.

Listing 5-15. *Shows the State class*

```
public class State {

    private String name;
    private String capital;
    private String flagImage;

    // getters and setters

    public State (String name, String capital){
        this.name = name;
        this.capital = capital;
        this.flagImage = "/images/states/flag_"+(name.toLowerCase()).replace(" ↵
            ", "")+".gif";
    }
}
```

We are done with the backend logic, or the model. We haven't yet implemented the listener that will return the suggested values. We will do that shortly. Let's now write the JSF page, shown in Listing 5-16.

Listing 5-16. *Write the JSF page*

```
<h:form>
    <rich:autocomplete layout="table" autocompleteMethod="#{statesSuggestionBean.suggest}"
        var="state" fetchValue="#{state.name}">
```

```
        <rich:column>
            <h:outputText value="#{state.name}"/>
        </rich:column>
        <rich:column>
            <h:outputText value="#{state.capital}"/>
        </rich:column>
        <rich:column>
            <h:graphicImage value="#{state.flagImage}"/>
        </rich:column>
    </rich:autocomplete>
</h:form>
```

This is where you can see the difference between using custom objects or just strings in the suggestion. As we are using custom objects, and can display multiple object properties (as we do in the example), the <rich:column> tag is used to define data columns in the pop-up. This also allows you display content other than text, such as images. Next, we need to create the suggest method that will return values based on input provided. Listing 5-17 shows the method that is placed inside the managed bean.

Listing 5-17. Shows the method that is placed inside the managed bean

```
public ArrayList <State> suggest (String input){
    ArrayList <State> result = new ArrayList <State>();
    for(State state : statesList) {
        if ((state.getName().toLowerCase()).startsWith(input.toLowerCase()))
            result.add(state);
        }
    return result;
}
```

All we are doing is going through the list of states and checking whether the current state name starts with the prefix entered. Because this is inside a managed bean, you are free to implement any other method of retrieving the suggested values. Figure 5-15 shows the result.

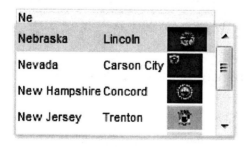

Figure 5-15. <rich:autocomplete> with complex content inside the pop-up

Another attribute we want to tell you about is fetchValue. As we show objects with multiple properties in a suggestions pop-up, we give a hint as to what to insert in the selection from the objects list. In this case a state name is used for insertion. If you don't specify fetchValue, then the object string representation will be inserted (State.toString() in this case).

We are also using the layout attribute. This attribute controls what markup the component will use for pop-up when a complex list is displayed. In our example, we use the *table* layout All possible layouts are shown in Table 5-3.

Table 5-3. <rich:autocomplete> Layouts

Layout Type	Description
table	Pop-up list content represented using HTML table. Columns should be used in order to define inner markup.
div	Suggestion markup will be wrapped in *<div>*. It will be more lightweight but in some cases you will have to do more work to align the content properly.
list	Suggestion markup will be wrapped in an HTML unordered list.

As you can see, the component is very flexible. You can display any type of information and in any number of columns.

JavaScript API

Table 5-4 shows component client-side JavaScript API.

Table 5-4. <rich:autocomplete> JavaScript API

Method Name	Description
showPopup()	Used to show suggestions pop-up
hidePopup()	Hides the suggestions pop-up
getValue()	Returns current component value
setValue(newValue)	Sets new string value to the input

Using <rich:select>

<rich:select> is a brand new component in RichFaces 4 and it is based on a standard UISelectOne component under the hood, as shown in Listing 5-18.

Listing 5-18. Using <rich:select>

```
<rich:select id="select" defaultLabel="Select Value..." value="#{selectBean.value}">>
    <f:selectItem itemValue="0" itemLabel="Banana" />
    <f:selectItem itemValue="1" itemLabel="Cranberry" />
    <f:selectItem itemValue="2" itemLabel="Blueberry" />
    <f:selectItem itemValue="3" itemLabel="Orange" />
    <f:selectItem itemValue="4" itemLabel="Strawberry" />
    <f:selectItem itemValue="4" itemLabel="Apple" />
</rich:select>
```

Figure 5-16 shows what will be rendered.

Figure 5-16. *<rich:select> component*

After clicking the component, it will show the list of options (as does the standard component), as in Figure 5-17.

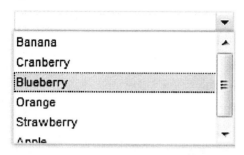

Figure 5-17. *<rich:select> pop-up selection*

You are probably wondering, why does RichFaces re-implement the standard `<h:selectOneMenu>` component? The answer is that the RichFaces component provides a number of extra features. The component is skinned using the RichFaces skins feature, unlike the standard component that renders differently in the various browsers and has styling limitations in some browsers The component provides a default label (common to all RichFaces inputs), and has direct keyboard-input features.

You will learn about skins in Chapter 12, so let's see how the direct keyboard-input feature works. All you need to activate this feature is to add `enableManualInput="true"`. After the component renders, you will be able to type into the input field directly and the component will filter the list according to the prefix entered, as shown in Figure 5-18.

Figure 5-18. *<rich:select> with direct typing enabled*

As the component provides select functionality, if you enter a value that can't be matched with any of selection items, the input will be highlighted as erroneous (the incorrect input will be shown in red) as shown in Figure 5-19 Keep in mind that such input will cause validation errors when the page is submitted.

Figure 5-19. *<rich:select> with incorrect input*

The selection change is a client-side operation. As for any other rich client component, we can attach an Ajax behavior to some component event to fire an Ajax request. Let's repeat the dependent selects example, but now using the `<rich:select>` component. The JSF page is shown in Listing 5-19.

Listing 5-19. The JSF page

```
<h:form>
   <h:panelGrid>
      <rich:select defaultLabel="Click to select items type" ↵
         value="#{selectBean.currentType}" ↵
         valueChangeListener="#{selectBean.valueChanged}"
         editEvent="dblclick">
         <f:selectItems value="#{selectBean.firstList}" />
         <a4j:ajax event="change" render="second" execute="@this" />
      </rich:select>
      <a4j:outputPanel id="second" layout="block">
         <rich:select value="#{selectBean.currentType}"
            defaultLabel="Click to select item"
            rendered="#{not empty selectBean.currentType}">
            <f:selectItems value="#{selectBean.secondList}" />
         </rich:select>
      </a4j:outputPanel>
   <h:panelGrid>
</h:form>
```

As you can see, the page code is completely the same as in the <rich:inplaceSelect> example (Listing 5-7). We just replaced the <rich:inplaceSelect> component with <rich:select>. Listing 5-20 shows the managed bean code, which is also unchanged.

Listing 5-20. Shows the unchanged managed bean code

```
@ManagedBean
@RequestScoped
public class SelectBean {
   private static final String[] FRUITS = { "Banana", "Cranberry", ↵
      "Blueberry", "Orange" };
   private static final String[] VEGETABLES = { "Potatoes", "Broccoli", ↵
      "Garlic", "Carrot" };
   private String currentItem = null;
   private String currentType = null;
   private List<SelectItem> firstList = new ArrayList<SelectItem>();
   private List<SelectItem> secondList = new ArrayList<SelectItem>();

   public SelectBean() {
      SelectItem item = new SelectItem("fruits", "Fruits");
      firstList.add(item);
      item = new SelectItem("vegetables", "Vegetables");
      firstList.add(item);
      for (int i = 0; i < FRUITS.length; i++) {
         item = new SelectItem(FRUITS[i]);
      }
   }
   public void valueChanged(ValueChangeEvent event) {
      secondList.clear();
      if (null != event.getNewValue()) {
         String[] currentItems;
         if (((String) event.getNewValue()).equals("fruits")) {
```

```
                currentItems = FRUITS;
            } else {
                currentItems = VEGETABLES;
            }
            for (int i = 0; i < currentItems.length; i++) {
                SelectItem item = new SelectItem(currentItems[i]);
                secondList.add(item);
            }
        }
    }
    //Getters and setters
}
```

Figure 5-20 shows the result. When the type selection is made in the first component, the second component list is updated based on the value selected in the first.

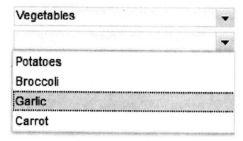

Figure 5-20. *Dynamic <rich:select> components*

JavaScript API

Table 5-5 shows component JavaScript API.

Table 5-5. *<rich:select> JavaScript API*

Method Name	Description
showPopup()	Shows the pop-up with select items.
hidePopup()	Closes the select items pop-up.
getValue()	Returns current value.
setValue(newValue)	Allows you to change the value. As it's the select component, remember to pass value and not a label as a parameter.

Using <rich:inputNumberSlider>

<rich:inputNumberSlider> renders a slider for inputting a number, as shown in Figure 5-21.

Figure 5-21. <rich:inputNumberSlider> component

The code is rather simple, that's all you need to render the component.

```
<rich:inputNumberSlider value="#{inputNumberBean.numberOfItems}" />
```

The InputNumberBean code is rather simple and contains just the single integer property with getter and setter, so it's omitted.

As this is basically just a rich input field, all the standard JSF rules, such as conversion/validation and event handling, apply to this component.

The component provides a number of rich features. You can easily set the minimum or maximum values, as well as the step value shown in Figure 5-22 (the amount by which the value will be increased or decreased when the handle is dragged).

Figure 5-22. <rich:inputNumberSlider> with custom boundary values

Listing 5-21 shows the component configured with the minimum and maximum value, as well as the step size.

Listing 5-21. Shows the component configured with minimum and maximum value

```
<rich:inputNumberSlider value="#{inputNumberBean.numberOfItems}"
    minValue="0"
    maxValue="500"
    step="2"/>
```

In order to disable manual input, set the enableManualInput attribute to false. This will force the user to use the component slider to set the value. Figure 5-23 shows the result.

Figure 5-23. <rich:inputNumberSlider> with manual input disabled

Listing 5-22 shows the component with the disabled manual input.

Listing 5-22. Shows the component with the disabled manual input

```
<rich:inputNumberSlider value="#{inputNumberBean.numberOfItems}"
    minValue="0"
    maxValue="500"
    step="2"
    enableManualInput="false"/>
```

To place the input field on the left side, set the inputPosition attribute, as shown in Figure 5-24.

Figure 5-24. *<rich:inputNumberSlider> with input shown on the left*

Listing 5-23 shows the code to position the input on the left.

Listing 5-23. *Shows the code to position the input*

```
<rich:inputNumberSlider value="#{inputNumberBean.numberOfItems}"
    minValue="0"
    maxValue="500"
    step="2"
    inputPosition="left"/>
```

The default value is right. To hide the input field completely, set showInput="false" as shown in Listing 5-24.

Listing 5-24. *Hiding the input field completely*

```
<rich:inputNumberSlider value="#{inputNumberBean.numberOfItems}"
    minValue="0"
    maxValue="500"
    step="2"
    showInput="false"/>
```

Figure 5-25 shows the component with the input field hidden.

Figure 5-25. *<rich:inputNumberSlider> with input not displayed*

In order to add additional arrow controls on the slider sides, use the showArrows attribute, as shown in Listing 5-25.

Listing 5-25. *Using the showArrows attribute*

```
<rich:inputNumberSlider value="#{inputNumberBean.numberOfItems}"
    minValue="0" maxValue="500"
    step="2" showArrows="true" />
```

Figure 5-26 shows the result.

| 0 | | 500 | | 300 |

Figure 5-26. *<rich:inputNumberSlider> with additional arrows next to boundary values*

Other attributes, such as showBoundaryValues, determine whether the minimum/maximum values are shown. If set to false, showToolTip will not display a tooltip when the handle is dragged. The tooltip shows the current value of the component when dragged.

As with any other input, <rich:inputNumberSlider> provides disabled attribute that allows a disabling component according to some permissions and so on. Figure 5-27 shows how a disabled component looks.

Figure 5-27. *<rich:inputNumberSlider> with manual input disabled*

JavaScript API

Table 5-6 shows the component JavaScript API.

Table 5-6. *<rich:inputNumberSlider> JavaScript API*

Method Name	Description
getValue()	Returns component current value
setValue(newValue)	Sets new value to component
increase()	Increments the value according to step defined
decrease()	Decreases the value according to step defined

Using <rich:inputNumberSpinner>

<rich:inputNumberSpinner> provides a familiar input field, but it renders a slider with up and down arrows to increase or decrease the value, as shown in Figure 5-28.

Figure 5-28. *<rich:inputNumberSpinner> component*

The code is rather simple again; that's all you need to do to render the *<rich:inplaceNumberSpinner>* component.

```
<rich:inputNumberSpinner value="#{inputNumberBean.numberOfItems}"/>
```

Listing 5-26 shows that similar attributes exist on <rich:inputNumberSpinner> as on <rich:inputNumberSlider>.

Listing 5-26. Shows that similar attributes exist

```
<rich:inputNumberSpinner value="#{inputNumberBean.numberOfItems}"
    maxValue="500"
    minValue="0"
    step="5"
    enableManualInput="false"/>
```

You can set the minimum and maximum values, set the step size, and disable manual input.

One other attribute available on this component is cycled. While set to true, when the value reaches one of the boundaries (minimum/maximum), it will be set to the next boundary or reversed.

JavaScript API

Table 5-7 shows the JavaScript API available on this component.

Table 5-7. *<rich:inputNumberSlide> JavaScript API*

Method Name	Description
getValue()	Returns component current value
setValue(newValue)	Sets new value to component
increase()	Increments the value according to step
decrease()	Decreases the value according to step

Using <rich:calendar>

The calendar component allows you to select the date and time values either inline or via a pop-up menu.

```
<rich:calendar value="#{calendarBean.today}"
    datePattern="dd/M/yy HH:mm:ss"/>
```

Where #{calendarBean.today} is of type java.util.Date with getter and setter methods.

▓ **Note** Calendar allows a value to be bound to different type of objects: String, Date, GregorianCalendar. It will convert the current value automatically depending on the type of value, or you could add a custom converter for custom date types.

Figure 5-29 shows an example of selecting a date. Note that by default the calendar is rendered with an input field. When activated, the calendar is shown in a pop-up.

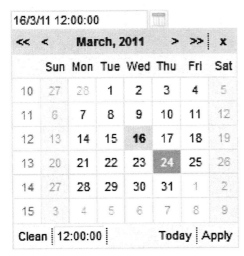

Figure 5-29. <rich:calendar> component

Figure 5-30 shows an example of how the month selection works.

Figure 5-30. Month selection with <rich:calendar>

Figure 5-31 shows an example of selecting time.

Figure 5-31. *Time selection with <rich:calendar>*

▥ **Note** The time selection turns on automatically when the pattern for calendar contains time. If it contains only the date, time controls will not appear.

All the examples shown so far in the calendar are pop-ups. Figure 5-32 shows an inline calendar.

<<	<		March, 2011			>	>>
	Sun	Mon	Tue	Wed	Thu	Fri	Sat
10	27	28	1	2	3	4	5
11	6	7	8	9	**10**	11	12
12	13	14	15	16	17	18	19
13	20	21	22	23	24	25	26
14	27	28	29	30	31	1	2
15	3	4	5	6	7	8	9
10/3/11	Clean	12:00:00					Today

Figure 5-32. *<rich:calendar>shown as rendered inline*

As you see in Figure 5-32, the calendar has the same look and feel, but no input field is displayed. Listing 5-27 shows the component code to render an inline calendar.

Listing 5-27. Shows the component code to render an inline calendar

```
<rich:calendar value="#{calendarBean.today}"
    datePattern="dd/M/yy hh:mm:a" popup="false"/>
```

Calendar Internationalization

The calendar component provides very rich UI, as shown in Figure 5-32, and comes with a large number of text labels and other internal controls. This brings us to a very important calendar feature: internationalization support. Table 5-8 shows attributes that are available in order to customize labels related to the dates pop-up representation.

Table 5-8. Calendar Labels Attributes

Attribute Name	Description
monthLabels	Defines full month names to be shown at month selection pop-up. Should be passed as comma-separated labels String or as List of Strings.
monthLabelsShort	Defines short month names to be shown in calendar header. Should be passed as comma-separated labels String or as List of Strings.
weekDayLabels	Defines week day labels. Not used in default markup but passed to event handlers with short labels. Should be passed as comma-separated labels String or as List of Strings.
weekDayLabelsShort	Defines week day short labels to be shown above the date grid. Should be passed as comma-separated labels String or as List of Strings.

By default, values from Table 5-8 are set with data from current Locale and should be used only if you want to define custom labels.

We also need to handle all the UI labels localization. The calendar component does not provide attributes for all the labels available on the component. The reason is rather simple. The set of the labels is very large and defining them all on the page would make the component look "heavy." Thus, the component uses message bundles for getting predefined localization properties. Table 5-9 lists available calendar properties.

Table 5-9. Calendar Message Bundle Keys

Property Name	Description
RICH_CALENDAR_APPLY_LABEL	Label for "apply" button on the month pop-up
RICH_CALENDAR_TODAY_LABEL	Label for "today" button on the month pop-up
RICH_CALENDAR_CLEAN_LABEL	Label for "clean" button on the month pop-up
RICH_CALENDAR_CANCEL_LABEL	Label for "cancel" button on month and time selection sub-pop-ups

Property Name	Description
RICH_CALENDAR_OK_LABEL	Label for "ok" button on month and time selection sub-pop-ups
RICH_CALENDAR_CLOSE_LABEL	Label for "close" button on month pop-up

These properties could be defined in either one of the two places, the choice is up to the developer. It could be an application message bundle (registered in a JSF configuration file) or it could be a separate message bundle that should be placed in an org.richfaces.renderkit package with name calendar.properties.

Let's look at an example shown in Figure 5- 33 using the component with an Italian locale.

Figure 5-33. <rich:calendar> with Italian locale

In order to achieve that, we created a bundle_it.properties file in a Java source root folder with content from Listing 5-28.

Listing 5-28. Creating a bundle_it.properties file in a Java source root folder

```
RICH_CALENDAR_APPLY_LABEL=Applica
RICH_CALENDAR_TODAY_LABEL=Oggi
RICH_CALENDAR_CLEAN_LABEL=Reimposta
RICH_CALENDAR_CANCEL_LABEL=Annulla
RICH_CALENDAR_OK_LABEL=Ok
RICH_CALENDAR_CLOSE_LABEL=Chiudi
```

Next, we added the registered file in *faces-config.xml*.

```
<application>
   <message-bundle>bundle</message-bundle>
</application>
```

And now set the calendar to use an Italian locale.

```
<rich:calendar datePattern="dd/M/yy hh:mm:ss" locale="it"/>
```

■ **Note** There is no need for explicit definitions of the locale attribute in most cases. Applying current locale will affect all calendars and corresponding bundles will be used for all of them. You should just provide those bundles.

Server-side Customization with CalendarDataModel

The calendar component supports a data model definition that allows customizing month markup according to a custom data model. In order to create a data model, we need to implement two interfaces: CalendarDataModel and CalendarDataModelItem. The class that implements CalendarDataModel will have the getData method implemented and responsible for returning instances (a range of dates, for example) of CalendarDataModelItem for a given date range. Each CalendarDataModelItem represents one calendar day. It also defines a getTooltip reserved method that will be used for future tooltip implementations. CalendarDataModelItem implementation has methods listed in Table 5-10.

Table 5-10. CalendarDataModel Item Interface

Method Name	Description
getStyleClass	Returns styleClass for single date cell.
isEnabled	Returns boolean flag that defines if the date is enabled for selection.
getData	Returns additional data map that could be used in client-side markup customization.
getTooltip	Returns the label for tooltip for given date. Not currently used, reserved for future versions.
getDay	Returns day number in that month.

All methods listed will be called by the calendar during month data-fetching in order to apply customizations to every date cell.

The calendar component works in two modes: Ajax and client. In client mode, the calendar switches between months on the client side, rebuilding the month markup every time it is switched on. In Ajax mode, new month data is fetched from the server. The dataModel is used in both cases if defined. In Ajax mode it's called when switching between months to load new months' data. For client mode we have to specify preloadDateRangeBegin and preloadDateRangeEnd attributes. Those attributes define a range of dates for which the data model will be loaded to the client. Then it will be used to construct the month on the client.

Let's look at an example of data model usage. We will use Ajax mode. The data model will define simple rules, as follows:

- Dates that are before the current date are disabled and styled correspondingly.

- Tuesdays and Thursdays are considered "busy" days that are disabled and styled in a special way.

- Saturdays and Sundays are disabled and also will have a special style.

Listing 5-29 shows the JSF page code.

Listing 5-29. The JSF page code

```
<style>
   .bdc {
      background-color: gray;
   }
   .wdc {
      font-weight: bold;
      font-style: italic;
   }
</style>
<h:form>
   <rich:calendar mode="ajax" popup="false"
      dataModel="#{calendarModel}" />
</h:form>
```

■ **Note** Don't forget to place `<rich:calendar>` inside `<h:form>` when using Ajax mode.

The managed bean code is shown in Listing 5-30.

Listing 5-30. The managed bean code

```
@ManagedBean
@ApplicationScoped
public class CalendarModel implements CalendarDataModel {
   private static final String WEEKEND_DAY_CLASS = "wdc";
   private static final String BUSY_DAY_CLASS = "bdc";
   private static final String BOUNDARY_DAY_CLASS = "rf-ca-boundary-dates";

   private boolean checkBusyDay(Calendar calendar) {
      return (calendar.get(Calendar.DAY_OF_WEEK) == Calendar.TUESDAY ||
      calendar.get(Calendar.DAY_OF_WEEK) == Calendar.THURSDAY);
   }

   private boolean checkWeekend(Calendar calendar) {
      return (calendar.get(Calendar.DAY_OF_WEEK) == Calendar.SUNDAY ||
      calendar.get(Calendar.DAY_OF_WEEK) == Calendar.SATURDAY);
   }

   public CalendarDataModelItem[] getData(Date[] dateArray) {
      CalendarDataModelItem[] modelItems = new CalendarModelItem[dateArray.length];
      Calendar current = GregorianCalendar.getInstance();
```

```java
            Calendar today = GregorianCalendar.getInstance();
            today.setTime(new Date());
            for (int i = 0; i < dateArray.length; i++) {
                current.setTime(dateArray[i]);
                CalendarModelItem modelItem = new CalendarModelItem();
                if (current.before(today)) {
                    modelItem.setEnabled(false);
                    modelItem.setStyleClass(BOUNDARY_DAY_CLASS);
                }
                else if (checkBusyDay(current)){
                    modelItem.setEnabled(false);
                    modelItem.setStyleClass(BUSY_DAY_CLASS);
                }
                else if (checkWeekend(current)){
                    modelItem.setEnabled(false);
                    modelItem.setStyleClass(WEEKEND_DAY_CLASS);
                }
                else{
                    modelItem.setEnabled(true);
                    modelItem.setStyleClass("");
                }
                modelItems[i] = modelItem;
            }
    return modelItems;
    }

    @Override
    public Object getToolTip(Date date) {
        return null;
    }
}

public class CalendarModelItem implements CalendarDataModelItem{

    private boolean enabled;
    private String styleClass;

    @Override
    public boolean isEnabled() {
        return enabled;
    }

    @Override
    public String getStyleClass() {
        return styleClass;
    }

    public void setEnabled(boolean enabled) {
        this.enabled = enabled;
    }

    public void setStyleClass(String styleClass) {
        this.styleClass = styleClass;
    }
```

```
    // All the other methods from interface just return null in this    ↵
       example
}
```

The calendar displayed is shown in Figure 5-34.

Figure 5-34. *<rich:calendar> with a custom data model*

Notice that our "busy" dates are disabled and styled with gray color. Weekends are styled in bold-italic. While creation of the data for the current month (see the getData method of the model) we are setting an enabled flag and style class according to the requirements we listed earlier. Also, the calendar that you see is displayed inline because we set the popup='false' attribute.

Client-side Customization with JavaScript

The calendar component also supports client-side customization. There are two attributes available: dayClassFunction and dayDisableFunction. These attributes should be defined with the JavaScript function names. The functions should accept a date parameter and return a CSS class and boolean flag, which indicates if the date is available for selection. Listing 5-31 shows a sample that achieves almost the same result as the previous one, which uses a data model but on the client side.

Listing 5-31. Using a data model but on the client side

```
<style>
.everyThirdDay {
    background-color: gray;
}

.weekendBold {
    font-weight: bold;
    font-style: italic;
}
</style>
    <script type="text/javascript">
```

```
        var curDt = new Date();
        function disablementFunction(day){
            if (day.isWeekend) return false;
            if (curDt==undefined){
                curDt = day.date.getDate();
            }
            if (curDt.getTime() - day.date.getTime() &lt; 0) return true; else return false;
        }
        function disabledClassesProv(day){
            if (curDt.getTime() - day.date.getTime() &gt;= 0) return 'rf-cal-boundary-day';
            var res = '';
            if (day.isWeekend) res+='weekendBold ';
            if (day.day%3==0) res+='everyThirdDay';
            return res;
        }
</script>
<rich:calendar dayDisableFunction="disablementFunction"
    dayClassFunction="disabledClassesProv"/>
```

The result is shown in Figure 5-35.

Figure 5-35. Client-side customization for the <rich:calendar>

Every third date is grayed, weekends have bold and italic styling, and all the dates before the current are disabled.

The calendar component also provides very rich JavaScript API, which allows you to control its state on the client. Listing 5-32 shows synchronizations between two calendars. Let's say that if a user has picked a start date, the user should pick a second date after the start date. In Listing 5-32, we are setting the same date in the second calendar by default. As we are using component JavaScript API, a #{rich:component('id')} function is used to reference the calendar and invoke a JavaScript method.

Listing 5-32. Using a `<rich:component(id)>` *function used to reference the calendar*

```
<h:panelGrid columns="2">
    From:
    <rich:calendar id="c1"
        onchange="#{rich:component('c2')}.
        setValue(#{rich:component('c1')}.getValue()))" />
    To:
    <rich:calendar id="c2" />
</h:panelGrid>
```

Figure 5-36 shows the result: after picking a start date in the first calendar component, the second calendar component is set to a start date automatically.

From: Mar 8, 2011

To: Mar 8, 2011

Figure 5-36. Using <rich:calendar> JavaScript API

JavaScript API

The component provides a very rich JavaScript API. Table 5-11 lists the most important methods. For a complete list of calendar JavaScript API, please visit the JBoss Community RichFaces web site at `http://jboss.org/richfaces/docs`.

Table 5-11. <rich:calendar> JavaScript API

`setValue(newDate)`	Sets new date according to passed date parameter
`resetSelectedDate()`	Clean selected date
`today()`	Sets today as new date
`getCurrentMonth()`	Returns the month currently shown in pop-up
`getCurrentYear()`	Returns the year currently shown in pop-up
`changeCurrentDate(date)`	Switches pop-up to month according to given date (does not perform date selection).
`showSelectedDate()`	Scrolls the pop-up to currently selected date
`showDateEditor()`	Populates year/month change pop-up
`hideDateEditor()`	Closes the year/month pop-up
`showTimeEditor()`	Populates time editor
`hideTimeEditor()`	Closes time editor

Component Facets

<rich:calendar> facets listed in Table 5-12 are used in order to redefine parts of the component.

Table 5-12. <rich:calendar> facets

Facet Name	Description
header	Allows you to redefine the header that contains the month changing controls and current month label.
footer	Allows you to redefine the footer that contains current date, time, and reset control.
optionalHeader	Allows you to add one more general header to pop-up above the month's switcher.
optionalFooter	Allows you to add another general footer to pop-up below the informational footer.

Uploading files with <rich:fileUpload>

<rich:fileUpload>, shown in Figure 5-37, is a component that provides asynchronous file input features and a highly customizable rich look and feel with uploading files information and progress indication.

Figure 5-37. <rich:fileUpload> component

The JSF page code that defines the component is shown in Listing 5-33.

Listing 5-33. The JSF page code

```
<h:form>
    <rich:fileUpload fileUploadListener="#{fileUploadBean.listener}"/>
<h:form>
```

The only attribute that you will have to use is `fileUploadListener`. It should be defined with a method expression, and the listener method will be responsible for processing uploaded files. It should be a void method that accepts a single parameter of `org.richfaces.event.FileUploadEvent` type. `FileUploadEvent` provides a `getUploadedFile` method that returns an instance of the uploaded file described in Listing 5-34.

Let's also look at a simple bean that stores an uploaded file object in session.

Listing 5-34. A simple managed bean

```
import org.richfaces.model.UploadedFile;
...
@ManagedBean
@SessionScoped
public class FileUploadBean {
    private UploadedFile file;
    public void listener(FileUploadEvent event) throws Exception {
        file = event.getUploadedFile();
    }
    //Getters and setters
}
```

Table 5-13 lists *UploadedFile* interface methods that can be used to obtain uploaded file information.

Table 5-13. UploadedFile Interface

Method Name	Return Type	Description
getContentType()	String	Returns content type for the uploaded file
getData()	byte[]	Returns uploaded file as byte array
getInputStream()	InputStream	Return uploaded file through InputStream
getName()	String	Returns file name
getSize()	long	Returns file size

Let's review a number of additional settings. At first, as with any component that sends Ajax requests to the server, you have to use a form to wrap the component. However, using the RichFaces file upload component, you don't need to make the form a multipart form, as it will be automatically handled by RichFaces. Using the standard `<h:form>` is sufficient.

File upload component has two options that are defined as application context-parameters in `web.xml` listed in Table 5-14.

Table 5-14. web.xml context parameters for <rich:fileUpload>

Parameter Name	Description
org.richfaces.fileUpload.maxRequestSize	Defines maximum size in bytes of files that could be uploaded across the application instance.
org.richfaces.fileUpload.createTempFiles	Defines whether the files should be stored in-memory or stored as application server temporary files before processed by upload listener.

Now let's add a limitation as to what kind of files can be uploaded, as in Listing 5-35.

Listing 5-35. Adding a limitation to what files can be uploaded

```
<rich:fileUpload id="fileUpload" acceptedTypes="jpg, gif, png"  ↵
    fileUploadListener="#{fileUploadBean.listener}"  ↵
    disabled="#{fileUploadBean.filesCountExceeded}"/>
```

Now the component will allow uploading only .jpg, .gif and .png images and once #{fileUploadBean.filesCountExceeded} evaluates to true, the component will be disabled and not allow any additional uploads. If #{fileUploadBean.filesCountExceeded} changes on the server, the component needs to be re-rendered in order to update its state on the client.

Let's look at another example uploading images with thumbnail support, as in Listing 5-36.

Listing 5-36. Uploading images with thumbnail support

```
<h:form>
    <h:panelGrid columns="2" columnClasses="top,top">
        <rich:fileUpload fileUploadListener="#{fileUploadBean.listener}"
            maxFilesQuantity="#{fileUploadBean.uploadsAvailable}" id="upload"
            acceptedTypes="jpg, gif, png, bmp">
            <a4j:ajax event="uploadcomplete" execute="@none" render="info" />
        </rich:fileUpload>
    <h:panelGroup id="info">
    <rich:panel bodyClass="info">
        <f:facet name="header">Uploaded Files Info</f:facet>
        <rich:dataGrid columns="1" value="#{fileUploadBean.files}" var="file" rowKeyVar="row">
            <rich:panel>
                <h:panelGrid columns="2">
                <a4j:mediaOutput element="img" mimeType="#{file.contentType}"
                    createContent="#{fileUploadBean.paint}" value="#{row}" style="width:100px;↵
height:100px;"
                    cacheable="false">
                    <f:param value="#{fileUploadBean.timeStamp}" name="time" />
                </a4j:mediaOutput>
                <h:panelGrid columns="2">
                    <h:outputText value="File Name:" />
                    <h:outputText value="#{file.name}" />
                    <h:outputText value="File Length(bytes):" />
                    <h:outputText value="#{file.size}" />
```

```
                </h:panelGrid>
                </h:panelGrid>
             </rich:panel>
           </rich:dataGrid>
       </rich:panel>
    </h:panelGroup>
    </h:panelGrid>
</h:form>
```

And the managed bean snippet is shown in Listing 5-37.

Listing 5-37. The managed bean snippet

```
@ManagedBean
@SessionScoped
public class FileUploadBean {
    private ArrayList<UploadedFile> files = new ArrayList<UploadedFile>();

    public void paint(OutputStream stream, Object object) throws IOException {
        stream.write(getFiles().get((Integer) object).getData());
    }

    public void listener(FileUploadEvent event) throws Exception {
        UploadedFile item = event.getUploadedFile();
        files.add(item);
    }

    public Date getTimeStamp(){
        return new Date();
    }

    // Getters and setters
}
```

After the files are uploaded, <a4j:ajax> performs an Ajax request to the server and updates the thumbnails panel, as shown in Figure 5-38.

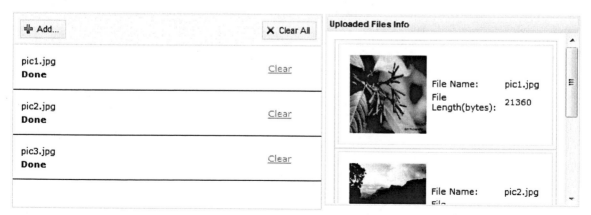

Figure 5-38. <rich:fileUpload> with thumbnails panel

Every uploaded file was stored in a list. We then iterate over the list using the *<rich:dataGrid>* component and pass the image to a *<a4j:mediaOutput>* component in order to output the image file thumbnail.

Component Facets

A single `progress` facet is available on the `<rich:fileUpload>` component. It allows you to redefine built-in `<rich:progressBar>` functionality in the component. You could place `<rich:progressBar>` inside the facet and customize its behavior or look and feel as you need.

Component JavaScript API

As of the writing of this book, the `<rich:fileUpload>` component doesn't provide public JavaScript API. JavaScript API might be added in future releases. Visit the JBoss Community RichFaces site at `http://richfaces.org` for updates.

Summary

This chapter covered RichFaces input components. All input components provide rich client functionality and some have built-in Ajax support. For input components that don't provide built-in Ajax support out of the box, you can easily add Ajax support by attaching `<a4j:ajax>` behavior to any event available on the component.

As you are working with these components, don't forget the rich JavaScript API many provide. Many components also provide facets to redefine some part of a component. All these features make RichFaces input components very powerful and flexible.

Under the hood, most components are just inputs so all the basic JSF concepts, such as conversion and validation, apply here as well. To see all the input components in action, view the components demo on the JBoss Community RichFaces site at `http://www.jboss.org/richfaces/demos`.

Now that we are done with rich input components, in the next chapter we will tell you about rich output components, such as pop-up panels, tabs, and more.

Rich Panel and Output Components

RichFaces offers a good number of out-of-the-box components for different data representation. This chapter will cover output components such as simple panels, collapsible panels, tabbed panels, toggle panels, and popup panels. Be prepared for numerous examples as well as common usages, such as how to use a popup panel to display a wizard or a status message.

Using <rich:panel>

`<rich:panel>` is just a panel or a container for any other content. You can place anything you want inside it, such as text or any other JSF components. A sample panel with text is shown in Figure 6-1.

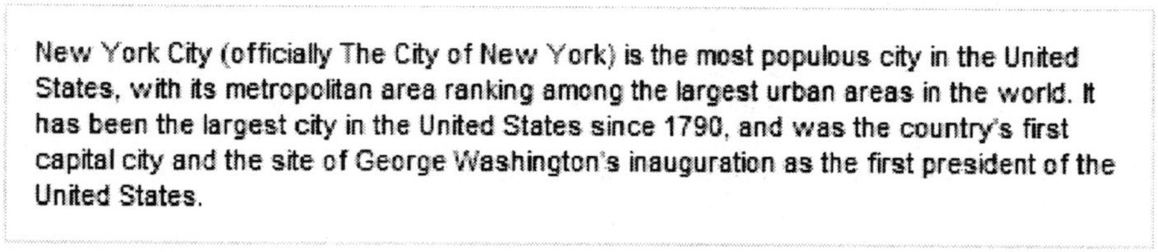

New York City (officially The City of New York) is the most populous city in the United States, with its metropolitan area ranking among the largest urban areas in the world. It has been the largest city in the United States since 1790, and was the country's first capital city and the site of George Washington's inauguration as the first president of the United States.

Figure 6-1. Panel without header

The code for this panel is shown in Listing 6-1.

Listing 6-1. Code for the panel without header

```
<rich:panel style="width:450px">
    New York City (officially The City of New York) is the most populous city
    in the United States, with its metropolitan area ranking among the largest
    urban areas in the world. It has been the largest city in the United
    States since 1790, and was the country's first capital city and the site
    of George Washington's inauguration as the first president of the United
    States...
</rich:panel>
```

You can easily add a panel *header* by setting *header* using attribute or using the same named `<f:facet>` as shown in Listing 6-2.

Listing 6-2. Adding a panel header with <f:facet>

```
<rich:panel style="width:450px">
    <f:facet name="header">New York City</f:facet>
    New York City (officially The City of New York) is the most populous city
    in the United States, with its metropolitan area ranking among the largest
    urban areas in the world. It has been the largest city in the United
    States since 1790, and was the country's first capital city and the site
    of George Washington's inauguration as the first president of the United
    States...
</rich:panel>
```

Figure 6-2 shows what it looks like.

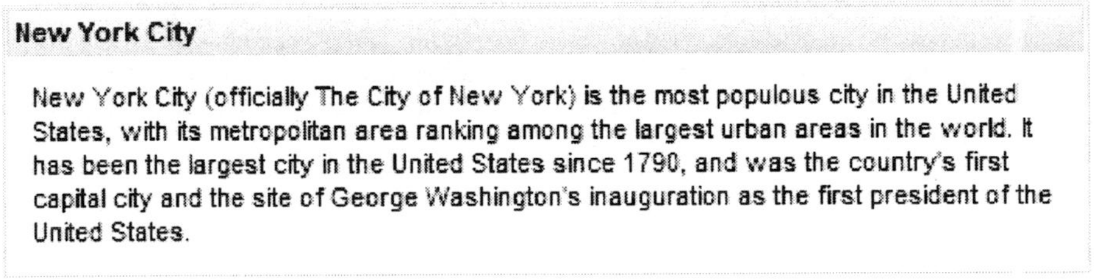

New York City

New York City (officially The City of New York) is the most populous city in the United States, with its metropolitan area ranking among the largest urban areas in the world. It has been the largest city in the United States since 1790, and was the country's first capital city and the site of George Washington's inauguration as the first president of the United States.

Figure 6-2. Panel with header

Keep in mind that you can place any other JSF components inside and the component is fully skinnable.

Listing 6-3 is an example of a second <rich:panel> nested inside the first one. In this example an image was placed inside the first panel and an image was placed inside the header for the second panel.

Listing 6-3. Example of a second <rich:panel> nested inside the first one

```
<rich:panel style="width:450px">
    <f:facet name="header">New York City</f:facet>
    <h:graphicImage value="/images/NY-flag.png" style="float:right" />
    New York City (officially The City of New York) is the most populous city
    in the United States, with its metropolitan area ranking among the largest
    urban areas in the world. It has been the largest city in the United
    States since 1790, and was the country's first capital city and the site
    of George Washington's inauguration as the first president of the United
    States...
    <rich:panel>
        <f:facet name="header">
            <h:panelGroup>
                <h:graphicImage value="/images/yellow_lamp.gif" />
                <h:outputText value="5 Boroughs" />
            </h:panelGroup>
        </f:facet>
    New York City comprises five boroughs, each of which is coextensive with a
    county: The Bronx, Brooklyn, Manhattan, Queens and Staten Island. With
    over 8.2 million residents within an area of 322 square miles (830 km),
    New York City is the most densely populated major city in the United
```

```
States.
    </rich:panel>
</rich:panel>
```

Figure 6-3 shows the result.

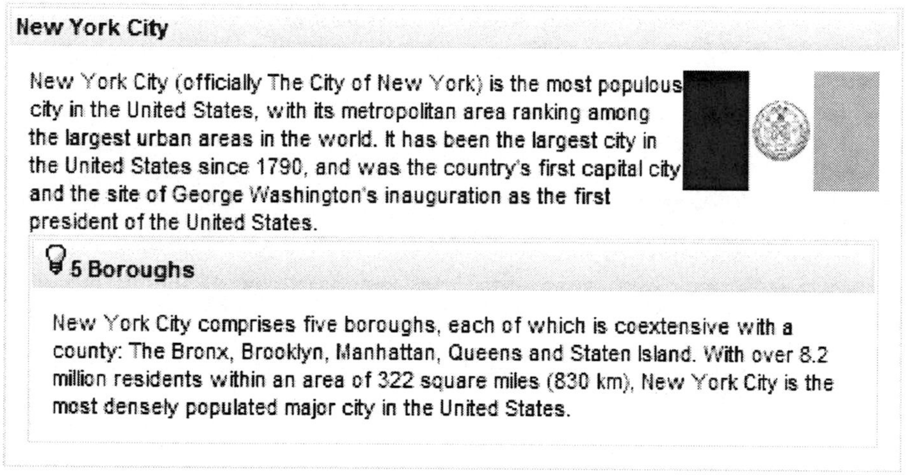

New York City

New York City (officially The City of New York) is the most populous city in the United States, with its metropolitan area ranking among the largest urban areas in the world. It has been the largest city in the United States since 1790, and was the country's first capital city and the site of George Washington's inauguration as the first president of the United States.

💡 5 Boroughs

New York City comprises five boroughs, each of which is coextensive with a county: The Bronx, Brooklyn, Manhattan, Queens and Staten Island. With over 8.2 million residents within an area of 322 square miles (830 km), New York City is the most densely populated major city in the United States.

Figure 6-3. Nested panels with various content

The component also supports all standard mouse and keyboard event handlers. Let's check one more example that shows how to use component event handlers in order to highlight the component content. The page code is shown in Listing 6-4.

Listing 6-4. Using component event handlers

```
<style>
.body:hover {
    font-weight:bold;
}
.highlight-font{
    text-decoration: underline;
}
</style>
<rich:panel bodyClass="body" headerClass="header" style="width:450px"
    onmouseover="jQuery('.header').addClass('highlight-font');"
    onmouseout="jQuery('.header').removeClass('highlight-font');">
        <f:facet name="header">New York City</f:facet>
    New York City (officially The City of New York) is the most populous
    city in the United States, with its metropolitan area
    ...
</rich:panel>
```

We are using the same panels, but with the *mouseover* event we make the font bold inside the panel, as shown in Figure 6-4.

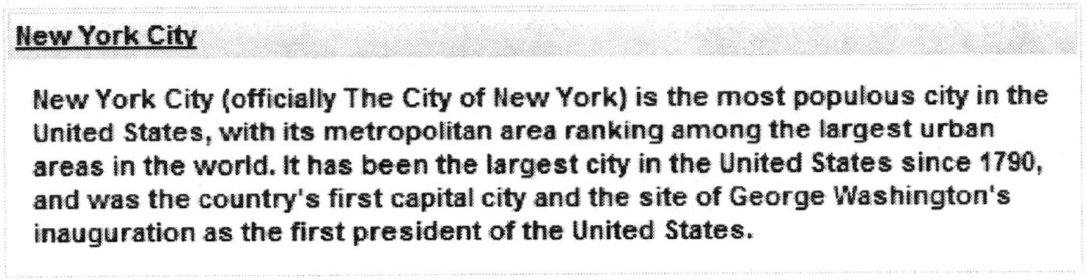

New York City

New York City (officially The City of New York) is the most populous city in the United States, with its metropolitan area ranking among the largest urban areas in the world. It has been the largest city in the United States since 1790, and was the country's first capital city and the site of George Washington's inauguration as the first president of the United States.

Figure 6-4. Panel with background color changed on mouseover

Two methods were used here. We added a CSS class by using simple jQuery statements to underline text in the header. We also applied a font weight change to the panel body by using a standard CSS hover selector.

Using <rich:collapsiblePanel>

<rich:collapsiblePanel> is similar to the <rich:panel> component with the additional functionality of being closed or open. Listing 6-5 shows an example.

Listing 6-5. <rich:collapsiblePanel> example

```
<h:form>
    <rich:collapsiblePanel width="450px" switchType="ajax" header="New York City">
    New York City (officially The City of New York) is the most populous city
    in the United States, with its metropolitan area ranking among the largest
    urban areas in the world. It has been the largest city in the United
    States since 1790, and was the country's first capital city and the site
    of George Washington's inauguration as the first president of the United
    States...
    </rich:collapsiblePanel>
</h:form>
```

You can see in Figure 6-5 and Figure 6-6 how the panel will look collapsed and expanded. In order to change the state of the panel, you can click anywhere in header.

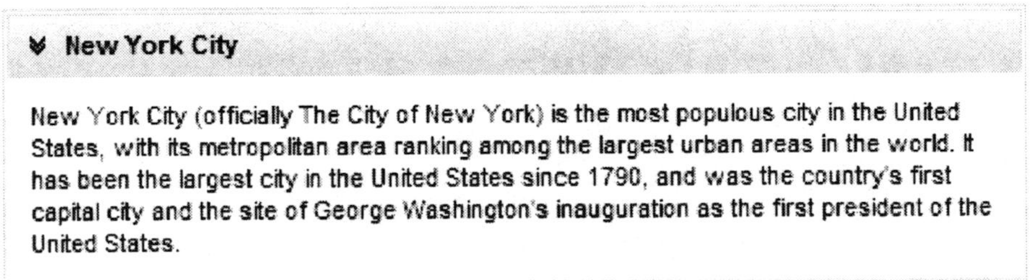

⊻ New York City

New York City (officially The City of New York) is the most populous city in the United States, with its metropolitan area ranking among the largest urban areas in the world. It has been the largest city in the United States since 1790, and was the country's first capital city and the site of George Washington's inauguration as the first president of the United States.

Figure 6-5. Expanded panel

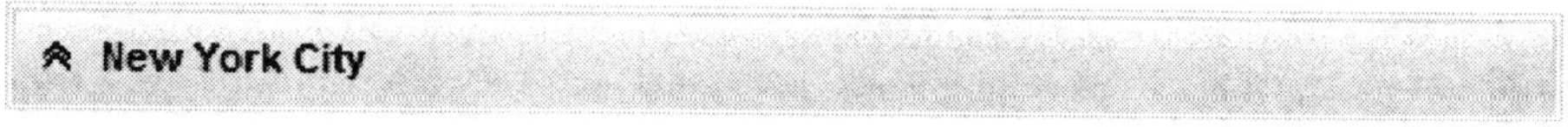

Figure 6-6. Collapsed panel

> **Note** As the panel has two states (open/close) you have the option to define different content for the header using two facets: headerExpanded (when open) and headerCollapsed (when closed). When using the header attribute, the header label will stay the same whether opened or closed.

Now let's change the indication icons in the header of the panel by using the other icons, as shown in Listing 6-6.

Listing 6-6. Changing the indication icons

```
<rich:collapsiblePanel rightCollapsedIcon="triangleUp"
  leftCollapsedIcon="/images/yellow_lamp.gif"
  leftExpandedIcon="/images/yellow_lamp.gif "
  rightExpandedIcon="triangleDown" style="width:450px" switchType="ajax"
  header="New York City">
```

The result is shown in Figures 6-7 and 6-8.

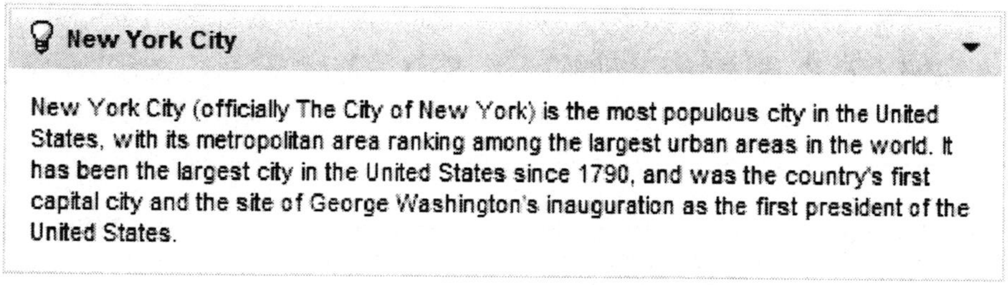

New York City

New York City (officially The City of New York) is the most populous city in the United States, with its metropolitan area ranking among the largest urban areas in the world. It has been the largest city in the United States since 1790, and was the country's first capital city and the site of George Washington's inauguration as the first president of the United States.

Figure 6-7. Expanded panel with customized and repositioned indication icon

New York City

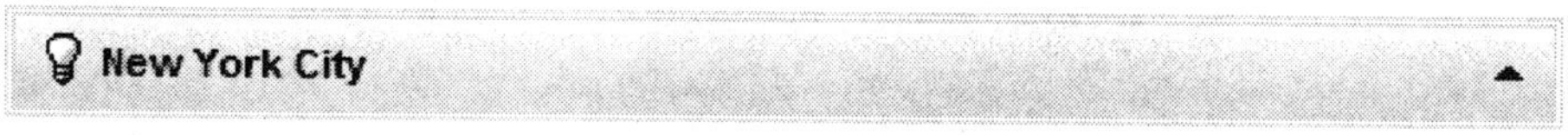

Figure 6-8. Collapsed panel with customized and repositioned indication icon

In addition to the values of triangleUp and triangleDown, leftcollapsedIcon and rightCollapsed-Icon attributes can be set to the following predefined icons: disc, grid, chevron, triangle, chevronUp, chevronDown, none, and transparent. none means there will be no icon and transparent helps the header look consistent when some panels use icons and others don't.

■ **Note** The built-in icons could be used across all the panels and some other components, such as `<rich:accordion>`, `<rich:panelMenu>`, and so on (some components are planned to be added with support after the first 4.0 release), which provide icon attributes. You will see some of them used later in this and other chapters. It's also possible to use custom icons—simply provide URI to the icon images, as shown in Listing 6-6. Also as you can see, you should use attributes in pairs to define left and right icons for both states.

Let's switch our attention to the `switchType` attribute used in Listing 6-6. There are three switch types available, which are listed in Table 6-1.

Table 6-1. Panels switchType Attribute Values

Value	Description
server	In this mode a full-page refresh will occur and the panel will be rendered with a proper state.
ajax	The default value. An Ajax request will be sent in order to load the panel content on states switching.
client	Component renders all content to the client and changes the state without any additional requests being sent.

■ **Caution** `<rich:collapsiblePanel>` and all the other switchable panels require `<h:form>` around them in server and Ajax modes to perform a submit. Also note that it's not possible to place a form inside each panel.

In Ajax and server modes, components will fire `org.richfaces.event.PanelToggleEvent`, which could be processed similarly to button and link action events by using the listener defined in the *panelToggleListener* attribute, as shown in Listings 6-7 and 6-8.

■ **Note** All the Ajax request customization and optimization attributes described in Chapter 3 can be used for the panel when switch mode is *Ajax*.

Listing 6-7. Using the listener defined in the panelToggleListener *attribute*

```
<rich:collapsiblePanel switchType="ajax" expanded="#{cityBean.isOpen}"
    panelToggleListener="#{bean.loadPanelData}">
    ...
</rich:collapsiblePanel>
```

Listing 6-8. Using org.richfaces.event.PanelToggleEvent

```
private void loadPanelData(PanelToggleEvent event){
    //refresh panel data if needed on expand, for example
}
```

To control whether the component is closed or opened when rendered for the first time, simply set the *expanded* attribute to either *true* or *false*, as follows:

```
<rich:collapsiblePanel switchType="ajax" expanded="false">
```

You can also point to an EL expression to control the attribute inside the managed bean, as follows:

```
<rich:collapsiblePanel switchType="ajax" expanded="#{cityBean.isOpen}">
```

JavaScript API

The component currently provides only one JavaScript API method, switchPanel(), which can be invoked on the client and switch the current state to opposite. Check the "RichFaces Component Reference" at www.jboss.org/richfaces/docs for new methods added by the RichFaces team.

Using <rich:tabPanel> and <rich:tab>

<rich:tabPanel> and <rich:tab> let you create tabbed panes on a page. <rich:tabPanel> is the container that consists of one or more tabs (<rich:tab>).

 <rich:tab> is the container for a single tab and can contain any other content and any JSF components.

 Listing 6-9 shows a sample tab panel.

Listing 6-9. A sample tab panel

```
<h:form>
    <rich:panel style="width:500px">
        <f:facet name="header">rich:tabPanel and rich:tab</f:facet>
        <rich:tabPanel switchType="ajax">
            <rich:tab header="New York City">
                Statue of Liberty
            </rich:tab>
            <rich:tab header="San Francisco">
                Golden Gate Bridge
            </rich:tab>
            <rich:tab header="Los Angeles">
                Hollywood
            </rich:tab>
        </rich:tabPanel>
    </rich:panel>
</h:form>
```

The result is shown in Figure 6-9.

```
rich:tabPanel and rich:tab

  New York City  San Francisco  Los Angeles

  Statue of Liberty
```

Figure 6-9. Simple tab panel

Headers for `<rich:tab>` are created in the same way as `<rich:panel>`, using an attribute with a header name.

It's easy to mark any tab as disabled by setting `disabled="true"`. Of course, the `disabled` attribute can point to an EL expression and be controlled via the model during runtime.

You can also use a facet named *header* instead of a corresponding attribute to define tab headers out of any number of components; for example, if you want to include images in the header for each tab, as shown in Figure 6-10.

```
rich:tabPanel and rich:tab

  ♀ New York City   ♀ San Francisco   ♀ Los Angeles

  Statue of Liberty
```

Figure 6-10. Tab panel with custom headers

Listing 6-10 shows the code used.

Listing 6-10. Code for tab panel with custom headers

```
<h:form>
    <rich:panel style="width:500px">        <f:facet name="header">rich:tabPanel and↵
rich:tab</f:facet>
        <rich:tabPanel switchType="ajax">
            <rich:tab>
                <f:facet name="header">
                    <h:panelGrid columns="2">
                        <h:graphicImage value="/images/yellow_lamp.gif"/>
                        <h:outputText value="New York City" />
                    </h:panelGrid>
                </f:facet>
                <h:outputText value="Statue of Liberty" />
            </rich:tab>
            <rich:tab>
                <f:facet name="header">...</f:facet>
                <h:outputText value="Golden Gate Bridge" />
            </rich:tab>
            <rich:tab disabled="true">
                <f:facet name="header">...</f:facet>
                <h:outputText value="Hollywood" />
```

```
        </rich:tab>
      </rich:tabPanel>
    </rich:panel>
</h:form>
```

For `<rich:collapsiblePanel>` you can use the same three `switchType`'s: *server*, *ajax* and *client*. Table 6-2 shows the available events and listeners information.

Table 6-2. tabPanel Server-Side Events and listeners

Component	Event	Listeners
tabPanel	ItemChangeEvent	itemChangeListener

By setting the *activeItem* attribute to point to the *name* of the tab to display, it's possible to control which tab opens when the page is loaded for the first time. Note that each tab will have *name* generated based on its *id* if *name* not set.

Listing 6-11 shows how to open a particular tab and render what is shown in Figure 6-11.

Listing 6-11. Shows how to open a particular tab and render the display

```
<h:form>
    <rich:panel style="width:500px">
        <f:facet name="header">rich:tabPanel and rich:tab</f:facet>
        <rich:tabPanel switchType="ajax" activeItem="sf">
            <rich:tab header="New York City" name="nyc">
                Statue of Liberty
            </rich:tab>
            <rich:tab header="San Francisco" name="sf">
                Golden Gate Bridge
            </rich:tab>
            <rich:tab header="Los Angeles" name="la">
                Hollywood
            </rich:tab>
        </rich:tabPanel>
    </rich:panel>
</h:form>
```

Figure 6-11. Tab panel with initial selected tab defined

A frequent question is: how do you control the selected tab inside the model? Well, that's very simple to do. Just point *activeItem* using EL expression to the bean property that will hold the currently active tab name, as shown in Listing 6-12.

Listing 6-12. Pointing activeItem *using EL expression to the bean property*

```
<h:form>
    <rich:panel style="width:500px">
        <h:selectOneRadio value="#{cityTabBean.city}"
            valueChangeListener="#{cityTabBean.changeCity}">
            <f:selectItem itemLabel="New York" itemValue="nyc" />
            <f:selectItem itemLabel="San Francisco" itemValue="sf" />
            <f:selectItem itemLabel="Los Angeles" itemValue="la" />
            <a4j:ajax event="change" render="cityTabs @this" />
        </h:selectOneRadio>
    </rich:panel>
    <rich:panel style="width:500px" header="rich:tabPanel and rich:tab">
        <rich:tabPanel switchType="ajax" id="cityTabs"
            activeItem="#{cityTabBean.selectedTab}">
            <rich:tab label="New York City" name="nyc">
                Statue of Liberty
            </rich:tab>
            <rich:tab label="San Francisco" name="sf">
                Golden Gate Bridge
            </rich:tab>
            <rich:tab label="Los Angeles" name="la">
                Hollywood
            </rich:tab>
        </rich:tabPanel>
    </rich:panel>
</h:form>
```

By selecting a radio button, an Ajax request (via *<a4j:ajax>*) is sent and the *selectedTab* property, which is bound to the *activeItem* attribute holding the name of the selected tab, gets updated in select *ValueChangeListener*. That's pretty simple, right?

The Java bean code is shown in Listing 6-13.

Listing 6-13. The Java bean code

```
@ManagedBean
@SessionScoped
public class CityTabBean {
    private String city = "sf";
    private String selectedTab = "sf";
    public void changeCity(ValueChangeEvent event) {
        selectedTab = (String)event.getNewValue();
    }
    // getters and setters
}
```

It renders as shown in Figure 6-12.

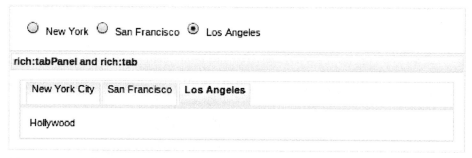

Figure 6-12. Tab panel switched outside

Another option for switching tab panels by external controls is to use its JavaScript API. Listing 6-14 shows the code to switch tabs with JavaScript API.

Listing 6-14. Shows the code to switch tabs with JavaScript API

```
<rich:panel style="width:500px" header="rich:tabPanel and rich:tab">
    <h:form>
        <rich:panel>
            <a4j:commandLink value="First"
                onclick="#{rich:component('tp')}.switchToItem('@first');
                return false;" />
            <a4j:commandLink value="Previous"
                onclick="#{rich:component('tp')}.switchToItem('@prev');
                return false;" />
            <a4j:commandLink value="New York City"
                onclick="#{rich:component('tp')}.switchToItem('nyc');
                return false;" />
            <a4j:commandLink value="San Francisco"
                onclick="#{rich:component('tp')}.switchToItem('sf');
                return false;" />
            <a4j:commandLink value="Los Angeles"
                onclick="#{rich:component('tp')}.switchToItem('la');
                return false;" />
            <a4j:commandLink value="Next"
                onclick="#{rich:component('tp')}.switchToItem('@next');
                return false;" />
            <a4j:commandLink value="Last"
                onclick="#{rich:component('tp')}.switchToItem('@last');
                return false;" />
        </rich:panel>
        <rich:tabPanel switchType="ajax" id="tp">
            <rich:tab header="New York City" name="nyc">
                Statue of Liberty
            </rich:tab>
            <rich:tab header="San Francisco" name="sf">
                Golden Gate Bridge
            </rich:tab>
            <rich:tab header="Los Angeles" name="la">
                Hollywood
```

```
        </rich:tab>
      </rich:tabPanel>
    </h:form>
  </rich:panel>
```

Figure 6-13 shows a tab panel that can be switched by links to a particular tab or to the first and last tabs using shortcut links (First/Previous, Next/Last).

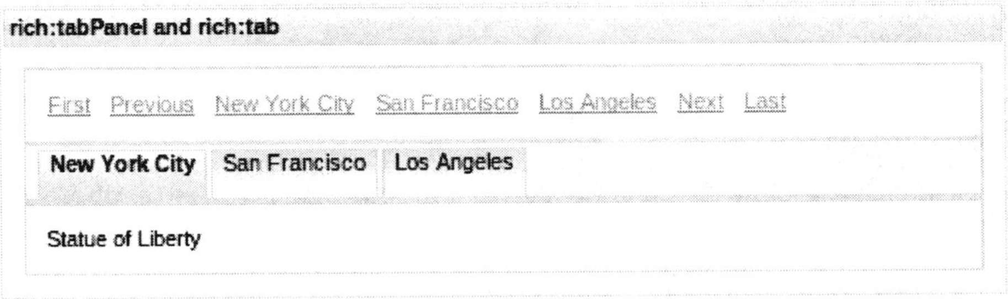

Figure 6-13. Switching the tab panel using JavaScript

The `<rich:tabPanel>` currently provides no icons attributes for tabs, and the tab component doesn't currently support tabs positioning on the right or along the side. These features are planned to be implemented in next release of RichFaces. Visit the RichFaces community often at `www.jboss.org/richfaces/docs` for updates and new features.

■ **Caution**   It's not possible to place a form inside the tab.

JavaScript API

The `<rich:tabPanel>` component provides the JavaScript API methods shown in Table 6-3.

Table 6-3. <rich:tabPanel> JavaScript API

Method Name	Description
getItems()	Used to get an array of the child tab objects.
getItemsNames()	Used to get an array of the child tab names.
switchToItem(tabName)	Used to switch to and display the tab identified by the tabName.

Using <rich:accordion>

`<rich:accordion>` allows you to create a set of panels that can be switched when a particular panel is selected to be opened and the currently opened panel is closed or collapsed. Content for each panel could be pre-rendered to the client. This means when you open or close the panels, the change occurs only on the client (the browser). This is an example of *switchType = "client"*. In addition to client switch type, the component can also be switched by using *ajax (default type now)* and *server* (full page reload) modes. Note that this component has to be inside a form to work properly.

Using the component is rather simple. An accordion consists of one or more accordion items, as shown in Listing 6-15.

Listing 6-15. An accordion consists of one or more accordion items

```
<h:form>
    <rich:panel style="width:550px" header="Using rich:accordion">
        <rich:accordion>
            <rich:accordionItem header="New York">
                Statue of Liberty
            </rich:accordionItem>
            <rich:accordionItem header="San Francisco">
                Golden Gate Bridge
            </rich:accordionItem>
            <rich:accordionItem header="Los Angeles">
                Hollywood
            </rich:accordionItem>
        </rich:accordion>
    </rich:panel>
</h:form>
```

The result is shown in Figure 6-14.

Figure 6-14. Simple accordion control

To define a header for each accordion item, a facet or attribute with the *header* name is used for panels. A facet is useful when you need to customize the header to include more than just simple text, such as images or more complex content. And for simpler text cases, you can use the *header* attribute. As with any panel, you can place any content inside each accordion item.

Figure 6-15 shows a sample of the component with a more complex layout and some customization already used in previous panels.

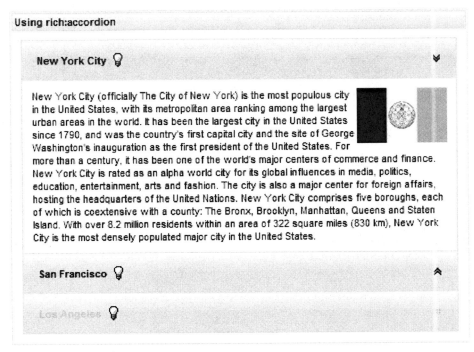

Figure 6-15. Customized accordion control

Listing 6-16 shows the code used.

Listing 6-16. Code used to customize accordion control

```
<h:form>
    <rich:panel style="width:500px" header="Using rich:accordion">
        <rich:accordion itemRightIconInactive="chevronUp"
            itemRightIconActive="chevronDown" itemRightIconDisabled="grid">
            <rich:accordionItem>
                <f:facet name="header">
                    <h:panelGrid columns="2">
                        <h:outputText value="New York City" />
                        <h:graphicImage value="/images/yellow_lamp.gif" />
                    </h:panelGrid>
                </f:facet>
                <h:graphicImage value="/images/NY-flag.png"
                    style="float:right" />
                New York City (officially The City of New York) is the most
                populous city in the United States, with its metropolitan area
                ranking among the largest urban areas in the world.
            </rich:accordionItem>
            ...
            <rich:accordionItem disabled="true">
                ...
            </rich:accordionItem>
```

```
            </rich:accordion>
        </rich:panel>
</h:form>
```

As you can see from the code in Listing 6-13, an accordion item can be disabled by setting `disabled="true"` attribute. Listing 6-17 shows how to define icons for the accordion item headers.

Listing 6-17. Shows how to define icons for the accordion item headers

```
<h:form>
    <rich:accordion itemRightIconInactive="chevronUp"
        itemRightIconActive="chevronDown"
        itemRightIconDisabled="grid">
        ...
    </rich:accordion>
</h:form>
```

For defining panel icons, you can use RichFaces built-in icons as shown in Listing 6-17. To use custom icons, you can point icon attributes to a custom image URI. The component also offers attributes to position the icons on either the left or right side on the accordion item or group. A complete list of built-in icon names and positioning attributes can be found in RichFaces documentation available at http://jboss.org/richfaces/docs.

As with other panels, switching between sets of states is possible via the *activeItem* attribute, which holds the name of the selected item, and can be bound to EL to control the selection in runtime. The panel switch modes are similar to other panels we covered: *ajax*, *server*, or *client* . When using *ajax* and server modes, the component fires a server-side *org.richfaces.event.ItemChangeEvent* event and provides an *itemChangeListener* attribute that is used to define the listener that will process it. Listing 6-18 shows how the listener is defined on the component.

Listing 6-18. Shows how the listener is defined on the component

```
<h:form>
    <rich:accordion activeItem="sf"
        itemChangeListener="#{panelsBean.processAccordionChange}"
        switchType="ajax">
        ...
    </rich:accordion>
</h:form>
```

Listing 6-19 shows the code for the listener inside the managed bean.

■ **Caution**   The accordion has to be placed inside a form in ajax and server mode.

Listing 6-19. Shows the code for the listener inside the managed bean

```
@ManagedBean
@RequestScoped
public class PanelsBean {
    public void processAccordionChange(ItemChangeEvent event){
```

```
        // Process the event...
    }
}
```

JavaScript API

The `<rich:accordion>` component provides the JavaScript API methods shown in Table 6-4.

Table 6-4. <rich:accordion> JavaScript API

Method Name	Description
getItems()	Used to get array of the child accordion item objects.
getItemsNames()	Used to get array of the child accordion item names.
switchToItem(accordionName)	Used to switch to and display the accordion identified by the accordionName.

Using <rich:togglePanel>

`<rich:togglePanel>` is actually the base component for `<rich:accordion>` and `<rich:tabPanel>`. It's covered last simply because the component is a pretty general implementation of panels with a states-switching feature and components that we covered previously.

`<rich:accordion>`, `<rich:tab>`, and `<rich:collapsiblePanel>`) are more popular and more often used. You define two or more panels using `<rich:togglePanelItem>` within the `<rich:togglePanel>` and add `<rich:toggleControl>` switching behavior to components (it can be inside or outside the panel), which switch those states.

Let's look at an example that uses famous quotes as the content for the panels. Figure 6-16 shows how the panel looks.

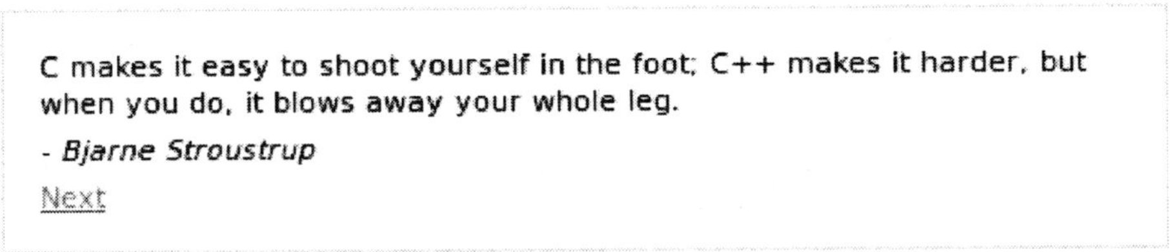

C makes it easy to shoot yourself in the foot; C++ makes it harder, but when you do, it blows away your whole leg.

- *Bjarne Stroustrup*

Next

Figure 6-16. Toggle panel initial state

Next, let's hide the current panel and show the next one using the link, as shown in Figure 6-17.

If you are going through hell, keep going.
- *Sir Winston Churchill (1874-1965)*

Next

Figure 6-17. Toggle panel switched to next item

Listing 6-20 shows the code to accomplish this.

Listing 6-20. Shows the code to toggle panel switched to next item

```
<h:form>
    <rich:panel style="width:450px">
        <rich:togglePanel id="quotes" switchType="ajax">
            <rich:togglePanelItem>
                <h:panelGrid>
                    <h:outputText value="C makes it easy to shoot yourself in the
                        foot; C++ makes it harder, but when you do, it blows away
                        your whole leg." />
                    <h:outputText value="- Bjarne Stroustrup"
                        style="font-style: italic" />
                    <h:commandLink value="Next">
                        <rich:toggleControl targetItem="@next" />
                    </h:commandLink>
                </h:panelGrid>
            </rich:togglePanelItem>
            <rich:togglePanelItem>
                <h:panelGrid>
                    <h:outputText value="If you are going through hell,
                        keep going." />
                    <h:outputText value="- Sir Winston Churchill (1874-1965)"
                        style="font-style: italic" />
                    <h:commandLink value="Next">
                        <rich:toggleControl targetItem="@next" />
                    </h:commandLink>
                </h:panelGrid>
            </rich:togglePanelItem>
            <rich:togglePanelItem>
                <h:panelGrid>
                    <h:outputText value="Life is pleasant. Death is peaceful. It's
                        the transition that's troublesome." />
                    <h:outputText value="- Isaac Asimov"
                        style="font-style: italic" />
                    <h:commandLink value="Next">
                        <rich:toggleControl targetItem="@next" />
                    </h:commandLink>
                </h:panelGrid>
            </rich:togglePanelItem>
            ...
        </rich:togglePanel>
    </rich:panel>
</h:form>
```

The panel is added by using a *<rich:panel>* component. The panel states (or the content) are defined by the addition of *<rich:togglePanel>* inside with the set of nested *<rich:togglePanelItem>* components (there isn't any predefined markup). Controls for switching are a simple *<h:commandLink>* with *<rich:toggleControl>* behavior. This adds greater flexibility and allows using the component in various use cases.

Behaviors are a great addition to JSF specification made in JSF 2. We could plug our *<rich:toggleControl>*'s behavior to any control on any event (*click* by default is used in this case), so we are not limited to just a button or a link anymore. In this example we use links and switched between states using the *@next* keyword, but you can also use the following predefined keywords: *@prev*, *@first*, and *@last*.

The order of switching defined by the order of child items within the component. The *cycledSwitching* attribute controls whether the panel will be switched from the boundary item to the opposite one if you continue switching in the same direction.

There is also another way to perform switching. The *<rich:togglePanelItem>* can be named using the *name* attribute. In *<rich:toggleControl>* you would then use the name in the *targetItem* attribute.

Finally, the controls with behavior are placed within the panel itself, but you can easily use them outside the panel component. You use the *targetPanel* attribute on the *<rich:toggleControl>* behavior defined with the corresponding panel *name*. In Listing 6-21, let's slightly change the previous sample.

Listing 6-21. *Using the* targetPanel *attribute on the* <rich:toggleControl> *behavior*

```
<h:form>
    <rich:panel style="width:450px">
        <rich:togglePanel id="tp2" switchType="ajax">
            <rich:togglePanelItem>
                <h:panelGrid>
                    <h:outputText value="C makes it easy to shoot yourself in the
                        foot; C++ makes it harder, but when you do, it blows away
                        your whole leg." />
                    <h:outputText value="- Bjarne Stroustrup"
                        style="font-style: italic" />
                </h:panelGrid>
            </rich:togglePanelItem>
            <rich:togglePanelItem>
                <h:panelGrid>
                    <h:outputText value="If you are going through hell, keep
                        going." />
                    <h:outputText value="- Sir Winston Churchill (1874-1965)"
                        style="font-style: italic" />
                </h:panelGrid>
            </rich:togglePanelItem>
            <rich:togglePanelItem name="einstein">
                <h:panelGrid>
                    <h:outputText value="Make everything as simple as possible,
                        but not simpler" />
                    <h:outputText value="- Albert Einstein (1879-1955)"
                        style="font-style: italic" />
                </h:panelGrid>
            </rich:togglePanelItem>
        </rich:togglePanel>
        <h:panelGrid columns="3">
            <h:commandButton value="Back">
                <rich:toggleControl targetPanel="tp2" targetItem="@prev" />
            </h:commandButton>
            <h:commandButton value="Einstein's quote">
                <rich:toggleControl targetPanel="tp2" targetItem="einstein" />
            </h:commandButton>
            <h:commandButton value="Next">
                <rich:toggleControl targetPanel="tp2" targetItem="@next" />
            </h:commandButton>
        </h:panelGrid>
    </rich:panel>
</h:form>
```

Note that we used buttons (instead of links) with *<rich:toggleControl>* behavior attached and placed them outside the toggle panel. Figure 6-18 shows the result after the Einstein button is clicked.

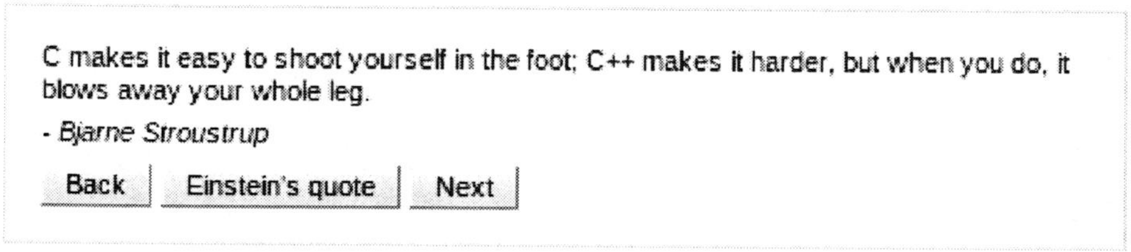

C makes it easy to shoot yourself in the foot; C++ makes it harder, but when you do, it blows away your whole leg.

- *Bjarne Stroustrup*

Back   Einstein's quote   Next

Figure 6-18. After clicking Bjarne's quote button

As with other panels, *<rich:togglePanel>* can be switched using three common modes: *server*, *ajax*, and *client*. And in the same way, it allows the *activeItem* attribute to bind the current panel id to the model and *itemChangeListener* to process the item switching in ajax or server mode.

■ **Caution**   The panel has to be placed inside a form in ajax and server mode.

Now let's create one more sample that will highlight the flexibility using this component. RichFaces provides the *<rich:tabPanel>* component out of the box but it does not provide a vertical tabs alignment feature. Let's create custom implementation using the *<rich:togglePanel>* component as shown in Figure 6-19.

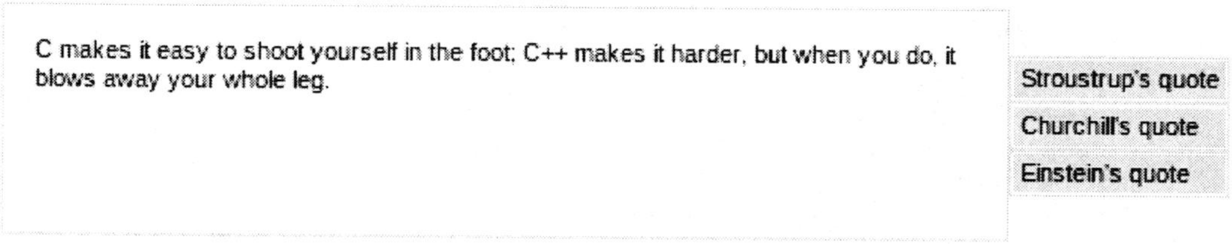

C makes it easy to shoot yourself in the foot; C++ makes it harder, but when you do, it blows away your whole leg.

Stroustrup's quote

Churchill's quote

Einstein's quote

Figure 6-19. Custom tab panel created using <rich:togglePanel>

This lightweight tab panel with vertically oriented tabs is really easy to build using the basic *<rich:togglePanel>* component, as shown in Listing 6-22.

Listing 6-22. Using the basic <rich:togglePanel> component

```
<style>
    .tab {
    padding: 2px 3px;
    background-color: #{richSkin.headerBackgroundColor};
}
    a.control {
    color: #{richSkin.headerTextColor};
    text-decoration:none;
}
</style>
```

```
<h:form>
    <h:panelGrid columns="2" cellpadding="0" cellspacing="0">
        <rich:panel style="width:450px; height:100px;">
            <rich:togglePanel id="tp2" switchType="ajax">
                <rich:togglePanelItem name="stroustrup">
                    <h:outputText value="C makes it easy to shoot yourself in the
                        foot; C++ makes it harder, but when you do, it blows away
                        your whole leg." />
                </rich:togglePanelItem>
                <rich:togglePanelItem name="churchill">
                    <h:outputText value="If you are going through hell, keep
                        going." />
                </rich:togglePanelItem>
                <rich:togglePanelItem name="einstein">
                    <h:outputText value="Make everything as simple as possible,
                        but not simpler."/>
                </rich:togglePanelItem>
            </rich:togglePanel>
        </rich:panel>
        <h:panelGroup>
            <rich:panel bodyClass="tab">
                <h:commandLink styleClass="control" value="Stroustrup's quote">
                    <rich:toggleControl targetPanel="tp2"
                        targetItem="stroustrup"/>
                </h:commandLink>
            </rich:panel>
            <rich:panel bodyClass="tab">
                <h:commandLink styleClass="control" value="Churchill's quote">
                    <rich:toggleControl targetPanel="tp2" targetItem="churchill"/>
                </h:commandLink>
            </rich:panel>
            <rich:panel bodyClass="tab">
                <h:commandLink styleClass="control" value="Einstein's quote">
                    <rich:toggleControl targetPanel="tp2" targetItem="einstein" />
                </h:commandLink>
            </rich:panel>
        </h:panelGroup>
    </h:panelGrid>
</h:form>
```

JavaScript API

The *<rich:togglePanel>* component provides the JavaScript API methods shown in Table 6-5.

Table 6-5. *<rich:togglePanel> JavaScript API*

Method Name	Description
getItems()	Used to get array of the child toggle panel item objects.
getItemsNames()	Used to get array of the child toggle panel item names.
switchToItem (panelName)	Used to switch to and display the panel identified by the panelName.

Using <rich:popupPanel>

The `<rich:popupPanel>` component implements a popup with various common features like dragging, resizing, screen blocking ability, and more. Popups can be called from one another and easily populated with dynamic content. Opening and closing the panel is done through client JavaScript code.

You can place any other content and any other JSF component inside the popup panel, but let's start with how you can choose the panel type and perform opening or closing the panel. You might also think about the popup panel as being just a *div* inside the current page that simply is shown or hidden.

Choosing Your Panel Type

A popup panel in RichFaces 4 can be either be modal (blocking the entire screen) or non-modal. RichFaces 3 came only with `<rich:modalPanel>`, which only provides a modal popup.

You could use the *modal* boolean attribute according to your use-case requirements. By default it will be opened as modal. To open the popup as non-modal, set *modal="false"*. Listing 6-23 shows an example.

***Listing 6-23.** To open the popup as non-modal*

```
<rich:popup modal="false">
    ...
</rich:popup>
```

Opening and Closing the Popup Panel

Listing 6-24 shows the simplest way to open and close the modal popup panel.

***Listing 6-24.** Simplest way to open and close the modal popup panel*

```
<a href="#" onclick="#{rich:component('modalPanel')}.show()">Open</a>

<rich:popupPanel id="modalPanel">
    <h:outputText value="Cool, I just opened a modal panel!" />
    <a href="#" onclick="#{rich:component('modalPanel')}.hide()">Hide</a>
</rich:popupPanel>
```

This code will produce the image shown in Figure 6-20.

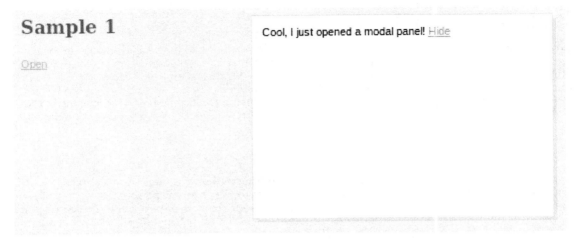

Figure 6-20. Simple modal popup

To open the popup panel, we used the *show()* JavaScript API method. The *#{rich:component(id)}* function is a RichFaces client-side EL function that enables you to reference any component. It is described more in Chapter 12.

To close it, you should use the *hide()* function, as follows:

```
<a href="#" onclick="#{rich:component('modalPanel')}.hide()">Hide</a>
```

Adding a Header

It's possible to add a panel header by adding a facet named header or an attribute with the same name. This is virtually identical to adding a header to <rich:panel>. With the header, you can now drag the component across the screen. The code in Listing 6-25 provides an example.

Listing 6-25. Code to drag the component across the screen

```
<a href="#" onclick="#{rich:component('modalPanel2')}.show()">Open</a>
<rich:popupPanel id="modalPanel2">
    <f:facet name="header">
      Modal panel
    </f:facet>
    <h:outputText value="Cool, I just opened a modal panel!" />
    <a href="#" onclick="#{rich:component('modalPanel2')}.hide()">Hide</a>
</rich:popupPanel>
```

This produces the image shown in Figure 6-21.

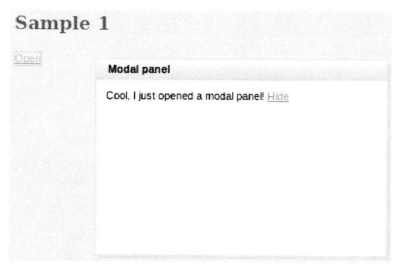

Figure 6-21. Modal panel with header

Adding Header Controls

You can also add a control on the right side of the header to close the popup panel. It's achieved by adding *control* facets to the popup panel, as shown in Listing 6-26.

Listing 6-26. Adding control *facets to the popup panel*

```
<a ref="#" onclick="#{rich:component('modalPanel3')}.show()">Open</a>
<rich:popupPanel id="modalPanel3">
    <f:facet name="header">
      Modal panel
    </f:facet>
    <f:facet name="controls">
       <h:outputLink value="#" style="font-size:large; color:black; text-
          decoration:none;" onclick="#{rich:component('modalPanel3')}.hide();
          return false;">
             X
       </h:outputLink>
    </f:facet>
    <h:outputText value="Cool, I just opened a modal panel!" />
    <a href="#" onclick="#{rich:component('modalPanel3')}.hide()">Hide</a>
</rich:popupPanel>
```

Inside the facet is an "X" symbol link that can be clicked to close the panel. The *onclick* event points to the panel *hide()* function to close the panel, as shown in Figure 6-22.

155

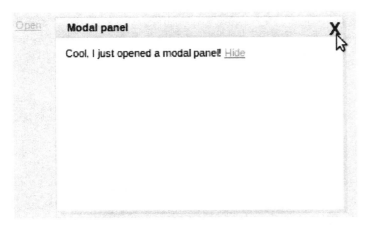

Figure 6-22. Modal panel with close control in header

Other Ways to Open/Close the Panel

Instead of using the *#{rich:component(id)}*, you can use the *<rich:componentControl>* component. As described in Chapter 12, it's a universal behavior that allows calling the JavaScript API on any RichFaces component based on a defined event supported by the parent component, such as *click* or *change*, as shown in Listing 6-27.

Listing 6-27. Using the <rich:componentControl> *component*

```
<h:commandButton value="Open">
    <rich:componentControl operation="show" target="modalPanel4" />
</h:commandButton>
<rich:popupPanel id="modalPanel4" modal="false">
    <f:facet name="header">
      Non-modal popup panel
    </f:facet>
    <f:facet name="controls">
       <h:graphicImage value="/modalPanel/close.png" style="cursor:pointer"
          onclick="Richfaces.hideModalPanel('modalPanel4')" />
    </f:facet>
    <h:outputText value="Cool, I just opened non-modal popup panel!" />
    <h:outputLink value="#">
       <h:outputText value="Hide" />
       <rich:componentControl event="click" operation="hide"
          target="modalPanel4" />
    </h:outputLink>
</rich:popupPanel>
```

Note that Figure 6-23 shows a popup in non-modal state.

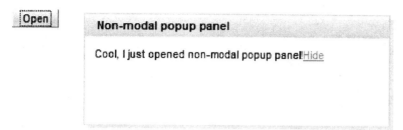

Figure 6-23. Non-modal popup called from button with <rich:componentControl>

This approach to showing and hiding the popup and the one we originally demonstrated are basically identical.

Open/Close Panel from Server-Side Action

One question that often arises in RichFaces related blogs and community forum threads is how to control the opening of a popup panel on the server. It's probably due to the control being client-side; you show or hide it on the client so it's not immediately clear how to control it from the server.

It's actually rather simple and is shown in Listing 6-28. This is an example of a welcome window (popup) shown to the user.

Listing 6-28. Example of a welcome window (popup)

```
<rich:popupPanel id="modalPanel7" autosized="true" header="Welcome!"
    show="#{simplePopupBean.justRegistered}">
    We hope you're getting much fun playing with RichFaces!!
    <a href="#" onclick="#{rich:component('modalPanel7')}.hide()">Hide</a>
</rich:popupPanel>
```

In this example, we use the *show* attribute to determine whether or not to show the component when the page is loaded. When the attribute is bound to EL, it's possible to control whether or not to show the component in runtime.

There is just one thing to keep in mind: if you are making changes via Ajax, don't forget to update the entire component in order for it to get re-initialized and shown or hidden based on a new value.

Component Customization

To manage the placement of an inserted popup, use the *zindex* attribute, which is similar to the standard HTML style and can specify window placement relative to the content. That is especially important in case multiple non-modal popups are opened from the different page controls. In case of opening one panel from another, the last will be automatically adjusted to be on top.

To manage window placement, use the *left* and *top* attributes. They define a window offset relative to the top-left corner of the window. These parameters (and some others, like *size* parameters) can be defined at tag level or passed to the *show()* method as we will show next. The last approach allows using a popup in a more dynamic way.

Popup panels can also support resize and move operations on the client side. To allow or disallow these operations, set the *resizeable* and *moveable* attributes to *true* or *false*. Popup resizing is also limited by the *minWidth* and *minHeight* attributes specifying the minimal sizes. Listing 6-29 shows an example.

Listing 6-29. Popup resizing

```
<h:commandButton value="Show popup">
    <rich:componentControl target="modalPanel5" operation="show">
        <a4j:param noEscape="true" value="event" />
        <rich:hashParam>
            <f:param name="minWidth" value="300px" />
            <f:param name="minHeight" value="150px" />
            <a4j:param noEscape="true" name="left"
                value="(jQuery(window).width()/2)-250" />
                <a4j:param noEscape="true" name="top"
                    value="(jQuery(window).height()/2)-150" />
        </rich:hashParam>
    </rich:componentControl>
</h:commandButton>
<rich:popupPanel id="modalPanel5" modal="false" resizeable="true"
    header="Dynamic popup panel" moveable="true">
    <p>Cool, I just opened non-modal popup panel passing parameters from
        script!</p>
    <p>It could be resized and moved to any part of the screen"</p>
    <a href="#" onclick="#{rich:component('modalPanel5')}.hide()">Hide</a>
</rich:popupPanel>
```

Figure 6-24 shows the result when the page is rendered.

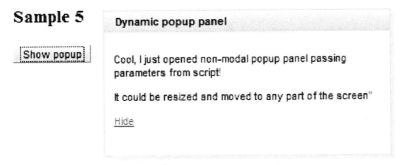

Figure 6-24. Popup panel with dynamic sizes

As you can see, we defined some functional parameters like *resizeable* and *moveable* at panel level, but passed positioning and size attributes from a concrete opening link. This adds more flexibility to component. Read more about *<a4j:param>* and *<rich:hashParam>* in corresponding sections about core (a4j:tags, features, and concepts) and miscellaneous (RichFaces functions, component control, miscellaneous) components.

Advanced Component Usage Samples

What we have shown you so far is how to open and close popup panels using various methods, as well as performing basic customization. Obviously, you want to use a panel for more interesting things, such as entering and saving input or maybe even building wizard-like behavior.

Performing Content Updates Inside <rich:popupPanel>

So far, you have been using the JavaScript API to open and close the popup panels. This works fine, but you probably want to display some server-side data, such as data from a managed bean. For the data to be updated every time you open the popup panel, the content has to be rendered by Ajax before opening the panel. To be able to update content, use already known Ajax controls such as *<a4j:commandlLink>* or *<a4j:commandButton>*.

Suppose you have added a time display to the popup panel, as shown in Listing 6-30.

Listing 6-30. Adding a time display to the popup panel

```
<a href="#" onclick="#{rich:component('modalPanel6')}.show()">Open</a>
<rich:popupPanel id="modalPanel6" autosized="true" header="Time Panel">    <h:panelGrid>
    <h:outputText value="Cool, I just opened a modal panel!" />
    <h:outputText id="time" value="Time: #{simplePopupBean.now}">
        <f:convertDateTime />
    </h:outputText>
  </h:panelGrid>
    <a href="#" onclick="#{rich:component('modalPanel6')}.hide()">Hide</a>
</rich:popupPanel>
```

#{simplePopupBean.now} simply returns the current server time, as shown in Listing 6-31.

Listing 6-31. Using #{simplePopupBean.now}

```
@ManagedBean
@RequestScoped
public class SimplePopupBean {
    public Date getNow(){
        return new Date();
    }
}
```

When the page is rendered for the first time, the time from the server will be rendered on the page. When the popup panel is opened, the value previously rendered will be shown. The time will not be the current time because you haven't updated it (re-rendered it). To solve this, you'll use *<a4j:commandLink>* to open the popup panel and re-render the component that shows the time. This way, each time the popup panel is opened you will get the latest time from the server, as demonstrated in Listing 6-32.

Listing 6-32. Using <a4j:commandLink>

```
<h:form>
    <a4j:commandLink value="Open"
        onclick="#{rich:component('modalPanel6')}.show()" render="time" />
</h:form>
<rich:popupPanel id="modalPanel6" autosized="true" header="Time Panel">
    <h:panelGrid>
        <h:outputText value="Cool, I just opened a modal panel!" />
        <h:outputText id="time" value="Time: #{simplePopupBean.now}">
            <f:convertDateTime />
        </h:outputText>
    </h:panelGrid>
    <a href="#" onclick="#{rich:component('modalPanel6')}.hide()">Hide</a>
</rich:popupPanel>
```

Figure 6-25 shows the popup opened using Ajax link.

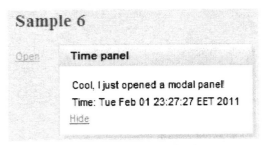

Figure 6-25. Popup panel with the content updated by Ajax

Again, it will help you to think about the popup panel as simply a section of the same page that can be shown or hidden. Other than that, all the rules for Ajax rendering apply as before.

Using Popup Panel As a Wizard

Let's look at an example where you can edit information in the popup panel. When you place input fields or buttons or links inside the popup panel, you need to make sure the popup panel has its own form. One thing to keep in mind is that it's not allowed to nest forms, so the popup panel must not be placed in some external form at the same time.

■ **Note** To avoid the problems of overlapping the popup panel with any z-index by the elements that are at upper DOM levels and have relative positioning (a common problem in Internet Explorer), the root node of the popup panel is moved to the top of a DOM tree. That's why you should use a separate <h:form> inside the popup panel if you want to perform submits from this panel.

Listing 6-33 shows an example using a popup panel as a wizard.

Listing 6-33. Popup panel as a wizard

```
<rich:popupPanel id="modalPanel8" header="Edit User Information"
    width="350" height="150" autosized="true">
    <h:form>
        <rich:tabPanel switchType="client">
            <rich:tab header="personal">
                <h:panelGrid columns="2">
                    <h:outputText value="Name:" />
                    <h:inputText value="#{userBean.name}" label="username"/>
                    <h:outputText value="Age:" />
                    <h:inputText value="#{userBean.age}" label="age"/>
                </h:panelGrid>
            </rich:tab>
```

```
            <rich:tab header="Location">
                <h:panelGrid columns="2">
                    <h:outputText value="City:" />
                    <h:inputText value="#{userBean.city}" id="city"/>
                    <h:outputText value="Country:" />
                    <h:inputText value="#{userBean.country}" label="country"/>
                </h:panelGrid>
            </rich:tab>
        </rich:tabPanel>
        <a4j:commandButton value="Close" id="close"
            onclick="#{rich:component('modalPanel8')}.hide(); return false;" />
        <a4j:commandButton value="Save and Close" id="save" render="input"
            oncomplete="if (#{facesContext.maximumSeverity==null})
            #{rich:component('modalPanel8')}.hide();" />
    </h:form>
</rich:popupPanel>
<a4j:outputPanel ajaxRendered="true">
    <rich:popupPanel id="msgPanel" modal="true" zindex="101" header="Correct
        your input!" autosized="true"
        show="#{facesContext.maximumSeverity!=null}">
        <h:messages style="color:red" />
        <a href="#" onclick="#{rich:component('msgPanel')}.hide()">Hide</a>
    </rich:popupPanel>
</a4j:outputPanel>
<h:form>
    <h:panelGrid id="input">
        <h:outputText value="Name: #{userBean.name}" />
        <h:outputText value="Age: #{userBean.age}" />
        <h:outputText value="City: #{userBean.city}" />
        <h:outputText value="Country: #{userBean.country}" />
        <a onclick="#{rich:component('modalPanel8')}.show()">Edit User
            wizard</a>
    </h:panelGrid>
</h:form>
```

The managed bean contains just simple *User* properties, as shown in Listing 6-34.

Listing 6-34. Managed bean

```
@ManagedBean
@RequestScoped
public class UserBean {
    @Length(min = 3, max = 15, message="Name should be defined(3 to 15
        characters)")
    private String name = "";
    @Min(value = 18, message = "You should be over 18 years to place orders")
    @NotNull(message="Age should be specified")
    private Integer age;
    @NotEmpty(message="City should be specified")
    private String city=null;
    @NotEmpty(message="Country should be specified")
    private String country=null;
    //getters and setters
}
```

A wizard is launched to enter values for #{userBean} properties. From the popup panel, you can cancel, edit, or save the value when closing the panel. If you save the value, the value entered is then updated in the main page.

One thing to note is that you need to point the *render* attribute of the Save and Close button to the <h:panelGrid> ID, as shown in Listing 6-33, to see the updated values in the parent page. Notice the separate <h:form> inside the popup panel.

Also notice that to save the input inside the popup panel, we are using <a4j:commandButton> to perform an Ajax submit of the values to the server. Once the request is done, the *oncomplete* event will be processed and will close the popup.

■ **Note** This sample shows you again how to open the panel as a result of server-side actions. The panel with messages that appear in the event of a failed validation are shown automatically, depending on whether messages are added to the context during request.

All the steps are shown here. Figure 6-26 shows the initial page state before opening the edit panel.

Name:
Age:
City:
Country:

Create/Edit User wizard

Figure 6-26. User details prior to filling the properties.

Figure 6-27 shows the edit popup.

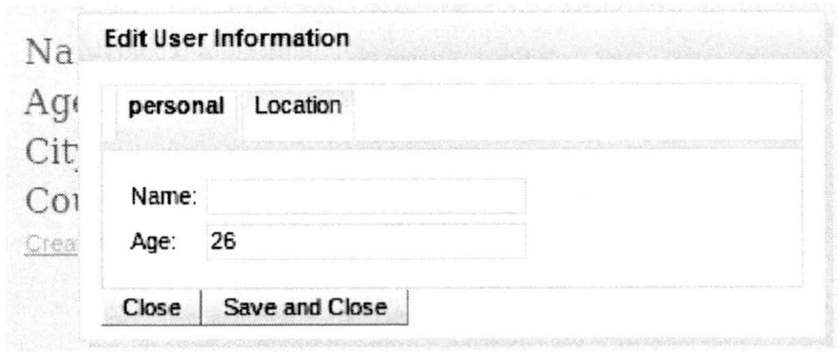

Edit User Information

| **personal** | Location |

Name:

Age: 26

Close | Save and Close

Figure 6-27. Popup panel which accepts user input shown

Figure 6-28 shows the second popup, which contains messages about failed form validation.

Figure 6-28. Popup panel with messages shown in the result of wrong input

In Figure 6-29 you see the result after successful user information entering.

Name: Ilya
Age: 26
City: Minsk
Country: Belarus

Create/Edit User wizard

Figure 6-29. User details after editing with popup wizard complete

Opening the Popup Panel from Within a Table

Another common usage is opening a popup panel from within a table to view or edit the selected record.
Figure 6-30 shows an example.

Airlines	
Name	**Actions**
American Airlines	View
United Airlines	View
Delta	View
Southwest Airlines	View
US Airways	View

Figure 6-30. Table with airlines information

After clicking a View link, a popup panel opens and shows the selected record information, as
shown in Figure 6-31.

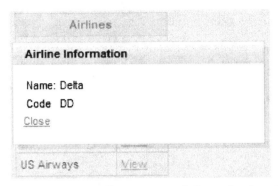

Figure 6-31. Details popup panel shown for the table row

The page source for these example figures is shown in Listing 6-35.

Listing 6-35. Page source

```
<h:form>
    <rich:dataTable value="#{airlinesBean.airlines}" var="airline">
        <f:facet name="header">Airlines</f:facet>
        <rich:column>
            <f:facet name="header">Name</f:facet>
                #{airline.name}
        </rich:column>
        <rich:column>
            <f:facet name="header">Actions</f:facet>
            <a4j:commandLink value="View"
                oncomplete="#{rich:component('popupPanel9')}.show()"
                render="airlineInfo">
                <f:setPropertyActionListener value="#{airline}"
                    target="#{airlinesBean.selected}" />
            </a4j:commandLink>
        </rich:column>
    </rich:dataTable>
</h:form>
<rich:popupPanel id="popupPanel9" width="250" height="100">
    <f:facet name="header">
        Airline Information
    </f:facet>
    <h:panelGrid id="airlineInfo" columns="2">
        <h:outputText value="Name:" />
        <h:outputText value="#{airlinesBean.selected.name}" />
        <h:outputText value="Code" />
        <h:outputText value="#{airlinesBean.selected.code}" />
    </h:panelGrid>
    <a href="#" onclick="#{rich:component('popupPanel9')}.hide();return
        false;">Close</a>
</rich:popupPanel>
```

The Java code is pretty simple. Note the AirlinesBean code in Listing 6-36.

Listing 6-36. AirlinesBean code

```
@ManagedBean
@SessionScoped
public class AirlinesBean {
    private Airline selected;
    private List<Airline> airlines;
    public AirlinesBean() {
        airlines = new ArrayList<Airline>();
        airlines.add(new Airline("American Airlines", "AA"));
        airlines.add(new Airline("United Airlines", "UA"));
        airlines.add(new Airline("Delta", "DD"));
        airlines.add(new Airline("Southwest Airlines", "WN"));
        airlines.add(new Airline("US Airways", "US"));
    }
    //Getters and setters
}
```

And the Airline object is shown in Listing 6-37.

Listing 6-37. Airline object

```
public class Airline {
    private String name;
    private String code;

    public Airline(String name, String code) {
        this.name = name;
        this.code = code;
    }
    //Getters and setters
}
```

We are using *<f:setPropertyActionListener>* to set the object that was selected in the table. The selected object is then updated inside the popup panel. This is no different from selecting the same object, and instead of showing it in a popup panel, you can display the object below the table, for example. To use a popup panel, it will help you to think that from the server perspective it's all one page.

■ **Note** Additional details about the iteration components are covered in Chapter 7.

Using the Popup Panel to Show Status

Another common usage for the popup panel is to show some operation status. Because the modal popup panel will block the underlying view, the user can't click any other buttons or links while the current operation is executed. The basic idea is that you click some function and a panel is shown. On completion of the operation, the panel is hidden. You are also going to use *<a4j:status>* to help with this. *<a4j:status>* will actually show and hide the popup panel. Listing 6-38 shows the page code.

Listing 6-38. Using <a4j:status>

```
<h:form>
    <a4j:commandButton actionListener="#{bean.calculate}" value="Calculate" />
</h:form>
<rich:popupPanel id="mp" style="text-align:center">
    <h:outputText value="Please wait..." style="font-weight:bold;font-
        size:large" />
</rich:popupPanel>
<a4j:status id="actionStatus"
    onstart="#{rich:component('mp')}.show('',{height:'80', width:'150'})"
    onstop="#{rich:component('mp')}.hide()" />
```

The calculate() method (which causes some long-running processing) will be defined, as shown in Listing 6-39.

Listing 6-39. calculate() method

```
@ManagedBean
@RequestScoped
public class Bean {
    public void calculate(ActionEvent event){
        // some long running calculations or this for testing:
        try {

            Thread.sleep(3000);

        } catch (InterruptedException e) {

            e.printStackTrace();

        }
    }
}
```

Figure 6-32 shows the result.

Figure 6-32. Popup panel used as blocking operation status window

When the button is clicked, the #{bean.calculate} listener is invoked. Let's assume it takes a few seconds to complete (you can put the current thread to sleep for a few seconds if you are testing). You know from before that you can use <a4j:status> to display any content while the Ajax request is being processed. In this example facets are not defined, but we are using <a4j:status>'s *start* and *stop* events to show and hide the popup panel. Again #{rich:component(id)} is the RichFaces client EL function that allows you to call the JavaScript API on the referenced component. That's exactly what the example does. On the request start, you call *show()* on the popup panel. When the request has been completed (*onstop* event handler called), you call *hide()* on the popup panel.

Popup Panels and Performance

Real-world applications are widely using various popups across the pages. There are some claims about performance downgrades when using <rich:popupPanel> on pages. Usually the reason for this is trying to pre-render every popup panel content to the client. In the past, most of the use-cases were implemented by using navigation between master and details pages. Today many rich controls like tooltip, popup, sliding panel, and so on are available to designers trying to keep as much content on the same page as possible in order to build single-page-like applications.

This is really convenient for the application users. But without mechanisms of lazy loading and some other optimization techniques, it could greatly influence performance. So the main thing you should keep in mind while using the component is to limit the number of instances (especially heavy-weight) as possible. And remember the following:

- Do not include popups in iteration components in order to simply generate popups with row details.

- Do not use several different panel instances in templates for all application pages. This is especially important if the panels themselves use other rich components.

- Do not add Ajax-rendered zones (via *<a4j:outputPanel>*) to every panel if only one will be actually updated in most view use-cases.

If you think about it, it all makes sense. First, every panel instance adds additional HTML to be rendered and loaded on the client. Second, every panel adds additional JavaScript initialization for the popup itself and for the components used in markup. Third, defining Ajax-rendered zones is good for panels in templates to catch all the changes without taking care about searching for the concrete panel that needs to be updated (re-rendered). But in that case, Ajax response size (and therefore time) will be increased and so will influence the Ajax performance.

Ideally, where possible, you should use something like Listing 6-40 in your applications.

Listing 6-40. Code to improve performance

```
<a4j:outputPanel id="updateMeToLoadPanel" layout="block">
    <rich:popupPanel rendered="#{controller.panelNeeded}">
        <a4j:outputPanel id="updateMeWhenPanelExist" layout="block">
            <ui:include src="#{controller.currentPanelURI}" />
        <a4j:outputPanel/>
    </rich:popupPanel>
</a4j:outputPanel>
```

A single panel instance is used and added only when it's needed. If the panel is already present in a view but has to be updated, then only inner *<a4j:outputPanel>* should be re-rendered to avoid JavaScript re-initialization of the popup. And *<ui:include>* src attribute, pointed to the subview, should be shown after the Ajax request. Then the panel could be shown using *oncomplete* of Ajax controls.

Ideally you should define only as many popups instances that you need nested panels for, and not for every separate case on the view.

JavaScript API

The `<rich:popupPanel>` component provides the JavaScript API methods shown in Table 6-6.

Table 6-6. <rich:popupPanel> JavaScript API

Method Name	Description
show ([event, options])	Used to show the panel. Could be used either without any options or providing event and hash map of visual parameters like sizes, minimum sizes and position.
hide()	Used to hide the panel.
getLeft()	Returns current horizontal position.
getTop()	Returns current vertical position.
moveTo (top, left)	Used to move the panel to new position.

Using <rich:toolTip>

`<rich:toolTip>` allows you to display a tooltip based on some event. The most common case would be when you move the mouse over some text label or icon image. The tooltip can contain any other JSF components and content.

Let's say you start with something like this and want to display information about New York City when the mouse cursor moves over the city name, as shown in Figure 6-33.

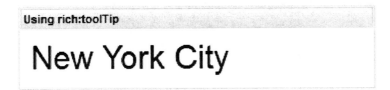

Figure 6-33. Panel with city name

Listing 6-41 shows how to define a simple tooltip for that case. The content of the tooltip is enclosed within <rich:toolTip>. If the tooltip content is just a small amount of text, you can use the *value* attribute of <rich:toolTip> instead. By default, the tooltip will be displayed when the *mouseover* event occurs. We will show you later in this chapter how you can specify the event implicitly.

Listing 6-41. Defining a simple tooltip

```
<rich:panel style="width:350px">
    <f:facet name="header">Using rich:toolTip</f:facet>
    <h:form>
        <h:outputText id="nyc" value="New York City" style="font-size: xx-
            large;" />
```

```
    <rich:tooltip mode="ajax" target="nyc">
        <h:panelGroup style="width:200px">
            New York City is the most populous city in the United States,
            with its metropolitan area ranking among the largest urban areas
            in the world. For more than a century, it has been one of the
            world's major centers of commerce and finance.
        </h:panelGroup>
    </rich:tooltip>
  </h:form>
</rich:panel>
```

The *target* attribute in Listing 6-41 points to the component whose event should activate the tooltip. It's also possible just to wrap the tooltip inside the actual component. We will show an example later in this chapter.

Finally, the loading mode used is *ajax*. In other words, when the mouse cursor moves over the text, an Ajax request is sent to the server to get the content of the tooltip. Another option is to use *client* mode. When using *mode="client"*, the tooltip content will be pre-rendered to the client. Tooltip does not provide *server* mode because there are no reasons to make a full-page refresh just to show the tooltip.

Figure 6-34 shows the result when *mouseover* occurs at panel body text.

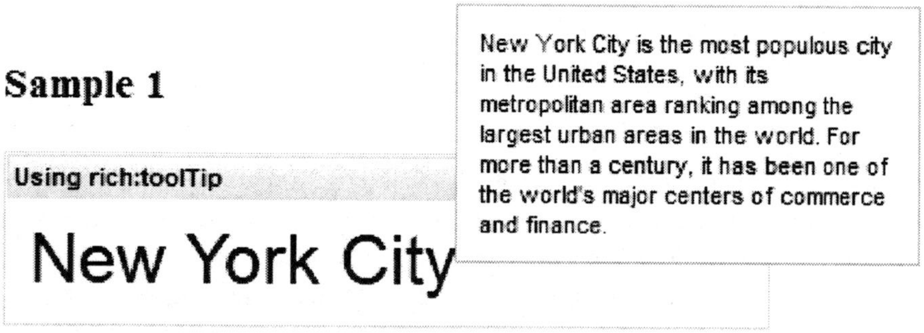

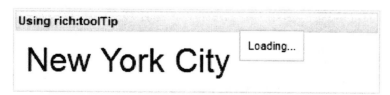

Figure 6-34. Tooltip above the text label

When using *ajax* mode, you can display a default message while the tooltip content is being retrieved from the server. This is useful if the operation to get the tooltip content might take a little while. To show the default content, you can use a facet named *loading*. Figure 6-35 shows how it looks in *ajax* mode when data for tooltip requested by default without even specifying the facet.

Using rich:toolTip

New York City   Loading...

Figure 6-35. Tooltip "loading" label

Another useful attribute is *followMouse*. When set to *true*, the tooltip will follow the mouse as long as it stays on the element, as shown in Listing 6-42.

Listing 6-42. followMouse

```
<h:form>
<rich:panel style="width:350px" id="panel">
   <f:facet name="header">Using rich:toolTip</f:facet>

       <rich:tooltip mode="client" followMouse="true">
           <f:facet name="loading">Loading...</f:facet>
           <h:panelGrid style="width:200px">
               New York City is the most populous city in the United States,
               with its metropolitan area ranking among the largest urban areas
               in the world. For more than a century, it has been one of the
               world's major centers of commerce and finance.
           </h:panelGrid>
       </rich:tooltip>
       <h:outputText id="nyc" value="New York City" style="font-size: xx-
           large;" />

   </rich:panel>
</h:form>
```

In this sample you also see the tooltip defined without *target* attribute usage. It is attached to the parent component (*<rich:panel>*).

■ **Note** There are components in JSF that don't encode its ID to the client unless you specify it explicitly. Two examples are <h:outputText> and <h:graphicImage>. If you are adding a tooltip to such components as a child and no ID is present, it will not work because it will not find an element to attach to. Adding a tooltip to a component requires that a client id is present. So a good practice is always to add an ID to parent components.

You can include any other JSF components inside the tooltip. Let's add the server time and a counter of the tooltip invocations, as well as an image. As shown in Listing 6-43, we will use *mode="ajax"*, so every time the tooltip is displayed, the time and counter should be updated.

Listing 6-43. Using mode="ajax"

```
<h:form>
   <rich:panel style="width:350px">
       <f:facet name="header">Using rich:toolTip</f:facet>
       <h:outputText id="nyc" value="New York City" style="font-size: xx-
           large;" />
       <rich:tooltip mode="ajax" for="nyc" followMouse="true"
           showEvent="click">
           <f:facet name="loading">Loading...</f:facet>
           <h:panelGrid style="width:200px">
               <b>#{tooltip.now}"</b>
               New York City is the most populous city in the United States,
               with its metropolitan area ranking among the largest urban
               areas in the world. For more than a century, it has been one
```

```
            of the world's major centers of commerce and finance.
            <h:graphicImage value="/images/NY-flag.png"/>
            <h:outputText value="Tooltip invoked #{tooltip.counter} times"
                style="font-weight:italic" />
        </h:panelGrid>
      </rich:tooltip>
   </rich:panel>
</h:form>
```

This code produces Figure 6-36.

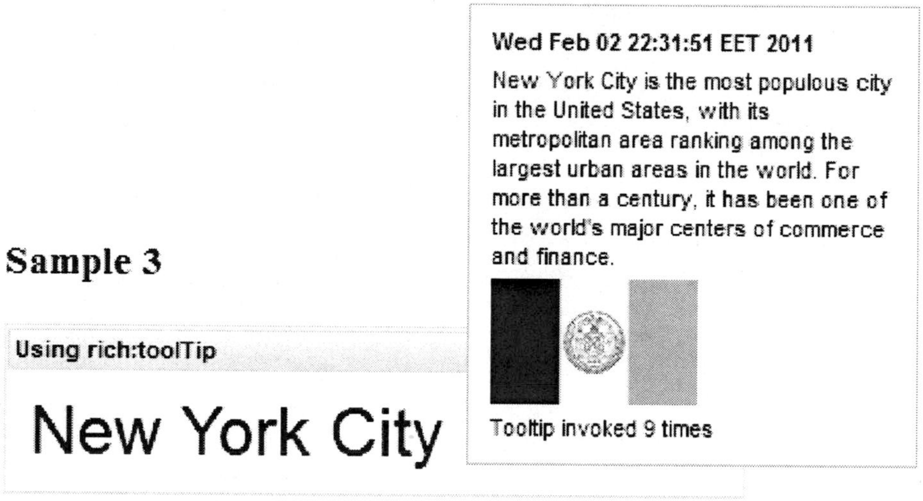

Sample 3

Figure 6-36. Tooltip with complex content and server-side data

You will see that the time was updated. *#{tooltip.now}* is bound to a getter that just returns the new time and *#{tooltip.counter}* increases every time the tooltip is requested, shown in Listing 6-44.

Listing 6-44. #{tooltip.now} *and* #{tooltip.counter}

```
@ManagedBean
@SessionScoped
public class Tooltip {
    private int counter = 0;

    public Date getNow() {
        return new Date();
    }

    public int getCounter() {
        return ++counter;
    }
}
```

If you switch to *mode="client"*, the tooltip content, including the time, will be pre-rendered and no longer updated. This also demonstrates how to show a tooltip for a component, and binding it on any event supported by that component.

There we use the *click* event as defined in the *showEvent* attribute, as follows:

```
<rich:tooltip mode="ajax" for="nyc" followMouse="true" showEvent="click">
```

■ **Note** You can use any component event to show the tooltip, but the event should provide positioning informa-tion. If a custom event on the component will not provide positioning information, the tooltip will not be positioned properly because it does not know where the event has occurred. *focus* event provides positioning information only if input was activated with a mouse. Currently, the tooltip can't be shown properly out of the box when the input gets focused using keyboard tabbing.

Using <rich:tooltip> with Data Iteration Components

Like the popup panel, the *<rich:toolTip>* component can be useful with data iteration components. For example, when mouse cursor is moved over a particular row cell, more information is displayed in the tooltip about that record.

One way to pre-render the content of the tooltip for each row is by setting *mode="client"*, as shown in Listing 6-45.

Listing 6-45. *Pre-render the content of the tooltip for each row*

```
<rich:dataTable id="statesTable"
    value="#{statesBean.statesList}" var="state">
    <h:column>
        <f:facet name="header">State</f:facet>
        <h:outputText value="#{state.name}" />
        <rich:tooltip mode="client" >
            <h:panelGrid>
                <h:outputText value="#{state.name}" style="font-weight:bold"/>
                <h:outputText value="#{state.capital}" />
                <h:graphicImage value="#{state.flagImage}"/>
            </h:panelGrid>
        </rich:tooltip>
    </h:column>
</rich:dataTable>
```

This produces Figure 6-37.

Figure 6-37. Tooltip over the table cell

You are probably wondering how to show the tooltip but not pre-render it to the client. That's definitely a good question as usage of tooltip pre-rendered inside iteration components could also affect the performance if the tooltip component contains complex markup and there are many rows in the iteration component, such as table. However, nothing complicated here—you should just change the mode to ajax and only the default facet will be pre-rendered. Tooltip content will be loaded via Ajax when the tooltip is requested.

▓ **Note** The best solution would be to define tooltip outside of the table and just show with particular cell information (ideally without any additional requests). But it's not so trivial with the current version of RichFaces. There is still no client templating feature implemented. And without that feature you will need to update the tooltip content using custom JavaScript before showing or updating via `ajax` anyway.

JavaScript API

The `<rich:tooltip>` component provides the JavaScript API method described in Table 6-7.

Table 6-7. <rich:tooltip> JavaScript API

Method Name	Description
show(event)	Used to show the tooltip.
hide()	Used to hide the tooltip.

Summary

RichFaces provides a wide range of rich output components, from a basic panel to popups and tool tips. This chapter showed you many different examples and tips on how to use and customize these components. As with any RichFaces component, you can customize the look and feel of these components with skins. Chapter 13 is dedicated to skins and their customization. To see these and other components in action, go to the RichFaces components demo application available at the JBoss Community RichFaces web site at www.jboss.org/richfaces.

Now that you have learned about output components, we are going to cover data iteration components in the next chapter.

CHAPTER 7

Rich Data Iteration Components

If you know how to use the standard JSF `<h:dataTable>` component, then you basically know how to use any data iteration components available in RichFaces. Now, RichFaces offers a number of features above and beyond what the standard data table component provides, such as advanced models, lazy loading, sorting, filtering, skins, and partial-table updates.

JSF 2 provides two components to iterate over data: `<h:dataTable>` and `<ui:repeat>`. The `<h:dataTable>` component generates an HTML `<table>..</table>` structure. The `<ui:repeat>` component allows you to iterate over collections wrapping with any HTML markup. However, when displaying collections in real enterprise applications, a simple table format is not always appropriate. You might also need to add scrolls to your tables, implement lazy loading, selection, or columns resizes, and order customization. Or, you might want to display various HTML lists, such as definition, ordered, or unordered. This is where RichFaces components come in.

Note Most screenshots in this chapter utilize the wine skin. Chapter 13 covers how to change skins.

RichFaces provides the following components to display collections:

1. `<rich:dataTable>`
2. `<rich:extendedDataTable>`
3. `<rich:collapsibleSubTable>`
4. `<rich:list>`
5. `<rich:dataGrid>`
6. `<a4j:repeat>`

All these components can be bound to the same data types as the standard `<h:dataTable>` component; however, the most common object that is bound to any type of data iteration component in simple cases is `java.util.List`. And, in more complex cases we will show you how to use advanced RichFaces data models.

Data Preparation

Let's start with the creation of the data that we will use across the examples. You might want to take a few minutes to review it (although it's pretty simple) because to save space, we will not repeat it in future code listings but will add only methods that should be added to the data bean to implement particular functionality. That simple List-based model will populate information about Olympic Games starting from 19th century. We will load the data from an XML file by using JAXB. (Java 6 was used for this example.) Listing 7-1 shows how the XML file looks.

■ **Tip** The Java Architecture for XML Binding (JAXB) provides a fast and convenient way to bind between XML schemas and Java representations, making it easy for Java developers to incorporate XML data and processing functions in Java applications. Learn more at http://jaxb.java.net/. You're free to skip this section if not familiar with JAXB or just not interested in XML-based data creation. Simply review the GameDescriptor class. Sample data in this chapter will consist of GameDescriptor class inside a java.util.List. In general, any Java bean with a couple of properties placed inside a list could be used as a data model object.

Listing 7-1. XML file

```
<games>
    <game>
        <city>Athens</city>
        <country>Greece</country>
        <continent>Europe</continent>
        <flag>greece_old</flag>
        <number>1</number>
        <season>Summer</season>
        <fromDate>4/6/1896</fromDate>
        <toDate>4/15/1896</toDate>
    </game>

<!-- other game entries-->
</games>
```

Listing 7-2 shows the GameDescriptor object that is used to store single-game information.

Listing 7-2. GameDescriptor object used to store single-game information

```
public class GameDescriptor implements Serializable {
    private String city;
    private String country;
    private String continent;
    private String flagName;
    private int number;
    private Calendar fromDate = new GregorianCalendar(Locale.US);
    private Calendar toDate = new GregorianCalendar(Locale.US);
    private seasons season;
    private statuses status = statuses.passed;
```

```
    private enum statuses {passed, future, canceled};
    private enum seasons {Winter, Summer};
    public int getYear() {
        return fromDate.get(Calendar.YEAR);
    }
    public String getFrom() {
        if (!status.equals(statuses.canceled)) {
            return fromDate.get(Calendar.DAY_OF_MONTH) + " "
                + fromDate.getDisplayName(Calendar.MONTH, Calendar.LONG, Locale.US);
        } else return "";
    }
    public String getTo() {
        if (!status.equals(statuses.canceled)) {
            return toDate.get(Calendar.DAY_OF_MONTH) + " "
                + toDate.getDisplayName(Calendar.MONTH, Calendar.LONG, Locale.US);
        } else return "";
    }
    public String getFlagURI() {
        return "/images/flags/" + flagName + ".png";
    }
    @XmlElement
    public String getCity() {
        return city;
    }
    // Getters and setters
}
```

As it mentioned, JAXB is used in the example to parse XML and create GameDescriptor objects. Note that all getters are marked with an @XmlElement annotation, such as getCity, as shown in listing 7-2.

getYear, getTo, and getFrom are used to get specific dates' representation, which will be used in the table. Images are placed in the WebApp/images/flags folder, and the getFlagURI method will transform an image name from an XML file to an image URI used inside a page.

fromDate and toDate getter methods are marked with the @XmlJavaTypeAdapter(value = CalendarConverter.class) annotation. CalendarConverter is used for unmarshalling the String date from XML to a java.util.Calendar property instance. It's pretty simple, as dates in XML are provided in a short format of US locales. CalendarConverter is shown in Listing 7-3.

Listing 7-3. CalendarConverter

```
public class CalendarConverter extends XmlAdapter<String, Calendar> {

    @Override
    public String marshal(Calendar v) throws Exception {
        return null;
    }
    @Override
    public Calendar unmarshal(String v) throws Exception {
        Calendar calendar = Calendar.getInstance(Locale.US);
        calendar.setTime(DateFormat.getDateInstance(DateFormat.SHORT, Locale.US).parse(v));
        return calendar;
    }
}
```

Let's review the GameParser.java class, which is used for parsing the data. It's shown in Listing 7-4.

Listing 7-4. GameParser.java class

```java
@ManagedBean
@ApplicationScoped
public class GamesParser {
    private List<GameDescriptor> gamesList;

    @XmlRootElement(name = "games")
    private static final class GameDescriptorsHolder {
        private List<GameDescriptor> games;

        @XmlElement(name = "game")
        public List<GameDescriptor> getGameDescriptors() {
            return games;
        }
        public void setGameDescriptors(List<GameDescriptor> games) {
            this.games = games;
        }
    }
    public synchronized List<GameDescriptor> getGameDescriptorsList() {
        if (gamesList == null) {
            ClassLoader ccl = Thread.currentThread().getContextClassLoader();
            URL resource = ccl.getResource("games.xml");
            JAXBContext context;
            try {
                context = JAXBContext.newInstance(GameDescriptorsHolder.class);
                GameDescriptorsHolder gamesHolder = (GameDescriptorsHolder) context
                    .createUnmarshaller().unmarshal(resource);
                gamesList = gamesHolder.getGameDescriptors();
            } catch (JAXBException e) {
                throw new FacesException(e.getMessage(), e);
            }
        }
        return gamesList;
    }
    public List<GameDescriptor> getGamesList() {
        if (gamesList == null){
            gamesList = getGameDescriptorsList();
        }
        return gamesList;
    }
    public void setGamesList(List<GameDescriptor> gamesList) {
        this.gamesList = gamesList;
    }
}
```

Listing 7-5 shows the managed bean that holds the GamesDescriptors list.

178

Listing 7-5. Managed bean of GamesDescriptors list

```
@ManagedBean
@ViewScoped
public class OlympicGamesBean implements Serializable{
    @ManagedProperty(value="#{gamesParser.gamesList}")
    private List<GameDescriptor> games = new ArrayList<GameDescriptor>();
    // Getters and setters
}
```

We are now ready to create all the samples for various RichFaces iteration components. We will start with the <rich:dataTable> in the next section.

▪ **Note** Covering JAXB is beyond the scope of this book. Refer to official JAXB documentation for additional information about how it works.

Using <rich:dataTable>

As we already mentioned, <rich:dataTable> basically provides the same functionally as <h:dataTable> with many additional features such as skins, partial-row update, and rows and columns spans. Let's start with the example in Listing 7-6.

Listing 7-6. <rich:dataTable>

```
<rich:panel style="width:650px" header="rich:dataTable sample">
    <rich:dataTable value="#{olympicGamesBean.games}" var="game">
        <f:facet name="header">Olympic Games List</f:facet>
        <rich:column>
            <f:facet name="header">Flag</f:facet>
            <h:graphicImage value="#{game.flagURI}" />
        </rich:column>
        <rich:column>
            <f:facet name="header">City</f:facet>
            #{game.city}
        </rich:column>
        <rich:column>
            <f:facet name="header">Country</f:facet>
            #{game.country}
        </rich:column>
        <!--More columns-->
    </rich:dataTable>
</rich:panel>
```

Figure 7-1 shows the table this code produces.

Olympic Games List									
Flag	City	Country	Continent	Season	Number	Year	From	To	Note
	Athens	Greece	Europe	Summer	1	1896	6 April	15 April	passed
	Paris	France	Europe	Summer	2	1900	14 May	28 October	passed
	St. Louis	United States	North America	Summer	3	1904	1 July	23 November	passed
	London	Great Britain	Europe	Summer	4	1908	27 April	31 October	passed
	Stockholm	Sweden	Europe	Summer	5	1912	5 May	27 July	passed
	Berlin	Germany	Europe	Summer	6	1916			canceled

Figure 7-1. Using <rich:dataTable>

Look-and-Feel Customization

Let's start a deeper component review with a look-and-feel customization. First, let's add a zebra-style, row hover-effect and additional column styling. For the zebra-style effect and column styling we will use attributes familiar if you used <h:dataTable> before. But, in order to add a row highlight for a hover, we will use events specific to a RichFaces table. For standard events such as onmouseover, onclick, and so on, the RichFaces table components also provides row events like onrowclick, onrowdblclick, and other like events.

As we will only add <rich:dataTable> attributes, let's look through the table definition in Listing 7-7. All the columns remain unchanged.

Listing 7-7. Adding <rich:dataTable> attributes

```
<style>
    .odd{
        background-color: #{richSkin.additionalBackgroundColor};
    }
    .even{
        background-color: #{richSkin.tableSubHeaderBackgroundColor};
    }
    .cityColumn{
        font-weight:bold;
    }
</style>

<rich:panel style="width:650px" header="rich:dataTable sample">
    <rich:dataTable value="#{olympicGamesBean.games}" var="game" rowClasses="odd, even"
        columnClasses=",cityColumn" onrowmouseover="this.style.fontWeight='bold'"
        onrowmouseout="this.style.fontWeight='normal'">
        ...
    </rich:dataTable>
</rich:panel>
```

The result is shown in Figure 7-2. Notice that the rowClasses attribute changed the backgrounds in both odd and even columns. That's a standard attribute and applies comma-separated class names sequentially to corresponding row elements. Also, columnClasses defines the second-column style class.

Finally, we are using two row event handlers—onrowmouseout and onrowmouseover—which are actually similar to standard HTML onmouseover and onmouseout, but define handlers for corresponding events on every component row. The handlers change all the cell fonts of the hovered row to bold and then back to normal (not bold) when the mouse leaves the row.

rich:dataTable sample

Olympic Games List									
Flag	City	Country	Continent	Season	Number	Year	From	To	Note
▪▪	Athens	Greece	Europe	Summer	1	1896	6 April	15 April	passed
▮▮	Paris	France	Europe	Summer	2	1900	14 May	28 October	passed
▬	St. Louis	United States	North America	Summer	3	1904	1 July	23 November	passed
▨	London	Great Britain	Europe	Summer	4	1908	27 April	31 October	passed
▪▪	Stockholm	Sweden	Europe	Summer	5	1912	5 May	27 July	passed
▬	Berlin	Germany	Europe	Summer	6	1916			canceled

Figure 7-2. Rich data table with column styling and row hover events

Now let's review the last and most interesting attribute related to CSS styling. rowClass is an attribute specific to RichFaces tables. It gets evaluated during iteration opposite to rowClasses, which gets evaluated prior to iterating the data model, so it can't be dynamically populated according to the model.

Let's change the background color of canceled game rows to the red. The code that adds such functionality is shown in Listing 7-8.

Listing 7-8. Changing the cancelled game row background color to red

```
.red{
    color:red;
}
</style>
<rich:panel style="width:650px" header="rich:dataTable sample">
    <rich:dataTable value="#{olympicGamesBean.games}" var="game"
        rowClasses="odd, even" columnClasses="cityColumn"
        onrowmouseover="this.style.fontWeight='bold'"
        onrowmouseout="this.style.fontWeight='normal'"
        rowClass="#{game.status == 'canceled' ? 'red' : ''}">
```

Figure 7-3 shows the result.

			Olympic Games List						
Flag	City	Country	Continent	Season	Number	Year	From	To	Note
▪▪	Athens	Greece	Europe	Summer	1	1896	6 April	15 April	
▮▮	Paris	France	Europe	Summer	2	1900	14 May	28 October	
▬	St. Louis	United States	North America	Summer	3	1904	1 July	23 November	
▨▨	London	Great Britain	Europe	Summer	4	1908	27 April	31 October	
▪▪	Stockholm	Sweden	Europe	Summer	5	1912	5 May	27 July	
▬	Berlin	Germany	Europe	Summer	6	1916			canceled

Figure 7-3. Rich data table with rows styled according to iteration data

That's it. Now you could easily apply any class to the whole row. Other use-cases that could require that feature include Task, Issue, or E-mail tables where rows should be styled according to item importance. In the past, you had to add the same class to all columns; that was not as easily maintainable and also caused much more HTML code to be rendered in the table markup.

Using Sub-Tables and Defining Complex Header Markups

In real applications, you will often have to deal with much more complex table-based data representations. Your tables could require using columns and rows spanning, which is the ability to define complex header structures to properly add the table content descriptions. Luckily, the RichFaces <rich:dataTable> component allows you to define rich, master-details tables using nested sub-tables.

Before we will start with the example, let us introduce the <rich:collapsibleSubTable> component. Used together with the <rich:dataTable>, it allows you to implement master-details tables of any complexity. It should be placed as either a child of <rich:dataTable> or <rich:collapsibleSubTable>, and iterate through a nested data model. And as you can probably guess, according to the name in RichFaces 4, it provides collapse/expand features right out of the box. So let's start with a simple example. The table we need to implement is shown in Figure 7-4.

Games by Continent								
			Place			Dates		Notes
Asia								
Season	Number	Flag	City	Country	Year	From	To	Status
Winter	5	●	Sapporo	Japan	1940			canceled
Summer	12	●	Tokyo	Japan	1940			canceled
Summer	18	●	Tokyo	Japan	1964	10 October	24 October	
Winter	11	●	Sapporo	Japan	1972	3 February	13 February	
Summer	24	⦂●⦂	Seoul	South Korea	1988	17 September	2 October	
Winter	18	●	Nagano	Japan	1998	7 February	22 February	
Summer	29	▨	Beijing	China	2008	8 August	24 August	
Europe								
Season	Number	Flag	City	Country	Year	From	To	Status
Summer	1	▦▦	Athens	Greece	1896	6 April	15 April	

Figure 7-4. Collapsible data table

Now, let's review Listing 7-9, which shows the code used to create this table.

Listing 7-9. Collapsible data table

```
<rich:dataTable value="#{olympicGamesBean.gamesMapKeys}" var="continent">
    <f:facet name="header">
        <rich:columnGroup>
            <rich:column colspan="9">Games by Continent</rich:column>
            <rich:column colspan="2" breakRowBefore="true"></rich:column>
            <rich:column colspan="3">Place</rich:column>
            <rich:column colspan="3">Dates</rich:column>
            <rich:column>Notes</rich:column>
        </rich:columnGroup>
    </f:facet>
    <rich:column colspan="9">#{continent}</rich:column>
    <rich:collapsibleSubTable value="#{olympicGamesBean.gamesMap[continent]}" var="game">
        <rich:column>
            <f:facet name="header">Season</f:facet>
                #{game.season}
        </rich:column>
        <rich:column>
            <f:facet name="header">Number</f:facet>
                #{game.number}
        </rich:column>
        <!--More columns-->
```

```
    </rich:collapsibleSubTable>
</rich:dataTable>
```

We added the code snippet shown in Listing 7-10 to OlympicGamesBean bean, previously shown in Listing 7-5.

Listing 7-10. Code snippet added to OlympicGamesBean bean

```
private Map<String, List<GameDescriptor>> gamesMap;

public Map<String, List<GameDescriptor>> getGamesMap(){
    if (gamesMap==null){
        gamesMap = new HashMap<String, List<GameDescriptor>>();
        for (GameDescriptor game : games) {
            List<GameDescriptor> gamesFromMap = gamesMap.get(game.getContinent());
                if (gamesFromMap == null){
                    gamesFromMap = new ArrayList<GameDescriptor>();
                }
                gamesFromMap.add(game);
                gamesMap.put(game.getContinent(), gamesFromMap);
        }
    }
    return gamesMap;
}

public List<String> getGamesMapKeys(){
    Map<String, List<GameDescriptor>> map = getGamesMap();
    List<String> continents = new ArrayList<String>();
    Iterator<String> it = map.keySet().iterator();
    while (it.hasNext()){
        continents.add(it.next());
    }
    Collections.sort(continents);
    return continents;
}
```

Let's look at the header. The <rich:columnGroup> component is used to encode a set of columns into a row that wraps them in a separate <tr>. Using colspan="9" on the first column and breakBefore="true" on the second, we stretched the first cell to table width and had the next cell encode as a new row prior to rendering. Again using colspan="3", we made the other cells group similar columns under common "Place" and "Dates" headers.

Let's slightly change the header layout using rowspan, assuming that the "Note" common header is not needed because it's applied to a single column with its own header.

To create the header shown in Figure 7-5, we changed the header definition, as shown in Listing 7-11.

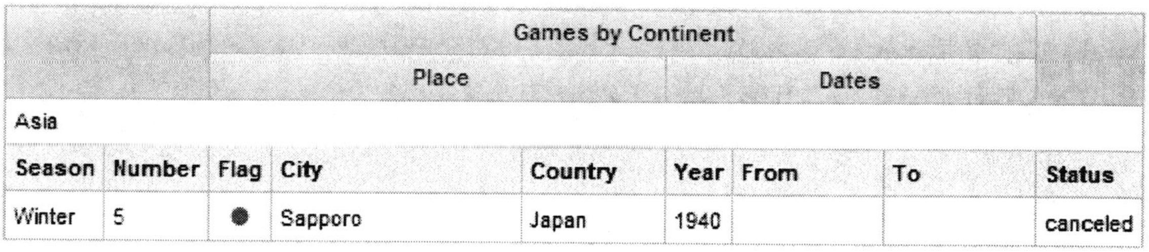

	Games by Continent							
	Place				Dates			
Asia								
Season	Number	Flag	City	Country	Year	From	To	Status
Winter	5	●	Sapporo	Japan	1940			canceled

Figure 7-5. Complex header in table

Listing 7-11. Changing the header definition

```
<f:facet name="header">
   <rich:columnGroup>
      <rich:column rowspan="2" colspan="2"></rich:column>
      <rich:column colspan="6">Games by Continent</rich:column>
      <rich:column rowspan="2" colspan="2"></rich:column>
      <rich:column colspan="3" breakRowBefore="true">Place</rich:column>
      <rich:column colspan="3">Dates</rich:column>
   </rich:columnGroup>
</f:facet>
```

That's all there is to header creation. Let's now look at the rest of the table.

Master-Details Tables with <rich:collapsibleSubTable>

According to the bean code changes, we have a list of continent names that are used as String keys for the map: public List<String> getGamesMapKeys(). The map consists of GameDescriptor object lists: public Map<String, List<GameDescriptor>> getGamesMap(). So, the <rich:dataTable> component iterates through the list of keys and encodes a single column with that key, which is getting stretched using colspan to the entire table length. Then, the <rich:collapsibleSubtable> iterates through every list from the map, retrieving them by the current continent name, and encodes the remaining columns with corresponding data.

■ **Note** Later you will see that <rich:dataTable> and <rich:extendedDataTable> share many features using similar definitions. However, the particular features of row and column spanning (both in the header and body) and <rich:collapsibleSubTable> usage are available only with <rich:dataTable>. This will be covered further in the <rich:extendedDataTable> section.

Now let's cover the <rich:collapsibleSubTable> component, which is used for expanding and collapsing content. All you need to be able to expand or collapse is to add <rich:collapsibleSubTableToggler> inside one of the table columns and point to the sub-table. Figure 7-6 shows the table with only the "Oceania" sub-table expanded.

Games by Continent								
	Place					Dates		
⩔ Asia								
⩔ Europe								
⩔ North America								
⩔ Oceania								
Season	**Number**	**Flag**	**City**	**Country**	**Year**	**From**	**To**	**Status**
Summer	16		Melbourne	Australia	1956	22 November	8 December	
Summer	27		Sydney	Australia	2000	15 September	1 October	
⩔ South America								

Figure 7-6. Table with collapsible sub-table

Listing 7-12 shows the code used to create this table.

Listing 7-12. Table with collapsible sub-table

```
<rich:dataTable value="#{olympicGamesBean.gamesMapKeys}" var="continent">
    <f:facet name="header">
        <!--header content-->
    </f:facet>
    <rich:column colspan="9">
        <rich:collapsibleSubTableToggler for="sbtable"/>
            #{continent}
    </rich:column>
    <rich:collapsibleSubTable id="sbtable" value="#{olympicGamesBean.gamesMap[continent]}"
        var="game">
    <rich:column>
        <f:facet name="header">Season</f:facet>
            #{game.season}
        </rich:column>
        <!--other columns-->
    </rich:collapsibleSubTable>
</rich:dataTable>
```

By default, toggle encoded as an icon (actually two icons shown for different states: one for expand and one for collapse). To customize the icon, use the expandedLabel, collapsedLabel, expandedIcon and collapsedIcon attributes. You can override the complete markup because you need to use the expanded and collapsed facets. The for attribute is used to point the toggle to the sub-table, which should be controlled via this component.

Now let's check <rich:collapsibleSubTable>, attributes which should be used to control its state switching. Let's first mention expandMode. As typical with RichFaces components with states switching, valid values for that attribute are ajax, server, and client. The initial and current sub-table state can be managed using the expanded attribute bound to a boolean property in your model. If set to true, the sub-table for the current row will be expanded.

That's all there is to basic `<rich:dataTable>` features usage. There are other advanced features, but because they are shared by other data iteration components, the "Iteration Components Advanced Usage" section found later in this chapter will cover features such sorting, filtering, pagination, and advanced data models.

`<rich:dataTable>` JavaScript API

The `<rich:dataTable>` component provides the JavaScript functions shown in Table 7-1.

Table 7-1. `<rich:dataTable> JavaScript API`

Method Name	Description
collapseAllSubTables()	Used to collapse all the sub-tables for the data table component.
expandAllSubTables ()	Used to expand all the sub-tables for the data table component.
switchSubTable(id)	Switches state of the sub-table with corresponding id.
sort(columnId, [direction, isClear])	Sorts the table according to the given column properties. direction allows you to define new sorting orders and isClear specifies if previous sorts should be reset.
filter(columnId, newFilterValue, [isClear])	Filters the table according to the given column properties. newValue specifies the filter value, and isClear specifies if previous filters should be reset.

`<rich:collapsibleSubTable>` JavaScript API

The `<rich:dataTable>` component provides the JavaScript functions shown in Table 7-2.

Table 7-2. `<rich:collapsibleSubTable> JavaScript API`

Method Name	Description
collapse()	Used to collapse the sub-table.
expand()	Used to expand sub-table.
switch ()	Used to switch the sub-table state to opposite.

Using <rich:extendedDataTable>

The <rich:extendedDataTable> component basically works just like <h:dataTable> and <rich:dataTable>. But, just based on its name, it adds a set of additional features to the standard implementation. The component provides vertical and horizontal scrolling for table body parts, frozen columns on the left side, lazy loading via Ajax while using vertical scroll, columns resizing and reordering, and selection features. That sounds pretty good for an out-of-the-box table component. So, let's start with a basic example and then we'll describe the features in more details.

We will use the same code as the first example of <rich:dataTable>, but will change the table tag to create an extended table. Figure 7-7 shows the result.

Olympic Games List								
Flag	City	Country	Continent	Season	Number	Year	From	To
■■	Athens	Greece	Europe	Summer	1	1896	6 April	15 April
■■	Paris	France	Europe	Summer	2	1900	14 May	28 October
■■	St. Louis	United States	North America	Summer	3	1904	1 July	23 November
■■	London	Great Britain	Europe	Summer	4	1908	27 April	31 October
■■	Stockholm	Sweden	Europe	Summer	5	1912	5 May	27 July
■■	Berlin	Germany	Europe	Summer	6	1916		

Figure 7-7. Extended data table

Listing 7-13 shows almost the same code that we used in the very first <rich:dataTable> example.

Listing 7-13. Creating an extended data table

```
<rich:panel style="width:1000px">
    <rich:extendedDataTable value="#{olympicGamesBean.games}" var="game">
        <f:facet name="header">Olympic Games List</f:facet>
        <rich:column>
            <f:facet name="header">Flag</f:facet>
            <h:graphicImage value="#{game.flagURI}" />
        </rich:column>
        <rich:column>
            <f:facet name="header">City</f:facet>
            #{game.city}
        </rich:column>
        <!--Other columns-->
    </rich:extendedDataTable>
</rich:panel>
```

That's it! There is really nothing specific that you need to know to start using this component.

Let's review features one by one, starting with the column resize feature. As you probably noticed in Figure 7-7, there are additional empty spaces on the right side. The reason for this is pretty simple. The feature to resize columns is always enabled for the component; every column has a default width if it not set explicitly. The table can be stretched to its parent element width (1000 pixels in our case). The remaining space is reserved with an empty column, without any styling, to be used if you try to resize any column. Resize is performed by a drag-and-drop of the column header.

■ **Note** If we decrease the panel width, we will see columns on the right become hidden behind the panel border. That's how the component works; the table gets stretched to the parent element size only until the sum of all the columns' width is not wider than the parent element, and then the table enlarges to fit them all. One solution is to set a smaller width for some concrete columns. But, if they are later resized by the user, the right columns become hidden again as the table width enlarges. The scrolling feature should be activated in this case.

Let's move on to the scrolling feature. The only options you need to specify on this component are the width and height attributes. The defined size attribute made the corresponding scroll active on the component. Let's review the example. We will decrease the wrapper panel and at the same time define the table size to fit that panel. The code shown in Listing 7-14.

Listing 7-14. Using the scrolling feature

```
<rich:panel style="width:650px" header="rich:extendedDataTable sample">
    <rich:extendedDataTable value="#{olympicGamesBean.games}" var="game" style="height:200px;
        width:620px;">
        <f:facet name="header">Olympic Games List</f:facet>
        <rich:column>
            <f:facet name="header">Flag</f:facet>
                <h:graphicImage value="#{game.flagURI}" />
        </rich:column>
        <rich:column>
            <f:facet name="header">City</f:facet>
                #{game.city}
        </rich:column>
        <!--Other columns-->
    </rich:extendedDataTable>
</rich:panel>
```

Figure 7-8 shows the result.

Figure 7-8. Extended data table

189

Using this code makes all the table data load on the client side and scroll without any additional data fetching. But, for large data sets it's not a good idea because it will greatly decrease performance. So, the next feature we are going to cover is lazy Ajax loading of rows while performing vertical scrolling. In order to use this feature we should define only one attribute, clientRows. The standard rows attribute determines the number of rows loaded on the client and allows you to implement pagination with external controls. The clientRows attribute tells the component the number of rows that should be preloaded on the client, and the number loaded after a vertical scroll. The following is a simple example:

```
<rich:extendedDataTable value="#{olympicGamesBean.games}" var="game"
    style="height:200px; width:620px;" clientRows="20">
```

Only 20 rows will be loaded while the component initially renders and when the vertical scroll position is changed. The next 20 rows corresponding to scroll position will be fetched via Ajax.

■ **Note**   As any other component that performs an Ajax request, <rich:extendedDataTable> requires <h:form> around it when Ajax lazy loading is used.

The ability to define the number of columns on the right as "fixed" or "frozen" is another feature. The frozenColumns attribute set to a number means that that number of columns will not be affected by horizontal scrolling. Let's look at the following example:

```
<rich:extendedDataTable value="#{olympicGamesBean.games}" var="game"
    frozenColumns="2" style="height:200px; width:620px;" clientRows="20">
```

This makes the table scroll horizontally, as illustrated in Figure 7-9. Notice that the columns flag and the city are still visible as the first two columns, even though the other columns scrolled.

Figure 7-9. Extended data table with "frozen" columns

The last unique feature of the <rich:extendedDataTable> is rows selection. It's controlled by the set of attributes shown in Table 7-3.

Table 7-3. Attributes to Control Row Selection

Name	Description
selectionMode	Turns the selection feature on/off and defines if the selection is available for a single row or for the set of rows. Available values are: none, single, multiple(default), and multipleKeyboardFree.
selection	Should point to the bean variable that will hold the collection of row keys for currently selected rows.
onselectionchange	JavaScript event fired after a new selection is made. Could be used to point Ajax behavior to process the selection.
onbeforeselectionchange	JavaScript event fired before changing the selection. It allows you to cancel the selection change by using return false.

Looking at the default value for the **selectionMode** attribute, the selection feature is turned on by default and multiple rows could be selected by using the SHIFT and CTRL keys together with row clicks.

Let's review the selection example. The page code is in Listing 7-15.

Listing 7-15. Using the selection feature

```
<h:form>
   <rich:panel style="width:600px" header="rich:extendedDataTable sample">
      <h:panelGrid columns="2" columnClasses="top, top">
         <rich:extendedDataTable value="#{olympicGamesBean.games}" var="game"
            frozenColumns="2" selection="#{olympicGamesBean.selection}" style="height:300px">
            <f:facet name="header">Olympic Games List</f:facet>
            <a4j:ajax event="selectionchange" render="details"
               listener="#{olympicGamesBean.showSelectionDetails}" />
            <rich:column>
               <f:facet name="header">Season</f:facet>
               #{game.season}
            </rich:column>
            <rich:column>
               <f:facet name="header">Number</f:facet>
               #{game.number}
            </rich:column>
            <rich:column>
               <f:facet name="header">Year</f:facet>
               #{game.year}
            </rich:column>
         </rich:extendedDataTable>
         <rich:dataTable value="#{olympicGamesBean.selectedGames}" var="sgame" id="details">
            <f:facet name="header">Selected Games Details</f:facet>
            <rich:column>
               <f:facet name="header">Flag</f:facet>
               <h:graphicImage value="#{sgame.flagURI}" />
            </rich:column>
            <rich:column>
```

```
            <f:facet name="header">Country</f:facet>
            #{sgame.country}
        </rich:column>
        <rich:column>
            <f:facet name="header">City</f:facet>
            #{sgame.city}
        </rich:column>
        <rich:column>
            <f:facet name="header">From</f:facet>
            #{sgame.from}
        </rich:column>
        <rich:column>
            <f:facet name="header">To</f:facet>
            #{sgame.to}
        </rich:column>
      </rich:dataTable>
    </h:panelGrid>
  </rich:panel>
</h:form>
```

We use `<a4j:ajax>` to send an Ajax request every time the selection is changed. Row keys for selected rows will be stored in the `#{olympicGamesBean.selection}` collection. After the `showSelectionDetails()` listener is invoked, it will place corresponding objects into the `#{olympicGamesBean.selectedGames}` list and the result table will be updated with the details of selected rows.

Listing 7-16 shows the bean code that we added to implement this functionality.

Listing 7-16. Java code to manage `<rich:extendedDataTable>` selection

```
private Collection<Object> selection = null;
private List<GameDescriptor> selectedGames = null;
...
public void showSelectionDetails(AjaxBehaviorEvent event){
    UIExtendedDataTable table = (UIExtendedDataTable)event.getComponent();
    selectedGames = new ArrayList<GameDescriptor>();
    Object storedRowKey = table.getRowKey();
    for (Object rowKey : selection) {
        table.setRowKey(rowKey);
        selectedGames.add((GameDescriptor)table.getRowData());
    }
    table.setRowKey(storedRowKey);
    ...

}
// Getters and setters
```

The result is shown in Figure 7-10.

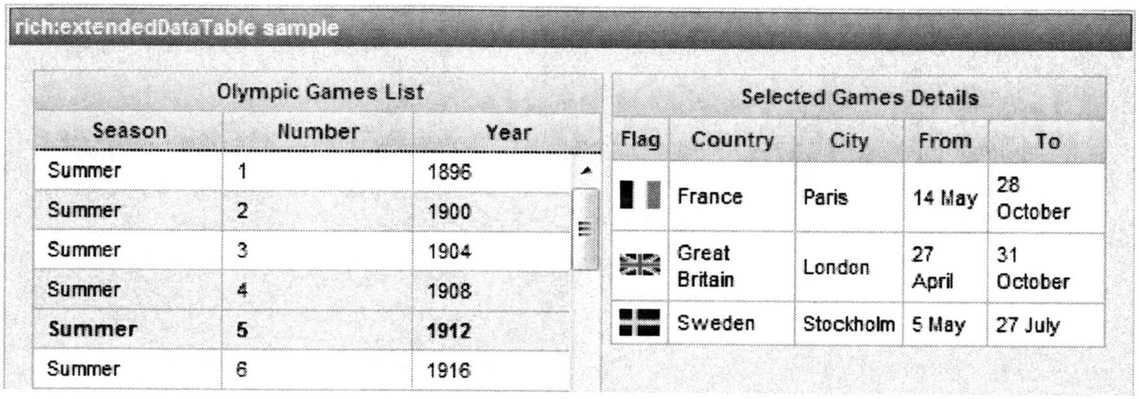

Figure 7-10. *Extended data table with row data selection*

■ **Note** The selection feature is not implemented for <rich:dataTable>. The selection feature might be added to the component in the future. For now, you can use <rich:extendedDataTable> just like <rich:dataTable> when you need the selection feature.

That covers the most important features in <rich:extendedDataTable>. We will cover additional and more advanced features in the "Iteration Components Advanced Usage" section later in this chapter.

<rich:extendedDataTable> JavaScript API

The <rich:extendedDataTable> component provides the JavaScript functions shown in Table 7-4.

Table 7-4. *<rich:dataTable> JavaScript API*

Method Name	Description
sort(columnId, [direction, isClear])	Sorts the table according to the given column properties. direction allows you to define a new sorting order and isClear specifies if previous sorts should be reset.
filter(columnId, newFilterValue, [isClear])	Filters the table according to the given column properties. newValue specifies filter value and isClear specifies if previous filters should be reset.
clearSorting()	Used to reset sorting.
clearFiltering	Used to reset filtering.

Method Name	Description
selectRow(index)	Used to select row according to specified index.
deselectRow(index)	Used to remove selection from the row according to specified index.
selectRows(startIndex, endIndex)	Used to select rows according to specified range.
setActiveRow(index)	Used to define row as active according to specified index. Active row used in case of multiple "range" selection (when performing selection with SHIFT+click).

Displaying Data in a List with <rich:list>

The <rich:list> component allows creating different HTML lists from the model. Figure 7-11 shows a simple example of a dynamically-populated unordered list.

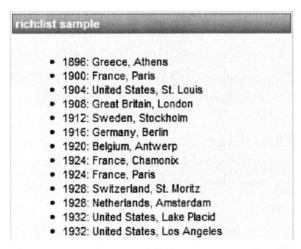

Figure 7-11. RichFaces <rich:list> as an unordered list

The page code used to create the list is shown in Listing 7-17.

Listing 7-17. RichFaces <rich:list> as an unordered list

```
<rich:panel style="width:280px" header="rich:list sample">
   <rich:list value="#{olympicGamesBean.games}" var="game">
     #{game.year}: #{game.country}, #{game.city}
   </rich:list>
</rich:panel>
```

The most interesting attribute on this component is type. It specifies the type of list to be rendered. It could be defined with ordered, unordered, and definitions values. As you can see from Listing 7-17, unordered is the default value. Figure 7-12 shows what will be rendered when the value is changed to ordered using

```
<rich:list type="ordered" …/>.
```

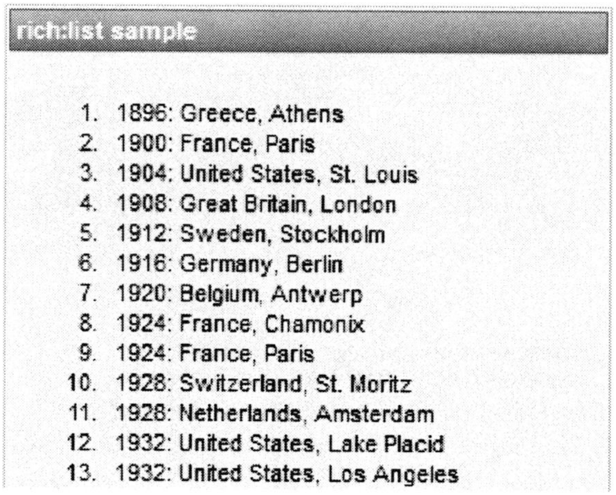

rich:list sample

1. 1896: Greece, Athens
2. 1900: France, Paris
3. 1904: United States, St. Louis
4. 1908: Great Britain, London
5. 1912: Sweden, Stockholm
6. 1916: Germany, Berlin
7. 1920: Belgium, Antwerp
8. 1924: France, Chamonix
9. 1924: France, Paris
10. 1928: Switzerland, St. Moritz
11. 1928: Netherlands, Amsterdam
12. 1932: United States, Lake Placid
13. 1932: United States, Los Angeles

***Figure 7-12.** RichFaces <rich:list> as an ordered list*

If we want to render a definition list, we need to use a facet for the list term. Listing 7-18 shows the code that populates the definition list.

***Listing 7-18.** Populating the definition list*

```
<rich:panel style="width:280px" header="rich:list sample">
    <rich:list type="definitions" value="#{olympicGamesBean.games}" var="game">
        <f:facet name="term"><b>#{game.year}</b></f:facet>
        #{game.country}, #{game.city}, #{game.from} - #{game.to}
    </rich:list>
</rich:panel>
```

In this example, we use the year property as a term. For a description, we list the country, city, and dates of the Olympics, as shown in Figure 7-13.

Figure 7-13. RichFaces <rich:list> as a definition list

That's all there is to cover for the <rich:list> component. As you can see, it's a pretty straightforward component. As for <rich:dataTable>, you could use either different class attributes (rowClasses, rowClass) or event handler attributes (onclick, onrowclick) in order to customize the basic look and feel and behavior.

Displaying Data in a Grid with <rich:dataGrid>

<rich:dataGrid> is a mix of <rich:dataTable> and <h:panelGrid>. While the component still iterates over a data model, just like all other components in this chapter, it outputs the component as <h:panelGrid>, placing a specified number of columns.

For example, every three records (objects) will take up one row using the following code from Listing 7-19.

Listing 7-19. Every three records (objects) will take up one row

```
<rich:panel style="width:650px" header="rich:dataGrid sample">
   <rich:dataGrid  value="#{olympicGamesBean.games}" var="game" columns="3">
      <rich:panel style="with:200px;">
         <h:graphicImage value="#{game.flagURI}" />
         <b>#{game.country} - #{game.city}</b><br/>
         <i>#{game.from} - #{game.to}</i>
      </rich:panel>
   </rich:dataGrid>
</rich:panel>
```

This code produces the result shown in Figure 7-14.

Figure 7-14. *<rich:dataGrid> iterating info panels*

If we change columns to "2" for example, we will see two objects (panels) in each row.

And, similar to the table component, you can add a header and footer to the grid using facets with header and footer names.

Iterating over Custom Markup with <a4j:repeat>

Even though the <a4j:repeat> component is part of the a4j: tag library, we decided to cover it in this section because it's the base component for all data iteration components in RichFaces. So why is it mentioned last, after all the other iteration components? We wanted to highlight the more popular concrete implementations first.

The idea behind the component is the same as in Facelets <ui:repeat>. It's used to iterate over a data model; however, it doesn't produce any HTML markup. You, the developer, are responsible for adding any content, HTML, or JSF tags to be iterated. If you ever need to iterate over a list of values but none of the out-of-the-box components provide what you need, this is the component you want to use.

The RichFaces team added special implementation in order to add features not available in <ui:repeat>. In addition to being able to bind to advanced RichFaces data models, it also supports partial-table rendering and pagination.

Let's cover some of the basic features. The more advanced features will be also covered in the "Iteration Components Advanced Usage" section.

Let's say we need the output to be similar to the one from the <rich:dataGrid> component from the previous section (or let's assume we didn't have <rich:dataGrid> at all). In addition, we want the columns count to depend on the browser window width. Resizing the window should increase the number of columns and setting less width should make it output fewer ones. Take a look at the code in Listing 7-20.

Listing 7-20. *Resizing the window and setting less width*

```
<a4j:repeat value="#{olympicGamesBean.games}" var="game"  >
   <rich:panel style="width:220px; height:60px; float:left; margin:5px;">
      <h:graphicImage value="#{game.flagURI}" />
      <b>#{game.country} - #{game.city}</b><br />
      <i>#{game.from} - #{game.to}</i>
   </rich:panel>
</a4j:repeat>
```

197

Notice that the component doesn't produce any markup, but will render a <rich:panel> for each data object. If we open the page and reduce the browser window to about 800 pixels, we will see the result in Figure 7-15.

Figure 7-15. Using <a4j:repeat> to create a grid

By making the browser window twice as big, we will see six columns in one row instead. So <a4j:repeat> is the best option when you need to implement any specific layout using the dynamic model iteration.

As it is the base component for all the other iteration components, most of the features covered in the rest of this book can be used with <a4j:repeat>, as well.

Iteration Components Advanced Usage

This section will show advanced features available on data iteration components. Most of the features are available for all RichFaces data iteration components.

Adding Pagination with <rich:dataScroller>

In the earlier examples, we didn't use a large data set (50+ Olympic Games since 1896). But in a real enterprise application, you deal with much larger data sets. One of the classical patterns to represent such data sets is adding a pagination control to the table, which allows using a fixed number of objects on each page. Fortunately, RichFaces comes with a component called <rich:datascroller> that provides pagination.

So, let's start with a simple example. We'll limit the number of games to 10 per page and add <rich:dataScroller> to our table footer. Figure 7-16 shows that in action.

Flag	City	Country	Continent	Season	Number	Year	From	To	Note
■■ ■■	Athens	Greece	Europe	Summer	1	1896	6 April	15 April	passed
■ ■	Paris	France	Europe	Summer	2	1900	14 May	28 October	passed
▬	St. Louis	United States	North America	Summer	3	1904	1 July	23 November	passed
▓	London	Great Britain	Europe	Summer	4	1908	27 April	31 October	passed
■■ ■■	Stockholm	Sweden	Europe	Summer	5	1912	5 May	27 July	passed
▬	Berlin	Germany	Europe	Summer	6	1916			canceled
■ ■	Antwerp	Belgium	Europe	Summer	7	1920	20 April	12 September	passed
■ ■	Chamonix	France	Europe	Winter	1	1924	25 January	4 February	passed
■ ■	Paris	France	Europe	Summer	8	1924	4 May	27 July	passed
✚	St. Moritz	Switzerland	Europe	Winter	2	1928	11 February	19 February	passed

Olympic Games List

《《《《 《《 《   1   2   3   4   5   6   》 》》 》》》》

Figure 7-16. Using the <rich:dataScroller> component

All we need to do is add the rows attribute with the number of rows per page, and add the
<rich:dataScroller> tag to the table footer without any additional attributes. (rows is a standard
attribute from the <h:dataTable> component.) Look through these changes in Listing 7-21.

Listing 7-21. Add the <rich:dataScroller> tag to the table footer

```
<h:form>
    <rich:dataTable value="#{olympicGamesBean.games}" var="game" rows="10">
        <f:facet name="header">Olympic Games List</f:facet>
            <rich:column>
                <f:facet name="header">Flag</f:facet>
                <h:graphicImage value="#{game.flagURI}" />
            </rich:column>
            <rich:column>
                <f:facet name="header">City</f:facet>
                #{game.city}
            </rich:column>
            <!--Other columns-->
        <f:facet name="footer">
            <rich:dataScroller />
        </f:facet>
    </rich:dataTable>
</h:form>
```

We added <h:form> around the table. Any component that sends an Ajax request needs to be placed
inside a form.

■ **Note** `<rich:extendedDataTable>` could use the same code to add pagination. It uses the same `rows` attribute to split the model into pages. As we mentioned in the `<rich:extendedDataTable>` section, this component also uses a separate `clientRows` attribute to add Ajax loading via vertical scroll. The component can even define both attributes. You should keep in mind, however, that Ajax loading done by `clientRows`-sized portions and is limited to "rows"—a defined number of rows. `<rich:dataScroller>` should be still used to switch pages.

We also need to mention that you can use `<rich:dataScroller>` defined outside the table; and even more than once instance of the scroller can be placed on a page. An example is shown in Figure 7-17.

Flag	City	Country	Continent	Season	Number	Year	From	To
	Atlanta	United States	North America	Summer	26	1996	19 July	4 August
	Nagano	Japan	Asia	Winter	18	1998	7 February	22 February
	Sydney	Australia	Oceania	Summer	27	2000	15 September	1 October
	Salt Lake City	United States	North America	Winter	19	2002	9 February	24 February
	Athens	Greece	Europe	Summer	28	2004	13 August	29 August

Figure 7-17. Using multiple scrollers outside of the table

To use the `<rich:dataScroller>` component outside the table, you should use the `for` attribute pointed to the table id. Updated code is shown Listing 7-22.

Listing 7-22. Using the for attribute pointed to the table id

```
<h:form>
    <rich:dataScroller for="table"/>
    <rich:dataTable value="#{olympicGamesBean.games}" var="game" rows="5" id="table">
        <!--Columns definitions-->
    </rich:dataTable>
    <rich:dataScroller for="table"/>
</h:form>
```

There are a few important attributes that should also be mentioned. First, the page attribute can be defined by the page that is currently shown. It allows you to restore the previous state when returning to the view with the table from a details screen. In order to allow such dynamic page setting, it could be defined with EL, as follows:

```
<rich:dataScroller for="table" page="#{viewController.gamesTablePage}"/>
```

■ **Note** If you will define a non-existent page number or a non-valid value, the component will reset to some of the boundary values. For example, if you set page 10 as the current page, and the table consists of only nine pages, then page 9, the last page, will set automatically. If the value is not valid, or less than 1, then the first page will be shown. When an incorrect value is used, a warning message about the correction is shown in the console.

Customizing the <rich:dataScroller> Look and Feel

`<rich:dataScroller>` allows flexible look-and-feel customization. It can be defined to be hidden if all values from the data model will fit onto just one page, as follows:

`<rich:dataScroller renderIfSinglePage="false"/>`

Forward and rewind button behavior can be customized in a similar way. There are three attributes to control them: boundaryControls (for first and next), fastControls (for switching to a few pages forward or back), and stepControls (previous and next).

All the attributes can take the following values: show (default), hide, and auto. If the value is hide, the corresponding controls will not be rendered. If the value is auto, the controls will not be rendered in boundary scroller states (first, rewind, and previous steps controls will not be encoded when the table is on the first page). And if the value is show, the controls will be rendered, but disabled if an action is not available.

By default, the fast-step control will switch to either the previous or next page. Using the fastStep attribute, you can configure how many pages to switch or jump. It should be defined with an integer value that indicates the number of pages that should be skipped on scrolling when using that control.

The following is an example that uses these attributes:

`<rich:dataScroller stepControls="hide" boundaryControls="auto" fastControls="auto" fastStep="3"/>`

This example demonstrates that the next/previous controls will not be rendered; the first/last and fast-step controls will always be rendered; and that three pages will be switched on any fast-step control activation.

In addition to controlling the behavior of the step and boundary buttons, you can also customize the look and feel of these buttons. The component offers various facets to control the appearance of the first, last, next, previous, fastforward, and fastrewind controls (and their disabled counterparts).

You can create a facet for active (clickable) and inactive (not clickable) controls. An inactive control is, for example, when you are looking at the last page and the next control is disabled.

Listing 7-23 shows an example with all the facets defined.

Listing 7-23. All control facets defined

```
<rich:dataScroller >
    <f:facet name="first">First</f:facet>
    <f:facet name="first_disabled">First</f:facet>
    <f:facet name="last">Last</f:facet>
    <f:facet name="last_disabled">Last</f:facet>
    <f:facet name="next">Next</f:facet>
    <f:facet name="next_disabled">Next</f:facet>
```

```
            <f:facet name="previous">Prev</f:facet>
            <f:facet name="previous_disabled">Prev</f:facet>
            <f:facet name="fastForward">FF</f:facet>
            <f:facet name="fastForward_disabled">FF</f:facet>
            <f:facet name="fastRewind">FR</f:facet>
            <f:facet name="fastRewind_disabled">FR</f:facet>
        </rich:dataScroller>
```

This code produces the result shown in Figure 7-18.

Flag	City	Country	Continent	Season	Number	Year	From	To	Note
■■	Athens	Greece	Europe	Summer	1	1896	6 April	15 April	passed
■	Paris	France	Europe	Summer	2	1900	14 May	28 October	passed
■	St. Louis	United States	North America	Summer	3	1904	1 July	23 November	passed
■	London	Great Britain	Europe	Summer	4	1908	27 April	31 October	passed
■■	Stockholm	Sweden	Europe	Summer	5	1912	5 May	27 July	passed

| First | «« | Prev | 1 | 2 | 3 | 4 | 5 | 6 | 7 | 8 | 9 | 10 | Next | »» | Last |

Figure 7-18. Customizing scroller controls using facets

This example uses text to create the controls, but it's possible to use any other components, as well as images, to create the controls.

That covers boundary and step buttons. Let's now look at page-number controls. If your data set contains hundreds of the pages, you definitely do not want to show page numbers for all of them. So it's possible to control the number of page numbers that are displayed by setting the maxPages attribute.

We also want to mention the lastPageMode attribute. It specifies the number of rows to display on the last page. If the last page contains only one row and you want the table to be the same size on any page, you should set the attribute to full. Let's say you have 42 records, and you display five objects on a page. When you switch to the last page, it will only list the final two objects. With lastPageMode set to full, the last page will display five objects, starting from row 38. If you want to display only the actual rows remaining, use the short value. Usage example for full mode will be shown in an upcoming JavaScript API example.

Using Other Data Components with <rich:dataScroller>

We have been using <rich:dataTable> to show how to use <rich:dataScroller>, but you can use <rich:datascroller> in a similar fashion with any other data iteration components.

Listing 7-24 is an example using <rich:list> with <rich:dataScroller>. Note that the for attribute points to <rich:list>.

Listing 7-24. Using <rich:list> with <rich:dataScroller>

```
<h:form>
    <rich:panel header="Using rich:datascroller">
        <rich:list type="definitions" value="#{olympicGamesBean.games}" var="game" rows="5"
        id="list">
```

```
        <f:facet name="term"><b>#{game.year}</b></f:facet>
            #{game.country}, #{game.city}, #{game.from} - #{game.to}
        </rich:list>
        <rich:dataScroller for="list" maxPages="4"/>
    </rich:panel>
</h:form>
```

Figure 7-19 shows what the code will produce.

Figure 7-19. *Using <rich:dataScroller> with <rich:list>*

Using <rich:dataScroller> with <rich:dataGrid>

Listing 7-25 shows an example of <rich:dataGrid> with scroller. There is one difference between using scroller with <rich:dataTable> and <rich:dataGrid>. The <rich:dataGrid> uses the elements attribute instead of rows.

Listing 7-25. *<rich:dataGrid> with scroller*

```
<h:form>
    <rich:dataGrid value="#{olympicGamesBean.games}" var="game" columns="3" elements="9"
        id="grid">
        <rich:panel>
            <h:graphicImage value="#{game.flagURI}" />
            <b>#{game.country} - #{game.city}</b> <br />
            <i>#{game.from} - #{game.to}</i>
        </rich:panel>
        <f:facet name="footer">
            <rich:dataScroller maxPages="4" />
        </f:facet>
    </rich:dataGrid>

</h:form>
```

203

We are using the `elements="9"` attribute in this example. It means the same as the rows attribute for all the other iteration components. It was renamed because `<rich:dataGrid>` renders objects in a line, and so the rows attribute wouldn't be a good fit. Figure 7-20 shows the result.

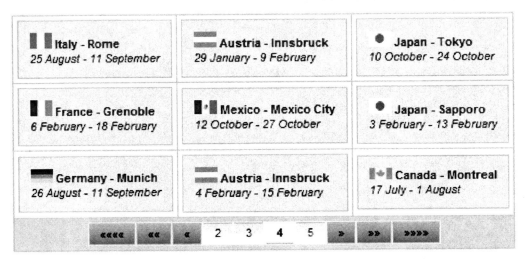

Figure 7-20. Using <rich:dataScroller> with <rich:dataGrid>

<rich:dataScroller> JavaScript API

The `<rich:dataScroller>` component provides the JavaScript functions shown in Table 7-5.

Table 7-5. <rich:collapsibleSubTable> JavaScript API

Method Name	Description
next()	Switches the table to next page.
previous()	Switches the table to previous page.
first()	Switches the table to first page.
last()	Switches the table to last page.
fastForward()	Switches the table forward according to number of pages specified using the fastStep attribute.
fastRewind()	Switches the table backward according to number of pages specified using the fastStep attribute.
switchToPage(pageNumber)	Switches the table to specified page.

Using Partial Table Updates

We are ready to cover partial updates for iteration components. This is a very important and powerful feature that allows you to update a limited set of components in defined rows instead of performing a full table update.

We'll start with the basics and learn how to do updates in the context of a current row. An Ajax component inside the current row can update any component inside the same row by pointing to the component id. You get this functionality out of the box.

In this section, let's move away from the Olympic Games list example and create a model that shows a simple, editable sales report. Listing 7-26 shows the code for SalesItem object.

Listing 7-26. SalesItem object

```java
public class SalesItem {
    private int productCode;
    private double proposedPrice;
    private double salesCost;
    private String reason;
    private double discount = 0;
    public ArrayList<SelectItem> getReasons() {
    ArrayList<SelectItem> reasons = new ArrayList<SelectItem>();
    if (proposedPrice != 0.0) {
        if (proposedPrice <= salesCost) {
            reasons.add(new SelectItem("Nobody Needs It"));
            reasons.add(new SelectItem("Bad Quality"));
            reasons.add(new SelectItem("Partly Broken"));
        } else {
            reasons.add(new SelectItem("Just Good"));
            reasons.add(new SelectItem("Everybody Asks for It"));
        }
    }
    return reasons;
}
    public SalesItem(int productCode, double salesCost) {
        super();
        this.productCode = productCode;
        this.salesCost = salesCost;
    }
    public double getProposedGrossMargin() {
        if (proposedPrice == 0)
            return 0;
        else {
            return (proposedPrice-salesCost)/proposedPrice ;
        }
    }
    // Getters and setters
}
```

Listing 7-27 shows the SalesReport bean code.

Listing 7-27. SalesReport bean code

```java
@ManagedBean
@ViewScoped
public class SalesReport {
    List<SalesItem> items = null;
    private void initData() {
        items = new ArrayList<SalesItem>();
        items.add(new SalesItem(1, 20.00));
        items.add(new SalesItem(2, 10.00));
        items.add(new SalesItem(3, 20.00));
        items.add(new SalesItem(4, 20.00));
    }
    public List<SalesItem> getItems() {
        if (items == null)
            initData();
        return items;
    }
    // Getters and setters
}
```

We will use this model for all examples in the "Using Partial Table Updates" section. Now, let's go through the page definition in Listing 7-28.

Listing 7-28. Page definition

```xml
<h:form>
    <rich:panel header="Partial updates in tables">
        <rich:dataTable value="#{salesReport.items}" var="item" rowKeyVar="key">
            <rich:column>
                <f:facet name="header">Product Code</f:facet>
                <h:outputText value="#{item.productCode}" />
            </rich:column>
            <rich:column>
                <f:facet name="header">Proposed Price</f:facet>
                <h:inputText value="#{item.proposedPrice}" size="7">
                    <a4j:ajax event="valueChange" render="reason, margin" />
                </h:inputText>
            </rich:column>
            <rich:column>
                <f:facet name="header">Sales Cost</f:facet>
                <h:outputText value="#{item.salesCost}" />
            </rich:column>
            <rich:column>
                <f:facet name="header">Reason</f:facet>
                <h:selectOneMenu id="reason" required="true" value="#{item.reason}">
                    <f:selectItems value="#{item.reasons}" />
                </h:selectOneMenu>
            </rich:column>
            <rich:column>
                <f:facet name="header">Proposed Gross Margin</f:facet>
                <h:outputText id="margin" value="#{item.proposedGrossMargin}">
                    <f:convertNumber pattern="$###0.000" />
```

```
            </h:outputText>
        </rich:column>
      </rich:dataTable>
    </rich:panel>
</h:form>
```

As you can see, we are setting the render attribute to reason and margin component ids in other columns, and updates in case it occurs in the same row. This is an example of partial-table rendering in the context of the row.

Figure 7-21 shows the result after a number of prices are modified.

Partial updates in tables				
Product Code	Proposed Price	Sales Cost	Reason	Proposed Gross Margin
1	18	20.0	Bad Quality ▼	-$0,111
2	12	10.0	Just Good ▼	$0,167
3	0.0	20.0	Just Good / Everybody Asks for it	$0,000
4	0.0	20.0	▼	$0,000

Figure 7-21. Partial updates of the components in context of row

The content of the Reason and Proposed Gross Margin columns are updated by sending it to the client.

Now let's review a more complex example. Suppose we have to update some subset of objects and want to render corresponding columns. As you know, you can define the render attribute for all the RichFaces Ajax components with an EL expression, which allows us to populate a dynamic list of ids of the component to be updated. That's one solution to populate a list of updated ids. But, it is not really a convenient or maintainable solution because the model needs know about table id's (including parent-naming container ids) and the ids of the component placed in columns.

RichFaces (starting with version 4.0) has a special @rows(rowKeysCollection) function available that should be used to define dynamic rows updates. You need a set of model row keys that will define the rows to be updated in the table. Let's use an actual example. Suppose we have a populated table and want to set discounts on all the items that have negative Proposed Gross Margin values. Listing 7-29 shows the changed page with a new discount column, as well as the button that we added to the form.

Listing 7-29. Changed page with a new discount column and button

```
<h:form>
    <rich:panel header="Partial updates in tables">
      <rich:dataTable value="#{salesReport.items}" var="item" rowKeyVar="key" id="table">
      <!--All the other columns -->
          <rich:column>
            <f:facet name="header">Discount</f:facet>
            <h:outputText id="discount" value="#{item.discount}">
               <f:convertNumber type="percent"/>
            </h:outputText>
```

```
        </rich:column>
      </rich:dataTable>
      <a4j:commandButton execute="@this" value="Set 20% discount to unprofitable products"
          action="#{salesReport.addDiscounts}"
          render="table:@rows(salesReport.updatedItems):discount"/>
    </rich:panel>
</h:form>
```

Let's review what we added to the code. The most important part is the render defined in the `<a4j:commandButton>`. It consists of a table id (table), a `@rows()` function, and a discount component id (discount), all separated with a naming container separator character (usually ":" although it could be configured per application, so be careful there). The updatedItems will be resolved to the rows id in which to update the discount component id. You might be wondering why the special `@rows()` syntax is used. We can't really use the standard EL, such as `#{rows()}`, because it would only give us a single string representation after evaluation. What was needed in our case was to have set of ids for render. And that specific function usage does the trick.

▪ **Tip** You don't deal with client ids or containers ids when performing partial table updates. RichFaces makes it very simple by letting you define everything with just component ids and row keys.

Now let's look at the `addDiscount` method and `updatedItems` list in Listing 7-30, which hold row keys from `SalesReport`.

Listing 7-30. addDiscount method and updatedItems list

```
private List<Integer> updatedItems = new ArrayList<Integer>();
public void addDiscounts() {
    for (SalesItem item : items) {
        if (item.getProposedGrossMargin() < 0) {
            item.setDiscount(0.2);
            updatedItems.add(items.indexOf(item));
        }
    }
}
// Getters and setters
```

Here we simply iterate over the model and are looking for objects with the negative `proposedGrossMargin` value. Then we add a discount to that object and put its `rowKey` in the `updatedItems` list. Note that for our simple, list-based model, `rowKey` will be equal to the index in the list. For more complex models (with filtering/sorting and so on) you should not return the index in the original collection, but with a separate object `rowKey`. We will cover this later in the chapter. When running this, we see only two components updated, as shown in Figure 7-22.

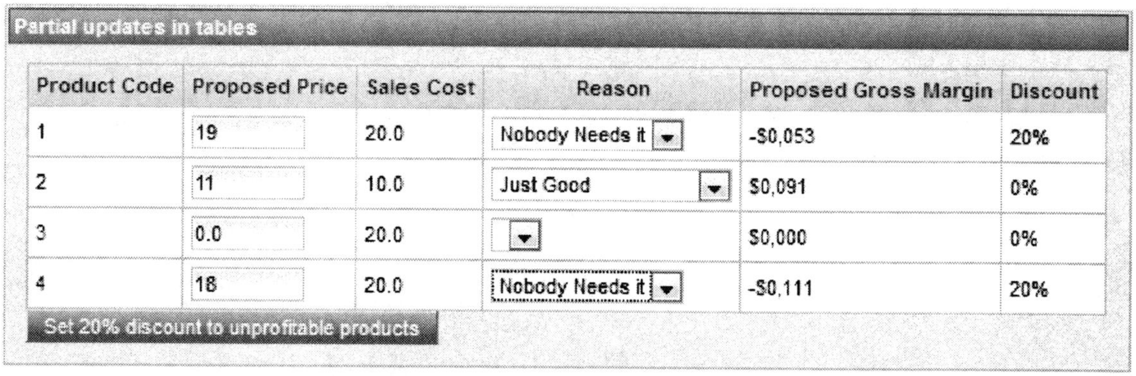

Product Code	Proposed Price	Sales Cost	Reason	Proposed Gross Margin	Discount
1	19	20.0	Nobody Needs it ▼	-$0,053	20%
2	11	10.0	Just Good ▼	$0,091	0%
3	0.0	20.0	▼	$0,000	0%
4	18	20.0	Nobody Needs it ▼	-$0,111	20%

Partial updates in tables

Set 20% discount to unprofitable products

Figure 7-22. Using partial-table update to update a set of rows

Both of the features we just described—updating components within the same row and updating components within a set of rows—works for any RichFaces iteration component, including base `<a4j:repeat>`.

There is another very handy partial-table update feature that RichFaces provides that allows you to update only the header, footer, or table body. To do this, RichFaces provides three pre-defined values: `@body`, `@header`, and `@footer`. They are supported by both `<rich:dataTable>` and `<rich:extendedDataTable>`.

For example, the following is placed outside the table and will update the entire table body; tableId will be replaced with actual table id.

```
<a4j:commandButton value="Update Data" render="tableId@body"/>
```

If the component is placed inside the table, then the table id doesn't need to be specified, as follows:

```
<a4j:commandButton value="Update Data" render="@body"/>
```

Request Variables of Iteration Components

Besides the standard var attribute, which provides a request scoped variable bound to the current iteration object, RichFaces components provide two more utility variables: rowKeyVar and iterationStatusVar.

rowKeyVar allows you to reference the rowKey of the current iteration objects. If you have your `<rich:dataTable>` bound to a simple List of objects, it will be equal to the row index of the object at the current iteration. Figure 7-23 shows a table in which the first column has object indexes.

Olympic Games List							
	Flag	City	Country	Continent	Season	Number	Year
0		Athens	Greece	Europe	Summer	1	1896
1		Paris	France	Europe	Summer	2	1900
2		St. Louis	United States	North America	Summer	3	1904
3		London	Great Britain	Europe	Summer	4	1908
4		Stockholm	Sweden	Europe	Summer	5	1912

Figure 7-23. Indexes of a row using rowKey

Listing 7-31 shows the page code.

Listing 7-31. Indexes of a row using rowKey

```
<rich:dataTable value="#{olympicGamesBean.games}" var="game"
   rowKeyVar="key" rows="10" id="table">
   <f:facet name="header">Olympic Games List</f:facet>
   <rich:column>#{key}</rich:column>
   ...
</rich:dataTable>
```

Note that this will only work when sorting and filtering are not used. (The rowKey is covered in more detail later in this chapter.) You will see this value is an identified object rather than a row index. When you sort or filter a table, the keys will not correspond to indexes because they will be filtered on the page along with bound objects.

Another example that actually shows more proper attribute usage is passing a rowKey as a parameter in order to identify or select an object inside a bean. An example of this is shown in Listing 7-32.

Listing 7-32. Passing a rowKey as a parameter in order to identify or select an object inside a bean

```
<h:form>
    <a4j:jsFunction name="updateDetails" render="details">
        <a4j:param name="rowKey" assignTo="#{olympicGamesBean.currentRow}" />
    </a4j:jsFunction>
    <rich:panel style="width:650px" header="rich:dataTable sample">
        <h:panelGrid columns="2">
            <rich:dataTable value="#{olympicGamesBean.games}" var="game" style="cursor:pointer;"
                rowKeyVar="key" rows="5" id="table" onrowclick="updateDetails(#{key})">
                <f:facet name="header">Olympic Games List</f:facet>
                <rich:column>
                    <f:facet name="header">Country</f:facet>
                    #{game.country}
                </rich:column>
                <!--Other columns-->
            </rich:dataTable>
            <rich:panel id="details" header="Selected Game:">
```

```
            <a4j:outputPanel layout="block" rendered="#{olympicGamesBean.currentGame ne null}">
                <h:graphicImage value="#{olympicGamesBean.currentGame.flagURI}" />
                <h:panelGrid columns="2">
                    <h:outputText value="Continent:" /> #{olympicGamesBean.currentGame.continent}
                    <h:outputText value="Country:" /> #{olympicGamesBean.currentGame.country}
                    <h:outputText value="City:" /> #{olympicGamesBean.currentGame.city}
                    <h:outputText value="From date:" /> #{olympicGamesBean.currentGame.from}
                    <h:outputText value="To date:" /> #{olympicGamesBean.currentGame.to}
                </h:panelGrid>
            </a4j:outputPanel>
        </rich:panel>
    </h:panelGrid>
  </rich:panel>
</h:form>
```

Notice that we used rowKey in order to pass the current row key to the server with an assignTo attribute of the <a4j:param>. Now let's look at a simple getter, which we need to add to our bean for the current sample. This method will return the current game using the passed object. Listing 7-33 shows the Java code.

Listing 7-33. *Java code*

```
private Integer currentRow; //Getter and setter

public GameDescriptor getCurrentGame(){
    return (currentRow==null) ? null : games.get(currentRow);
}
```

It will return a valid object even if you sorted or filtered the table using built-in sorting or filtering, because as we mentioned, row keys are always bound to the same objects. We will show you another example using the database key later in this chapter.

Figure 7-24 shows the page after clicking on a row.

Olympic Games List					Selected Game:
Country	Season	Number	Year		▬▬
Greece	Summer	1	1896		Continent: North America
France	Summer	2	1900		Country: United States
United States	Summer	3	1904		City: St. Louis
Great Britain	Summer	4	1908		From date: 1 July
Sweden	Summer	5	1912		To date: 23 November

Figure 7-24. *Passing a rowKey to the server to identify the clicked row, showing details*

iterationStatusVar is another request variable. It allows you to reference an iteration status object, which provides a set of useful properties to get information about current iteration properties. Table 7-6 is a list of properties that can be used on a page.

211

Table 7-6. Properties Available from the iterationStatusVar Variable

Method	Description
begin	Returns first row index of the current page of the table.
end	Returns last row index of the current page of the table.
count	Returns count of the objects shown at page.
index	Returns current object index.
rowCount	Returns number of rows in the model.
step	Returns 1, reserved for complex components.
even	Returns boolean flag if the currently iterated row is even.
first	Returns boolean flag if the current iteration is the first one on the page.
last	Returns boolean flag if the current iteration is the last one on the page.
odd	Returns boolean flag if the currently iterated row is odd.

This variable is a lot more useful if you just need to output index as done in the first example using rowKey.

Listing 7-34 is an example using iterationStatusVar.

Listing 7-34. Using iterationStatusVar

```
<style>
.odd {
   background-color: #{richSkin.additionalBackgroundColor};
}
.even {
   background-color: #{richSkin.tableSubHeaderBackgroundColor};
}
</style>
<h:form>
    <rich:panel style="width:650px" header="rich:dataTable sample">
      <rich:dataTable value="#{olympicGamesBean.games}" var="game" rows="10"
          iterationStatusVar="iter" rowClass="#{iter.even?'even':'odd'}">
          <f:facet name="header">Olympic Games List</f:facet>
          <rich:column>#{iter.index+1}</rich:column>
          <rich:column>
             <f:facet name="header">Flag</f:facet>
             <h:graphicImage value="#{game.flagURI}" />
          </rich:column>
          <rich:column>
             <f:facet name="header">City</f:facet>
```

```
                #{game.city}
            </rich:column>
            <!--Other Columns-->
            <f:facet name="footer">
                <rich:dataScroller />
            </f:facet>
        </rich:dataTable>
    </rich:panel>
</h:form>
```

We perform two tasks using this variable. First, we render column styles based on whether it's an even or odd row. Second, we render the current row index inside one of the columns. Using this variable, the row indexes will always be correct and will not be affected by pagination, sorting, or filtering. Figure 7-25 shows the result.

	Flag	City	Country	Continent	Season	Number	Year	From	To
				Olympic Games List					
1		Athens	Greece	Europe	Summer	1	1896	6 April	15 April
2		Paris	France	Europe	Summer	2	1900	14 May	28 October
3		St. Louis	United States	North America	Summer	3	1904	1 July	23 November
4		London	Great Britain	Europe	Summer	4	1908	27 April	31 October
5		Stockholm	Sweden	Europe	Summer	5	1912	5 May	27 July

Figure 7-25. iterationStatusVar usage for styling and row indexes output

---

■ **Note** When using the index property to display row numbers, it will start at 0. Most likely, you want to start at 1, so #{iter.index+1} should be used. This should be fixed in a future RichFaces release, or another variable that starts at 1 will be introduced.

Table Sorting

This section will cover sorting functionality available in RichFaces data iteration components. We will use a List-based example and cover a more complex example with a custom data model in the "Iteration Components Advanced Models" section.

Basic sorting functionality can be implemented in two ways: by using JavaScript API or by using external controls.

213

> ■ **Note** No built-in controls for sorting and filtering are implemented as of writing of this book. We will cover basic API. Please check the JBoss Community's RichFaces Component Reference at www.jboss.org/richfaces/docs and other informational resources to learn when such controls might be added.

To start sorting, all you need to do is add the sortBy attribute, with it pointing to some object property (based on what you want to sort) to the <rich:column> tag. In order to store the sorting state between requests, use the sortOrder attribute, which should be bound to the server-side object with the values from the org.richfaces.component.SortOrder set (unsorted, ascending or descending).

comparator is another <rich:column> attribute that you can use to customize the sorting. It can be used instead of sortBy in order to define a custom comparator that will be called by the component during sorting for comparison of the objects according to your rules.

> ■ **Tip** We use <rich:dataTable> in the examples; however, the same code can be used with the <rich:extendedDataTable> component.

To start, let's review sorting using external controls. Listing 7-35 is the code we used to define three columns of the sortable, Olympic Games table.

Listing 7-35. Defining three columns of a table

```
<h:form>
    <rich:panel style="width:650px" header="rich:dataTable sample">
        <rich:dataTable value="#{olympicGamesBean.games}" var="game" id="table" rows="10">
            <f:facet name="header">Olympic Games List</f:facet>
            <rich:column>
                <f:facet name="header">Flag</f:facet>
                <h:graphicImage value="#{game.flagURI}" />
            </rich:column>
            <rich:column sortBy="#{game.city}" sortOrder="#{sortingBean.sortOrders['city']}">
                <f:facet name="header">
                    <a4j:commandLink value="City" render="table" action="#{sortingBean.sort}">
                        <a4j:param name="sortProperty" value="city" />
                    </a4j:commandLink>
                </f:facet>
                #{game.city}
            </rich:column>
            <rich:column sortBy="#{game.country}"
                sortOrder="#{sortingBean.sortOrders['country']}">
                <f:facet name="header">
                    <a4j:commandLink value="Country" render="table"
                        action="#{sortingBean.sort}">
                        <a4j:param name="sortProperty" value="country" />
                    </a4j:commandLink>
```

```
                        </f:facet>
                        #{game.country}
                </rich:column>
                <rich:column>
                        <f:facet name="header">Season</f:facet>
                        #{game.season}
                </rich:column>
                <rich:column>
                        <f:facet name="header">Number</f:facet>
                        #{game.number}
                </rich:column>
                <rich:column sortOrder="#{sortingBean.sortOrders['year']}"
                        comparator="#{sortingBean.yearComparator}">
                        <f:facet name="header">
                                <a4j:commandLink value="Year" render="table" action="#{sortingBean.sort}">
                                        <a4j:param name="sortProperty" value="year" />
                                </a4j:commandLink>
                        </f:facet>
                        #{game.year}
                </rich:column>
                <rich:column>
                        <f:facet name="header">From</f:facet>
                                #{game.from}
                </rich:column>
                <rich:column>
                        <f:facet name="header">To</f:facet>
                        #{game.to}
                </rich:column>
        </rich:dataTable>
    </rich:panel>
</h:form>
```

Listing 7-36 shows the SortingBean bean followed by more explanation of this example.

Listing 7-36. SortingBean bean

```
@ManagedBean
@ViewScoped
public class SortingBean implements Serializable{

    private Map<String, SortOrder> sortOrders = new HashMap<String, SortOrder>();
    private static final String SORT_PROPERTY = "sortProperty";

    // getters and setters

    private void modifySortProperty(Map<String, SortOrder> orders, String sortProperty, SortOrder
        currentOrder) {
        if ((currentOrder == null) || (currentOrder == SortOrder.ascending)) {
            orders.put(sortProperty, SortOrder.descending);
        } else {
            orders.put(sortProperty, SortOrder.ascending);
        }
    }
}
```

```
    private String getSortProperty() {
        String sortProperty = FacesContext.getCurrentInstance()
            .getExternalContext().getRequestParameterMap().get(SORT_PROPERTY);
        return sortProperty;
    }
    public Comparator<GameDescriptor> getYearComparator() {
        return new Comparator<GameDescriptor>() {
            @Override
            public int compare(GameDescriptor o1, GameDescriptor o2) {
                return o1.getFromDate().compareTo(o2.getFromDate());
            }
        };
    }
    public void sort() {
        String sortProperty = getSortProperty();
        SortOrder currentOrder = sortOrders.get(sortProperty);
        sortOrders.clear();
        modifySortProperty(sortOrders, sortProperty, currentOrder);
    }
}
```

Let's review the code, starting with the city column. We added sortOrder pointing to #{game.city}, so the city string value will be used for sorting. We pointed the sortOrder attribute to the map object and placed it under the city key. Actually, any key could be used there and you are free to implement any kind of object for storing the sort order. We just used a more convenient and simple code for that simple case.

Next, we added the <a4j:commandLink> control, which will perform an Ajax request for sorting the table. After the sorting the entire table will be changed, so we've added its id to the render attribute of that link.

Now, let's look through our Java code. We are placing the sortOrder of the currently clicked column header link into the map to which we mapped sort orders; or we revert it in case it is already there. The name that we are using on the page to get the sort order from the map passed with <a4j:param> tag. So, all the naming definitions are actually made at view level and we are using a constant to get the column name for sorting from the request variables.

The same simple definitions are used for the country column. The year column is more interesting. We can set sortBy to the year property and rely on built-in sorting because we want the column to be sorted considering month and day properties when the year is the same. To accomplish this, we are going to add a comparator. Objects are passed (#{game} in this case) into the comparator so that any property can be checked and compared. In our bean we use the default Date object comparator method, as follows:

```
    return o1.getFromDate().compareTo(o2.getFromDate());
```

Now we are sure that as longs as the year is the same, we will compare start dates that consider the month and day, as well.

Figure 7-26 shows the result after sorting by year.

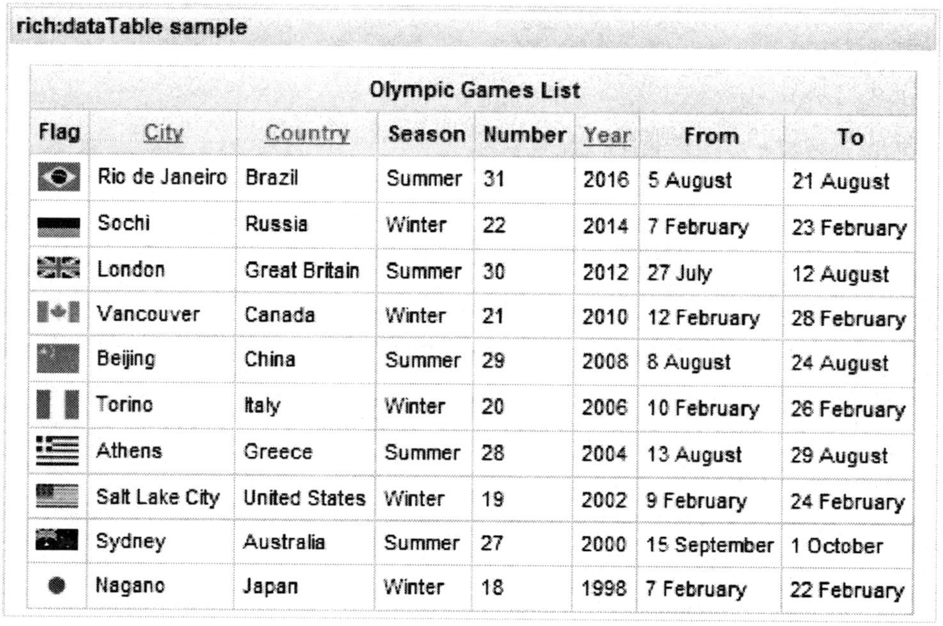

Figure 7-26. Table sorting with the year property

There is one important note about built-in sorting using the sortBy attribute. While sorting string properties, you can use Collator to perform local-sensitive strings comparison. In this case, just set the org.richfaces.datatableUsesViewLocale context parameter to true in your web.xml application.

Table Sorting by Multiple Columns

Almost nothing special needs to be done in order to sort by multiple columns. As you remember in the previous example, we cleared the map used to store sort orders before placing a new one there. Basically, all we need to do is remove that code, as shown at Listing 7-37.

Listing 7-37. Removing the code

```
<h:form>
    <rich:panel style="width:650px" header="rich:dataTable sample">
        <rich:dataTable value="#{olympicGamesBean.games}" var="game" id="table2" rows="10"
            sortPriority="#{sortingBean.sortPriorities}">
            <f:facet name="header">Olympic Games List</f:facet>
            ...
            <rich:column sortBy="#{game.city}" id="city"
                sortOrder="#{sortingBean.sortOrdersMultiple['city']}">
                <f:facet name="header">
                    <a4j:commandLink value="City" render="table2"
                        action="#{sortingBean.sortMultiple}">
                        <a4j:param name="sortProperty" value="city" />
                    </a4j:commandLink>
                </f:facet>
```

```
            </f:facet>
            #{game.city}
        </rich:column>
        <!--More columns-->
    </rich:dataTable>
    <a4j:commandButton value="Reset Sorting" render="table2"
        action="#{sortingBean.resetSorting}"/>
    </rich:panel>
</h:form>
```

Notice that we use the sortPriority attribute in <rich:dataTable>. That attribute should be bound to a collection of the column ids. It's used to define which order sorting will be performed. So the order of the ids in that collection will mean the order of the column sorts. Figure 7-27 shows the result after sorting by country and then by city. Note that cities are now also sorted in connection to the country.

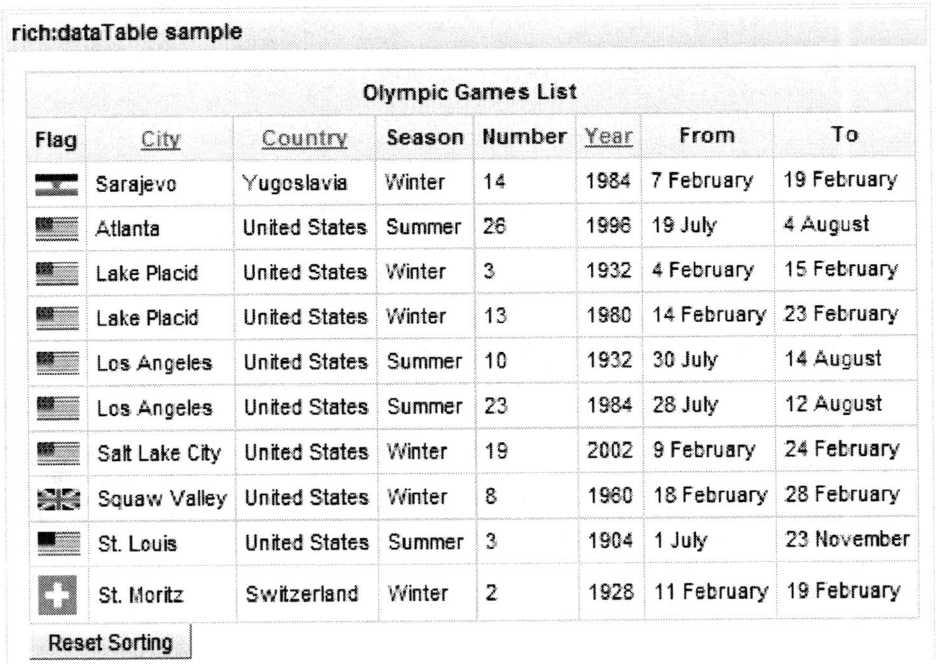

rich:dataTable sample

			Olympic Games List				
Flag	City	Country	Season	Number	Year	From	To
	Sarajevo	Yugoslavia	Winter	14	1984	7 February	19 February
	Atlanta	United States	Summer	26	1996	19 July	4 August
	Lake Placid	United States	Winter	3	1932	4 February	15 February
	Lake Placid	United States	Winter	13	1980	14 February	23 February
	Los Angeles	United States	Summer	10	1932	30 July	14 August
	Los Angeles	United States	Summer	23	1984	28 July	12 August
	Salt Lake City	United States	Winter	19	2002	9 February	24 February
	Squaw Valley	United States	Winter	8	1960	18 February	28 February
	St. Louis	United States	Summer	3	1904	1 July	23 November
	St. Moritz	Switzerland	Winter	2	1928	11 February	19 February

Reset Sorting

Figure 7-27. Table sorting by multiple properties

The Java code is shown in Listing 7-38.

Listing 7-38. The Java code

```
@ManagedBean
@ViewScoped
public class SortingBean implements Serializable{

    private Map<String, SortOrder> sortOrdersMultiple = new HashMap<String, SortOrder>();
    private List<String> sortPriorities = new ArrayList<String>();
```

```
    private static final String SORT_PROPERTY = "sortProperty";
    private void modifySortProperty(Map<String, SortOrder> orders,

    public void resetSorting() {
        this.sortOrdersMultiple.clear();
        this.sortPriorities.clear();
    }
    String sortProperty, SortOrder currentOrder) {
    if ((currentOrder == null) || (currentOrder == SortOrder.ascending)) {
        orders.put(sortProperty, SortOrder.descending);
        } else {
        orders.put(sortProperty, SortOrder.ascending);
        }
    }
    private String getSortProperty() {
        String sortProperty = FacesContext.getCurrentInstance()
            .getExternalContext().getRequestParameterMap().get(SORT_PROPERTY);
        return sortProperty;
    }
    public Comparator<GameDescriptor> getYearComparator() {
        return new Comparator<GameDescriptor>() {
            @Override
            public int compare(GameDescriptor o1, GameDescriptor o2) {
                return o1.getFromDate().compareTo(o2.getFromDate());
            }
        };
    }
    public void sortMultiple() {
        String sortProperty = getSortProperty();
        SortOrder currentOrder = sortOrdersMultiple.get(sortProperty);
        modifySortProperty(sortOrdersMultiple, sortProperty, currentOrder);
        if (!sortPriorities.contains(sortProperty))
            sortPriorities.add(sortProperty);
    }
}
}
```

As we mentioned, we introduced a new sortPriorities list and added the column id to it after sorting on that column was invoked (but only in case it was not added before). Now we are not removing anything from the map prior to adding or changing the sortOrder. Also, you see a simple resetSorting method that clears both the sortOrders map and the sortPriorities list.

Now that we have covered all the attributes, you have full control over the table component sorting state. You will apply the same basic attributes when using more complex custom data models in upcoming sections.

One other example we want to cover is sorting using JavaScript API. It's optimal for simple cases where you do not need to use links with custom Ajax request options. In fact, the examples we used are simple and JavaScript API usage is sufficient.

The table client object provides the sort() method, which should take three parameters: a column id, sort order, and a clearance boolean flag. The last two parameters are optional. Basically, you define it by which column table should be sorted. Then if needed, define a new sort order for that column (it will be reverted if not passed). The last parameter, clearance flag, tells the table if you want all the previous sorts to be reset prior to when the new sorting was applied.

Listing 7-39 shows the JavaScript API sorting example.

Listing 7-39. JavaScript API sorting

```
<h:form>
    <rich:panel style="width:650px" header="rich:dataTable sample">
        <rich:dataTable value="#{olympicGamesBean.games}" var="game" id="table3" rows="10">
            <f:facet name="header">Olympic Games List</f:facet>
            <rich:column>
                <f:facet name="header">Flag</f:facet>
                <h:graphicImage value="#{game.flagURI}" />
            </rich:column>
            <rich:column sortBy="#{game.city}" id="city">
                <f:facet name="header">
                    <h:commandLink value="City">
                        <rich:componentControl target="table3" operation="sort">
                            <f:param name="column" value="city" />
                            <f:param value="" />
                            <f:param name="reset" value="true" />
                        </rich:componentControl>
                    </h:commandLink>
                </f:facet>
                #{game.city}
            </rich:column>
            <rich:column sortBy="#{game.country}" id="country">
                <f:facet name="header">
                    <h:commandLink value="Country">
                        <rich:componentControl target="table3" operation="sort">
                            <f:param name="direction" value="country" />
                            <f:param value="" />
                            <f:param name="reset" value="true" />
                        </rich:componentControl>
                    </h:commandLink>
                </f:facet>
                #{game.country}
            </rich:column>
            <!--more columns-->
            <rich:column comparator="#{sortingBean.yearComparator}" id="year">
                <f:facet name="header">
                    <h:commandLink value="Year">
                        <rich:componentControl target="table3" operation="sort">
                            <f:param name="column" value="year" />
                        </rich:componentControl>
                    </h:commandLink>
                </f:facet>
                #{game.year}
            </rich:column>
            <!--more columns-->
        </rich:dataTable>
    </rich:panel>
</h:form>
```

We've used <rich:componentControl> (described in detail in Chapter 12) in order to define JavaScript calls declaratively, and passed parameters using nested <f:param> tags. We do not use sortOrder because while sorting from a client API we rely on component-state saving, which stores sort orders while staying on the same view. Sorting by city and country resets all previous sorting and performs a new one according to the link clicked. Clicking the date sorts the table by the date without resetting previous city or country sorting. Figure 7-28 shows how the table looks after sorting by country and then by year.

rich:dataTable sample							
Olympic Games List							
Flag	City	Country	Season	Number	Year	From	To
	Sarajevo	Yugoslavia	Winter	14	1984	7 February	19 February
	St. Louis	United States	Summer	3	1904	1 July	23 November
	Lake Placid	United States	Winter	3	1932	4 February	15 February
	Los Angeles	United States	Summer	10	1932	30 July	14 August
	Squaw Valley	United States	Winter	8	1960	18 February	28 February
	Lake Placid	United States	Winter	13	1980	14 February	23 February
	Los Angeles	United States	Summer	23	1984	28 July	12 August
	Atlanta	United States	Summer	26	1996	19 July	4 August
	Salt Lake City	United States	Winter	19	2002	9 February	24 February
	St. Moritz	Switzerland	Winter	2	1928	11 February	19 February

Figure 7-28. Table sorted by City and Country columns using JavaScript API

▦ **Note** Even though there are no Ajax controls on the page, it's still important to have the table wrapped with `<h:form>`, because after calling the `sort()` method, `<rich:dataTable>` itself will perform an Ajax request for sorting the data.

You're probably wondering how to reflect the sorting on the page. All our examples thus far lack visual information about the current state. RichFaces doesn't (yet) provide such a feature, so it's left to be implemented by us. The simplest way is to use conditional rendering for markers that depend on the same sortOrder values. Listing 7-40 shows an example for sorting where we add a simple text indication to the headers. In your application, you could add some icons that point up and down.

Listing 7-40. Adding a simple text indication to the headers

```
<h:form>
    <rich:panel style="width:650px" header="rich:dataTable sample">
        <rich:dataTable value="#{olympicGamesBean.games}" var="game" id="table" rows="10">
```

```
            <f:facet name="header">Olympic Games List</f:facet>
            <rich:column>
                <f:facet name="header">Flag</f:facet>
                <h:graphicImage value="#{game.flagURI}" />
            </rich:column>
            <rich:column sortBy="#{game.city}" sortOrder="#{sortingBean.sortOrders['city']}">
                <f:facet name="header">
                    <a4j:commandLink value="City" render="table" action="#{sortingBean.sort}">
                        <a4j:param name="sortProperty" value="city" />
                    </a4j:commandLink>
                    <h:outputText value="(a)"
                       rendered="#{sortingBean.sortOrders['city']=='ascending'}"
                       style="font-weight:bold"/>
                    <h:outputText value="(d)"
                       rendered="#{sortingBean.sortOrders['city']=='descending'}"
                       style="font-weight:bold"/>
                </f:facet>
                #{game.city}
            </rich:column>
            <!--More columns-->
        </rich:dataTable>
    </rich:panel>
</h:form>
```

The result after sorting will look like Figure 7-29.

rich:dataTable sample

Flag	City(a)	Country	Season	Number	Year	From	To
▮▮	Albertville	France	Winter	16	1992	8 February	23 February
▬▬	Amsterdam	Netherlands	Summer	9	1928	17 May	12 August
▮▮	Antwerp	Belgium	Summer	7	1920	20 April	12 September
▮▮	Athens	Greece	Summer	1	1896	6 April	15 April

Figure 7-29. Table sorted by City column with simple text indication for sorted state

Table Filtering

This section describes the basics of table filtering in RichFaces. We take a similar approach as the sorting section, showing the main, basic filtering features that can be applied to either <rich:dataTable> or <rich:extendedDataTable> components. We will cover a more complicated case in the "Iteration Components Advanced Models" section, including using a database based filtering.

Analogous to sorting tables, filtering functionality can be implemented in two ways: using JavaScript API or using RichFaces action controls.

Let's start with basic attributes that should be used for filtering implementation. We will then build two different examples.

The first attribute is the filterExpression. It is an attribute on <rich:column>. For simple cases where a table's built-in filtering is used, it should be set to an EL expression that is evaluated to a boolean value, and return true if the current iteration object matches the condition for filtering for that column. You could use JSTL, Seam, or any custom function in this attribute.

An alternative to the declarative approach is using the filter attribute. This attribute should be defined with an EL expression pointing to an object that implements the org.richfaces.model.Filter<T> interface. This object should implements a single accept(T t) method, which should be passed with the row object and return a similar boolean result that shows whether the object satisfies the filter condition or not.

Now that we have covered the concepts, let's review an example of filtering implementation using inputs in headers that are plugged with <a4j:ajax> behavior in order to filter the table when values get changed.

In this example, we will use JSTL functions, so we need to add proper namespace to the page, as follows:

```
xmlns:fn="http://java.sun.com/jsp/jstl/functions"
```

Listing 7-41 shows the page code.

Listing 7-41. Page code

```
<h:form>
    <rich:panel style="width:650px" header="rich:dataTable sample">
        <rich:dataTable value="#{olympicGamesBean.games}" var="game" id="table">
            <f:facet name="header">Olympic Games List</f:facet>
            <rich:column>
                <f:facet name="header">Flag</f:facet>
                <h:graphicImage value="#{game.flagURI}" />
            </rich:column>
            <rich:column filterExpression="#{fn:startsWith(game.city,
                filteringBean.cityFilterString)}">
                <f:facet name="header">
                    <h:inputText value="#{filteringBean.cityFilterString}">
                        <a4j:ajax render="table@body" />
                    </h:inputText>
                </f:facet>
                #{game.city}
            </rich:column>
            <rich:column filterExpression="#{fn:containsIgnoreCase(game.country,
                filteringBean.countryFilterString)}">
                <f:facet name="header">
                    <h:inputText value="#{filteringBean.countryFilterString}">
```

```
                                    <a4j:ajax render="table@body" />
                                </h:inputText>
                        </f:facet>
                        #{game.country}
                    </rich:column>
                    <rich:column>
                        <f:facet name="header">Season</f:facet>
                        #{game.season}
                    </rich:column>
                    <rich:column filter="#{filteringBean.centuryFilter}">
                        <f:facet name="header">
                            <h:selectOneMenu value="#{filteringBean.centuryFilterNumber}">
                                <a4j:ajax render="table@body" />
                                <f:selectItem itemLabel="" itemValue="0" />
                                <f:selectItem itemLabel="19th century" itemValue="19" />
                                <f:selectItem itemLabel="20th century" itemValue="20" />
                                <f:selectItem itemLabel="21st century" itemValue="21" />
                            </h:selectOneMenu>
                        </f:facet>
                        #{game.year}
                    </rich:column>
                </rich:dataTable>
            </rich:panel>
        </h:form>
```

On the page we see three columns, which get defined as filterable. The City column uses the fn:startWith JSTL function and the Country column uses fn:containsIgnoreCase. The third column uses the filter attribute bound to a centuryFilter object in our FilteringBean. Current filtering values for the first two columns are stored in two string properties bound to inputs cityFinteringString and countryFilteringString and an integer property stored in the centuryFilteringNumber field of FilteringBean. As a result of filtering, we should update only data in the table and not loose our input focus. We updated only the body of the table from <a4j:ajax> using the body meta-component, which were mentioned in the "Using Partial Table Updates" section of this chapter.

Listing 7-42 shows the bean code.

Listing 7-42. The bean code

```
@ManagedBean
@ViewScoped
public class FilteringBean implements Serializable{

    private String cityFilterString;
    private String countryFilterString;
    private int centuryFilterNumber;

    public Filter<GameDescriptor> getCenturyFilter() {
        return new Filter<GameDescriptor>() {
            @Override
            public boolean accept(GameDescriptor t) {
                switch (centuryFilterNumber) {
                    case 19:
                        return (t.getYear() >= 1800) && (t.getYear() < 1900);
                    case 20:
```

```
                    return (t.getYear() >= 1900) && (t.getYear() < 2000);
                case 21:
                    return (t.getYear() >= 2000);
                default:
                    return true;
            }
        }
    };
}
//Getters and Setters
}
```

cityFilteringString and countryFilteringString properties get compared with every Olympic Game corresponding property, according to JSTL functions defined in filterExpression attributes. The CenturyFilter object is probably of most interest to us. As we said earlier, analogous to the sorting comparator usage, the iteration object (GameDescriptor) is passed to the accept method on every iteration to check whether it satisfies filter conditions or not. We use a simple switch statement according to possible select component values to check whether the year for the current object is matching the chosen century.

Figure 7-30 shows how the table looks after filtered by country and century.

Olympic Games List			
Flag		**Unit**	**Season**	20th century ▼
	St. Louis	United States	Summer	1904
	Lake Placid	United States	Winter	1932
	Los Angeles	United States	Summer	1932
	Squaw Valley	United States	Winter	1960
	Lake Placid	United States	Winter	1980
	Los Angeles	United States	Summer	1984
	Atlanta	United States	Summer	1996

Figure 7-30. Table filtering

Pretty simple isn't it? Now let's show you the second approach, using JavaScript API. The table client object provides the filter() API method. This method should be passed with three parameters: column id, current filter value, and clearance flag. The first and the second parameter are required and don't need an explanation. The third parameter determines if the other filtering rules should be cleared on a new filtering call or be added to previous ones.

Listing 7-43 shows the page code for the API usage example.

Listing 7-43. API usage

```
<h:form>
    <rich:panel style="width:650px" header="rich:dataTable sample">
        <a4j:outputPanel ajaxRendered="true" layout="block">
            <a4j:repeat value="#{filteringBean.continents}" var="cont">
                <h:outputLink value="#"
                    styleClass="#{filteringBean.continentFilterString==cont ?
                    'bold':''}">
                    #{cont}
                    <rich:componentControl target="table2" operation="filter" event="click">
                        <f:param value="contCol"/>
                        <f:param value="#{cont}"/>
                    </rich:componentControl>
                </h:outputLink> |
            </a4j:repeat>
        </a4j:outputPanel>
        <a4j:outputPanel ajaxRendered="true" layout="block">
            <h:outputLink value="#" styleClass="#{filteringBean.centuryFilterNumber==0 ?
                'bold':''}"
                onclick="#{rich:component('table2')}.filter('centCol', 0); return false;">
                All available
            </h:outputLink> |
            <h:outputLink value="#" styleClass="#{filteringBean.centuryFilterNumber==19 ?
                'bold':''}"
                onclick="#{rich:component('table2')}.filter('centCol', 19); return false;">
                19th century
            </h:outputLink> |
            <h:outputLink value="#" styleClass="#{filteringBean.centuryFilterNumber==20 ?
                'bold':''}"
                onclick="#{rich:component('table2')}.filter('centCol', 20); return false;">
                20th century
            </h:outputLink> |
            <h:outputLink value="#" styleClass="#{filteringBean.centuryFilterNumber==21 ?
                'bold':''}"
                onclick="#{rich:component('table2')}.filter('centCol', 21); return false;">
                21st century
            </h:outputLink> |
        </a4j:outputPanel>
        <rich:dataTable value="#{olympicGamesBean.games}" var="game" id="table2">
            <f:facet name="header">Olympic Games List</f:facet>
            <!--Other columns-->
            <rich:column id="contCol" filterValue="#{filteringBean.continentFilterString}"
                filterExpression="#{(filteringBean.continentFilterString=='') ||
                (game.continent==filteringBean.continentFilterString)}">
                <f:facet name="header">Continent</f:facet>
                    #{game.continent}
            </rich:column>
            <!--Other columns-->
            <rich:column filter="#{filteringBean.centuryFilter}"
                filterValue="#{filteringBean.centuryFilterNumber}" id="centCol">
                <f:facet name="header">Year</f:facet>
```

```
            #{game.year}
        </rich:column>
    </rich:dataTable>
    </rich:panel>
</h:form>
```

We added the same century filter from Listing 7-42, and for the continents we used empty or equals conditions. In order to perform filtering, we called the `filter()` API method with target column id and filter value parameters.

All we added to the bean was a `continents` array with a getter method in order to populate our filter panel dynamically, as follows:

```
public final static String[] continents = { "Europe", "Asia", "North America", "South
America", "Oceania" };
```

Figure 7-31 shows the result after clicking the "North America" and "21st Century" links.

Figure 7-31. Table filtered via JavaScript API

As we have no inputs defined for the filter, we need to define the `filterValue` attribute with the EL expression set to the bean property, which will be updated with the current filtering value, and so could be used in the `Filter` object and defined in the `filterExpression`.

If the filter returns no data, you can use the `noDataLabel` attribute or the `noData` facet in order to define the content to be shown in such case. Adding a facet is shown in Listing 7-44.

Listing 7-44. Adding a Facet to Table Filtered via JavaScript API.

```
<f:facet name="noData">
    <h:outputText value="No games for current filter found" style="font-weight:bold"/>
</f:facet>
```

The result will be as shown in Figure 7-32 after clicking "Asia" and "19th Century."

Figure 7-32. No results to display after filtering

Iteration Components Advanced Models

If you previously worked with JSF tables, you know that you can pass not only a simple List to the <rich:dataTable> value, but also point the table to the data model that is an object of a class that extends the javax.faces.model.DataModel<E> abstract class.

RichFaces adds the following two data models:

- org.ajax4jsf.model.ExtendedDataModel<E>: A base model abstract class. It defines the abstract model contract, which helps to manage complex data structures like trees, spreadsheets, and so on, in complex iteration components.

- org.richfaces.model.ArrangeableModel: A model implementation that extends ExtendedDataModel and implements the org.richfaces.model.Arrangeable interface. This model adds filtering and sorting operations.

Let's go over why we need these special data models.

The ExtendedDataModel adds the rowKey entity to a JSF model and uses rowKey instead (in some cases together with) of rowIndex. This key is an abstract property that allows us to identify the object among a wrapped collection. This key can be your database entity id for example. Using keys instead of just indexes guarantees that we will easily and correctly get the object from the wrapped model, in the case of a paginated model, with built-in component selection enabled. Using javax.faces.model.DataModel, which uses indexes, we will need to design and implement additional "model index" or "database object" lookup functionality. When using ExtendedDataModel, all the necessary methods and default implementation are already provided.

ExtendedDataModel has org.ajax4jsf.model.SequenceDataModel<E> simple implementation used as the default model for the iteration components (when sorting and filtering features are not activated). It extends with org.richfaces.model.TreeSequenceKeyModel<V>, which is also an abstract class with implementations used in tree components.

Finally, ArrangeableModel extends the ExtendedDataModel, providing default implementation for abstract classes and implementing the Arrangeable interface. It uses the same methods from the extended model and with an additional arrange() method used to set sorting and filtering rules to the model from the component level.

Let's review both models by creating two examples.

Data Preparation

In order to get close to a real-world application, we will add a database layer to our application and use Hibernate to work with the data.

We will use HSQLDB (version 1.8.0.2) for the database in our example, and Hibernate Core (version 3.6.2).

The next step is to add the Hibernate configuration file (hibernate.cfg.xml) to the application resources. Its content is shown in Listing 7-45.

Listing 7-45. Adding the Hibernate configuration file to application resources

```
<?xml version='1.0' encoding='utf-8'?>
<!DOCTYPE hibernate-configuration PUBLIC
"-//Hibernate/Hibernate Configuration DTD//EN"
"http://hibernate.sourceforge.net/hibernate-configuration-3.0.dtd">
<hibernate-configuration>
    <session-factory>
        <property name="hibernate.connection.driver_class">org.hsqldb.jdbcDriver</property>
        <property name="hibernate.connection.url">jdbc:hsqldb:mem:iteration-sample</property>
        <property name="hibernate.connection.username">sa</property>
        <property name="hibernate.connection.password"></property>
        <property name="hibernate.connection.pool_size">10</property>
        <property name="show_sql">true</property>
        <property name="dialect">org.hibernate.dialect.HSQLDialect</property>
        <property name="hibernate.hbm2ddl.auto">create</property>
        <mapping resource="gameDescriptor.hbm.xml" />
    </session-factory>
</hibernate-configuration>
```

That's a pretty a simple Hibernate configuration file, so we will not spend much time on it. If you need more information on Hibernate, please visit the JBoss Community's Hibernate page at http://hibernate.org. Most interesting is the mapping that is defined using the <mapping> element. Listing 7-46 shows that mapping.

Listing 7-46. Mapping the hibernate configuration file

```
<?xml version="1.0" encoding="UTF-8"?>
<!DOCTYPE hibernate-mapping PUBLIC
    "-//Hibernate/Hibernate Mapping DTD 3.0//EN"
    "http://hibernate.sourceforge.net/hibernate-mapping-3.0.dtd">
<hibernate-mapping>
    <class name="org.richfaces.book.examples.model.GameDescriptor">
        <id name="id">
            <generator class="increment" />
        </id>
        <property name="city" />
        <property name="country" />
        <property name="continent" />
        <property name="flagName" />
        <property name="number" />
        <property name="season" />
        <property name="status" />
        <property name="fromDate" />
        <property name="toDate" />
    </class>
</hibernate-mapping>
```

It's the GameDescriptor class, id field definition for the class objects and fields definitions. You are already familiar with the class itself, as we used it across the entire chapter, and we just mapped it to the database using that descriptor. One thing we also performed in the code is defining that the

GameDescriptor class extends the BaseDescriptor class. And that BaseDescriptor is a simple class, shown in Listing 7-47, which provides a single id property together with accessor methods. So we are using that id property in mapping.

Listing 7-47. BaseDescriptor

```
public class BaseDescriptor implements Serializable{
    private Integer id;
    public Integer getId() { return id; }
    public void setId(Integer id) { this.id = id; }
}
```

You are probably wondering why we didn't use annotations. We could have added the same mappings via annotations in the GameDescriptor class itself to look more modern. But, we just didn't want to add more annotations to the class that already defined a couple of JAXB annotations (to initialize it from XML).

The easiest way for us to populate the database is to persist the collection we already initialized from XML and used for all the samples earlier. Listing 7-48 shows the application scoped bean, which populates the database.

Listing 7-48. Application scoped bean

```
@ApplicationScoped
@ManagedBean(eager = true)
public class GamesHibernateBean {

    @ManagedProperty(value = "#{gamesParser.gamesList}")
    private List<GameDescriptor> games = new ArrayList<GameDescriptor>();
    private static final String[] GAME_FIELDS = {"country", "city", "continent", "season",
        "number", "year"};

    @PostConstruct
    public void fillDatabase(){
        Session hibernateSession = HibernateUtils.getSessionFactory().openSession();
            for (BaseDescriptor game : games) {
                try {
                    hibernateSession.persist(game);
                }catch (HibernateException e){
                    e.printStackTrace();
                }
            }
        hibernateSession.flush();
        hibernateSession.close();
    }

    public String[] getGameFields(){
        return GAME_FIELDS;
    }

    public void setGames(List<GameDescriptor> games) {
        this.games = games;
    }
```

```
    public List<GameDescriptor> getGames() {
        return games;
    }
}
```

According to the eager=true definition, an application scoped bean will be created on application start. The gamesList will be injected from the GameParser, which was used in the beginning of this chapter. We just iterate over the injected list and persist every object into the database.

In order to obtain the Hibernate session, we used the popular HibernateUtils class, which provides basic implementation of session factory programmatic lookup from the Hibernate documentation, as shown in Listing 7-49.

Listing 7-49. HibernateUtils

```
public class HibernateUtils {
    private static final SessionFactory sessionFactory;
    static {
        try {
            sessionFactory = new Configuration().configure().buildSessionFactory();
        } catch (Throwable ex) {
            System.err.println("Initial SessionFactory creation failed." + ex);
            throw new ExceptionInInitializerError(ex);
        }
    }

    public static SessionFactory getSessionFactory() {
        return sessionFactory;
    }

}
```

■ **Note** We intentionally decided to go with a very basic JSF-Hibernate configuration. Showing different advanced options of plugging Hibernate or JPA, for example, into the JSF application is beyond the scope of this book; we want to concentrate on the UI components data model.

ExtendedDataModel Implementation for Paging

The topic of ExtendedDataModel implementation for paging is one of the most popular among those who play with iteration components and JSF/RichFaces in general. All the component library references show pretty simple examples of pointing the table component to the list from a managed bean and implementing additional functionality on top of that model. But later, getting such a bean connected to the database layer appears too time consuming, for example, to get a complete list to show only 10 to 20 rows using the first and rows table attributes.

The same problem applied to the RichFaces <rich:dataTable>–<rich:dataScroller/> components pair. Simple usage of the tables pointed to List for example and wrapped to the SequenceDataModel by default, obtains the entire list and partially encodes it using the first, rows, and page properties. But a common task for a real application is to optimize database calls and fetch only the data that corresponds to the current page to be displayed. Next, we will implement the model properly to achieve that result.

> ■ **Note** This is a very common question (or even expectation) from new developers. Developers expect the table to be able to perform partial data fetching because it provides a data scrolling component. A UI component in JSF, however, doesn't know anything about the underlying model and completely relies on the default if proper custom implementation is not provided. The default gets a complete list, wraps it as a model, and makes it available for the page.

Let's review more of the ExtendedDataModel abstract class in Listing 7-50.

Listing 7-50. ExtendedDataModel Abstract Class

```
public abstract class ExtendedDataModel<E> extends DataModel<E> {
    public abstract void setRowKey(Object key);
    public abstract Object getRowKey();
    public abstract void walk(FacesContext context, DataVisitor visitor, Range range, Object
        argument);
}
```

It defines three new methods extending the standard JSF DataModel. Having only the rowIndex isn't really enough for complex data models and features. Furthermore, the walk() method should be implemented and provide functionality of iteration over the model using the "Visitor" pattern. Concrete iteration components that use the models based on this will call the walk() method a few times at different request phases. The following parameters will be passed to the method: a FacesContext instance, a visitor object that will perform current iteration data processing, and a range object that specifies the range of iteration component and can accept one more argument depending on implementation.

When we know which methods we should compare to the standard DataModel, let's look at Listing 7-51, which shows our custom model (other methods will be explained soon).

Listing 7-51. Custom model

```
public abstract class BasePageableHibernateModel<T extends BaseDescriptor> extends

    ExtendedDataModel<T> {
    protected Class<T> entityClass;
    protected SequenceRange cachedRange = null;
    protected Integer cachedRowCount = null;
    protected List<T> cachedItems = null;
    protected Object rowKey;

    public BasePageableHibernateModel(Class<T> entityClass) {
        super();
        this.entityClass = entityClass;
    }

    @Override
    public Object getRowKey() {
        return rowKey;
    }
```

```java
    @Override
    public void setRowKey(Object key) {
        this.rowKey = key;
    }

    protected Criteria createCriteria(Session session) {
        return session.createCriteria(entityClass);
    }

    @Override
    public void walk(FacesContext facesContext, DataVisitor visitor, Range range, Object
        argument) {
        // Will be described in details later in the chapter
    }

    @Override
    public int getRowCount() {
        if (this.cachedRowCount == null) {
            Session session = HibernateUtils.getSessionFactory().openSession();
            try {
                Criteria criteria = createCriteria(session);
                this.cachedRowCount = criteria.list().size();
            } finally {
                session.close();
            }
        }
        return this.cachedRowCount;
    }

    @Override
    public T getRowData() {
        for (T t : cachedItems) {
            if (t.getId().equals(this.getRowKey())) {
                return t;
            }
        }
        return null;
    }

    @Override
    public boolean isRowAvailable() {
        return (getRowData() != null);
    }
    // other methods see note below
}
```

▨ **Note** To keep the code shorter, we skipped a few methods that are not used in this implementation.

That's a generic model. It's marked as abstract and parameterized with t he object class. This allows you to later use the same model code for all our various objects across the application.

Let's review the methods overridden from the ExtendedDataModel. As we said before, the id of the wrapped object from the database is used as a rowKey for the object. getRowData() simply iterates the cached items (collected during the walk() method execution) and performs lookup for an object id equals to the current rowKey.

The isRowAvailable() is a standard method from DataModel and simply returns the result from checking the current rowData for value. Let's review another getRowCount() simple method before looking at the walk() method.

We're using Hibernate Criteria API for retrieving entities. We created Criteria without any new Criterions added in order to get the size of the result set. We're performing simple caching of that size in session using the cachedRowCount bean property.

Notice that very important parts—getRowIndex() and setRowIndex()—are not required to be implemented properly when using a simple <rich:dataTable> component. We only added them as stub methods. However, if you will want to use <rich:extendedDataTable>, it requires these methods to have proper implementation for selection functionality. The reason for this is rather simple: as the table allows sequential selection of row ranges (for example standard UI SHIFT key + mouse click selection), it can't use only rowKeys because you can't characterize a range using anything except indexes. If you require selection, the following two methods need to be implemented:

1. setRowIndex(index): This method calls the setRowKey(rowKey) method and passes the rowKey of the object, which corresponds to the index for a given range and sorting/filtering rules applied to the wrapped model.

2. getRowIndex(): This returns the index in the wrapped model of the object for a currently set rowKey.

In Listing 7-52, let's review in detail the most important walk() method, as well as one helper method.

Listing 7-52. walk() method as well as one helper method

```
protected static boolean areEqualRanges(SequenceRange range1, SequenceRange range2) {
    if (range1 == null || range2 == null) {
        return range1 == null && range2 == null;
    } else {
        return range1.getFirstRow() == range2.getFirstRow() && range1.getRows() ==
range2.getRows();
    }
}

@Override
public void walk(FacesContext facesContext, DataVisitor visitor, Range range, Object argument)
{
    SequenceRange sequenceRange = (SequenceRange) range;
    if (this.cachedItems == null || !areEqualRanges(this.cachedRange, sequenceRange)) {
        Session session = HibernateUtils.getSessionFactory().openSession();
        try {
            Criteria criteria = createCriteria(session);
            if (sequenceRange != null) {
                int first = sequenceRange.getFirstRow();
                int rows = sequenceRange.getRows();
                criteria.setFirstResult(first);
                if (rows > 0) {
```

```
            criteria.setMaxResults(rows);
        }
    }
    this.cachedRange = sequenceRange;
    this.cachedItems = criteria.list();
    } finally {
        session.close();
    }
}
for (T item : this.cachedItems) {
    visitor.process(facesContext, item.getId(), argument);
}
}
```

As you can see, the idea is pretty simple. First, we are checking that we haven't already cached the data. Even if the data is cached, we then check whether the cached data range matches the current range passed by the table. . If no match, the component is getting rendered first time or it was switched to a different page using the <rich:dataScroller> component or by changing first and/or rows attributes. In this case we use Criteria API, setting parameters from Range as criteria parameters (first object index to fetch and number of objects which should be fetched). After getting the result. we cache it in a session with the current Range object.

Finally, we are iterating over the result set that we just obtained, calling the process() method of the Visitor.

■ **Note** The rowKey passed to the visitor is added to the clientId of nested components for every iteration. getRowKey() has to return a value that is a string-based and is compatible with javax.faces.component. UIComponent#getClientId(FacesContext ctx). In other cases, you have to provide the rowKeyConverter using a corresponding iteration component attribute.

Finally, we need to check the model class for specific GameDescriptor objects and the page that defines the <rich:dataTable> component. Listing 7-53 shows the PageableHibernateModel class.

Listing 7-53. PageableHibernateModel class

```
@ManagedBean
@SessionScoped
public class PageableHibernateModel extends BasePageableHibernateModel<GameDescriptor> {

    public PageableHibernateModel() {
        super(GameDescriptor.class);
    }

}
```

Have you ever seen a simpler model class? By now you should realize how important it is to provide a generic model for your data objects. Once implemented, it usually makes concrete models implementations the easiest task. We just passed the GameDescriptor class to initialization. An abstract model we reviewed earlier implements everything we need.

■ **Note** We wanted to keep the examples simple, but keep in mind that placing data in a session scope is not always a good idea because you may run into concurrent access problems.

In Listing 7-54, let's look at the page that uses that model, and render the table with a limited page size and <rich:dataScroller> control.

Listing 7-54. Render the table with a limited page size and <rich:dataScroller> control

```
<rich:dataTable value="#{pageableHibernateModel}" var="game" rows="10" id="table">
    <f:facet name="header">Olympic Games List</f:facet>
    <c:forEach items="#{gamesHibernateBean.gameFields}" var="column">
        <rich:column id="#{column}">
            <f:facet name="header">
                <h:outputText value="#{column}"/>
            </f:facet>
            <h:outputText value="#{game[column]}"/>
        </rich:column>
    </c:forEach>
    <f:facet name="footer">
        <rich:dataScroller/>
    </f:facet>
</rich:dataTable>
```

Things are pretty simple here. We are using a registered data model as a table value, and using the rows attribute, limiting the number of rows per page to 10.

Most notable there is <c:forEach> usage, which provides a way to iterate over the gameFields (column names stored in GamesHibernateBean) and dynamically add columns to the table.

■ **Note** Using <c:forEach> instead of <ui:repeat> is needed in this case. <c:forEach> has to be used in cases where we need to create the actual components in a JSF tree during the view creation phase, rather than iterating over a single instance at the render response phase (as would happen with <ui:repeat>). There are many good JSF-related resources that can provide more information.

The footer facet contains the <rich:dataScroller> component.
Figure 7-33 shows how it will looks on initial rendering.

Olympic Games List					
country	city	continent	season	number	year
Greece	Athens	Europe	Summer	1	1896
France	Paris	Europe	Summer	2	1900
United States	St. Louis	North America	Summer	3	1904
Great Britain	London	Europe	Summer	4	1908
Sweden	Stockholm	Europe	Summer	5	1912
Germany	Berlin	Europe	Summer	6	1916
Belgium	Antwerp	Europe	Summer	7	1920
France	Chamonix	Europe	Winter	1	1924
France	Paris	Europe	Summer	8	1924
Switzerland	St. Moritz	Europe	Winter	2	1928

Figure 7-33. <rich:dataTable> with dynamic columns and backed by custom model

When we click to some other page, the table will be switched, as shown in Figure 7-34.

Olympic Games List					
country	city	continent	season	number	year
Italy	Torino	Europe	Winter	20	2006
China	Beijing	Asia	Summer	29	2008
Canada	Vancouver	North America	Winter	21	2010
Great Britain	London	Europe	Summer	30	2012
Russia	Sochi	Europe	Winter	22	2014
Brazil	Rio de Janeiro	South America	Summer	31	2016

Figure 7-34. <rich:dataTable> with dynamic columns and backed by custom model after page change

You can easily check with debug or adding some logging code to the model that database calls are performed only in the following ways:

1. Twice on initial rendering in order to cache all the object counts and to get the first 10 records.

2. Once for a page change, when the next 10 records are loaded. In complex cases, a row count should not be cached in such a simple way because the table size could change; but it works for simple cases with static tables.

It turns out that the walk() method is called a few times per request; as many times as the component needed to iterate over the value according to JSF specification (decode, render). And rowCount also gets called a few times by the <rich:dataTable> and <rich:dataScoller> components. So, as previously mentioned, if a table points to a database result set directly, rather than using the model like we created, you will see numerous database calls on initial rendering or a single request. The performance of such implementations will be extremely low.

ArrangeableModel Implementation for Filtering and Sorting

This section shows you ArrangeableModel implementation in order to implement in-database sorting and filtering. ArrangeableModel is based on the same ExtendedDataModel but also implements the Arrangeable interface. We will not implement all the base functionality in our ArrangeableModel from scratch. Instead, we will extend our BasePageableModel.

But first, in Listing 7-55, let's see how the page will be changed.

Listing 7-55. Code for ArrangeableModel implementation

```
<h:form>
    <a4j:outputPanel ajaxRendered="true" layout="block">
        <a4j:repeat value="#{filteringBean.continents}" var="cont">
            <h:outputLink value="#" styleClass="#{filteringBean.continentFilterString==cont ?
                'bold':''}">
                #{cont}
                <rich:componentControl target="table" operation="filter" event="click">
                    <f:param value="continent" />
                    <f:param value="#{cont}" />
                </rich:componentControl>
            </h:outputLink> |
        </a4j:repeat>
    </a4j:outputPanel>
    <rich:dataTable value="#{arrangeableHibernateModel}" var="game" rows="10" id="table">
        <f:facet name="header">Olympic Games List</f:facet>
        <c:forEach items="#{gamesHibernateBean.gameFields}" var="column">
            <rich:column id="#{column}" sortBy="#{column}" filterExpression="#{column}">
                <f:facet name="header">
                    <h:commandLink value="#{column}">
                        <rich:componentControl target="table" operation="sort">
                            <f:param value="#{column}" />
                            <f:param value="" />
                            <f:param name="reset" value="true" />
                        </rich:componentControl>
                    </h:commandLink>
                </f:facet>
                <h:outputText value="#{game[column]}"/>
            </rich:column>
        </c:forEach>
        <f:facet name="footer">
            <rich:dataScroller/>
        </f:facet>
    </rich:dataTable>
</h:form>
```

The differences include the following:

1. The sortBy and `filterExpression` properties for the column are from the filtering and sorting section. Instead of setting them to object properties or simple boolean expressions, we passed column names as parameters in order to pick the column names that were activated on the model level.

2. The FilteringBean remained the same as in the previous example. It contains the same static continents array.

3. The block of links for filtering that use a simple JavaScript API.

4. The links in headers for sorting are also based on a simple JavaScript API.

It's now time to dig into the code for BaseArrangeableHibernateModel is just a concrete implementation of the generic one), as shown in Listing 7-56. It extends the BasePageableHibernateModel so that all the base model methods remain at a super-class level and we will see only additional and changed methods. In order to make the code cleaner, we skipped a few utility methods, but will explain them after the initial model review.

Listing 7-56. Code for BaseArrangeableHibernateModel

```
public abstract class BaseArrangeableHibernateModel<T extends BaseDescriptor> extends
   BasePageableHibernateModel<T> implements Arrangeable {
  private List<FilterField> filterFields;
  private List<SortField> sortFields;

  public BaseArrangeableHibernateModel(Class<T> entityClass) {
    super(entityClass);
  }

  private void appendFilters(FacesContext context, Criteria criteria) {
      // Described in details later. Adds filters to the Criteria.
  }

  private void appendSorts(FacesContext context, Criteria criteria) {
      // Described in details later. Adds sorts to the Criteria.
  }

  private String getPropertyName(FacesContext facesContext, Expression expression) {
      // Described in details later. Used to get properties names defined in sortBy and
filterExpression
  }

  @Override
  public void walk(FacesContext facesContext, DataVisitor visitor, Range range, Object
argument) {
    SequenceRange sequenceRange = (SequenceRange) range;
    if (this.cachedItems == null || !areEqualRanges(this.cachedRange, sequenceRange)) {
      Session session = HibernateUtils.getSessionFactory().openSession();
        try {
          Criteria criteria = createCriteria(session);
          appendFilters(facesContext, criteria);
          appendSorts(facesContext, criteria);
          if (sequenceRange != null) {
```

```
                int first = sequenceRange.getFirstRow();
                int rows = sequenceRange.getRows();
                criteria.setFirstResult(first);
                if (rows > 0) {
                    criteria.setMaxResults(rows);
                }
            }
            this.cachedRange = sequenceRange;
            this.cachedItems = criteria.list();
        } finally {
            session.close();
        }
    }
    for (T item : this.cachedItems) {
      visitor.process(facesContext, item.getId(), argument);
    }
  }
}

@Override
public int getRowCount() {
  if (this.cachedRowCount == null){
        Session session = HibernateUtils.getSessionFactory().openSession();
        try {
            Criteria criteria = createCriteria(session);
            appendFilters(FacesContext.getCurrentInstance(), criteria);
            cachedRowCount = criteria.list().size();
        } finally {
            session.close();
        }
    }
  return this.cachedRowCount;
}

public void arrange(FacesContext facesContext, ArrangeableState state) {
  if (state != null) {
    this.filterFields = state.getFilterFields();
    this.sortFields = state.getSortFields();
    this.cachedItems = null;
    this.cachedRange = null;
    this.cachedRowCount=null;
  }
 }
}
```

Let's now review what we have here, starting from the getRowCount() method. It creates Criteria and gets the list size in case the row count is still not marked as cached. It only appends filters to the Criteria prior to getting the result set size.

The new arrange() method accepts the FacesContext and ArrangeableState objects as parameters. The ArrangeableState object provides three methods: getFilterFields(), getSortFields(), and getLocale(). The filter fields contain information about filterValue, filterExpression, and Filter objects attached to the column. The sort fields contain information about sortValue, sortBy, and defined Comparators.

If you check RichFaces sources, you will see that in default ArrangeableModel implementation, the arrange() method, performs sorting and filtering. But that's not usually the case for the custom model.

Because of the difference with the default, it doesn't operate on a full list, but partially loads it according to the current page range in walk(). So we store sorting and filtering fields for further processing in walk() in that method.

Let's review the walk() method, which looks very similar to the walk() method from the pageable model; the only difference is that it appends sorting and filtering to Criteria prior to fetching the result list.

We'll look at the trimmed methods in more detail in Listing 7-57.

Listing 7-57. Trimmed methods

```
private String getPropertyName(FacesContext facesContext, Expression expression) {
    try {
    return (String) ((ValueExpression) expression).getValue(facesContext.getELContext());
    } catch (ELException e) {
     throw new FacesException(e.getMessage(), e);
    }
}

private void appendSorts(FacesContext context, Criteria criteria) {
  if (sortFields != null) {
    for (SortField sortField : sortFields) {
      SortOrder ordering = sortField.getSortOrder();
      if (SortOrder.ascending.equals(ordering) || SortOrder.descending.equals(ordering)) {
        String propertyName = getPropertyName(context, sortField.getSortBy());
        Order order = SortOrder.ascending.equals(ordering) ? Order.asc(propertyName) :
          Order.desc(propertyName);
        criteria.addOrder(order.ignoreCase());
      }
    }
  }
}


private void appendFilters(FacesContext context, Criteria criteria) {
  if (filterFields != null) {
    for (FilterField filterField : filterFields) {
      String propertyName = getPropertyName(context,filterField.getFilterExpression());
      String filterValue = (String)filterField.getFilterValue();
      if (filterValue != null && filterValue.length() != 0) {
        criteria.add(Restrictions.like(propertyName, filterValue,
          MatchMode.ANYWHERE).ignoreCase());
      }
    }
  }
}
```

This method seems fairly self-explanatory. Every append*() method iterates over the sort or filter fields, obtains the current values for filtering or sorting, and applies it to the criteria by using its API. The getPropertyName() method obtains the column names that were passed using sortBy and filterExpression by getting value from the given ValueExpression.

It's time to see the result, first looking at the simple concrete object model class shown in Listing 7-58.

Listing 7-58. Simple concrete object model class

```
@ManagedBean
@SessionScoped
public class ArrangeableHibernateModel extends BaseArrangeableHibernateModel<GameDescriptor> {
    public ArrangeableHibernateModel() {
        super(GameDescriptor.class);
    }
}
```

Figure 7-35 shows the table after initial rendering.

Europe | Asia | North America | South America | Oceania |

	Olympic Games List				
country	city	continent	season	number	year
Greece	Athens	Europe	Summer	1	1896
France	Paris	Europe	Summer	2	1900
United States	St. Louis	North America	Summer	3	1904
Great Britain	London	Europe	Summer	4	1908
Sweden	Stockholm	Europe	Summer	5	1912
Germany	Berlin	Europe	Summer	6	1916
Belgium	Antwerp	Europe	Summer	7	1920
France	Chamonix	Europe	Winter	1	1924
France	Paris	Europe	Summer	8	1924
Switzerland	St. Moritz	Europe	Winter	2	1928
Netherlands	Amsterdam	Europe	Summer	9	1928
United States	Lake Placid	North America	Winter	3	1932
United States	Los Angeles	North America	Summer	10	1932
Germany	Garmisch-Partenkirchen	Europe	Winter	4	1936
Germany	Berlin	Europe	Summer	11	1936

1 2 3 4

Figure 7-35. Table backed by ArrangeableModel custom implementation

Figure 7-36 shows the table after sorting (by city) and filtering (by continent).

Europe | Asia | North America | South America | Oceania |

	Olympic Games List				
country	city	continent	season	number	year
China	Beijing	Asia	Summer	29	2008
Japan	Nagano	Asia	Winter	18	1998
Japan	Sapporo	Asia	Winter	11	1972
Japan	Sapporo	Asia	Winter	5	1940
South Korea	Seoul	Asia	Summer	24	1988
Japan	Tokyo	Asia	Summer	18	1964
Japan	Tokyo	Asia	Summer	12	1940

Figure 7-36. *Filtered and sorted table*

That's all the coverage related to models and the advanced features they provide. We believe you now have all the information to implement complex data models with RichFaces data iteration components.

Summary

This chapter introduced various data iteration components, from the most basic `<a4j:repeat>`, which doesn't produce any markup, to complex components such as `<rich:extendedDataTable>`. One unique feature that all data iteration components have is partial-table update, where you can specify which specific row(s) to update. The look and feel of all components can be greatly customized via skins, which are covered in Chapter 13. At the end we covered the usage of custom models implementations for complex, in-database paging/sorting/filtering operations in data table components.

CHAPTER 8

Rich Menu Components

In this chapter, you'll explore the various menu components available in RichFaces. First we'll first cover toolbar and drop-down menu components, and then we'll show you a panel menu component. The context menu unfortunately was not included into the RichFaces 4.0 final release, but will definitely be added in one of the first 4.x updates.

▧ **Note** Component images in this chapter use a slightly customized blueSky skin with a larger general font size. If you want to use it, create a new skin and overwrite the font size as follows:

```
baseSkin=blueSky
generalSizeFont=12px
```

If you are not sure how to use this custom skin, Chapter 13 covers skins in detail.

Using <rich:toolbar>

<rich:toolbar> creates a horizontal bar that can hold any other JSF component, including any action components.

You can easily use <rich:toolbar> in conjunction with <rich:panel>, where the panel holds some information associated with a link in the toolbar. Figure 8-1 shows how it looks.

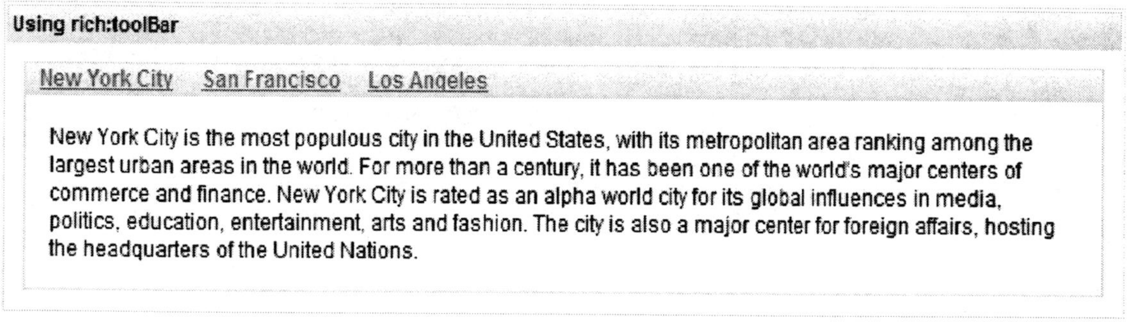

Figure 8-1. Simple toolbar

The code is shown in Listing 8-1.

Listing 8-1. *Simple toolbar code*

```
<h:form>
   <rich:toolbar>
      <a4j:commandLink id="nyc" value="New York City" actionListener=
"#{toolbarBean.cityListener}" />
      <a4j:commandLink id="sf" value="San Francisco" actionListener=
"#{toolbarBean.cityListener}" />
      <a4j:commandLink id="la" value="Los Angeles" actionListener=
"#{toolbarBean.cityListener}" />
   </rich:toolbar>
</h:form>
<rich:panel>
   <a4j:outputPanel ajaxRendered="true">
      <h:panelGrid rendered="#{toolbarBean.nyc}">
         New York City is the most populous city in the United States, with its metropolitan
         area ranking among the largest urban areas in the world. For more than a century,
         it has been one of the world's major centers of commerce and finance. New York
         City is rated as an alpha world city for its global influences in media, politics,
         education, entertainment, arts and fashion. The city is also a major center for
         foreign affairs, hosting the headquarters of the United Nations.
      </h:panelGrid>
      <h:panelGrid rendered="#{toolbarBean.sf}">
         San Francisco is the fourth most populous city in California and the 14th most
         populous city in the United States. San Francisco is a popular international
         tourist destination renowned for its steep rolling hills, an eclectic mix of
         Victorian and modern architecture, and famous landmarks, including the Golden
         Gate Bridge, Alcatraz Island, the cable cars, Coit Tower, and Chinatown.
      </h:panelGrid>
      <h:panelGrid rendered="#{toolbarBean.la}">
         Los Angeles is the largest city in the state of California and the second-largest
         in the United States. Los Angeles is one of the world's centers of culture,
         technology, media, business, and international trade.
      </h:panelGrid>
   </a4j:outputPanel>
</rich:panel>
```

Two attributes, width and height, are available on components in order to allow simple definitions for those basic properties without using CSS. We will use height across all the examples and width will be set to 100% by default. Besides the attributes usage, you could define the same sizes using Skins CSS (rf-tb class) in order not to repeat the definition for all the toolbars. Skins will be described in later chapter, but for now just keep in mind that you may use CSS instead of the sizes attributes used there.

In this example, the toolbar contains three command links, but keep in mind that any JSF component can be placed inside the toolbar. The links simply change the rendered panel content, and after <a4j:outputPanel> get automatically updated (because of ajaxRendered=true) and corresponding description is rendered. In order for the example to be complete, see the bean code in Listing 8-2.

Listing 8-2. The bean code

```
@ManagedBean
@ViewScoped
public class ToolbarBean implements Serializable {
    private boolean nyc = true;
    private boolean sf = false;
    private boolean la = false;

    public void cityListener(ActionEvent event){
        if (event.getComponent().getId().equals("nyc")) nyc = true; else nyc = false;
        if (event.getComponent().getId().equals("sf")) sf = true; else sf = false;
        if (event.getComponent().getId().equals("la")) la = true; else la = false;
    }
    // Getters and setters
}
```

It's also possible to specify a separator between items (components) on the toolbar. Four built-in separators are available: none, line, square, and disc. We set the toolbar to use the line separator using the following:

```
<rich:toolbar height="24px" itemSeparator="line">
```

The result shown in Figure 8-2.

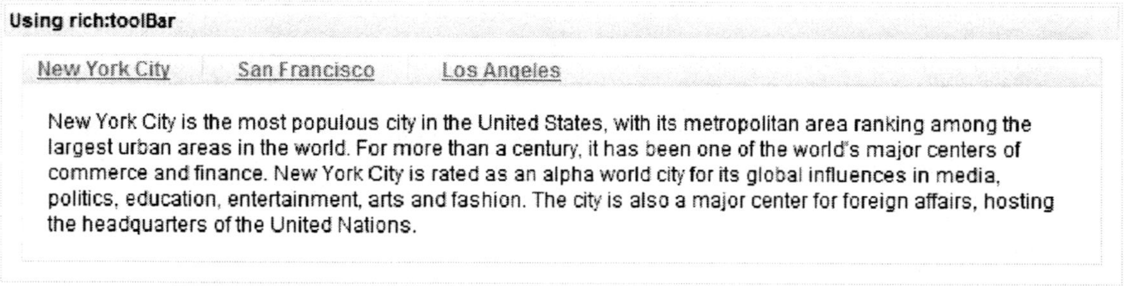

Using rich:toolBar

| New York City | San Francisco | Los Angeles |

New York City is the most populous city in the United States, with its metropolitan area ranking among the largest urban areas in the world. For more than a century, it has been one of the world's major centers of commerce and finance. New York City is rated as an alpha world city for its global influences in media, politics, education, entertainment, arts and fashion. The city is also a major center for foreign affairs, hosting the headquarters of the United Nations.

Figure 8-2. Toolbar with items separator

You could also use a custom separator image. Let's say we slightly modify the declaration again to the following:

```
<rich:toolbar itemSeparator="/img/ico.gif">
```

We see our corresponding custom icon applied instead of the line ones from the Figure 8-2.

It's also possible to place a custom separator by creating a facet named itemSeparator. An example shown in Listing 8-3.

Listing 8-3. Placing a custom separator

```
<rich:toolbar height="24px">
    <f:facet name="itemSeparator">
        <h:outputText value="|"/>
    </f:facet>
    ...
<rich:toolbar>
```

The result is shown in Figure 8-3.

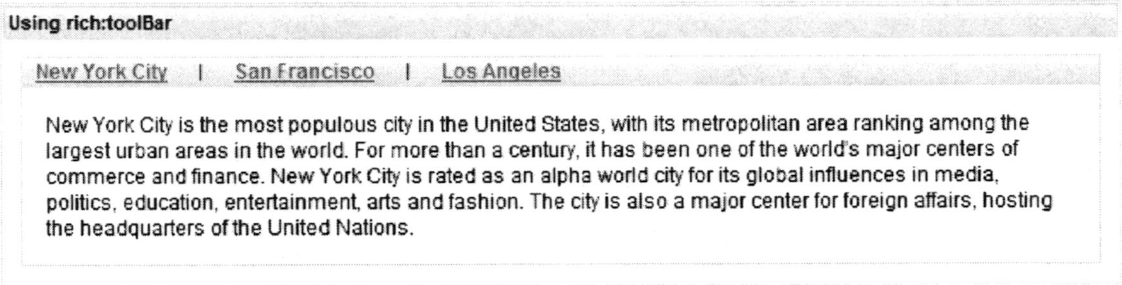

Using rich:toolBar

New York City | San Francisco | Los Angeles

New York City is the most populous city in the United States, with its metropolitan area ranking among the largest urban areas in the world. For more than a century, it has been one of the world's major centers of commerce and finance. New York City is rated as an alpha world city for its global influences in media, politics, education, entertainment, arts and fashion. The city is also a major center for foreign affairs, hosting the headquarters of the United Nations.

Figure 8-3. Toolbar with custom items separator

You can place any components inside a facet. Just remember that a facet can hold only one child. If you need to place more than one component inside, use <h:panelGroup> to wrap them (JSF limitation).

It is also possible to group items on the toolbar when needed. Suppose you want to group together cities on the West Coast, as it's done in Listing 8-4.

Listing 8-4. Grouping together cities on the West Coast

```
<h:form>
    <rich:toolbar itemSeparator="disc" height="24px">
        <a4j:commandLink id="nyc" value="New York City" actionListener=↵
            "#{toolBarBean.cityListener}" />
        <rich:toolbarGroup itemSeparator="square" location="right">
            <a4j:commandLink id="sf" value="San Francisco" actionListener=↵
                "#{toolBarBean.cityListener}" />
            <a4j:commandLink id="la" value="Los Angeles" actionListener=↵
                "#{toolBarBean.cityListener}" />
        </rich:toolbarGroup>
    </rich:toolbar>
<h:form>
<!-- content panels -->
```

When grouping, you can specify a different itemSeparator for the group, as well as the location of the group. In the previous example, the group is placed to the right, which produces the result shown in Figure 8-4.

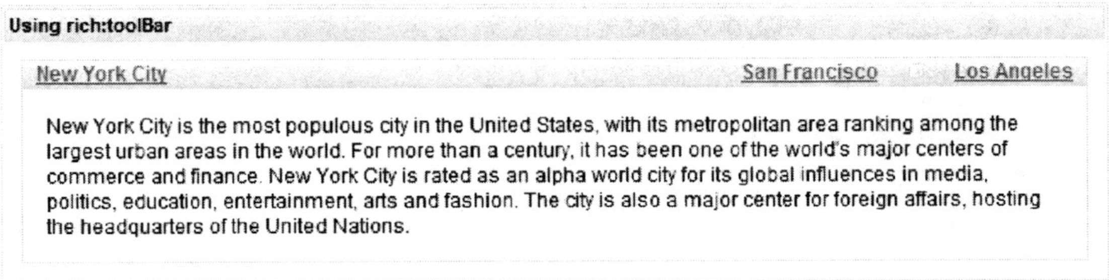

Using rich:toolBar

New York City   San Francisco   Los Angeles

New York City is the most populous city in the United States, with its metropolitan area ranking among the largest urban areas in the world. For more than a century, it has been one of the world's major centers of commerce and finance. New York City is rated as an alpha world city for its global influences in media, politics, education, entertainment, arts and fashion. The city is also a major center for foreign affairs, hosting the headquarters of the United Nations.

Figure 8-4. Toolbar with the group aligned to the right

You could define any number of left and right aligned groups within the toolbar and they will be aligned according to the order of definition on the page.

You can as easily place any JSF component inside the toolbar. For example, Listing 8-5 shows how to use images inside.

Listing 8-5. Placing any JSF component inside the toolbar

```
<rich:panel>
    <rich:toolbar itemSeparator="line" height="24px">
        <h:graphicImage value="/images/states/flag_california.gif" width="24" height="21"/>
         <h:graphicImage value="/images/states/flag_newyork.gif" width="24" height="21"/>
         <h:graphicImage value="/images/states/flag_florida.gif" width="24" height="21"/>
         <h:graphicImage value="/images/states/flag_massachusetts.gif" width="24" height="21"/>
    </rich:toolbar>
</rich:panel>
```

This result produced is shown in Figure 8-5.

Figure 8-5. Toolbar with images

Of course in order for the toolbar to become useful, we need to wrap the images with links or add some click-handling behaviors.

Let's create a more interesting usage sample. You already know about the `<rich:popupPanel>` component from Chapter 6. Let's attach it to `<rich:toolbar>` and have it activated on a corresponding link click. Let's take a look at it in Listing 8-6.

Listing 8-6. Attaching `<rich:popupPanel>` to `<rich:toolbar>`

```
<rich:toolbar height="24px">
    <h:outputLink value="#" id="ll">
        <rich:componentControl event="click" operation="show" target="loginPane">
            <a4j:param name="event" value="event" noEscape="true" />
            <rich:hashParam>
                <a4j:param noEscape="true" name="top"
                    value="jQuery(#{rich:element('ll')}.parentNode).offset().top +
                    jQuery(#{rich:element('ll')}.parentNode).height()" />
                <a4j:param noEscape="true" name="left"
                    value="jQuery(#{rich:element('ll')}.parentNode).offset().left" />
            </rich:hashParam>
        </rich:componentControl>
        Account
    </h:outputLink>
</rich:toolbar>
<rich:messages/>
<rich:popupPanel id="loginPane"  modal="false" autosized="true">
    <h:form>
        <h:panelGrid columns="2">
            Name:
            <h:inputText value="#{userBean.userName}" />
            Password:
```

```
            <h:inputSecret value="#{userBean.password}" />
        </h:panelGrid>
        <h:commandButton value="Login"
            onclick="#{rich:component('loginPane')}.hide();" action="#{userBean.login}"/>
    </h:form>
</rich:popupPanel>
```

This allows you to attach a popup component (`<rich:popupPanel>`) to the `<rich:toolbar>` control, as shown in Figure 8-6.

Figure 8-6. Toolbar with attached popup panel

We used the `<rich:popupPanel>` Java Script API and passed position coordinates dynamically from JavaScript.

▪ **Note** `<rich:hashParam>` is described in detail in Chapter 12. All you need to understand in this example is that it groups the nested parameters to JavaScript hash (similar to Java hash map). It's used because the `<rich:popupPanel>` show() API method accepts two parameters, event and hash map, with named options (we passed left and top position there).

The UserBean code is shown in Listing 8-7.

Listing 8-7. UserBean code

```
@ManagedBean
@SessionScoped
public class UserBean {

    private String userName;
    private String password;

    public void login() {
        FacesContext.getCurrentInstance().addMessage(null,
            new FacesMessage(FacesMessage.SEVERITY_INFO, userName + " logged!", userName +
                " logged!"));
    }
    //Getters and setters
}
```

When the button is clicked, a login() action will be executed and a message about a successful login will appear below the toolbar.

That's it for the <rich:toolbar> component. We will continue using it when we cover the <rich:dropDownMenu> component in the next section.

Using <rich:dropDownMenu>

<rich:dropDownMenu> produces a drop-down menu, as shown in Figure 8-7.

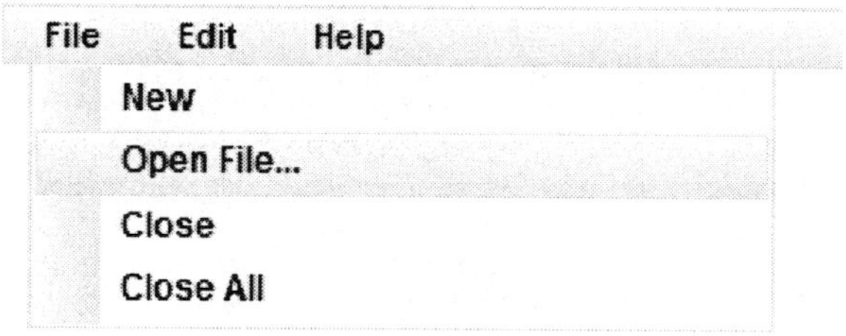

Figure 8-7. Simple drop-down menu

Every menu item can be associated with a particular action or action listener to be invoked via a standard POST request with a full page update or via Ajax. All the standard Ajax concepts apply here as well, such as render, execute, and other Ajax options.

The code to create this menu is shown in Listing 8-8.

Listing 8-8. The code to create the simple drop-down menu

```
<h:form>
    <rich:toolbar>
        <rich:dropDownMenu mode="ajax" label ="File">
            <rich:menuItem label="New" />
            <rich:menuItem label="Open File..." />
            <rich:menuItem label="Close" />
            <rich:menuItem label="Close All" />
        </rich:dropDownMenu>
        <rich:dropDownMenu mode="ajax" >
            <f:facet name="label">
                <h:outputText value="Edit" />
            </f:facet>
            <rich:menuItem label="Undo" />
        </rich:dropDownMenu>
        <rich:dropDownMenu mode="ajax" >
            <f:facet name="label">
                <h:outputText value="Help" />
            </f:facet>
            <rich:menuItem label="About" />
        </rich:dropDownMenu>
    </rich:toolbar>
</h:form>
```

<rich:toolbar> is the container component, which we have covered before. Inside, you place one or more <rich:dropDownMenu> components. You use the label facet or attribute to define the top menu label. From there, you use <rich:menuItem> to create each menu item. That's pretty simple.

■ **Note** You are not required to use <rich:toolbar> as a drop-down menu parent. You may choose any other wrapper component or even create your own instead.

Notice that the mode attribute is set to ajax. It has three possible values: ajax, server, and client. client means no request will be sent to the server. In such case you should handle click events on your own using some custom JavaScript handler methods, behaviors or by attaching <a4j:ajax>, for example. You can also set the mode attribute on a particular <rich:menuItem>, which will override the mode on the parent <rich:dropDownMenu> component.

You want to make each menu actually do something. We'll show you how to add an action listener for each menu. Just to demonstrate that a listener is actually called, you can display the menu name selected each time.

The changes are rather minor. You'll add an action listener to each menu item. This means you will need to create a managed bean first, so let's start with the code in Listing 8-9.

Listing 8-9. Creating a managed bean

```
@ManagedBean
@RequestScoped
public class DropDownBean {

    private String menuSelected;

    public String getMenuSelected() {
        return menuSelected;
    }
    public void listenerNew(ActionEvent event) {
        menuSelected = "New";
    }
    public void listenerOpenFile(ActionEvent event) {
        menuSelected = "Open File...";
    }
    public void listenerClose(ActionEvent event) {
        menuSelected = "Close";
    }
    public void listenerCloseAll(ActionEvent event) {
        menuSelected = "Close All";
    }
    public void listenerUndo(ActionEvent event) {
        menuSelected = "Undo";
    }
}
```

With the code in Listing 8-9, you have defined a listener for each menu item and also created a property to display the selected menu item that you'll display on a page. Let's see what changes are needed on the JSF page. The changes are shown in Listing 8-10.

Listing 8-10. JSF page

```
<h:form>
    <h:panelGrid columns="2">
        <rich:toolbar width="150px">
            <rich:dropDownMenu mode="ajax" label="File">
                <rich:menuItem label="New" actionListener="#{dropDownBean.listenerNew}"
                    render="menu" />
                <rich:menuItem label="Open File..." actionListener="#{dropDownBean.listener↵
                    OpenFile}"
                    render="menu" />
                <rich:menuItem label="Close" actionListener="#{dropDownBean.listenerClose}"
                    render="menu" />
                <rich:menuItem label="Close All" actionListener="#{dropDownBean.listenerCloseAll}"
                    render="menu" />
            </rich:dropDownMenu>
            <rich:dropDownMenu label="Edit" mode="ajax">
                <rich:menuItem label="Undo" actionListener="#{dropDownBean.listenerUndo}"
                    render="menu" />
            </rich:dropDownMenu>
            <rich:dropDownMenu label="Help">
                <rich:menuItem mode="ajax" label="About" />
            </rich:dropDownMenu>
        </rich:toolbar>
        <h:panelGroup id="menu">
            <h:outputText value="#{dropDownBean.menuSelected}" />
        </h:panelGroup>
    </h:panelGrid>
</h:form>
```

Every menu item has an action listener associated with it, and the menuSelected property is updated on selection to show what was selected. That's it!

Figure 8-8 shows what the page would look like after Edit ➤ Undo were selected. Now select File ➤ Open File, also as shown in Figure 8-8.

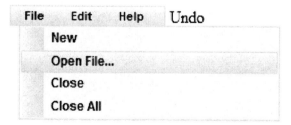

Figure 8-8. Label updated after Undo item selected

"Open File. . ." is now displayed on the right side of the menu, as shown in Figure 8-9.

File   Edit   Help   Open File...

Figure 8-9. Label updated after Open File item selected

> ■ **Note** In Listing 8-10, we used a different action listener for each menu item. We could also have used just one action listener for each menu, such as `actionListener="#{dropDownBean.select}"`. In this case we would need to use `ActionEvent` passed to the listener to determine which component activated. It's also possible to use `action` to invoke a method on the server. `action` can also be used for navigation.

You have left the About menu item in the Help menu without any action. Let's use what we have already covered and use client mode to open a modal popup when Help ➤ About is selected.

First, you need to create the popup panel, as done in Listing 8-11.

Listing 8-11. Creating a popup panel

```
<rich:popupPanel id="about">
    <f:facet name="header">
        <h:panelGroup>
            <h:graphicImage value="/images/icons/yellow_lamp.gif" />
            <h:outputText value="About" />
        </h:panelGroup>
    </f:facet>
    <h:panelGrid>
        <h:outputText value="About text goes here" />
        <a href="#" onclick="#{rich:component('about')}.hide();return false">OK </a>
    </h:panelGrid>
</rich:popupPanel>
```

Next, you need to open the menu when Help ➤ About is selected. That's pretty simple to do. Just change the About menu item declaration to the next, as follows:

```
<rich:menuItem mode="client" label="About" onclick="#{rich:component('about')}.show();" />
```

`#{rich:component('about')}.show()` is used to show the popup. Running the application will produce what you see in Figure 8-10 when Help ➤ About is selected.

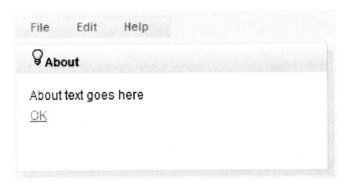

Figure 8-10. Popup opened on menu-item click

Now let's add some icons to our menu items. `<rich:menuItem>` provides `icon` and `iconDisabled` attribute for that purpose. A simple usage is shown in Listing 8-12.

Listing 8-12. Adding icons to the menu items

```
<rich:toolbar width="150px">
    <rich:dropDownMenu mode="ajax" label="File">
        <rich:menuItem label="New" icon="/images/icons/new.gif" />
        <rich:menuItem label="Open File..." icon="/images/icons/open.gif" />
        <rich:menuItem label="Save" icon="/images/icons/save.gif" />
        <rich:menuItem label="Save All" icon="/images/icons/save_all.gif" />
    </rich:dropDownMenu>
</rich:toolbar>
```

The result is shown in Figure 8-11.

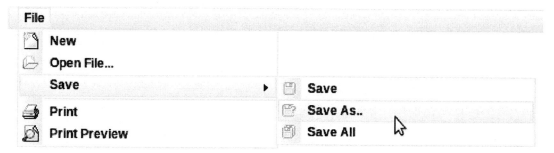

Figure 8-11. Menu items with icons

Using <rich:menuGroup> and <rich:menuSeparator>

There are two more components available for rich menu creation: `<rich:menuGroup>` and
`<rich:menuSeparator>`.

`<rich:menuGroup>` allows you to define a sub-menu and `<rich:separator>` allows you to add a
horizontal line separator between two items. Note that menu groups could be nested as needed. Using
these components, you will be able to create menus of any depth and complexity. Let's look at the
example in Figure 8-12.

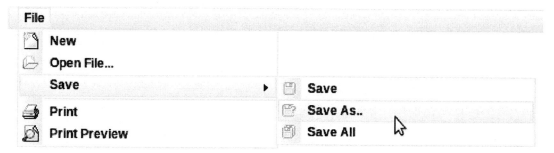

Figure 8-12. Complex menu with nested sub-menus and items separators

The code for this menu creation is shown in Listing 8-13.

Listing 8-13. Code for creating complex menu

```
<rich:toolbar>
    <rich:dropDownMenu mode="ajax" label="File">
        <rich:menuItem label="New" icon="/images/icons/new.gif" />
        <rich:menuItem label="Open File..." icon="/images/icons/open.gif" />
        <rich:menuGroup label="Save">
            <rich:menuItem label="Save" icon="/images/icons/save.gif" />
            <rich:menuItem label="Save As.." icon="/images/icons/save_as.gif" />
            <rich:menuItem label="Save All" icon="/images/icons/save_all.gif" />
        </rich:menuGroup>
        <rich:menuSeparator />
        <rich:menuItem label="Print" icon="/images/icons/print.gif"/>
        <rich:menuItem label="Print Preview" icon="/images/icons/print_preview.gif"/>
    </rich:dropDownMenu>
</rich:toolbar>
```

Using <rich:menuItem> as a Standalone Component

<rich:menuItem> is not only used to construct the menu items for <rich:dropDownMenu>, but can also be used as a standalone component. You are probably wondering when and why you would use it.

Let's say you are using a toolbar, but in addition to menus you also want to place other items, such as About link—which is just a top level link, without menu popups. In such case you can place a link inside the toolbar as we showed in the <rich:toolbar> section. But, at the same time, you want it to look consistent with other items in the menu. So, you would have to add styling and hover CSS selectors. You would also need to add an icon and align it with the link. That's probably a better job for a composite component. Going back to <rich:menuItem>, being able to use this component as a standalone, we can achieve the same functionality without doing any extra work. An example is shown in Figure 8-13.

Figure 8-13. Menu items in toolbar

The very simple code that creates such a toolbar is shown in Listing 8-14.

Listing 8-14. Simple code to create toolbar

```
<rich:toolbar width="100px;">
    <rich:menuItem label="New" icon="/images/icons/new.gif" />
    <rich:menuItem label="Open File..." icon="/images/icons/open.gif" />
</rich:toolbar>
```

Using Menu Components JavaScript API

<rich:dropDownMenu> provides JavaScript API, as shown in Table 8-1.

Table 8-1. <rich:dropDownMenu> JavaScript API

Method Name	Description
show()	Used to show the menu.
hide()	Used to hide the menu.
activateItem(itemClientId)	Used to activate one of the menu items with the *menuItemId* identifier. Useful for hot-key implementation.

`<rich:menuItem>` provides a single `activate()` method that can be useful to call directly if used as a standalone component.

Using <rich:panelMenu>

`<rich:panelMenu>` builds a vertical, collapsible menu with any depth level. Let's look at Figure 8-14.

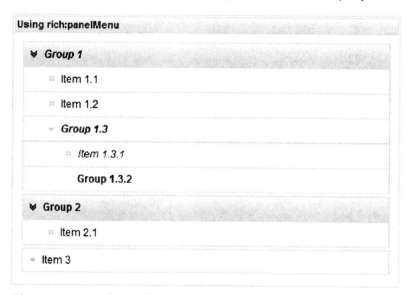

Figure 8-14. Simple panel menu

To start building this menu, you first start with `<rich:panelMenu>`, which acts as the main container for all menu items or nodes. Inside the container, you can place any number of menu items (`<rich:panelMenuItem>`) or groups (`<rich:panelMenuGroup>`). Each group in turn can have many menu items or additional groups, and so on. There is no limit to the depth of the menu that you can create.

Listing 8-15 shows the code for creation of the menu shown in Figure 8-14.

Listing 8-15. Shows code for simple panel menu

```
<h:form>
    <rich:panel style="width:450px" header="Using rich:panelMenu">
        <rich:panelMenu mode="ajax" topItemLeftIcon="disc" itemLeftIcon="grid"
            topGroupExpandedLeftIcon="chevronDown" groupExpandedLeftIcon="triangleDown"
            expandSingle="false">
            <rich:panelMenuGroup label="Group 1">
                <rich:panelMenuItem label="Item 1.1" />
                <rich:panelMenuItem label="Item 1.2" />
                <rich:panelMenuGroup label="Group 1.3">
                    <rich:panelMenuItem label="Item 1.3.1" />
                    <rich:panelMenuGroup label="Group 1.3.2">
                        <rich:panelMenuItem label="Item 1.3.2.1" />
                    </rich:panelMenuGroup>
                </rich:panelMenuGroup>
            </rich:panelMenuGroup>
            <rich:panelMenuGroup label="Group 2">
                <rich:panelMenuItem label="Item 2.1" />
            </rich:panelMenuGroup>
            <rich:panelMenuItem label="Item 3" />
        </rich:panelMenu>
    </rich:panel>
</h:form>
```

You can use a facet with the label name instead of the corresponding attribute in `<rich:panelMenuGroup>`. The content of `<rich:panelMenuItem>` could be customized using any other nested components. The code in Listing 8-16 will render the same menu shown in Figure 8-14.

Listing 8-16. Code to render the menu shown in Figure 8-14

```
<h:form>
    <rich:panelMenu mode="ajax" topItemLeftIcon="disc" itemLeftIcon="grid"
        topGroupExpandedLeftIcon="chevronDown" groupExpandedLeftIcon="triangleDown"
        expandSingle="false">
        <rich:panelMenuGroup>
            <f:facet name="label">
                <h:outputText value="Group 1" />
            </f:facet>
            <rich:panelMenuItem>
                <h:outputText value="Item 1.1" />
            </rich:panelMenuItem>
            <rich:panelMenuItem>
                <h:outputText value="Item 1.2" />
            </rich:panelMenuItem>
            ...
        </rich:panelMenuGroup>
        ...
    </rich:panelMenu>
</h:form>
```

Note the expandSingle attribute used at `<rich:panelMenu>`. If it's set to true, only one group at the same level could be expanded and the next expansion will collapse the previous one. We set it to false there so you could see both top groups opened.

The next interesting attribute is bubbleSelection. If it's set to true, all the parent groups will be visually highlighted if some child item is selected. In other cases only the currently selected menu item will be selected.

Any group or item can be disabled using the disabled="true" declaration.

One last feature related to the look and feel of the component is using the icon attributes. Looking at Figure 8-14, you can see that the groups and items at the higher level are displayed with a special look and feel that is different from the look and feel of their children groups and items (a separate style and icon attributes were used for top level and nested items and groups). Also, groups and items can have both right- and left-side icons and can also have different ones for all the states—collapsed, expanded and disabled. Because the number of attributes to customize this is rather large, see the RichFaces Reference Guide at www.jboss.org/richfaces/docs, or just use your IDE content assist to find all the available attributes. Icon attributes can be defined with the standard icons mentioned in Chapter 6 (we already used them in the earlier example) and, of course, defined with URI to custom icons. An example using icons is shown in Figure 8-15.

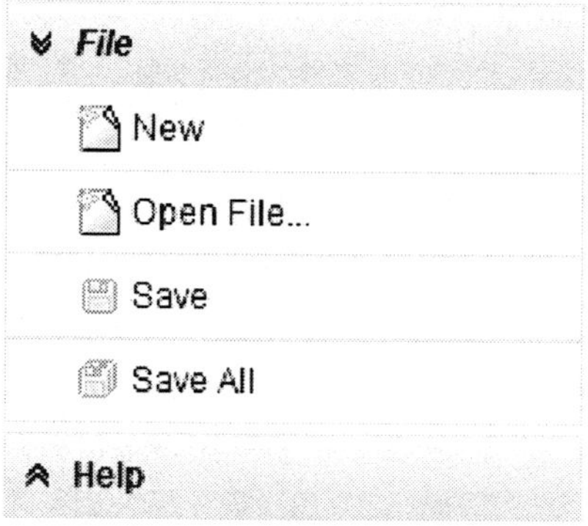

Figure 8-15. Panel menu with both standard and custom icons used

The code to create the menu in Figure 8-15 is shown in Listing 8-17. We used standard RichFaces icons for top groups and custom ones for items.

Listing 8-17. Code to create the menu in Figure 8-15

```
<h:form>
    <rich:panelMenu topGroupCollapsedLeftIcon="chevronUp" width="200px"
        topGroupExpandedLeftIcon="chevronDown">
        <rich:panelMenuGroup label="File">
            <rich:panelMenuItem label="New" leftIcon="/images/icons/new.gif"/>
            <rich:panelMenuItem label="Open File..." leftIcon="/images/icons/new.gif"/>
            <rich:panelMenuItem label="Save" leftIcon="/images/icons/save.gif"/>
            <rich:panelMenuItem label="Save All" leftIcon="/images/icons/save_all.gif" />
        </rich:panelMenuGroup>
        <rich:panelMenuGroup label="Help">
            <rich:panelMenuItem label="About" leftIcon="/images/icons/yellow_lamp.gif" />
        </rich:panelMenuGroup>
    </rich:panelMenu>
</h:form>
```

Invoking User Actions for Groups and Items

Let's finish with UI related features review and proceed with functional part of the component. Items and groups could be configured to use different modes. Let's check the attributes available on <rich:panelMenu> component in Table 8-2.

Table 8-2. Mode Attributes of the Panel Menu

Name	Description
groupMode	Specifies the mode for groups' expansion. Possible values are server, ajax and client. Client mode used by default.
itemMode	Specifies the mode for item activation. Possible values are server, ajax and client. Ajax mode is used by default.

Modes could be defined for all the groups and items at panel level, but could also be redefined for a particular group or item using the mode attribute on the group or item tag.

Let's also review server-side events and listeners provided by the components shown in Table 8-3.

Table 8-3. Server-Side Events and Listener Attributes of Panel Menu Components

Component	Event	Listener attributes
<rich:panelMenu>	ItemChangeEvent	itemChangeListener
<rich:panelMenuGroup>	ActionEvent	action/actionListener
<rich:panelMenuItem>	ActionEvent	action/actionListener

That's enough theory—now we will build an example of using server-side actions and listeners for the component. We will use the code that is pretty similar to one that we used in the <rich:dropDownMenu> section. Let's take a look at the page code in Listing 8-18.

Listing 8-18. The page code

```
<h:form>
    <h:panelGrid columns="2">
        <rich:panelMenu topGroupCollapsedLeftIcon="chevronUp" width="200px"
            topGroupExpandedLeftIcon="chevronDown">
            <rich:panelMenuGroup selectable="true" mode="ajax" label="File" render="menu"
                action="#{panelMenuBean.listenerFileGroup}">
                <rich:panelMenuItem label="New" leftIcon="/images/icons/new.gif"
                    actionListener="#{panelMenuBean.listenerNew}" render="menu" />
                <rich:panelMenuItem label="Open File..." leftIcon="/images/icons/new.gif"
                    actionListener="#{panelMenuBean.listenerOpenFile}" render="menu" />
                <rich:panelMenuItem label="Save" leftIcon="/images/icons/save.gif"
                    actionListener="#{panelMenuBean.listenerSave}" render="menu" />
                <rich:panelMenuItem label="Save All" leftIcon="/images/icons/save_all.gif"
```

```
                    actionListener="#{panelMenuBean.listenerSaveAll}" render="menu" />
            </rich:panelMenuGroup>
            <rich:panelMenuGroup label="Help">
                <rich:panelMenuItem label="About" leftIcon="/images/icons/yellow_lamp.gif" />
            </rich:panelMenuGroup>
        </rich:panelMenu>
        <h:panelGroup id="menu">
            <h:outputText value="#{panelMenuBean.menuSelected}" />
        </h:panelGroup>
    </h:panelGrid>
</h:form>
```

The managed bean code is shown in Listing 8-19.

Listing 8-19. The managed bean code

```
@ManagedBean
@RequestScoped
public class PanelMenuBean {

    private String menuSelected;

    public String getMenuSelected() {
        return menuSelected;
    }

    public PanelMenuBean() {
    }

    public void listenerNew(ActionEvent event) {
        menuSelected = "New";
    }

    public void listenerOpenFile(ActionEvent event) {
        menuSelected = "Open File...";
    }

    public void listenerSave(ActionEvent event) {
        menuSelected = "Save";
    }

    public void listenerSaveAll(ActionEvent event) {
        menuSelected = "Save All";
    }

    public void listenerFileGroup() {
        menuSelected = "File Group";
    }
}
```

Basically we are just storing the label of the group or item activated and updating it on the page. The result after expanding the File group is shown in Figure 8-16.

File Group

Figure 8-16. *Label updated after File group expansion*

The result of the Open File menu item activation is shown in Figure 8-17.

Open File...

Figure 8-17. *Label updated after Open File menu item activation*

There is one more interesting attribute that influences menu behavior as well as its look and feel. selectable="true" in the File group means that the group will function as an item when selected and any previously selected item will be cleared. The activeItem attribute, which holds the currently selected item, will be set to the selected group name. In other words group became not just item's container but also a higher level item.

When would you use this? It's useful when expanding the group updates on some part of the page with group-related content. And when clicking a item in this group, it will show updated content specific to that item. If selectable is set to *false*, the group will still expand and collapse, but the action or listener on the group will not be invoked and the activeItem attribute will not be set to that menu group name after the group expansion. In other words, only item could be stored in the model as active in case group has selectable="false". A group simply becomes an item container in such case.

In Chapter 6 we showed you how to manage currently selected item using the activeItem attribute. It should be set to some menu group name (if groups are selectable) or some menu item name. Also, for the groups you could use the expanded attribute to control its current state (if true, the group will be rendered expanded). Both attributes support EL so you could easily manage the <rich:panelMenu> state in your actions.

Listings 8-20 and 8-21 show how the selected item or group could be defined.

Listing 8-20. Defining a group

```
<rich:panelMenu activeItem="fileGroup">
    ...
    <rich:panelMenuGroup name="fileGroup" selectable="true" label="File">
    ...
```

Listing 8-21. Defining an item

```
<rich:panelMenu activeItem="aboutItem">
    ...
    <rich:panelMenuItem name="aboutItem" label="About">
    ...
```

The expansion state could be controlled in the same manner, as follows:

```
<rich:panelMenuGroup expanded="true" label="File">
```

As we've already done in drop-down menu section, let's add an About item that is using client mode with a client-side action. We have no handlers defined for the menu item in the previous sample. So let's modify it, as shown in Listing 8-22.

Listing 8-22. Modifying the menu items

```
<rich:panelMenuGroup label="Help">
    <rich:panelMenuItem label="About" leftIcon="/images/icons/yellow_lamp.gif" mode="client"
        onclick="#{rich:component('about')}.show()"/>
</rich:panelMenuGroup>
```

And we should add the popup to the page, as shown in Listing 8-23.

Listing 8-23. Adding the popup to the page

```
<rich:popupPanel id="about" header="About">
    <h:outputText value="That popup opened from &lt;rich:panelMenuItem&gt; component. " />
    <h:commandLink value="Hide" onclick="#{rich:component('about')}.hide();return false;"/>

</rich:popupPanel>
```

The result of clicking the About menu item is shown in Figure 8-18.

Figure 8-18. Popup panel opened from panel menu

Using Panel Menu Components JavaScript API

`<rich:panelMenu>` provides JavaScript API, as shown in Table 8-4.

Table 8-4. <rich:panelMenu> JavaScript API

Method Name	Description
collapseAll	Used to collapse all the menu groups.
expandAll	Used to expand all the menu groups.
selectItem(itemId)	Used to set new selection

`<rich:panelMenuGroup>` provides JavaScript API, as shown in Table 8-5.

Table 8-5. <rich:panelGroup> JavaScript API

Method Name	Description
collapse	Used to collapse the menu group.
expand	Used to expand the menu group.
select	Used to select the group if it's defined as selectable.

`<rich:panelMenuItem>` provides only `select()` method, which is used to select an item.

Summary

This chapter covered various RichFaces menu components. We used them in different modes for calling some server-side actions and performing simple JavaScript calls. Any time a menu item fires an Ajax request, all the basic principles we covered for `<a4j:ajax>`, such as render, execute, and client queue usage, apply as well.

Even though `<rich:contextMenu>` is not available at the time of writing, it will surely be added in a future RichFaces release. Check the JBoss Community RichFaces site at `www.jboss.org/richfaces` for updates.

Rich Tree Components

Trees are ideal components to represent hierarchical data. They are one of the most popular complex components in any UI library (probably next to tables). Trees are very useful for building menus, building hierarchical filters, and so on. RichFaces tree components provide everything you need to represent data in a tree-like structure. This chapter will explain the basics and provide advanced examples using RichFaces tree components.

Using <rich:tree>

<rich:tree> is an implementation of a common component designed to display hierarchical data. As any other JSF iteration component, it has to be bound to a model that provides the data for the tree. Figure 9-1 shows the tree component in action.

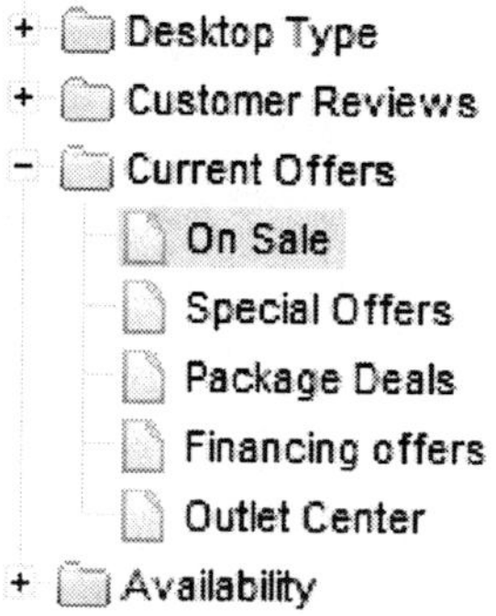

Figure 9-1. A simple RichFaces tree

One thing to keep in mind is that this component can't be designed in a static way simply from page code (putting a component on a page without binding to a model is usually possible with other components). The ability to place the component on a page without binding to a data model could be added to RichFaces in the future.

Creating a Tree Model Based on the Swing TreeNode Interface

Let's start with data model creation. If you ever used Swing's javax.swing.tree.TreeNode, then you already know how to create a model for the RichFaces tree component. Let's start with Swing tree node support and explore RichFaces' proprietary org.richfaces.model.TreeNode interface in upcoming sections.

■ **Note** If you have a project where data is organized using Swing's TreeNode, you should be able to use the data and classes from the project here.

Let's create a simple SwingTreeNodeImpl class that implements a javax.swing.tree.TreeNode interface. Listing 9-1 shows the class.

Listing 9-1. Shows the class

```
public class SwingTreeNodeImpl implements TreeNode {
    private List<SwingTreeNodeImpl> childNodes;
    private String data;

    // Getters and setters

    public SwingTreeNodeImpl(String data) {
        super();
        this.data = data;
    }
    public void addChild(SwingTreeNodeImpl child) {
        if (child != null) {
            if (childNodes == null) {
                childNodes = new ArrayList<SwingTreeNodeImpl>();
            }
            childNodes.add(child);
        }
    }
    @Override
    public TreeNode getChildAt(int childIndex) {
        return (childNodes == null) ? null : childNodes.get(childIndex);
    }
    @Override
    public int getChildCount() {
        return (childNodes == null) ? null : childNodes.size();
    }
    @Override
    public TreeNode getParent() {
        return null;
    }
    @Override
    public int getIndex(TreeNode node) {
        return (childNodes == null) ? null : childNodes.indexOf(node);
```

```
    }
    @Override
    public boolean getAllowsChildren() {
        return true;
    }
    @Override
    public boolean isLeaf() {
        return (childNodes == null);
    }
    @Override
    public Enumeration children() {
        return Iterators.asEnumeration(childNodes.iterator());
    }
    @Override
    public String toString() {
        return data;
    }
}
```

If you are familiar with TreeNode, then this code should be self-explanatory. Every node has a list that stores child nodes and a simple string data field that contains information on that node. All other methods are implementation methods of the TreeNode interface and return all the needed information to process the node and allow data modifications.

___

■ **Note** Instead of implementing the Swing TreeNode, you can also extend the default

org.richfaces.model.SwingTreeNodeImpl<T> implementation provided by RichFaces.

___

Now that we have covered tree node implementation, let's look at Listing 9-2 to see how we can populate the tree shown in SwingTreeNodeBean.

Listing 9-2. Populate the tree shown in SwingTreeNodeBean

```
@ManagedBean
@ViewScoped
public class SwingTreeNodeBean {

    List<SwingTreeNodeImpl> rootNodes = null;

    public void initNodes() {
        rootNodes = new ArrayList<SwingTreeNodeImpl>();
        SwingTreeNodeImpl node = new SwingTreeNodeImpl("Desktop Type");
        node.addChild(new SwingTreeNodeImpl("Compact"));
        node.addChild(new SwingTreeNodeImpl("Everyday"));
        node.addChild(new SwingTreeNodeImpl("Gaming"));
        node.addChild(new SwingTreeNodeImpl("Premium"));
        rootNodes.add(node);
        node = new SwingTreeNodeImpl("Customer Reviews");
        node.addChild(new SwingTreeNodeImpl("Top Rated"));
        rootNodes.add(node);
```

```
        node = new SwingTreeNodeImpl("Current Offers");
        node.addChild(new SwingTreeNodeImpl("On Sale"));
        node.addChild(new SwingTreeNodeImpl("Special Offers"));
        node.addChild(new SwingTreeNodeImpl("Package Deals"));
        node.addChild(new SwingTreeNodeImpl("Financing offers"));
        node.addChild(new SwingTreeNodeImpl("Outlet Center"));
        rootNodes.add(node);
        node = new SwingTreeNodeImpl("Availability");
        node.addChild(new SwingTreeNodeImpl("In store & Online"));
        node.addChild(new SwingTreeNodeImpl("Online only"));
        rootNodes.add(node);
    }
    public void setRootNodes(List<SwingTreeNodeImpl> rootNodes) {
        this.rootNodes = rootNodes;
    }
    public List<SwingTreeNodeImpl> getRootNodes() {
        if (rootNodes == null){
            initNodes();
        }
        return rootNodes;
    }
}
```

Now that we have the data initialized, let's see the RichFaces tree in action. Listing 9-3 shows the page code for displaying the tree.

Listing 9-3. Page code for displaying the tree

```
<h:form>
    <rich:tree value="#{swingTreeNodeBean.rootNodes}" var="node" />
</h:form>
```

Pretty simple isn't it? The tree rendered is shown in Figure 9-2.

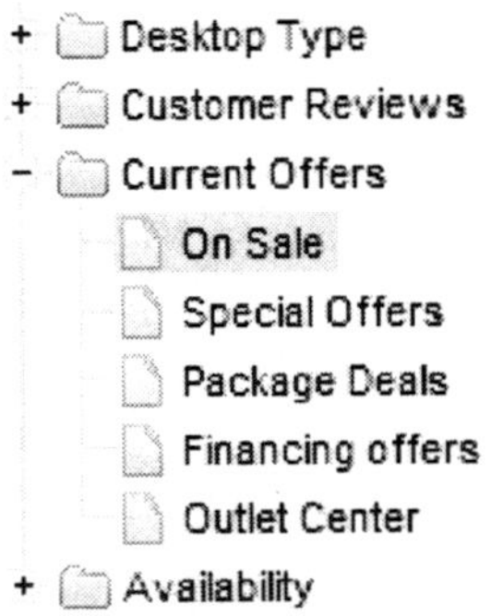

+ ☐ Desktop Type
+ ☐ Customer Reviews
− ☐ Current Offers
    ☐ On Sale
    ☐ Special Offers
    ☐ Package Deals
    ☐ Financing offers
    ☐ Outlet Center
+ ☐ Availability

Figure 9-2. <rich:tree> built using Swing TreeNode

Note that we don't need to define any markup for tree nodes. The tree is rendered using default implementation and with the help of the SwingTreeNodeImpl toString() method, it returns a string value for the node name. That's fine when you are just getting started, but still would like to have more flexibility in defining tree nodes such as binding to a different property in the node data model object.

Creating a Tree Model Based on the RichFaces TreeNode Interface

RichFaces also supports the `org.richfaces.model.TreeNode` interface and provides default implementation for this interface. Listing 9-4 shows the interface.

Listing 9-4. The `org.richfaces.model.TreeNode` interface

```java
public interface TreeNode {
    public TreeNode getChild(Object key);
    public int indexOf(Object key);
    public Iterator<Object> getChildrenKeysIterator();
    public boolean isLeaf();
    public void addChild(Object key, TreeNode child);
    public void insertChild(int idx, Object key, TreeNode child);
    public void removeChild(Object key);
}
```

Assuming you already read about the RichFaces data iteration components in Chapter 7, you should notice the main difference between that interface and Swing's. It uses a key–child node relation instead of an index–child node relation. It's similar to the `<rich:dataTable>` row key–row data relation explained in the data models section in Chapter 7. As you remember, all the iteration components in RichFaces, including complex components like trees, use `ExtendedDataModel` as the base abstract model and uses `rowKeys` to identify the data in the model. That makes the components better integrated with the database layer. Actually, even when defining the Swing-based model you are still using `ExtendedDataModel` under the hood, as the tree automatically wraps your model to it.

Let's return to the code. This time we will not work on all interface methods implementation. Instead we will extend default `TreeNodeImpl` implementation, as shown in Listing 9-5.

Listing 9-5. Extend default `TreeNodeImpl` implementation

```java
public class RichFacesTreeNode extends TreeNodeImpl {

    private String data;

    public RichFacesTreeNode(String data) {
        super();
        this.data = data;
    }
    public String getData() {
        return data;
    }
    public void setData(String data) {
        this.data = data;
    }
    @Override
    public String toString() {
        return data;
    }

}
```

■ **Note** We will be using the RichFaces TreeNode object across all the samples in the remainder of the chapter.

Listing 9-6 shows a bean in which we populate the tree. It looks very similar to the one we created using the Swing tree model.

Listing 9-6. Shows a bean used to populate the tree

```
@ManagedBean
@ViewScoped
public class RichFacesTreeNodeBean {

    private TreeNode rootNode = null;

    public void initNodes() {
        rootNode = new TreeNodeImpl();
        RichFacesTreeNode node = new RichFacesTreeNode("Desktop Type");
        node.addChild("1_1",new RichFacesTreeNode("Compact"));
        node.addChild("1_2",new RichFacesTreeNode("Everyday"));
        node.addChild("1_3",new RichFacesTreeNode("Gaming"));
        node.addChild("1_4",new RichFacesTreeNode("Premium"));
        rootNode.addChild("1",node);
        // other initialization code
    }

    public void setRootNode(TreeNode rootNode) {
        this.rootNode = rootNode;
    }

    public TreeNode getRootNode() {
        if (rootNode == null) {
            initNodes();
        }
        return rootNode;
    }
}
```

The RichFaces TreeNode-based model should have the only root node (the Swing model Collection of root nodes was supported as value binding). It is not an actual root, but simply a fake node that is not getting rendered to the view, and so should not contain any data. It's only a placeholder for the set of child nodes that will be the actual set of root nodes (it's designed this way to support backward compatibility with previous RichFaces version).

Listing 9-7 shows the page, which still looks very simple.

Listing 9-7. The simple page

```
<h:form>
    <rich:tree value="#{richFacesTreeNodeBean.rootNode}" var="node"/>
</h:form>
```

The tree rendered is shown in Figure 9-3.

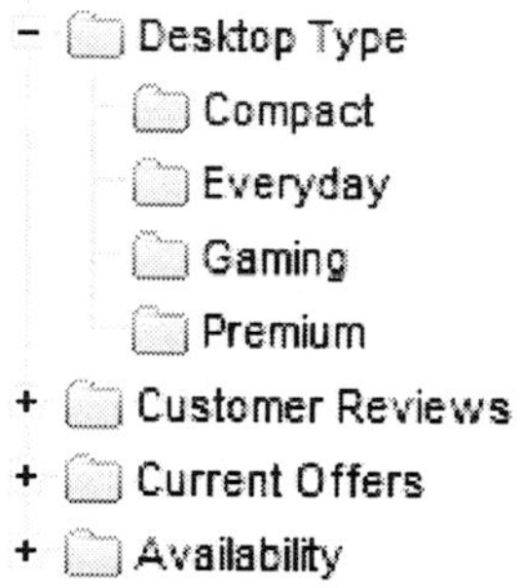

Figure 9-3. *<rich:tree> built using the RichFaces TreeNode*

You are probably curious why the leaf nodes have the same representation as the nodes with children and are not shown as leafs? That's how it's designed. When we implemented Swing's TreeNode interface, we implemented the isLeaf() method to return a boolean value, which determines if the collection is empty. RichFaces default Swing node implementation does the same.

On the other hand, org.richfaces.model.TreeNodeImpl doesn't make the decision if the node is a leaf according to the presence of its children. It has to be defined with a flag passed to the constructor or have its isLeaf() method properly overridden. This is done to allow the developers to manually specify the leaf node property if the developer wants to implement lazy node loading or just needs to have an empty nodes representation. Thus, a node can have no children initialized, but have isLeaf() returning true by default. We will show you a little later how to initialize the RichFaces TreeNodeImpl to be a leaf.

Using <rich:treeNode> to Define Tree Nodes Markup

Let's see now how we can replace using the toString() method and encode iteration object properties instead. We just need to add a <rich:treeNode> object to the <rich:tree> and define the content of the node inside using the var attribute in the same way as the <rich:column> content inside tables. Then every node will be rendered using that markup. In order to create the same representation but which does not rely on the toString() method, we only make changes to the page code. Listing 9-8 shows the page code.

Listing 9-8. *The page code*

```
<h:form>
  <rich:tree value="#{richFacesTreeNodeBean.rootNode}" var="node">
    <rich:treeNode>
      #{node.data}
    </rich:treeNode>
  </rich:tree>
</h:form>
```

Using this code, we get the tree rendered in Figure 9-4.

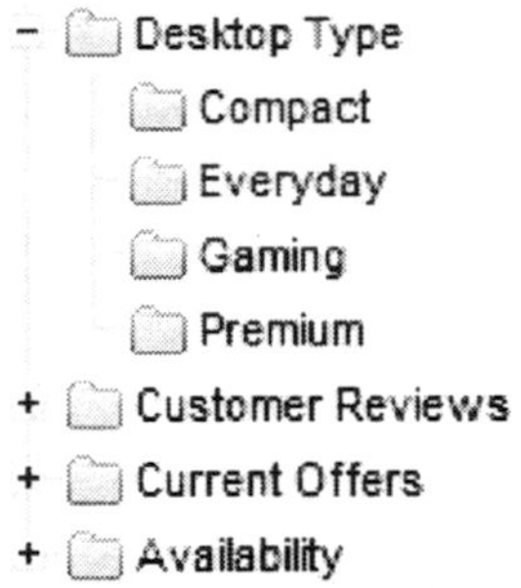

- ☐ Desktop Type
  - ☐ Compact
  - ☐ Everyday
  - ☐ Gaming
  - ☐ Premium
+ ☐ Customer Reviews
+ ☐ Current Offers
+ ☐ Availability

Figure 9-4. Creating a custom node using <rich:treeNode>

Using <rich:treeNode> allows you to place outputs such as links, images, formatted text, and so on. The next section will introduce you to another feature of the <rich:treeNode> and demonstrate different ways to render nodes.

Using Different Types of Nodes in a Tree

Suppose we need to show the nodes in a different way according to some conditions or properties of the model node. <rich:tree> easily allows you to do that. <rich:treeNode> provides the type attribute, which should be used for that purpose. All you need to do to use different kinds of nodes is add a property to the node's model objects, which will identify the node type. It could be any property with any values. Then you need to add a set of <rich:treeNode> components as child components to the <rich:tree> with the type attributes defined according to possible model types. Finally, define the markups inside every <rich:treeNode>.

In order to make a decision about which node should be rendered for the current iteration, the <rich:tree> component provides the nodeType attribute. You should use it to define the property on the node that stores its type. Or, alternatively, use a simple EL expression that will be evaluated to possible types.

In the previous sample we added a single string data property to our RichFacesTreeNode, which was used to represent a node on the client. Now let's add another property that will identify the node type, as shown in Listing 9-9.

Listing 9-9. Adding another property that will identify the node type

```
public class TypifiedRichFacesTreeNode extends TreeNodeImpl {
    private String data;
    private SimpleTreeNodeTypes type;

    public TypifiedRichFacesTreeNode(String data, SimpleTreeNodeTypes type) {
        super(type.equals(SimpleTreeNodeTypes.LEAF));
        this.data = data;
        this.type = type;
    }

    public String getData() {
        return data;
    }
```

```
    public void setData(String data) {
        this.data = data;
    }

    public SimpleTreeNodeTypes getType() {
        return type;
    }

    public void setType(SimpleTreeNodeTypes type) {
        this.type = type;
    }
}
```

■ **Note** TreeNodeImpl provides constructor with a leaf parameter. In our object, which extends TreeNodeImpl, we call super() passing the leaf parameter according to our type definition. So it will be properly rendered as a leaf by the component for the objects initialized with a true leaf value.

Listing 9-10 shows an Enum for note types.

Listing 9-10. Shows an Enum for note types

```
public enum SimpleTreeNodeTypes {
    NODE, LEAF
}
```

The modified bean that initializes data for the tree is shown in Listing 9-11.

Listing 9-11. The modified bean

```
@ManagedBean
@ViewScoped
public class TypifiedRichFacesTreeNodeBean {

    private TreeNode rootNode = null;

    public void initNodes() {
        rootNode = new TreeNodeImpl();

        TypifiedRichFacesTreeNode node = new TypifiedRichFacesTreeNode(
            "Desktop Type", SimpleTreeNodeTypes.NODE);
        node.addChild("1_1", new
            TypifiedRichFacesTreeNode("Compact",SimpleTreeNodeTypes.LEAF));
        node.addChild("1_2", new
            TypifiedRichFacesTreeNode("Everyday",SimpleTreeNodeTypes.LEAF));
        node.addChild("1_3", new
            TypifiedRichFacesTreeNode("Gaming",SimpleTreeNodeTypes.LEAF));
```

```
            node.addChild("1_4", new
                TypifiedRichFacesTreeNode("Premium",SimpleTreeNodeTypes.LEAF));
            rootNode.addChild("1", node);
            //Other nodes initialization
        }
        public void setRootNode(TreeNode rootNode) {
            this.rootNode = rootNode;
        }
        public TreeNode getRootNode() {
            if (rootNode == null) {
                initNodes();
            }
            return rootNode;
        }
    }
}
```

Notice that we don't need the toString() method anymore, as we are defining the representation using a set of nested <rich:treeNode> tags. Looking through Listing 9-12, notice the nodeType attribute of <rich:tree> and the type attribute defined on every <rich:treeNode>. This is the way to point the <rich:treeNode> to our model type for every iterated tree node.

Listing 9-12. Defining the representation using a set of nested <rich:treeNode> tags

```
<rich:tree value="#{typifiedRichFacesTreeNodeBean.rootNode}" var="node"
    nodeType="#{node.type}"
    toggleType="client" selectionType="client">
    <rich:treeNode type="NODE">
        <h:outputText value="#{node.data}" />
    </rich:treeNode>
    <rich:treeNode type="LEAF">
        <h:outputLink value="#">
            #{node.data}
        </h:outputLink>
    </rich:treeNode>
</rich:tree>
```

And finally, Figure 9-5 shows the result. Notice the links rendered at the second level opposite the plain text labels at the root nodes.

+ 🗀 Desktop Type
+ 🗀 Customer Reviews
+ 🗀 Current Offers
− 🗀 Availability
    🗋 In store & Online
    🗋 Online only

Figure 9-5. Different custom nodes within <rich:tree>

During data model iteration, the EL expression defined at the nodeType attribute is evaluated using the current object defined in the var attribute. A lookup is then performed for the node with the same type among nested components. If the node with a corresponding type is found, it will be used for node markup rendering. If the node is not found, the tree will lookup the node without the type specified, and it will become the default node for all the objects, which can't be associated with any type. If neither default node is found, the tree will create a default one, as was done in previous examples where <rich:treeNode> was not used.

▨ **Note**　If a `<rich:treeNode>` has the `rendered` attribute evaluated as `false` in context of an iteration, the node will not be rendered and no default nodes will be used or created.

Tree Toggling and Selection Modes

A RichFaces tree can be defined with different modes to be used while the user performs tree nodes expansion or selects a particular node. Table 9-1 shows the attributes that should be used to define the modes.

Table 9-1. Tree Node Selection Modes

Attribute	Description
toggleType	Defines the mode to be used for expanding/collapsing the tree node. Possible values are server, ajax, and client.
selectionType	Defines the selection mode. Possible values are server, ajax, and client.

　　`toggleType` defines how every tree node child will be loaded. With the `client` type, the complete tree will be rendered on page load and nodes toggling will be done through JavaScript (on the client). In `ajax` and `server` modes, `<rich:tree>` will perform form submission via Ajax or standard POST in order to load the child components when the tree nodes get expanded.

　　`selectionType` can be set to the similar values—client, ajax, server—but for the selection user action. We will use `ajax` `selectionType` in all the later samples created in order to show you different options for processing tree events on the server side.

▨ **Note**　`<rich:tree>` needs to be placed inside `<h:form>` to perform an Ajax (or standard) request.

▨ **Tip**　A popular question is how to implement a simple navigation tree that does not perform actions, but redirects to another view through simple links. Set `selectionType=client` and use `<h:outputLink>` as the tree node. The tree itself won't send an Ajax request, but you can navigate via `<h:outputLink>`.

Selection Event Handling

In a real application, in addition to rendering the tree, we also need to know how to handle the user action when a particular tree node is selected.

In addition to the selectionType definition we need to point the tree to a server-side listener method. <rich:tree> provides the selectionChangeListener attribute in order to do that. That attribute should be defined with the method expression and the method accepts TreeSelectionChangeEvent as a parameter. That event provides two methods that should be used in order to process selection: getOldSelection() and getNewSelection(). These methods return the collection of rowKeys to identify previous and new selections.

Listing 9-13 shows the tree definition with the listener defined.

Listing 9-13. *Shows the tree definition*

```
<h:form>
    <rich:tree value="#{richFacesTreeNodeBean.rootNode}" var="node" toggleType="client"
        selectionType="ajax"
            selectionChangeListener="#{richFacesTreeNodeBean.selectionChanged}">
        <rich:treeNode>
            #{node.data}
        </rich:treeNode>
    </rich:tree>
</h:form>
```

Now we will need to add some code to the RichFacesTreeNodeBean bean that will be used to process user selection. We will add the list in which we store selected objects, such as the panel and the listener method, as shown in Listing 9-14.

Listing 9-14. *The bean that will be used to process user selection*

```
private List<String> selection = new ArrayList<String>();

public void selectionChanged(TreeSelectionChangeEvent event){
    selection.clear();
    UITree tree = (UITree)event.getComponent();
    Object storedRowKey = tree.getRowKey();
    for (Object rowKey : event.getNewSelection()) {
        tree.setRowKey(rowKey);
        selection.add(((RichFacesTreeNode)tree.getRowData()).getData());
    }
    tree.setRowKey(storedRowKey);
}
```

Looks pretty straightforward, doesn't it? We are just iterating through a collection of rowKeys for newly-selected objects that are passed to the listener, getting the object from the tree model object that corresponds to that key, and placing its data into a result list.

■ **Note** In our example, getData() only returns the selected node object, but you can also get any other object property or complete object.

Now we just need to add a component that will iterate through the result list to show the selection on the page. We will use <a4j:repeat> for that, as Listing 9-15 shows.

Listing 9-15. Using <a4j:repeat>

```
<a4j:outputPanel layout="block" ajaxRendered="true">
    <rich:panel header="Current selection:" rendered="#{not empty
        richFacesTreeNodeBean.selection}">
        <a4j:repeat value="#{richFacesTreeNodeBean.selection}" var="nodeData">
            #{nodeData}
        </a4j:repeat>
    </rich:panel>
</a4j:outputPanel>
```

That's all for now. If the selection list is filled, the panel will be rendered and repeat defined inside that panel will iterate over the selection list. Figure 9-6 shows the result of the node selected.

Figure 9-6. Tree with nodes selection

■ **Note** event.getNewSelection() returns a Collection even though only single node selection is supported right now. This is done because a future version of the component should support multiple selections.

Expansion Event Handling

Next, let's add similar processing for nodes expansion or collapse. You just need to add toggleListener to the <rich:tree> page definition. Listing 9-16 shows a simple page used to create such a sample.

Listing 9-16. Adding toggleListener to the <rich:tree> page definition

```
<h:form>
    <rich:tree value="#{richFacesTreeNodeBean.rootNode}" var="node" toggleType="ajax"
        toggleListener="#{richFacesTreeNodeBean.nodeToggled}">
        <rich:treeNode>
            #{node.data}
        </rich:treeNode>
    </rich:tree>
</h:form>
```

We are using the same richFacesTreeNode bean that holds the tree constructed using the simple RichFacesTreeNode. We will add the property that will hold the data of the node that changed state, and the listener that will populate the data, as shown in Listing 9-17.

Listing 9-17. *Adding the listener that will populate the data*

```
private String toggledNodeData = null;

public void nodeToggled(TreeToggleEvent event) {
    toggledNodeData =
((RichFacesTreeNode)((UITree)event.getComponent()).getRowData()).getData();
}
```

Listing 9-18 shows an additional output component to show the changes in the page.

Listing 9-18. *Shows an additional output component to show the changes in the page*

```
<a4j:outputPanel layout="block" ajaxRendered="true">
    <h:outputText value="#{richFacesTreeNodeBean.toggledNodeData} has the state changed!"
        rendered="#{not empty richFacesTreeNodeBean.toggledNodeData}" />
</a4j:outputPanel>
```

Figure 9-7 shows the rendered result.

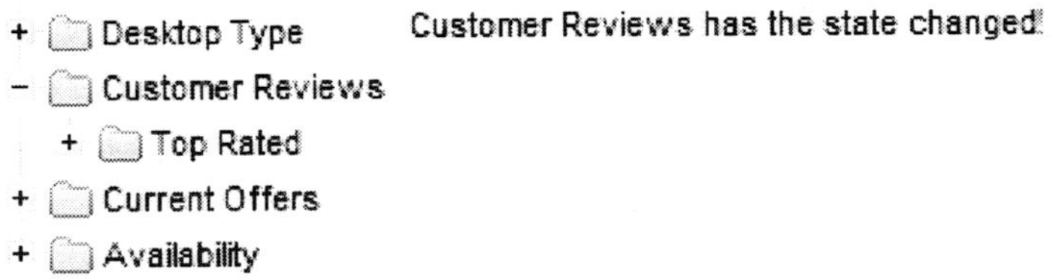

Figure 9-7. *Tree nodes toggling processing*

Tree Nodes Lazy Loading

Now let's create a more interesting sample where we handle node events. Let's implement simple lazy loading for the nodes when additional nodes get added to the model only on expansion of the parent node. This is a great example, as you will be able to apply these concepts when working with large data sets, such as getting data from a database or a from a remote service call.

First let's create the bean that holds the org.richfaces.model.TreeNode-based model, as shown in Listing 9-19.

Listing 9-19. *Creating the bean that holds the org.richfaces.model.TreeNode-based model*

```
@ManagedBean
@ViewScoped
public class LazyTreeBean {

    private TreeNode rootNode = null;

    public void initNodes() {
```

```
        rootNode = new TreeNodeImpl();
        RichFacesTreeNode node = new RichFacesTreeNode("Node 1");
        rootNode.addChild("1", node);
        node = new RichFacesTreeNode("Node 2");
        rootNode.addChild("2", node);
        node = new RichFacesTreeNode("Node 3");
        rootNode.addChild("3", node);
        node = new RichFacesTreeNode("Node 4");
        rootNode.addChild("4", node);
    }
    public void setRootNode(TreeNode rootNode) {
        this.rootNode = rootNode;
    }
    public TreeNode getRootNode() {
        if (rootNode == null) {
            initNodes();
        }
        return rootNode;
    }
}
```

As you can see, we're initially instantiating only four root nodes without any children. Now let's put a tree on a page that will use this data model, as shown in Listing 9-20.

Listing 9-20. Putting a tree on a page that will use this data model

```
<h:form>
    <rich:tree value="#{lazyTreeBean.rootNode}" var="node" toggleType="ajax">
        <rich:treeNode>
            #{node.data}
        </rich:treeNode>
    </rich:tree>
</h:form>
```

Figure 9-8 shows that when rendered, the tree will be shown as usual; but on node expansion nothing will be shown because the node is just a leaf without children.

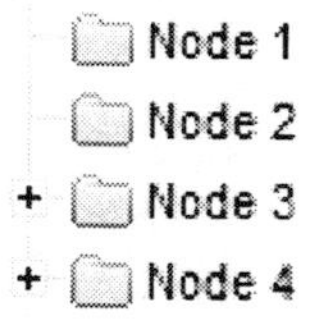

```
   📁 Node 1
   📁 Node 2
 + 📁 Node 3
 + 📁 Node 4
```

Figure 9-8. Tree without child nodes

Next, let's create a toggle listener that will add child nodes to the node that was expanded. The listener is shown in Listing 9-21.

Listing 9-21. Creating a toggle listener that will add child nodes

```
public void toggleListener(TreeToggleEvent event) {
    UITree tree = (UITree) event.getComponent();
    RichFacesTreeNode modelNode = (RichFacesTreeNode)tree.getRowData();
```

```
for (int i = 0; i < 5; i++) {
    RichFacesTreeNode node =
        new RichFacesTreeNode(modelNode.getData() + "." + i);
    modelNode.addChild(i, node);
  }
}
```

Notice that we are getting the UITree instance from the event and not the currently toggled node object. It's passed to the listener by design, as toggled node data could be easily accessed via the getRowData() method, but at the same time you have the option to operate with a complete tree instance using its API.

After we get the toggled node data object, we simply create five dummy child nodes and add them as child nodes to the current node. <rich:tree> will automatically mark the toggled node to be updated on the client, so we don't need to add any additional render definitions on the page. The only thing we need to do is point the tree component to the listener method.

```
<rich:tree ... toggleListener="#{lazyTreeBean.toggleListener}">
```

We are now ready to try this example. After opening the page and a few expand actions, you should see the result shown in Figure 9-9.

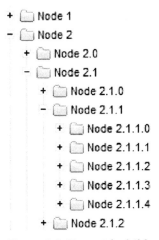

Figure 9-9. *Tree with child nodes lazy loaded*

This is really simple and could be easily used in any scenario in which you need to load new nodes during runtime.

Now let's proceed to the next sections, which describe declarative models usage.

Using <rich:tree> Adaptors to Build the Data Model

RichFaces provides two adaptors to construct <rich:tree> data model. Both <rich:treeModelRecursiveAdaptor> and <rich:treeModelAdaptor> allow you to point the tree to an existent, non-hierarchical data model declaratively. It means that if you already have a model that is Collection- or Map-based, you have no need to convert them manually into the hierarchical models in the way we showed earlier. You could easily use all that data to create a tree, as is, with the help of adaptor tags.

Using <rich:treeModelAdaptor>

<rich:treeModelAdaptor> allows you to point the tree to some Collection or Map with any objects and add them as a nodes to the tree model. It has a nodes attribute that's used to point the adaptor to the data. Tree could be defined with any number of adaptors at the same level, and adaptors can also be nested in order to define child nodes as needed.

Let's create an example. First, we will create the model that will store data in a List. Listing 9-22 shows the base object, which will define an abstract entity (we called it Entry) with a set of properties defined.

Listing 9-22. Shows an example of the base object

```
public class Entry {
    private String name;

    private List<String> properties;
    // Getters and setters

    public Entry(String name) {
        super();
        this.name = name;
    }

}
```

The class defines two properties: the properties list, representing a list of simple string properties related to an entry, and the name string, which stores the name of the entry. Next, in Listing 9-23, let's create the managed bean that will initialize the collection of entries and that we will use to build the tree.

Listing 9-23. The managed bean

```
@ManagedBean
@SessionScoped
public class DeclarativeTreeNodesBean {

    private List<Entry> entries = null;

    public void initEntries(){
        entries = new ArrayList<Entry>();

        Entry entry = new Entry("Desktop Type");
        List<String> childEntries = new ArrayList<String>();
        childEntries.add("Compact");
        childEntries.add("Everyday");
        childEntries.add("Gaming");
        childEntries.add("Premium");
        entry.setProperties(childEntries);
        entries.add(entry);

        entry = new Entry("Customer Reviews");
        childEntries = new ArrayList<String>();
        childEntries.add("Top Rated");
        entry.setProperties(childEntries);
```

```
        entries.add(entry);

        //More initialization stuff
    }
    public List<Entry> getEntries() {
        if (entries == null) {
            initEntries();
        }
        return entries;
    }
    public void setEntries(List<Entry> entries) {
        this.entries = entries;
    }
}
```

We have a list of Entry objects, and every Entry is initialized with its properties. We used the same data as from the previous example. In Listing 9-24, let's review the page code, which defines <rich:tree> and points it to the plain data model using <rich:treeModelAdaptor> tag.

Listing 9-24. Review the page code

```
<rich:tree var="node" toggleType="client">
    <rich:treeModelAdaptor nodes="#{declarativeTreeNodesBean.entries}">
        <rich:treeNode>
            #{node.name}
        </rich:treeNode>
        <rich:treeModelAdaptor nodes="#{node.properties}"/>
    </rich:treeModelAdaptor>
</rich:tree>
```

Figure 9-10 shows how it looks. Go ahead review the code more closely.

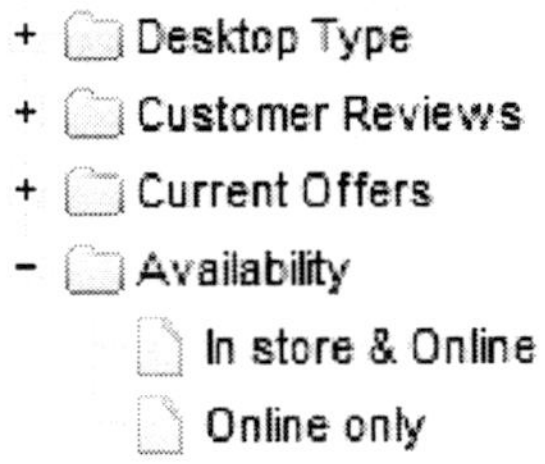

```
+  Desktop Type
+  Customer Reviews
+  Current Offers
-  Availability
       In store & Online
       Online only
```

Figure 9-10. Tree built using model adaptor

▪ **Note** The adaptor doesn't provide a var attribute. The <rich:tree> var variable can be used at any level.

That's definitely what we expected to see. Notice that we achieved the result by only using page tags and without any modifications at model level or without creation of any kind of TreeNode objects and storing them hierarchically.

Let's look at the page code again. The first <rich:treeModelAdaptor> iterates over our list of entries and constructs the first level of the tree. We are using <rich:treeNode> as usual in order to define the markup of the created tree nodes. In our case, we need to name the property of the Entry to be rendered as a node label.

As we mentioned before, adaptors could be nested without any restrictions. In our case, a nested adaptor iterates the list of properties for the currently iterated Entry. Properties objects are just string objects, so we have no need for it in <rich:treeNode> usage, as each will be only used as the labels.

Using <rich:treeModelRecursiveAdaptor>

<rich:treeModelRecursiveAdaptor> is an extension of a <rich:treeNodesAdaptor> component. According to the name, it provides a simple way to create a tree model iterating over an existing model recursively. It should be defined using two base attributes: the roots attribute defines the collection or map used at the top of the recursion, and the nodes is used to add nested nodes recursively.

The most common and probably most often used example for such model is the file system representation. We will show you how to create such a sample using the code, which has no tree-specific objects. The tree data model will again be automatically created by the component with the help of the adaptors tags.

In our example, we will get all the directories and file listings from our application web root folder. Listing 9-25 shows the code for the base FileSystem node class.

Listing 9-25. *Shows the code for the base* FileSystem *node class*

```
public class FileSystemNode {
    private String path;
    private List<FileSystemNode> directories;
    private List<String> files;
    private String shortPath;

    private static final Function<String, FileSystemNode> FACTORY =
        new Function<String, FileSystemNode>() {
            public FileSystemNode apply(String from) {
                return new FileSystemNode(from.substring(0, from.length() - 1));
            };
    };
    private static final Function<String, String> TO_SHORT_PATH = new
        Function<String, String>() {
        public String apply(String from) {
            int idx = from.lastIndexOf('/');
            if (idx < 0) {
                return from;
            }
            return from.substring(idx + 1);
        };
    };
    public FileSystemNode(String path) {
        this.path = path;
        int idx = path.lastIndexOf('/');
        if (idx != -1) {
```

```
                shortPath = path.substring(idx + 1);
            } else {
                shortPath = path;
            }
        }
    public synchronized List<FileSystemNode> getDirectories() {
        if (directories == null) {
            directories = Lists.newArrayList();
            Iterables.addAll(directories,
            Iterables.transform(Iterables.filter(getResourcePaths(),
Predicates.containsPattern("/$")),
                FACTORY));
        }
        return directories;
    }
    public synchronized List<String> getFiles() {
        if (files == null) {
            files = new ArrayList<String>();
            Iterables.addAll(files, Iterables.transform(
            Iterables.filter(getResourcePaths(),
                Predicates.not(Predicates.containsPattern("/$"))),
                TO_SHORT_PATH));
        }
        return files;
    }
    private Iterable<String> getResourcePaths() {
        FacesContext facesContext = FacesContext.getCurrentInstance();
        ExternalContext externalContext = facesContext.getExternalContext();
        Set<String> resourcePaths = externalContext.getResourcePaths(this.path);
        if (resourcePaths == null) {
            resourcePaths = Collections.emptySet();
        }
        return resourcePaths;
    }
    public String getShortPath() {
        return shortPath;
    }
}
```

The FileSystemNode object returns the list of directories and files at given levels and defines a set of utility methods used in order to transform path strings, providing simple representation for them. It uses Google's Guava libraries, which make working with collections much simpler. You can learn more about the project from Guava: Google Core Libraries for Java 1.5+ at http://code.google.com/p/guava-libraries.

The bean that defines the root level and operates with the FileSystemNode objects to get the file system structure starting from the root directory is shown in Listing 9-26.

Listing 9-26. The bean that defines the root level and operates with the FileSystemNode objects

```
@ManagedBean
@RequestScoped
public class FileSystemBean {

    private List<FileSystemNode> rootDirs;
```

```
    private List<String> rootFiles;
    private FileSystemNode rootNode = new FileSystemNode("/");

    public List<FileSystemNode> getRootDirs() {
        if (rootDirs == null) {
            rootDirs = rootNode.getDirectories();
        }
        return rootDirs;
    }
    public List<String> getRootFiles() {
        if (rootFiles == null) {
            rootFiles = rootNode.getFiles();
        }
        return rootFiles;
    }
}
```

Let's look at what we have. The bean returns a list of files and directories for the root level. Besides every FileSystemNode, which actually represents a directory, it's also possible to create a list of directories and files inside. Now we just need to reflect that in the <rich:tree> page definition using adaptor tags shown in Listing 9-27.

Listing 9-27. Create a list of directories and files inside

```
<rich:tree toggleType="client" var="item">
    <rich:treeModelRecursiveAdaptor roots="#{fileSystemBean.rootDirs}"
        nodes="#{item.directories}">
    <rich:treeNode>
      #{item.shortPath}
    </rich:treeNode>
        <rich:treeModelAdaptor nodes="#{item.files}">
        <rich:treeNode>#{item}</rich:treeNode>
    </rich:treeModelAdaptor>
  </rich:treeModelRecursiveAdaptor>
        <rich:treeModelAdaptor nodes="#{fileSystemBean.rootFiles}">
        <rich:treeNode>#{item}</rich:treeNode>
  </rich:treeModelAdaptor>
</rich:tree>
```

The recursive tree node adaptor defined first, iterates over the directories starting from rootDirs and recursively retrieving directories as defined in the nodes attribute. In addition to nested <rich:treeModelAdaptor>, adaptor iterates over the files inside every directory.

The second adapter, which is nested inside <rich:tree>, iterates over root-level directory files. Figure 9-11 shows the result after the tree gets rendered and we expanded a few nodes.

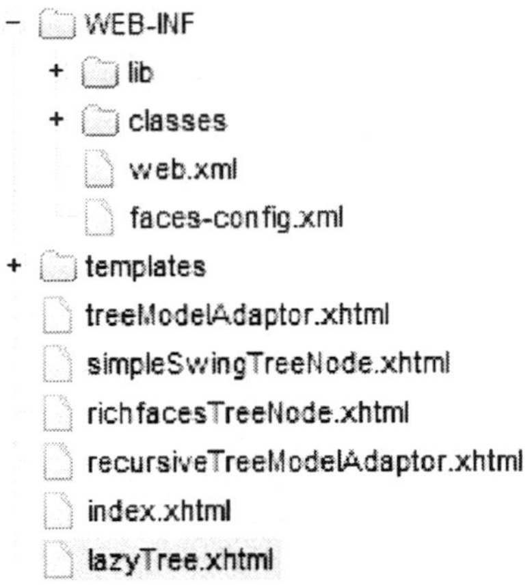

```
-  📁 WEB-INF
   +  📁 lib
   +  📁 classes
      📄 web.xml
      📄 faces-config.xml
+  📁 templates
   📄 treeModelAdaptor.xhtml
   📄 simpleSwingTreeNode.xhtml
   📄 richfacesTreeNode.xhtml
   📄 recursiveTreeModelAdaptor.xhtml
   📄 index.xhtml
   📄 lazyTree.xhtml
```

Figure 9-11. Tree built using the recursive model adaptor

■ **Note** As of writing of this book and the first release of RichFaces version 4.0, tree components don't provide JavaScript API. We anticipate such API will be added in a future RichFaces release.

Summary

This chapter covered one of the most important components in RichFaces: tree. Although also considered one of the most difficult to use (in any framework), RichFaces provides a number of features that make working with trees rather simple, but at the same time flexible and powerful.

RichFaces allows you to build and display a tree structure based on an existing Swing model, but also allows you to build custom models. We have also shown you how to expand and collapse nodes and invoke server-side listeners when a node is selected. Finally, we covered how to take a list structure and present it in a tree structure using the powerful RichFaces tree adaptors.

CHAPTER 10

Rich Drag-and-Drop Components

Being able to drag and drop items inside a browser is cool and becoming an important feature. RichFaces provides a set of features that enable you to drag and drop almost any JSF component. The available drag-and-drop components provide everything you need, so you won't have to deal with any JavaScript. Although drag-and-drop is happening on the client side, RichFaces allows binding drag-and-drop events to server-side listeners. Another thing to keep in mind is that drag-and-drop components are actually just functional components (similar to the Core tag library in JSF), so they don't provide a lot in terms of UI, only the functionality to drag-and-drop other components.

Using <rich:dragSource> and <rich:dropZone>

Enabling drag-and-drop in JSF pages using RichFaces can be done by only using two tags: <rich:dragSource> and <rich:dropTarget>. <rich:dragSource> is nested inside the component that you want to drag and <rich:dropTarget> is nested inside the component that should become the drop zone. Let's first cover some of the basic attributes and then run through an example.

As we mentioned, these drag and drop components are added as children to any components, and will encode all the necessary JavaScript to make the source draggable and the target a drop zone. Listing 10-1 shows an example of making the image component draggable.

Listing 10-1. An example of making the image component draggable

```
<h:graphicImage value="/images/nikon-dx3100.png" id="dragImage">
    <rich:dragSource/>
</h:graphicImage>
```

An image is rendered but it is also now draggable. Drag it with the mouse as you usually do with any desktop items. The result is shown in Figure 10-1.

Figure 10-1. Dragged image

■ **Note** Two examples of components in JSF that don't encode an id to the client unless you specify it explicitly are `<h:outputText>` and `<h:graphicImage>`. If you are adding drag-and-drop capability to such components and no id is present, drag-and-drop will not work. Adding drag-and-drop capability to component requires that the client id is present. So, a good practice is always to specify the id for a component.

So far nothing is happening after we release the element. The dragged image simply disappears from the screen; but that's what is supposed to happen. RichFaces drag-and-drop components do not provide client-side reordering of elements within a DOM tree or any sort of absolute position change. To process the drop of the component, we need to define a drop zone. Once a component is dropped into this zone, we can send an Ajax request in order to process the drop event. Basically, `<rich:dropTarget>` provides a way to attach a client-side listener for a drop operation that will send a standard Ajax request. Let's add `<rich:dropTarget>` to the page. Remember that both tags register listeners on parent components, so we will use `<rich:panel>` as a drop zone. Listing 10-2 shows the code.

Listing 10-2. Adding `<rich:dropTarget>` to the page

```
<h:form>
    <a4j:status startText="Processing drop event"/>
    <rich:panel id="dropZone" header="Drop Here">
        <rich:dropTarget/>
    </rich:panel>
</h:form>
```

The result shown in Figure 10-2.

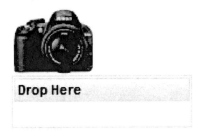

Figure 10-2. <rich:panel> as a drop zone

As you see we also added `<a4j:status>` to show the Ajax request status. However, after we drag the image and drop it into the panel, we still don't see status component activation. So the request is not being sent. We are still missing one thing to make it work.

You can attach the drag component to any component and also attach the drop component to any component. It's required to declare which drag sources correspond to which drop zones. In other words, you need to define that items of type A, for example, can be dropped into only one particular drop zone and not any other.

To make this work, we need to define a type attribute on the `<rich:dragSource>` component. It should be any string identifier that will be used to attach it to the drop target. Then we should define an acceptedTypes attribute for `<rich:dropTarget>`. It should be set to all accepted drag sources. You can use a comma or a space to separate string values or bind the attribute to a bean property that holds Set or List of types.

Listing 10-3 shows the code with all the updates.

Listing 10-3. *Shows the updated code*

```
<h:graphicImage value="/images/nikon-dx3100.png" id="dragImage">
    <rich:dragSource type="img"/>
</h:graphicImage>
<a4j:status startText="Processing drop event" />
<h:form>
    <rich:panel id="dropZone" header="Drop Here">
        <rich:dropTarget acceptedTypes="img"/>
    </rich:panel>
</h:form>
```

Finally, after dropping the image into the panel, the Ajax request status should be shown as illustrated in Figure 10-3.

Figure 10-3. *Ajax request sent after drop event*

In this example we set the drag source type (type="img") and then defined acceptedTypes="img" to make sure that only the component of that type can be dropped into this drop zone. If you have a drop zone that should accept any types of draggable components, then, instead of listing each accepted type, we could set the drop zone to accept any type, such as the following:

```
acceptedTypes="@all"
```

Even though any component can now be dropped into this drop zone, we still need to define the drag source type for every <rich:dragSource> component.

Invoking Server-side Listener on Drop

Things are looking good—we can drag-and-drop components—but we are still missing something. The missing part is the ability to invoke server-side listeners when a drop occurs, in order to add some business logic to those operations.

To add a server-side listener, we define the dropListener attribute for <rich:dropTarget> with a method expression to the listener inside the bean. The listener method signature is as follows:

```
public void listenerName(org.richfaces.event.DropEvent event)
```

We will touch on DropEvent and the information it exposes in listener code shortly, but for now let's cover two more attributes that should be used to handle a drop operation on the server side and which are related to the DropEvent. dragValue defined on <rich:dragSource> and dropValue defined on <rich:dropTarget> are used in order to pass additional information to the listener.

Now let's review DropEvent closer. Table 10-1 lists methods available on the DropEvent object.

Table 10-1. DropEvent Object API

Method	Description
getDragSource()	Returns UIComponent to which <rich:dragSource> is bound.
getDropTarget()	Returns UIComponent to which <rich:dropTarget> is bound.
getDropValue()	Returns the dropValue defined at <rich:dropTarget>.
getDragValue()	Returns the dragValue defined at <rich:dragSource>.

■ **Note** It's also possible to use <f:param> or <a4j:param> tags to pass parameters to <rich:dropTarget> as we do for JSF links, buttons, or any other action component. However, because <rich:dragSource> is not an action component, it will not process the additional parameters.

Shopping Cart Example

Let's create an example that consists of a list of products and a shopping cart. Moving products into the cart will be implemented using drag and drop. Listing 10-4 shows the Product object.

Listing 10-4. Shows the Product object

```
public class Product {

    private static final String IMAGES_EXT = ".jpg";
    private static final String IMAGES_DIR = "/images/";
    private String title;
    private String description;
    private String img;

    public Product(String title, String description, String img) {
        super();
        this.title = title;
        this.description = description;
        this.img = img;
    }

    public String getIconURI() {
        return IMAGES_DIR + this.img +  IMAGES_EXT;
    }
    // Getters and setters
}
```

The Product object provides three properties—name, description, and icon—all used to represent it in the list.

Listing 10-5 shows a bean that initializes a collection of products.

Listing 10-5. Shows a bean that initializes a collection of products

```
@ManagedBean
@RequestScoped
public class ShoppingCartBean {
    public List<Product> items;
    public List<Product> cartItems;

    public String getProductsCountString() {
        return cartItems.size() + " products in cart";
    }
    public ShoppingCartBean() {
        items = new ArrayList<Product>();
        cartItems = new ArrayList<Product>();
        items.add(new Product("Nikon D3100",
            "14.2MP Digital SLR Camera with 18-55mm f/3.5-5.6 AF-S DX VR Nikkor
                Zoom Lens", "nikon-d3100"));
        items.add(new Product("Canon Rebel XS",
            "10.1MP Digital SLR Camera with EF-S 18-55mm f/3.5-5.6 IS Lens
                (Black)", "canon-xs"));
        //More items initialization code
    }
    //Getters and setters
}
```

Not much to explain here. We create shopping items and place them in a list.

Now, let's create the page that will display a list of items and add drag-and-drop to it. Listing 10-6 shows the initial page code.

Listing 10-6. Shows the initial page code

```
<h:form>
    <h:panelGrid columns="2" id="panel">
        <rich:panel header="Products" style="width:300px">
            <rich:dataGrid value="#{shoppingCartBean.items}" var="item">
                <rich:panel style="width:275px">
                    <rich:dragSource type="products" dragValue="#{item}" />
                        <h:panelGrid columns="2">
                            <h:graphicImage value="#{item.iconURI}" />
                                <fieldset>
                                <legend><b>#{item.title}"</b></legend>
                                #{item.description}
                                </fieldset>
                        </h:panelGrid>
                </rich:panel>
            </rich:dataGrid>
        </rich:panel>
        <rich:panel header="Shopping Cart">
            <rich:dropTarget render="panel" acceptedTypes="products"
```

```
            dropListener="#{shoppingCartBean.processDrop}" />
        <h:panelGrid>
            <h:outputText value="#{shoppingCartBean.productsCountString}"
                rendered="#{not empty shoppingCartBean.cartItems}" />
            <h:graphicImage value="#{empty shoppingCartBean.cartItems ?
                '/images/empty_cart.png' :
                '/images/cart.png'}" />
            <h:link outcome="checkout" rendered="#{not empty
                shoppingCartBean.cartItems}">
                Checkout
            </h:link>
        </h:panelGrid>
    </rich:panel>
    </h:panelGrid>
</h:form>
```

Now let's review the code. We created two panels. The left panel will display a list of products using the `<rich:dataGrid>` component. Inside every cell, a panel is displayed with product details. We then add drag capability to the panel using `<rich:dragSource>`. The `<rich:dragSource>` component is defined with the `products` type and also defines the drag value (using `dragValue` attribute) as the current iteration object.

The right panel contains an icon of a shopping cart and will get updated when items are dropped into it. It will display an added products count, and the link to the checkout page will become enabled once an item is added to the cart. `<rich:dropTarget>` defines the entire panel as a drop zone and defines the same `products` as an accepted type.

Figure 10-4 shows how the page is rendered initially.

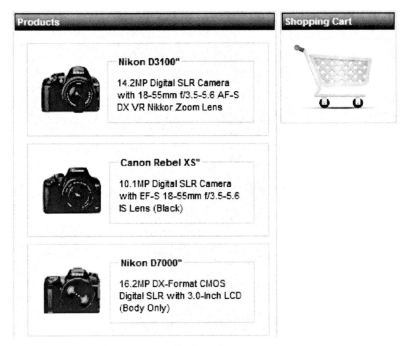

Figure 10-4. *Products page with shopping cart*

The only thing we are missing is the drop listener method implementation. So let's add it to the ShoppingCartBean class, as defined in Listing 10-7.

Listing 10-7. Adding the drop listener method to the ShoppingCartBean class

```
public void processDrop(DropEvent event) {
    Product dragValue = (Product)event.getDragValue();
    cartItems.add(dragValue);
    items.remove(dragValue);
}
```

Recall that we are passing the Product object exposed as an iteration variable and as a drag value (#{item}). Inside the listener, we are getting the object and adding it to the cartItems list, and then removing it from items list. Figure 10-5 shows the page after we drag-and-drop two items.

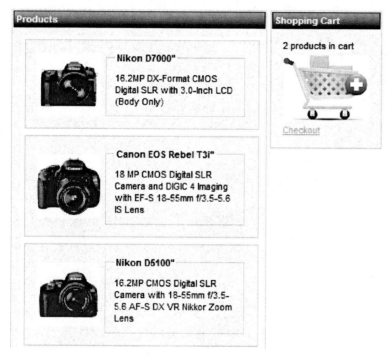

Figure 10-5. A few products were dropped into the shopping cart.

Looks pretty simple, doesn't it? And finally, to complete the example, let's navigate to the checkout page by using <h:link> with a checkout outcome. This means that we have the checkout.xhtml page in the same directory as the shopping page. Listing 10-8 shows the page.

Listing 10-8. Navigating to the checkout page by using <h:link> with a checkout outcome

```
<rich:dataTable value="#{shoppingCartBean.cartItems}" var="item">
  <f:facet name="header">Items for checkout</f:facet>
  <rich:column>#{item.title}</rich:column>
```

```
<rich:column>#{item.description}</rich:column>
</rich:dataTable>
```

We use a table that is bound to the cartItems list in the ShoppingCartBean object. When we click on the checkout link in the cart, we should see the result shown in Figure 10-6.

Items for checkout	
Nikon D3100	14.2MP Digital SLR Camera with 18-55mm f/3.5-5.6 AF-S DX VR Nikkor Zoom Lens
Canon Rebel XS	10.1MP Digital SLR Camera with EF-S 18-55mm f/3.5-5.6 IS Lens (Black)

Figure 10-6. Checkout page

Two-way Drag-and-Drop Operations

Let's improve our example and ability to remove some items from the shopping cart and place them back in the products list. There is nothing complicated here; we will just need the same drag support on the target items (shopping cart) and define drop support on the source list (products list).

Let's review page changes in segments, starting with changes to the products size. Listing 10-9 shows the products panel modified.

Listing 10-9. Shows the modified products panel

```
<rich:panel header="Products" style="width:300px">
   <rich:dropTarget acceptedTypes="targetProducts"
      dropListener="#{shoppingCartBean.processRemove}" render="panel"/>
   <rich:dataGrid value="#{shoppingCartBean.items}" var="item">
      <rich:panel style="width:275px">
         <rich:dragSource type="products" dragValue="#{item}" />
         <h:panelGrid columns="2">
            <h:graphicImage value="#{item.iconURI}" />
            <fieldset>
               <legend><b>#{item.title}"</b></legend>
               #{item.description}
            </fieldset>
         </h:panelGrid>
      </rich:panel>
   </rich:dataGrid>
</rich:panel>
```

It's almost the same as before, but now we have added <rich:dropTarget> to the entire products panel, which accepts dragged elements of the targetProducts type and calls the processRemove() drop listener from the same ShoppingCartBean bean. Listing 10-10 shows the method code.

Listing 10-10. The method code

```
public void processRemove(DropEvent event) {
   Product dragValue = (Product)event.getDragValue();
   cartItems.remove(dragValue);
   items.add(dragValue);
}
```

Listing 10-11 shows the modified panel with shopping cart.

Listing 10-11. The modified panel with shopping cart

```
<rich:panel header="Shopping Cart">
    <h:panelGrid>
        <h:outputText value="#{shoppingCartBean.productsCountString}"
            rendered="#{not empty shoppingCartBean.cartItems}" />
        <h:graphicImage value="#{empty shoppingCartBean.cartItems ?
            '/images/empty_cart.png' : '/images/cart.png'}" />
        <h:link outcome="checkout" rendered="#{not empty
            shoppingCartBean.cartItems}">
            Checkout
        </h:link>
        <rich:dataGrid value="#{shoppingCartBean.cartItems}" var="item">
            <a4j:outputPanel layout="block">
                <rich:dragSource type="targetProducts" dragValue="#{item}" />
                <h:panelGrid columns="2">
                    <h:graphicImage value="#{item.iconURI}" style="width:30px; height:30px;" />
                    #{item.title}
                </h:panelGrid>
            </a4j:outputPanel>
        </rich:dataGrid>
    </h:panelGrid>
    <rich:dropTarget render="panel" acceptedTypes="products"
        dropListener="#{shoppingCartBean.processDrop}" />
</rich:panel>
```

There, we added a small list of items that appear below the cart. Every item was added with drag capability using <rich:dragSource> with targetProducts as the type and the current iteration object (#{item}) as the value. Now we are able to pass the items either way between the lists. Figure 10-7 shows the page when two items are added to the cart.

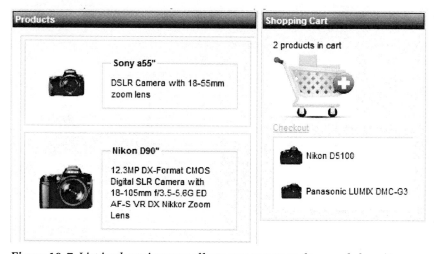

Figure 10-7. List in shopping cart allows you to return drag-and-drop items

Now you can take any item in the shopping cart, remove it from the shopping cart, and put it back into the products list via drag and drop.

Customizing the Drag Indicator

Figure 10-8 shows what you see when an item is dragged on the page using the default drag indicator.

Figure 10-8. Dragged state default indication

By default, the drag indication element is achieved by cloning the DOM section that is being dragged.

Using the default is fine, but we would like to have the option to customize the object that's being dragged with some styling, for example, and other options.

Luckily, as with everything else in RichFaces, it's pretty easy to do. The RichFaces drag-and-drop feature adds a set of predefined CSS classes (the same as with UI-rich components) that are applied to the cloned indicator element in different states. Table 10-2 shows the style names and explains when they should be used.

Table 10-2. Predefined CSS Classes for Drag Indicator

Class Name	Description
.rf-ind-drag	Applied to root DOM element of dragged object by default.
.rf-ind-acpt	Added to root DOM element of dragged object when it hovers over the drop zone accepting its type.
.rf-ind-rejt	Added to root DOM element of dragged object when it hovers over the drop zone rejecting its type.

Now it should be a pretty easy task to make the indicator change in different states in order to better notify the user about current action options. In Listing 10-12, let's add the CSS classes to our previous sample page.

Listing 10-12. Adding the CSS classes to our previous sample page

```
<style>
  .rf-ind-drag{
  }
  .rf-ind-acpt{
    border:3px solid green;
  }
  .rf-ind-rejt{
    border:3px solid red;
  }
</style>
```

Based on this styling, the indicator is defined to look as it is when just dragged. A green border is added when hovering over the drop zone that accepts this object. And, a red border is shown when hovering the components over a drop zone that doesn't accept this object type. So when we hover one of the items over the cart, we will see it updated with a green border, as shown in Figure 10-9.

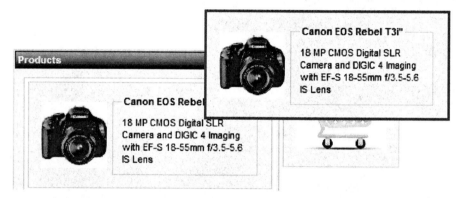

Figure 10-9. Drag indicator customized with green border in accept state

Being able to style in this way looks a lot more user-friendly.

The next section describes how to customize the drag indicator with custom content using a special `<rich:dragIndicator>` component.

Using `<rich:dragIndicator>`

`<rich:dragIndicator>` is a pretty simple component that allows you to define some custom static content that is shown under the mouse cursor when you perform a drag operation.

There are two things you need to know to start using this component. First, the content of indicator should be defined using any nested components. Second, the indicator itself should be attached to `<rich:dragSource>` using same named `dragIndicator` attribute on the `<rich:dragSource>` behavior with the indicator id specified.

So, let's proceed with an example. Using the cart sample, we will add the indicator anywhere on the page, as shown in Listing 10-13.

Listing 10-13. Adding the indicator anywhere on the page using the cart sample

```
<rich:dragIndicator id="indicator">
    <rich:panel>
        <h:outputText value="Drop product to cart" />
    </rich:panel>
</rich:dragIndicator>
```

Now you need only to point our drag behaviors to it using code as follows:

```
<rich:dragSource ... dragIndicator="indicator" />
```

When you drag any product, you will no longer see the panel. Instead, you will see a smaller panel with only the content defined. And, if we don't remove our style class definitions for rf-ind-drag and two other styles (drop accepted, drop not accepted), we should see the results shown in Figures 10-10 and 10-11.

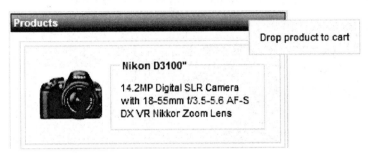

Figure 10-10. Panel with static indicator dragged

Figure 10-11. Panel with static indicator over the drop zone

Besides the rf-* classes, which are applied to all the indicators in the page, you can use <rich:dragIndicator> component attributes to define specific styles for that particular indicator. Those attributes are acceptClass, draggingClass, and rejectClass.

■ **Note** As of the writing of this book, there are no options to redefine markup for different indicator states, only the option of restyling it using CSS. In other words, if you need to show a different icon to indicate the reject or accept state inside the indicator, it can be done—but only by using CSS selectors (to hide and show some elements in some states) or by using background images defined in CSS classes. The option to redefine markup could be added in a future release, so check the JBoss Community RichFaces page at `www.jboss.org/richfaces` often for new updates.

Using Drag-and-Drop with Tree Components

Drag-and-drop with tree components might sound complicated; however, once you finish this section, you will see that it's actually not that difficult. All we are doing is combining knowledge from Chapter 9 with knowledge from this chapter. We will implement moving the leaf nodes between different parent nodes. Although this is a basic example, you should be able to extend it to any more complicated case.

Let's create a simple tree model, as we did in Chapter 9. Listing 10-14 shows the code for Swing's TreeNode implementation, which will be used to create a tree model.

Listing 10-14. Shows the code for the Swing's TreeNode implementation

```
public class FileSystemNode extends org.richfaces.model.SwingTreeNodeImpl<Object> {
    private String label;

    public FileSystemNode(String label) {
        super();
        this.label = label;
    }

    public String getNodeType() {
        return isLeaf() ? "leaf" : "node";
    }
}
```

■ **Note** We use the SwingTreeNodeImpl default implementation class from richfaces-api as it is more convenient for that specific sample because it already provides the getParent() method implemented. We will use that method to perform moving between nodes more easily. org.richfaces.TreeNodeImpl doesn't have such a method and we would have to add it if we wanted to switch to that implementation.

It's as simple as possible. It will store either the file or directory name and will return two string types, leaf and node, according to the isLeaf() method. Later, we will use a different type of node on the page.

Now, let's look at the bean that initializes the model in Listing 10-15.

Listing 10-15. The bean that initializes the model

```
@ManagedBean
@SessionScoped
public class TreeDnDBean {

    private List<SwingTreeNodeImpl<Object>> nodes;

    public TreeDnDBean() {
        nodes = new ArrayList<SwingTreeNodeImpl<Object>>();
        for (Integer i = 1; i < 5; i++) {
            FileSystemNode rootNode = new FileSystemNode("folder " + i);
            for (Integer j = 1; j <= 5; j++) {
                FileSystemNode leafNode =
                    new FileSystemNode("pic" + i + "." + j + ".jpg");
                rootNode.addChild(leafNode);
            }
            nodes.add(rootNode);
        }
    }
    public List<SwingTreeNodeImpl<Object>> getNodes() {
        return nodes;
    }
}
```

This bean creates a set of "folder" nodes and adds numerous "pic" leaf nodes inside. We already know how to create tree models using SwingTreeNodeImpl and other options, thus let's just jump to the JSF page, shown in Listing 10-16.

Listing 10-16. The JSF page

```
<h:form>
    <rich:tree value="#{treeDnDBean.nodes}" nodeType="#{node.nodeType}" var="node"
        id="tree" toggleType="client">
        <rich:treeNode type="leaf">
            <h:outputText value="#{node.label}" />
        </rich:treeNode>
        <rich:treeNode type="node">
            <h:outputText value="#{node.label}" />
        </rich:treeNode>
    </rich:tree>
</h:form>
```

Note that we are using two <rich:treeNode> tags on the page, with the same content in them. Why did we do that? We are going to implement drag-and-drop of leafs between different nodes. The simplest way to achieve this is to define leafs as draggable and nodes as drop zones. An easy way to do it is to have different placeholders for the drag-and-drop behaviors. In a more complicated case where you might need to support moving folders, you would need to have folders as drag sources and as drop zones at the same time, plus be able to handle a restriction such as not being able to drop the node on itself.

Now let's see the result of the page rendered. We should check that our tree was created successfully before proceeding with adding drag-and-drop functionality. The correct tree is shown in Figure 10-12.

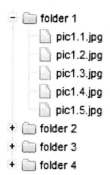

Figure 10-12. Tree component

Now we are ready to add drag-and-drop to the tree. The updated page is shown in Listing 10-17 and followed by an explanation of what we did.

Listing 10-17. Adding drag-and-drop to the tree

```
<style>
    .rf-ind-acpt {
        border: 2px solid green;
    }
</style>
<h:form>
    <rich:tree value="#{treeDnDBean.rootNode}" nodeType="#{node.type}" var="node"
        toggleType="client" id="tree">
        <rich:treeNode type="node">
            <a4j:outputPanel>
                <rich:dropTarget acceptedTypes="file" render="tree" execute="tree"
                    dropListener="#{treeDnDBean.moveFile}" dropValue="#{node}" />
                <h:outputText value="#{node.label}" />
            </a4j:outputPanel>
        </rich:treeNode>
        <rich:treeNode type="leaf">
            <a4j:outputPanel>
                <rich:dragSource type="file" dragValue="#{node}" />
                <h:outputText value="#{node.label}" />
            </a4j:outputPanel>
        </rich:treeNode>
    </rich:tree>
</h:form>
```

Leafs are marked as draggable using `<rich:dragSupport>` and nodes became drop zones using `<rich:dropTarget>`. We pointed value attributes (dragValue, dropValue) of both components to the #{node} iteration variable, so we will get corresponding node objects inside listeners.

`<rich:dropTarget>` performs a complete tree re-render in order to update the markup after the nodes movement. We set the execute attribute to the tree itself to save its state during submission. (Nodes toggling occurs on the client according to the toggleType attribute, so by default, we will lose the state.)

Ideally you may want to use partial rendering of the updated nodes. But that just out of scope for this sample and will make the code more complicated. We want to concentrate on drag-and-drop functionality instead. Partial rendering using the @rows() function described in iteration components chapter can also work for trees.

■ **Note** We wrapped the content of the draggable node with an additional `<a4j:outputPanel>` because the drag indicator created by default is just a clone of the dragged element, and we wouldn't want a nested tree structure together with the selection and connecting lines (in the case of a draggable node with child nodes) to be cloned. In the current markup, only a `<span>` with a text label will be moved when dragged. The same goes for a drop zone node. We want just the node without its child components to become drop target.

The last step is to create the drop listener method that will actually perform movement of the leaf node from one parent to another. Let's look at the code in Listing 10-18.

Listing 10-18. Creating the drop listener method

```
public void moveFile(DropEvent event) {
    FileSystemNode draggedNode = (FileSystemNode) event.getDragValue();
    FileSystemNode droppedNode = (FileSystemNode) event.getDropValue();
    ((FileSystemNode) draggedNode.getParent()).removeChild(draggedNode);
    droppedNode.addChild(draggedNode);
}
```

As you can see in the code, DropEvent provides two values: the drag value and drop value. As we are passing complete node objects (referencing it using tree iteration var) in the value attribute, we are getting those objects in the listener. Next, we remove the node that we dragged from its parent and add it to the node to which it was dropped. Figure 10-13 shows the tree after two files from "folder 1" get dropped into "folder 2."

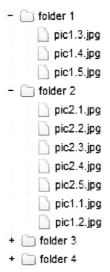

Figure 10-13. Nodes from one folder moved via drag-and-drop to another

As you can see, drag-and-drop with trees is not that complicated. We are defining some node components to be draggable and some node components to act as a drop zone. The only difference is that we are now working with tree nodes and leafs; other than that, all the concepts are the same.

Dragging and Dropping Within Tables

Using drag-and-drop within tables is not difficult (it's actually even easier than dragging and dropping within a tree), we will give you a few pointers in this short section.

As we already know, drag and drop is always added to parent component. This means that drag and drop can either be added to the table itself or a column inside the table, but not to a row. That is, if we add `<rich:dragSupport>` as an immediate child of table, the entire table will be draggable—probably not what we need. If we add `<rich:dragSupport>` to a `<rich:column>`, we will be able to drag only that single column; other columns will not be draggable.

If you want to achieve "row dragging" functionality, the solution is to embed a drag support component within every column of the table. Basically, we get the functionality of the entire row with drag support when we add drag support to each column.

It's also a good idea to create a good drag indicator, so that you don't just drag the current column content (the default drag indicator is the same content that's being dragged). With the custom indicator, no matter which column is actually selected when dragged, the indicator will show the same information and it will appear as only the row is being dragged.

■ **Note** Functionality to enable native drag-and-drop support for iteration components is planned in the future. For example, a feature such as row context that can be dragged and dropped might be added. Check the JBoss Community RichFaces page at `www.jboss.org/richfaces` for updates.

Summary

In this chapter we showed you that adding drag-and-drop capability to your JSF application is very simple with RichFaces. To be able to drag any component on the page, we add the `<rich:dragSource>` behavior. To make any are on the page to act as a drop zone, we add a `<rich:dragTarget>` behavior. Although drag-and-drop is happening on the client side, to communicate the drag-and-drop action to the server, we use the standard listener approach. In addition, RichFaces provides options to enforce which items can be dropped into which particular drop zones, as well as the ability to customize the drag indicator. Finally, we showed you how to add drag-and-drop functionality to trees and provided tips on how to achieve drag-and-drop within tables.

CHAPTER 11

Rich Validation

Validating user input is a major part of any web application. JSF provides a number of tags to enable basic validation and makes it pretty easy to build custom validators. JSF 2 makes validation even simpler by providing out-of-the-box support for popular Bean Validation (JSR 303). RichFaces takes validation to the next level and extends Bean Validation by providing client-side validation. Client-side validation allows validation to be performed on the client based on Bean Validation constraints. This is a must-have feature for high-performance enterprise web sites. In addition to client-side validation, RichFaces also provides a cross-field or object validation feature where one or two fields can be validated together. That's exactly what we are going to cover in this chapter.

Bean Validation

To start with client-side validation, we first need to tell you about Bean Validation support in JSF 2. Bean Validation is part of a Java EE stack and was born from Hibernate Validator. In fact, Hibernate Validator is the reference implementation for Bean Validation. Instead of putting validation in the view, place validation constraints on the model and have the view call those validations. For example, in Listing 11-1, Bean Validation constraints are applied to three properties. name has to be at least three characters long, age has to be between two and 120, and email has to match the regular expression.

Listing 11-1. Bean Validation constraints are applied to three properties

```java
@ManagedBean
@RequestScoped
public class ValidationBean {

    @Size (min=3)
    private String name;

    @Min (2) @Max (120)
    private Integer age;

    @Pattern (regexp=".+@.+\\.[a-z]+")
    private String email;

    // getters and setters
}
```

■ **Note** Regular expression for the e-mail we use is rather simple. You can find a more strict expression for validating an e-mail address.

Why is this better than placing validation in the JSF page? If you will be accessing the model from various JSF views, but also in other ways not from a JSF view, then you don't need to repeat validation definitions and validation can be reused. Luckily, Bean Validation support in JSF 2 is built-in; in other words, there is nothing you need to do. Just bind a JSF component to a property with Bean Validation annotation and the validation will be invoked during the Process Validation phase as usual. Listing 11-2 shows the JSF page where components are bound to properties from Listing 11-1.

Listing 11-2. Shows the JSF page

```
<h:form>
    <h:panelGrid columns="3">
        <h:outputText value="Name:" />
        <h:inputText id="name" value="#{validationBean.name}" >
            <a4j:ajax render="nameMsg"/>
        </h:inputText>
        <h:message for="name" id="nameMsg"/>

        <h:outputText value="Email:" />
        <h:inputText id="email" value="#{validationBean.email}" >
            <a4j:ajax render="emailMsg"/>
        </h:inputText>
        <h:message for="email" id="emailMsg"/>

        <h:outputText value="Age:" />
        <h:inputText id="age" value="#{validationBean.age}" >
            <a4j:ajax render="ageMsg"/>
        </h:inputText>
        <h:message for="age" id="ageMsg"/>
    </h:panelGrid>
</h:form>
```

■ **Tip** Using <a4j:ajax>, you can also set bypassUpdates="true". This will bypass or skip the Update Model phase and the Invoke Application phase, even if the values are valid. This is useful when only validating the form. When only validating, you rarely have a need to update the model and invoke the application. bypassUpdates is covered in more detail in Chapter 3.

There is nothing new here; it looks like a very standard JSF page. Validation (Ajax request) will be sent on a change event. To display the error message we use the <h:message> component. We don't have any validation on the page itself. Instead, when the page will be submitted, user-entered values will be checked against the constraints specified in the managed bean via Bean Validation annotations. Again, you get all this with JSF 2, out of the box. Running the page will produce the result shown in Figure 11-1.

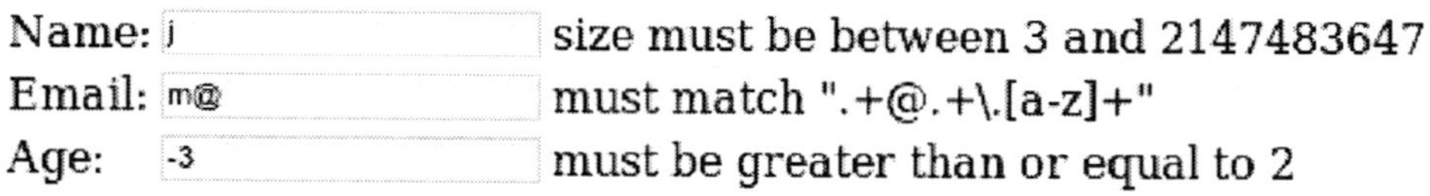

Name: j   size must be between 3 and 2147483647

Email: m@   must match ".+@.+\.[a-z]+"

Age: -3   must be greater than or equal to 2

Figure 11-1. Bean Validation standard error messages

A note on the error messages: the messages that are rendered are the standard messages from Bean Validation. One way to customize the error messages is by setting the message property on the validation annotation. For more ways to customize the messages, refer to Bean Validation documentation (see the following Tip for suggestions found on the internet). For example, changing the message for e-mail validation can be done like the following:

```
@Pattern (regexp=".+@.+\\.[a-z]+", message="Email has invalid format")
```

■ **Tip**   Learn more about Bean Validation (JSR 303) at the Java Community Process Program web site at www.jcp.org/en/jsr/detail?id=303 and from the Java EE 6 Tutorial: Using Being Validation page at http://download.oracle.com/javaee/6/tutorial/doc/gircz.html.

RichFaces Client-side Validation

RichFaces takes validation to the next level by providing client-side validation. In other words, validation can be done on the client without sending an Ajax request. How does RichFaces do it? RichFaces extends standard Bean Validation by bringing the validation to the client. You might be wondering why you need client-side validation when you can "quickly" validate with Ajax? It's true that validating with Ajax can be fast, but an Ajax request is still sent to the server. In high-performance, high-traffic applications, being able to validate on the client and without sending an Ajax request can greatly improve performance.

Let's take our page and add client-side validation to it. To add client-side validation to a form is very easy, probably too easy. All we need to do is place the <rich:validator> tag inside the input component that's being validated. By default, client validation will be invoked on the change event, but we can use any other event by setting the event attribute. The only other thing we need to do is use <rich:message> or <rich:messages> tags to display the error message. Client-side validation error messages will not be displayed with the standard <h:message> tag. There are no changes in the bean because we use the same Bean Validation but now bring it to the client.

Listing 11-3 shows the update page with client-side validation.

Listing 11-3. Shows the update page with client-side validation

```
<h:form>
   <h:panelGrid columns="3">
      <h:outputText value="Name:" />
      <h:inputText id="name" value="#{validationBean.name}" >
         <rich:validator/>
      </h:inputText>
      <rich:message for="name" />
```

```
    <h:outputText value="Email:" />
    <h:inputText id="email" value="#{validationBean.email}" >
        <rich:validator/>
    </h:inputText>
    <rich:message for="email"/>

    <h:outputText value="Age:" />
    <h:inputText id="age" value="#{validationBean.age}" >
        <rich:validator/>
    </h:inputText>
    <rich:message for="age"/>
  </h:panelGrid>
</h:form>
```

As you can see, <rich:validator> is now nested inside each input field. In fact, it's a client behavior just like <a4j:ajax>. And, being a behavior, it attaches to a parent UI component event, just like <a4j:ajax>. As validation is performed on input components, the default event to which <rich:validator> attaches is change. We also replaced <h:message> with <rich:message> because client-side validation messages will be displayed only when using either <rich:message> or <rich:messages>. When the page is rendered, RichFaces will render all the necessary JavaScript to the client to perform validation by looking at bean property and its annotation. Running the page will produce the result shown in Figure 11-2.

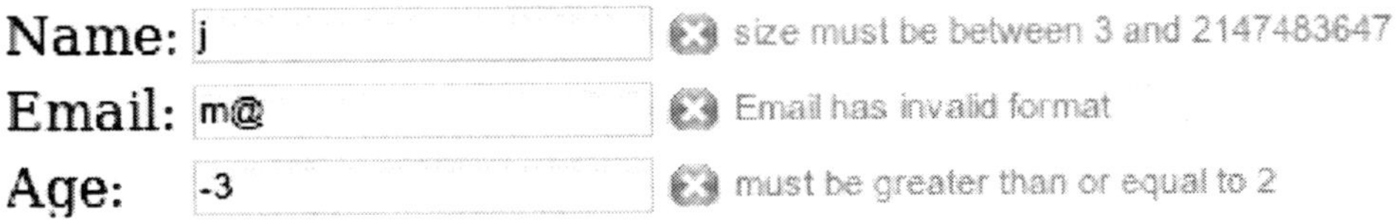

Name: j ⊗ size must be between 3 and 2147483647

Email: m@ ⊗ Email has invalid format

Age: -3 ⊗ must be greater than or equal to 2

Figure 11-2. RichFaces client-side validation

To change the event that triggers client-side validation, set the event attribute. For example, the code that follows will invoke client-side validation on a blur event:

```
<rich:validator event="blur"/>
```

Caution <rich:message> or <rich:messages> must be used when using client-side validation. These components provide the necessary JavaScript to be updated on the client. And, of course, they also work with standard server-side validation as well.

Although Bean Validation is the preferred way to add validation in JSF 2, RichFaces client validation still supports standard JSF validation. This makes it possible to add client-side validation to a page where standard JSF validator tags are already used.

As of writing of this book, client-side validation only supports single field-based validation. What this means is that it's possible to invoke client-side validation when a change event (default event) or blur event (or any other event supported by the UI component) occurs on a particular field. If there is a control to submit the entire form, such as when a button or link is clicked, client-side validation will not be performed but the standard server-side validation will be. There are plans to add client-side validation support when a form is submitted in the future.

Using <rich:message> and <rich:messages>

`<rich:message>` and `<rich:messages>` are used to display messages or error messages and work just like the standard `<h:message>` and `<h:messages>` tags, but with a number of extra features. Just to remind you, `<h:message>` or `<rich:message>` displays a message for a particular component via the for attribute. On the other hand, `<h:messages>` or `<rich:messages>` displays all current messages from a current JSF request.

As for differences, one major difference is that the messages are automatically rendered, which means you don't need to point to component via the render attribute. If you remember, we can achieve a similar result where we don't need to use render using `<a4j:outputPanel ajaxRendered="true">`. Listing 11-4 shows such an example.

Listing 11-4. An example

```
<a4j:outputPanel ajaxRendered="true">
   <h:message for="email"/>
</a4j:outputPanel>
```

`<a4j:outputPanel ajaxRendered="true">` is always automatically rendered. So, the following is identical to Listing 11-4:

```
<rich:message for="email"/>
```

This message will be rendered automatically. We can summarize it like this. Where `<a4j:outputPanel ajaxRendered="true">` is an auto-rendered panel, `<rich:message>` or `<rich:messages>` is an auto-rendered message.

■ **Note** It's possible to turn off auto-rendered panels or messages by setting the `limitRender="true"` attribute on action components and `<a4j:ajax>` behavior. This `limitRender` attribute is covered in Chapter 2.

Customizing Message Icons

Another extra feature that you probably noticed is that the error message in Figure 11-2 now has an icon. That's again because we used the `<rich:message>` tag. To remove the icon, we have to overwrite one of the Skin CSS classes used by the component, as shown in Listing 11-5.

Listing 11-5. Overwrite one of the Skin CSS classes used by the component

```
<style>
.rf-msg-err {
   background-image: none;
}
</style>
```

Of course, instead of removing the icon, you could point that CSS property to your own image to be used as an icon.

The CSS class we have shown applies to messages with ERROR severity; for messages with other severity levels, use the following CSS classes: .rf-msg-ftl (FATAL), .rf-msg-inf (INFO), and .rf-msg-wrn (WARNING).

Also remember that <rich:messages> uses rf-msgs-* classes while <rich:message> uses rf-msg-* classes.

Separating Summary and Details Styling

Another simple but cool look-and-feel customization improvement is rendering details and summary parts of messages as separate HTML elements and support for separately styling them. Listing 11-6 shows the page where there is a button and messages. Let's say the button needs to add user-friendly messages when some services required for business action are not responsive. Look closely at the two predefined classes used in the example.

Listing 11-6. Shows the page where there is a button and messages

```
<style>
    .rf-msgs-sum{
        font-weight: bold;
    }
    .rf-msgs-det{
        font-style: italic;
    }
</style>

<h:form>
    <h:panelGrid>
        <!--Form elements-->
        <rich:messages showDetail="true" showSummary="true"/>
        <a4j:commandButton value="Submit"
            action="#{beanValidation2.serviceAction}"/>
    </h:panelGrid>
</h:form>
```

Code for the action is shown in Listing 11-7.

Listing 11-7. Code for the action

```
public void serviceAction(){
    //Business code
    FacesMessage message = new FacesMessage("Service Error. ",
        "Sorry, you caught us doing maintenance.");
    FacesContext.getCurrentInstance().addMessage(null, message);
}
```

The message consists of two parts. Summary reflects message category, such as services error, and the details provide more specific information. Using different CSS classes, it's possible to style summary and details differently. Everything together is shown in Figure 11-3.

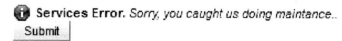

Services Error. *Sorry, you caught us doing maintance..*

[Submit]

Figure 11-3. *Displaying summary and details parts*

Changing <rich:messages> Layout

By default `<rich:messages>` is rendered as a set of `<span>` elements with the `display="block"` CSS property defined. Messages are aligned vertically with icon images on the left. If you want to show the messages as a simple HTML unordered list, you can change those `<span>` element display properties to be list-items, as shown in Listing 11-8.

Listing 11-8. *Changing those <span> element display properties to be list-items*

```
<style>
.rf-msgs-err{
   display:list-item;
   margin-left:20px;
   padding-left:0px;
   background-image:none;
}
</style>
<h:form>
   <rich:messages/>
   <h:panelGrid columns="2">
      <h:outputText value="Name:" />
      <h:inputText label="Name" id="name" required="true">
         <f:validateLength minimum="3" />
      </h:inputText>
      <h:outputText value="Job:" />
      <h:inputText label="Job" id="job" required="true">
         <f:validateLength minimum="3" maximum="50" />
      </h:inputText>
      <f:facet name="footer">
         <a4j:commandButton value="Ajax Validate"/>
      </f:facet>
   </h:panelGrid>
</h:form>
```

On the page there are two inputs with some validation applied using JSF tags, and an Ajax button, which validates the form and the `<rich:messages>` components.

Notice that we added `<style>` definition. We are just changing the `display` property to `list-item`, removing the icon and making minor adjustments required because of its span-based markup. The result is shown in Figure 11-4.

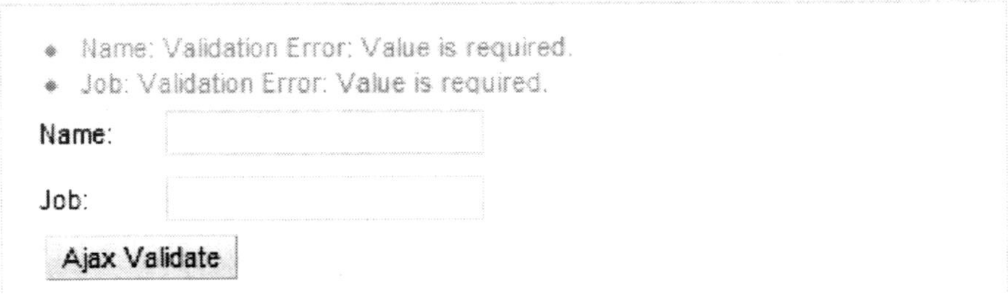

Figure 11-4. Displaying messages as a simple list

If you need table-based markup, update the `display` property to have `table-row` value and make CSS adjustments considering that span as a table row.

Falling Back to Server Validation

When you use a validation that doesn't have its client-side implementation, such as when a custom validation is used, RichFaces will automatically fall back to server-side Ajax validation. You don't have to do anything. Currently RichFaces only provides client-side implementations for all validations from Bean Validation (JSR 303) specification. If we take Hibernate Validator, which is the reference implementation (used in our examples), it goes beyond the specification and provides additional validations, such as `@Email`. `@Email` will make sure the input has a valid e-mail format. RichFaces currently doesn't support this annotation and in our examples we used a `@Pattern` annotation. But, using `@Email`, we can precisely see when client-side validation is used and when server-side validation is used.

■ **Note** RichFaces provides client-side implementation for all validators in a `javax.validation.*` package. The list of annotations can be found at The Java EE 6 Tutorial: Using Bean Validation page at

`http://download.oracle.com/javaee/6/tutorial/doc/gircz.html`.

First, we need to update the bean. Listing 11-9 shows using `@Email` instead of the `@Pattern` annotation on an `email` property (only partial code is shown, related to `@Email` annotation).

Listing 11-9. Updated managed bean

```
import org.hibernate.validator.constraints.Email;
// other imports

@ManagedBean

@RequestScoped

public class ValidationBean {
    @Email
    private String email;
```

```
    // Other properties, getters and setters
}
```

You will notice that @Email annotation is coming from a org.hibernate.validator.* package.

When you run the page, you won't see any difference and that's the desired result. Even though there is no client-side implementation for the @Email constraint, everything worked as expected; validation for email fell back to the server-side behind the scenes. Placing <a4j:log> tag on the page is a very quick and easy way to see when client-side validation is invoked and when server-side validation is invoked. If you remember, <a4j:log> shows the Ajax request and response information. If client-side validation is used, then the <a4j:log> won't display any output. If server-side validation is used, then the <a4j:log> will display the Ajax request and response information.

Graph Validator

Validating a component's value is simple in JSF, but comparing whether two inputs are equals or against any other validation rules, unfortunately, is not an easy task. No built-in JSF feature allows us to "look" at two or more values during validation. You can find workarounds, but RichFaces makes this task a lot simpler with its <rich:graphValidator> tag. The simplest way to understand would be to look at an example, and the simplest example is to see whether two string inputs are equal. Let's start with the JSF page shown in Listing 11-10.

Listing 11-10. The JSF page

```
<rich:messages />
<h:form>
    <h:panelGrid columns="2">
        <h:outputText value="Text 1:" />
        <h:inputText id="text1" value="#{graphValidationBean.text1}" />

        <h:outputText value="Text 2:" />
        <h:inputText id="text2" value="#{graphValidationBean.text2}" />
    </h:panelGrid>
    <h:commandButton action="result.xhtml" value="Check Input" />
</h:form>
```

The page is very simple; it has only two inputs. Our goal is to validate each input individually but also make sure both inputs are equals. This is very similar to confirming a password field that you see on many forms today. One more thing to note is that the error messages are displayed at the top of the page using <rich:messages>.

When the button is clicked, we navigate to the result.xhtml page, if the input is valid and also equal. This page can be as simple as displaying the following:

```
<h4>Inputs are equal.</h4>
```

Validation constraints are defined in Listing 11-11.

Listing 11-11. Defining validation constraints

```
@ManagedBean
@RequestScoped
public class GraphValidationBean implements java.lang.Cloneable{
```

```
@NotNull
@Size (min=3,max=10, message="Text 1 must be between {min} and {max}.")
private String text1;

@NotNull
@Size (min=3,max=10, message="Text 2 must be between {min} and {max}.")
private String text2;

@AssertTrue (message="Text 1 and Text 2 are not equal")
public boolean isTextEqual (){
    return text1.equals(text2);
}
@Override
public Object clone() throws CloneNotSupportedException {
    return super.clone();
}
// Getters and setters
}
```

We can go ahead and run the page. Validation should be invoked as expected. However, we are also able to navigate to the next page, even if the values in the inputs are not equals. If you look carefully at the page and bean, you will notice that input components are bound to text1 and text2 properties. But, there is another constraint defined with @AssertTrue. It's not bound to any UI component on the page, but that's also the constraint that we need. It will check whether the two inputs are the same. How do we make sure this constraint is checked? We enclose all the inputs inside <rich:graphValidator> and set the tags value attribute to point to the managed bean named graphValidator, as shown in Listing 11-12.

Listing 11-12. Using <rich:graphValidator>

```
<rich:messages for="gv"/>
<h:form>
    <rich:graphValidator value="#{graphValidatorBean}" id="gv">
        <h:panelGrid columns="2">
            <h:outputText value="Text 1:" />
            <h:inputText id="text1" value="#{graphValidationBean.text1}" />

            <h:outputText value="Text 2:" />
            <h:inputText id="text2" value="#{graphValidationBean.text2}" />
        </h:panelGrid>
    </rich:graphValidator>
    <h:commandButton action="result.xhtml" value="Check Input" />
</h:form>
```

When the page is submitted, each component is validated, as usual, during the Process Validations phase. Error messages are displayed at the top of the page, as shown in Figure 11-5.

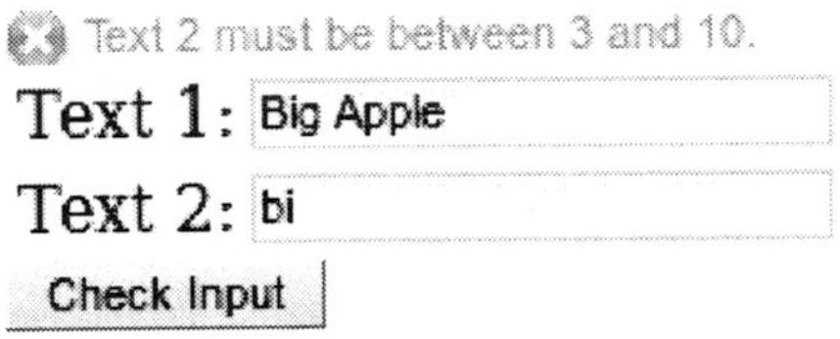

Figure 11-5. Validating each input separately

If every single component passes its validation, that's when the graph validator comes into play. As you can see, the `<rich:graphValidator>` value property is bound to the managed bean. That's what triggers the validation to be run for the entire bean again, including the constraint that wasn't bound to any UI component. So basically, all the properties that are bound are validated again, and they already hold the valid values. Plus, we validate all the other constraints in the bean. In our example, that would be `@AssertTrue`, as shown in Figure 11-6.

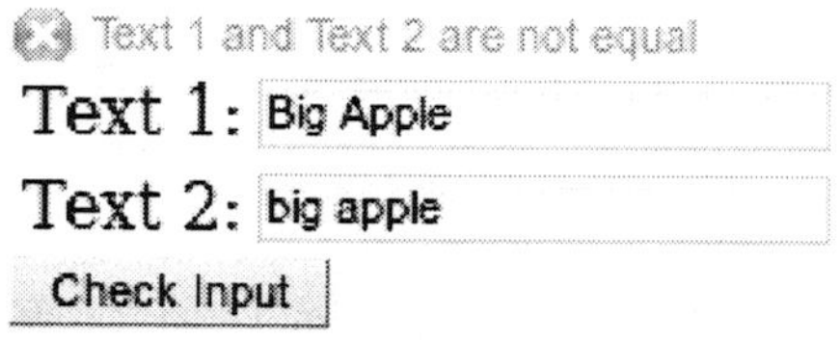

Text 1 and Text 2 are not equal

Text 1: Big Apple

Text 2: big apple

Check Input

Figure 11-6. Graph validator error message

Where does this validation happen? It happens during the Process Validations phase. You are probably wondering, how can validation be invoked on the entire bean if the values are not yet set in the properties because we haven't passed the Update Model phase? RichFaces makes a copy or clones (called `clone()`) the bean, the values submitted are copied into the cloned copy, and then the validation is invoked on the cloned copy. That's the reason we need to wrap all the inputs that bound to that bean's properties with the `<rich:graphValidator>` tag, and the bean has to implement the `java.lang.Cloneable` interface. The only exception to this is noted in the following caution.

■ **Caution** If the bean doesn't implement `Cloneable`, `CloneNotSupportedException` exception is thrown. In this case, when RichFaces attempts to clone the object, then validation will be done during the Update Model phase (after the model will be actually updated so all the values available). Don't worry, you won't see this exception because RichFaces will catch it and will perform validation during the Update Model phase.

■ **Note** For graph validator to be invoked during the Process Validations phase, the `clone()` method has to be overwritten and be public. In a case of simple properties, you don't need to do anything and just call `super()`. If there are other properties—such as custom object (so a deep clone needed), lists, or maps—the clone mechanism has to be implemented by the developer.

Summary

Validation is a crucial part of any web application. JSF 2 makes validation easy with out-of-the-box support for powerful and popular Bean Validation. RichFaces takes validation to the next level by providing client-side validation. RichFaces simply extends the Bean Validation model by bringing it to the client. Validation can be performed on the client without sending an Ajax request. In situations where client-side implementation for a particular validation is not available, RichFaces quietly falls back to server-side validation without the developer needing to do anything. Finally, RichFaces provides graph validator, which enables validation of the entire bean again. The graph validator validates all properties bound to UI components, as well as properties not bound to UI components. Graph validator is useful for conditional validation, such as comparing whether two inputs satisfy a validation rule.

CHAPTER 12

Rich Components JavaScript API, Client Functions, and Using jQuery

In this chapter we are going to cover a number of miscellaneous but important components and functions. We will start with the widely used #{rich:component()} client function and <rich:componentControl> behavior. Both make it possible to call the JavaScript API available on a component. We will then cover other client functions. We will finally cover two remaining components: <rich:jQuery>, which integrates the jQuery JavaScript framework into a JSF application, and <rich:hashParam>, which allows passing a group of client-side parameters to a client-side component.

Invoking a Component's JavaScript API

In this section, we are going to show you two different ways to invoke the component's JavaScript API.

Using #rich:component(id) Function

We already covered #{rich:component()} in Chapter 4 when we introduced rich components. But let's cover it here briefly again. As you know by now, many RichFaces components provide JavaScript API. When a component provides JavaScript API, it's possible to control the component on the client, such as switching tabs in case of a tab component, or showing and hiding in the case of a popup component. Before we can invoke a JavaScript function on a component, we need to get a reference to that component on the client, and that's exactly what #{rich:component()} does. When placed on a page, it renders a JavaScript that obtains a reference to the component in the browser.

Let's see how it works in an example. We will start with one of the most popular components in RichFaces: <rich:popupPanel>. This popup is usually rendered on the page, but it is hidden from view. Showing and hiding a popup is done on the client-side (e.g., the browser). Listing 12-1 shows a popup panel.

Listing 12-1. A popup panel

```
<h:outputLink value="#"
   onclick="#{rich:component('popup')}.show();return
      false;">Open</h:outputLink>
   <rich:popupPanel header="RichFaces" id="popup">
      <h:panelGrid>
```

```
            <h:outputText value="This is a RichFaces popup" />
            <h:outputLink value="#"
                onclick="#{rich:component('popup')}.hide();">Close</h:outputLink>
        </h:panelGrid>
</rich:popupPanel>
```

The most important code is in the onclick event in both open and close links. As we already mentioned, showing and hiding a panel is done on the client, so we need to get a reference to the popup component on the client and invoke JavaScript API. That's exactly what we do with #{rich:component()}. #{rich:component()} gives a reference to all the component JavaScript API. With this reference, we can invoke any available function. In our example, we call show() to show the component, and hide() to hide the component. How do you know what API is available? RichFaces documentation lists all functions for each component. Whenever you need to get a reference to the component's JavaScript API, you use #{rich:component()}, passing it the component id, as follows:

#{rich:component(id)}

It's important to point out that the function takes the component id, not the client id.

Tip   RichFaces documentation at www.jboss.org/richfaces lists all JavaScript API for each component.

So far we used show() without any arguments. If we want to pass any arguments to the popup panel, we have to use this signature: show(event, {param1:value, param2:value}). Listing 12-2 shows the updated popup example.

Listing 12-2. Passing arguments to the popup panel

```
<h:outputLink value="#" onclick="#{rich:component('popup')}.show(event,
    {top:5,left:5,width:200,height:250});">Open</h:outputLink>

<rich:popupPanel header="RichFaces" id="popup">
    <h:panelGrid>
        <h:outputText value="This is a RichFaces pop-up" />
        <h:outputLink value="#"
            onclick="#{rich:component('popup')}.hide();">Close</h:outputLink>
    </h:panelGrid>
</rich:popupPanel>
```

event is a variable and the parameters are passed in JSON format.

Tip   Any component JavaScript function that takes arguments should either be invoked with no arguments (if supports calls with just default values) or should pass all the arguments with event being the first: foo(event, options).

Let's try another example using the accordion component. When using an accordion, to switch to a different item we just click that item. Another way to switch items is to use the JavaScript API that the component provides. Figure 12-1 shows the accordion followed by the code listing.

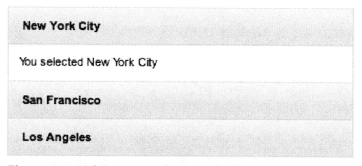

Figure 12-1. RichFaces accordion panel with three major U.S. cities

Listing 12-3 shows the page code.

Listing 12-3. The page code

```
<h:form>
    <rich:panel style="width:350px">
        <rich:accordion id="cities">
            <rich:accordionItem header="New York City" name="nyc">
                <h:outputText value="You selected New York City" />
            </rich:accordionItem>
            <rich:accordionItem header="San Francisco" name="sf">
                <h:outputText value="You selected San Francisco" />
            </rich:accordionItem>
            <rich:accordionItem header="Los Angeles" name="la">
                <h:outputText value="You selected Los Angeles" />
            </rich:accordionItem>
        </rich:accordion>
    </rich:panel>
</h:form>
```

Accordion provides JavaScript API for switching items. We are going to add a button for each city and when the button is clicked, the item corresponding to a city will be selected. Listing 12-4 shows the three buttons.

Listing 12-4. Shows the three buttons

```
<h:form>
    <rich:panel style="width:350px">
        <rich:accordion id="cities">
            <rich:accordionItem header="New York City" name="nyc">
                <h:outputText value="You selected New York City" />
            </rich:accordionItem>
            <rich:accordionItem header="San Francisco" name="sf">
                <h:outputText value="You selected San Francisco" />
            </rich:accordionItem>
```

```
        <rich:accordionItem header="Los Angeles" name="la">
            <h:outputText value="You selected Los Angeles" />
        </rich:accordionItem>
    </rich:accordion>

    <input type="button" value="New York City"
        onclick="#{rich:component('cities')}.switchToItem('nyc')" />
    <input type="button" value="San Francisco"
        onclick="#{rich:component('cities')}.switchToItem('sf')" />
    <input type="button" value="Los Angeles"
        onclick="#{rich:component('cities')}.switchToItem('la')" />
  </rich:panel>
</h:form>
```

We again use the #{rich:component()} client function to get a reference to the accordion component first (cities id). Once we have a reference, we can invoke any available JavaScript function on the component. In our example, we call switchToItem(), passing it the name of the accordion item to which we want to switch.

In Listing 12-4, the buttons were placed inside the form. That's not required and the buttons could have been placed outside the form. Usually, when invoking a JavaScript function, the form is not required because we are not making any requests to the server. However it's possible that the component itself will send an Ajax request according to the API called. The default switch type for an accordion is ajax. This means that when a button is clicked it calls the API method on <rich:accordion> to switch the item, and an Ajax request is sent by the <rich:accordion> to the server. An easy way to check this is to place an <a4j:log> component on the page. Whenever an Ajax request is sent, this component will output request/response information. If we change accordion's switchType="client", then no request will be sent because all the items are rendered on first page load and further switching is done entirely on the client.

In addition to switching to a named item like we did in our example, Listing 12-4, accordion also supports switching to first, last, next, and previous items. Listing 12-5 shows these four buttons.

Listing 12-5. Shows the first, last, next, and previous items buttons

```
<input type="button" value="First"
    onclick="#{rich:component('cities')}.switchToItem('@first')" />
<input type="button" value="Next"
    onclick="#{rich:component('cities')}.switchToItem('@next')" />
<input type="button" value="Previous"
    onclick="#{rich:component('cities')}.switchToItem('@prev')" />
<input type="button" value="Last"
    onclick="#{rich:component('cities')}.switchToItem('@last')" />
```

The accordion provides predefined names for switching to these tabs, such as @first, and this naming format closely follows JSF 2 convention.

■ **Tip**   Other RichFaces components that can be switched and are built out of "items" such as <rich:accordionItem>, which provide the same switchToItem() API and the same predefined names.

Using <rich:componentControl>

In the previous section we showed you how to invoke component's JavaScript API using the #{rich:component()} function. There is another way to invoke the API. This second approach is more declarative and uses <rich:componentControl> behavior. The name of the component implies what it does. It makes it possible to control a component from another component that is done via JavaScript.

Let's take two examples from previous sections and update them to use <rich:componentControl>. Listing 12-6 shows the popup panel example updated using <rich:componentControl> instead of the #{rich:component()} function.

Listing 12-6. *Shows the popup panel example updated using <rich:componentControl> instead of the #{rich:component()} function*

```
<h:outputLink value="#">
   <h:outputText value="Open" />
   <rich:componentControl event="click" target="popup" operation="show" />
</h:outputLink>

<rich:popupPanel header="RichFaces" id="popup">
   <h:panelGrid>
      <h:outputText value="This is a RichFaces pop-up" />
      <h:outputLink value="#">
      <h:outputText value="Close" />
         <rich:componentControl event="click" target="popup"
            operation="hide" />
      </h:outputLink>
   </h:panelGrid>
</rich:popupPanel>
```

Let's take a closer look at the opening link. Instead of using #{rich:component()} we nest <rich:componentControl> behavior inside. <rich:componentControl> attaches itself to the parent component and then invokes a JavaScript function on another component. We specified the following three attributes: event="click" indicates which event to listen on the parent component; target="popup" indicates on which component to invoke the function; operation="show" indicates which function to invoke on the component. This looks very similar to using #{rich:component()}, simply done in a more declarative fashion. To close (hide) the popup, we use the same setup, but instead of invoking the show operation (show() function), we invoke the hide operation (hide() function). One major difference between these two approaches is that the #{rich:component()} function can be used with any HTML tag, but being a behavior, <rich:componentControl> can be attached only to another JSF component.

■ **Tip**   When specifying operation in <rich:componentControl>, only the operation (function) name is used, without parenthesis ().

Passing Parameters with <a4j:param>

Now let's update the accordion example to use <rich:componentControl>. We are not going to repost the accordion markup because it stays the same. We will only update the buttons. When we switched accordion items, we passed the item's name to the switchToItem() function. Let's see how we can do the same using `<rich:componentControl>`. Listing 12-7 shows using `<rich:componentControl>` on external buttons to control the items.

Listing 12-7. Using `<rich:componentControl>` on external buttons to control the items

```
<h:commandButton value="New York">
   <rich:componentControl event="click" target="cities"
      operation="switchToItem">
      <a4j:param value="nyc" />
   </rich:componentControl>
</h:commandButton>
<h:commandButton value="San Francisco">
   <rich:componentControl event="click" target="cities"
      operation="switchToItem">
      <a4j:param value="sf" />
   </rich:componentControl>
</h:commandButton>
<h:commandButton value="Los Angeles">
   <rich:componentControl event="click" target="cities"
      operation="switchToItem">
      <a4j:param value="la" />
   </rich:componentControl>
</h:commandButton>
```

Notice that for the operation attribute, we specify only the function name; there is no option to pass parameters there. How do we pass the parameter? We include `<a4j:param>` with the accordion item's name inside `<rich:componentControl>`. It's possible to pass multiple parameters; they will be applied in the order the `<a4j:param>` tag is listed.

Instead of `<a4j:param>`, we can also use the standard `<f:param>` tag. Both will give us the same result. Listing 12-8 shows using `<f:param>` with a button.

Listing 12-8. Using `<f:param>` with a button

```
<h:commandButton value="New York">
   <rich:componentControl event="click" target="cities"
      operation="switchToItem">
      <f:param value="nyc" />
   </rich:componentControl>
</h:commandButton>
```

However, `<a4j:param>` adds one very important feature. In addition to passing parameters evaluated from server-side expressions to client functions, the `<a4j:param>` value can also be evaluated as a client-side JavaScript expression when the noEscape attribute is set to true. We show an example of this in next section.

Passing JavaScript Hash with `<rich:hashParam>`

In previous sections we saw how to pass string-based parameters. However, it's also possible to pass a JavaScript hash to a function. RichFaces now comes with a new component called `<rich:hashParam>`, which allows you to pass a JavaScript hash or hash table to a JavaScript function. A hash table is very similar to a hash map; it consists of keys and associated values.

Let's look at an example in Listing 12-9, which shows opening a popup panel and passing information such as width, height, and positioning via the <rich:hashParam> tag.

Listing 12-9. Opening a popup panel and passing information via the <rich:hashParam> tag

```
<h:outputLink value="#">
    <h:outputText value="Open" />
    <rich:componentControl event="click" target="popup" operation="show">
        <a4j:param noEscape="true" value="event" />
        <rich:hashParam>
            <a4j:param name="width" value="500" />
            <a4j:param name="height" value="300" />
            <a4j:param name="minWidth" value="300" />
            <a4j:param name="minHeight" value="150" />
            <a4j:param noEscape="true" name="left"
                value="(jQuery(window).width()/2)-250" />
            <a4j:param noEscape="true" name="top"
                value="(jQuery(window).height()/2)-150" />
        </rich:hashParam>
    </rich:componentControl>
</h:outputLink>

<rich:popupPanel header="RichFaces" id="popup">
    <h:panelGrid>
        <h:outputText value="This is a RichFaces pop-up" />
        <h:outputLink value="#">
            <h:outputText value="Close" />
            <rich:componentControl event="click" target="popup"
                operation="hide"/>
        </h:outputLink>
    </h:panelGrid>
</rich:popupPanel>
```

From Listing 12-9, all parameters passed to the popup are inserted into a JavaScript hash tab with the <rich:hashParam> tag. The actual parameter is defined with the <a4j:param> tag but you can also use the standard <f:param> for all except top, left, and event parameters. For top and left, the value is not a string-based value but a jQuery function that calculates the positioning based on the current browser window size. Setting noEscape="true" is required in those cases; otherwise, the parameters will be treated as server-side expressions and the jQuery function will not be invoked.

■ **Note**   As of writing of this book, only <rich:popupPanel> component accepts a JavaScript hash table as an argument to its API. We anticipate more components will support JavaScript hash table arguments in the future.

■ **Note**   You might be wondering why we pass <a4j:param noEscape="true" value="event"> as the first parameter. This is required because the show method has the following signature: show(event, options). You can invoke show() without any arguments, but if you do provide arguments, both must be specified.

Other RichFaces Client Functions

In addition to the widely used #{rich:component()} to invoke client JavaScript API, RichFaces provides the following client-side functions:

- #{rich:clientId(id)}: Returns a client id for a component from passed component id

- #{rich:element(id)}: Returns a DOM element from passed component id

- #{rich:findComponent(id)}: Returns a server-side component instance for passed component id

- #{rich:isUserInRole(role)}: Returns if the user has a specified role

Let's try the first three in an example and then come back to the #{rich:userInRole()} function. To start, we are going to place a <rich:calendar> on the page, shown in Listing 12-10, and use this component with all the functions.

Listing 12-10. Placing a <rich:calendar> on the page

```
<h:form id="form">
    <rich:calendar popup="true" id="calendar" />
</h:form>
```

First, as these are client-side functions, they are invoked via EL, inside #{}. If we need to get the calendar's client id, we place this on a page, as follows:

```
#{rich:clientId('calendar')}
```

And we get the following output:

```
form:calendar
```

We place them on a page because it's an easy way to test and see what they produce. However, in real applications, you will most likely use them from inside a JavaScript function.
If we need to get a calendar's DOM element, we place this on a page, as follows:

```
#{rich:element('calendar')}
```

And we get the following output:

```
document.getElementById('form:calendar')
```

Let's also try #{rich:component} and see what we get. So, we place the following on a page:

```
#{rich:component('calendar')}
```

And we get the following result:

```
RichFaces.$('form:calendar')
```

Behind the scenes this is a jQuery selector that will let us call the available JavaScript functions on this component. We don't recommend using JavaScript from #{rich:component(id)} directly anywhere.

#{rich:component(id)} is a shortcut and in case of changes to implementation or refactoring, you won't have to make any changes to the application.

Let's now try #{rich:findComponent}, which is best demonstrated in an example shown in Listing 12-11.

Listing 12-11. Using #{rich:findComponent}

```
<h:form id="form">
   <h:panelGrid>
      <h:outputText value="Text:" />
      <h:inputText id="input">
         <a4j:ajax event="keyup" render="echo"/>
      </h:inputText>
      <h:outputText value="Echo:" />
      <h:outputText id="echo" value="#{rich:findComponent('input').value}" />
   </h:panelGrid>
</h:form>
```

This example shows a somewhat typical echo-like example. Any input typed is echoed immediately on the next line because we use the keyup event. What's interesting is that there is no managed bean or managed property bound and used in this example. The page in our example is submitted as always and the value entered is set into the component. As we don't bind the input component to a managed bean property, the value just stays in the component. Using #{rich:findComponent(id)}, we find that input component in a JSF component tree, get its value, and then display it on the page with #{rich:findComponent(id).value}. In other words, we are working directly with a JSF component tree, without needing a backing bean. This could be useful if you need to test something quickly without having to build and bind to a model.

The last function is called #{rich:isUserInRole(role)}. It provides a shortcut to a standard Java EE security feature, which in turn makes the following call:

```
facesContext.getExternalContext.getUserInRole(role)
```

What's good about this function is that it doesn't care how and where roles are defined. Roles can be defined in web.xml but can also be defined somewhere else, depending on application configuration. The function returns *true* if current user is in the provided role. For example, suppose only the administrator should see some part of a page, as shown in Listing 12-12.

Listing 12-12. Example of the administrator's defined role

```
<rich:panel header="Admin panel" rendered="#{rich:isUserInRole('admin')}">
  Very sensitive information
</rich:panel>

<rich:panel header="User panel">
  General information
</rich:panel>
```

In the above example, unless the current user is authenticated as admin, the top panel will not be rendered. For this to work, appropriate security roles need to be defined in the web.xml file.

Using jQuery with <rich:jQuery>

jQuery JavaScript framework is at the heart of RichFaces because it's the only JavaScript framework used (and extended) by RichFaces. The following is a jQuery description from jQuery.com: "jQuery is a fast and concise JavaScript Library that simplifies HTML document traversing, event handling, animating, and Ajax interactions for rapid web development."[1]

We also would like to add that jQuery is one of the most popular JavaScript frameworks out there. We highly recommend that you do some reading about how jQuery works. A good starting point is the JQuery: The Write Less, Do More, JavaScript Library web site at http://jquery.com. You can also find a number of good books out there. One of them is *jQuery: Novice to Ninja* by Earle Castledine and Craig Sharkie (SitePoint, 2010).

jQuery works with the browser DOM. With jQuery, you first select a single element or group of elements in the DOM and then do something with it or query it. If this particular query should be done when a button is clicked, for example, then we also attach this selector/query to some HTML element. There are many different tools, easy and advanced, to select an element, and many different things you can "perform" on the selection. Why do we need the <rich:jQuery> tag? <rich:jQuery> allows a more convenient and declarative way of adding jQuery queries to a page and its elements. One last thing to mention, jQuery being a JavaScript framework, it works in the client or the browser. Let's do an easy example with <rich:panel> shown in Listing 12-13.

Listing 12-13. Example with <rich:panel>

```
<rich:panel header="New York" id="nycInfo" style="width:50%">
    New York is the most populous city in the United States and the center of the New York
    Metropolitan Area, one of the most populous metropolitan areas in the world. New York
    exerts a significant impact upon global commerce, finance, media, culture, art, fashion,
    research, technology, education, and entertainment. As the home of the United Nations
    Headquarters, it is also an important center for international affairs. The city is often
    referred to as New York City or the City of New York to distinguish it from the state of New
    York, of which it is a part. Source: http://en.wikipedia.org/wiki/New_York_City.
</rich:panel>
```

Let's say we would like to change the header title from "New York" to "New York City." This is easily done with jQuery. We first attach jQuery to a button, on button click we select the panel, and then we do the content change. Listing 12-14 shows a button that does that.

Listing 12-14. Attaching jQuery to a button

```
<input type="button" id="changeButton" value="Update panel" />
<rich:jQuery selector="#changeButton"
    query="click(function(){
        $('#nycInfo .rf-p-hdr').text('New York City');
})"/>
```

The selector attribute is used to select one or more elements on the page. In our example, selector="#changeButton" selects the button that will be clicked. query binds the handler function to the click event on the selected button. Inside the handler function, we first select the panel (#nycInfo), then we select its header by its CSS class (.rf-p-hdr) and invoke the text() function to modify the header. You might be wondering why we first select #nycInfo and then .rf-p-hdr. A rich panel is a complex

---

[1] http://jquery.com/.

component and consists of a number of HTML tags. jQuery allows you to filter elements, and only returns the elements that you need. #nycInfo would return the entire panel—and that's not what we need. However, once we have the panel and search for .rf-p-hdr, we get the header element which we want to modify.

▒ **Note** $('id') is a shortcut for jQuery('id').

Let's also change the text color inside the panel to blue. Listing 12-15 shows the changes.

Listing 12-15. Change the text color inside the panel

```
<input type="button" id="changeButton" value="Update panel" />

<rich:jQuery selector="#changeButton"
    query="click(function(){
        $('#nycInfo .rf-p-hdr').text('New York City');
        $('.rf-p-b').css('color', 'blue');
})"/>
```

Notice that we didn't specify a panel id before; this means we are not selecting a particular panel, and if we had other panels on the page, they would also change body color. To test this, just add another <rich:panel> to the page, for example, as shown in Listing 12-16.

Listing 12-16. Testing which panels would change body color

```
<rich:panel>
    This panel will also turn blue.
</rich:panel>
```

If you look at the query attribute value in Listing 12-15, it looks rather long and somewhat complicated. We can simplify the markup by setting the event via the event attribute, as shown in Listing 12-17. That attribute allows us to bind the query defined in the corresponding attribute to a specified event without an additional definition in query itself.

Listing 12-17. Simplify the markup by setting the event via the event attribute

```
<input type="button" id="changeButton" value="Update panel" />
<rich:jQuery selector="#changeButton" event="click"
    query="$('#nycInfo .rf-p-hdr').text('New York City');
              $('.rf-p-b').css('color', 'blue');" />
```

Let's add one more jQuery effect: add a button that hides the panel. Listing 12-18 shows the page code.

Listing 12-18. Adding a button that hides the panel

```
<input type="button" id="hideButton" value="Hide panel"/>
<rich:jQuery selector="#hideButton" event="click" query="$
    ('#nycInfo').hide()"/>
```

We use a built-in jQuery hide() function to hide the panel. The only other difference, instead of specifying the event in query, we use a separate event attribute to set the click event, which makes the tag markup even simpler. We can't leave this without adding a show button, as shown in Listing 12-19.

Listing 12-19. Using a built-in jQuery hide() function to hide the panel

```
<input type="button" id="showButton" value="Show panel"/>
<rich:jQuery selector="#showButton" event="click" query="$
    ('#nycInfo').show()"/>
```

While using event attributes to define the query as an event handler, you might want to define the binding type because jQuery allows different binding types for event handlers. The attachType attribute is used for that. bind type is the default type and means that the event handler will be bound to all elements returned by the selector and currently present on the page. live type works the same as bind and also means that the event handler defined in the query will be bound to all elements that will appear on the page later (for example, created using JavaScript or loaded via Ajax). And one type means the event handler is bound to all elements currently defined by the selector attribute. After the first invocation of the event, the handler of one type is unbound such that it no longer fires when the event occurs.

Everything we just did can be written directly with jQuery, without using the <rich:jQuery> tag. Listing 12-20 shows everything we just did, but directly with jQuery.

Listing 12-20. Example using jQuery

```
<script>
$('#changeButton').click(function(){
    $('#nycInfo .rf-p-hdr').text('New York City');
    $('.rf-p-b').css('color', 'blue');
});
$('#hideButton').click(function(){
        $('#nycInfo').hide();
});
$('#showButton').click(function(){
        $('#nycInfo').show();
});
</script>
```

What is the difference between using jQuery directly and <rich:jQuery>? The differences are very minor. One difference is that using <rich:jQuery> has a more declarative syntax. Also, when <rich:jQuery> is used, the actual jQuery script file is automatically rendered into the page. However, if jQuery is used directly, it's necessary to load the JavaScript file manually. There are a number of ways to do that. You can use @ResourceDependency or use the standard <h:outputScript> tag to load the file.

■ **Caution** You should be careful when loading external libraries using standard JSF 2 loading mechanisms. In case the library you loaded manually conflicts with RichFaces built-in libraries, application pages may not work as expected, if at all.

Another option is to place <rich:jQuery> on the page as follows:

```
<rich:jQuery rendered="true"/>
```

This will render the script file, but will not render anything for the component.

Finally, there is one more difference when `<rich:jQuery>` is used and we search for some id in the selector attribute, as follows:

```
selector="#changeButton"
```

We can specify a component id and RichFaces will resolve it to the client id. When we use jQuery directly, we always need to specify the client id. In cases when the component is nested, the client id might be long.

■ **Tip** If you need to select an element with client id such as `form:img`, it could conflict with CSS selector syntax. A work-around using double backslashes can be used to escape the colon character such that the identifier is read correctly instead of being interpreted as CSS selector syntax. For example: `selector="#form\\:img"`.

So far we have shown you how to attach event handlers. This means something is activated and the jQuery query is invoked. It's also possible to define an inline statement to be evaluated while a page is loading or when loaded. For example, let's look at Listing 12-21, which shows a classic addition of the zebra style to a table using jQuery.

Listing 12-21. Shows a classic addition of the zebra style to a table using jQuery

```
<style>
    .even-row {
        background-color: #FCFFFE;
    }
    .odd-row {
        background-color: #ECF3FE;
    }
</style>
<rich:dataTable id="gamesTable" value="#{olympicGamesBean.games}"
    var="game">
    <rich:column>
        <f:facet name="header">
            <h:outputText value="City" />
        </f:facet>
        <h:outputText value="#{game.city}" />
    </rich:column>
    <rich:column>
        <f:facet name="header">
            <h:outputText value="Country" />
        </f:facet>
        <h:outputText value="#{game.country}" />
    </rich:column>
    <rich:column>
        <f:facet name="header">
```

```
            <h:outputText value="Year" />
        </f:facet>
        <h:outputText value="#{game.year}" />
    </rich:column>
</rich:dataTable>

<rich:jQuery selector="#gamesTable tr:odd" query="addClass('odd-row')" />
<rich:jQuery selector="#gamesTable tr:even" query="addClass('even-row')" />
```

After rendering, the table will look like Figure 12-2.

City	Country	Year
Atlanta	United States	1996
Sydney	Australia	2000
Athens	Greece	2004
Beijing	China	2008
London	United Kingom	2012
Rio de Janeiro	Brazil	2016

Figure 12-2. Table with zebra style added with <rich:jQuery>

In this example, once the page is rendered, `<rich:jQuery>` will be invoked; it will select the table based on its id and add a CSS class to odd rows and a different CSS class to even rows. In this example, the query will be triggered when the DOM has been loaded and ready. Timing can be changed via the `timing` attribute. `domready` is the default value (used in our example) and will trigger the query once the DOM is ready. On the other hand, the value of `immediate` will trigger the query immediately after the JavaScript code is rendered.

Another way to use `<rich:jQuery>` is a named query. If we give `<rich:jQuery>` a name by using a corresponding attribute, we can then invoke the query as a regular JavaScript function from any other component. This is called a named query. An example is shown in Listing 12-22.

Listing 12-22. An example of a named query

```
<h:graphicImage width="100" value="/images/venice.png"
    onmouseover="larger(this, {})" onmouseout="normal(this, {})" />

<rich:jQuery name="larger" query="animate({width:'241px'})" />
<rich:jQuery name="normal" query="animate({width:'100px'})"/>
```

When the mouse is over the image (onmouseover), we call the `larger()` function, which is the name of the function defined by the `<rich:jQuery>` tag. When the mouse moves outside the image (onmouseout), we call the `normal()` function, also defined by `<rich:jQuery>`. For the named query to work, the object on which the query will be invoked has to be passed and that's why we pass this object as the first argument. The second argument allows you to pass parameters to the jQuery function in the query shown in Listing 12-23.

Listing 12-23. Passing parameters to the jQuery function in the query

```
<h:graphicImage width="100" value="/images/venice.png"
    onmouseover="larger(this, {imageWidth:'241'})" onmouseout="normal(this,
        {})" />

<rich:jQuery name="larger" query="animate({width:options.imageWidth})" />
<rich:jQuery name="normal" query="animate({width:'100px'})"/>
```

Parameters are passed in JSON syntax as a second parameter in the JavaScript call. The options namespace is then used in the <rich:jQuery> query to access the passed function parameters.

■ **Tip**   Named <rich:jQuery> will produce JavaScript evaluated only after the call to the function is made. It will not be invoked on page rendering.

Summary

Even though this is a miscellaneous chapter, we covered a number of very important RichFaces features. We first learned how to invoke JavaScript API on components, as well as various ways for passing parameters to these functions. We then covered other RichFaces client functions, such as #{rich:isUserInRole(role)}, which provides a super-easy way to check whether the current user is in a particular defined role. In the last part of this chapter we covered <rich:jQuery>, which allows you to bind to an element and invoke jQuery queries in a declarative approach.

CHAPTER 13

Skins

RichFaces comes with a built-in skins feature that allows you to control the look and feel of your entire application from a single place. The skins feature is sometimes called *themes*, and in this context they're the same thing.

You are probably wondering why you wouldn't just use good old CSS to change the look and feel of your application. CSS is not going anywhere; you are still going to use it. The basic idea is to provide more abstraction when working with the look and feel. Instead of repeating the same color in the CSS file, you will be able to dictate that all panel headers or tab labels will be this style or all table headers will have that color, and so on. In situations where you need more control and flexibility, you can still use CSS and overwrite skin generated styles. However, when using skins, by changing just a few parameters, it is possible to alter the appearance of RichFaces components in a synchronized fashion without messing up the user interface consistency. Skins is a high-level extension of standard CSS, which can be used together with regular CSS declarations.

In this chapter we will show you how to use skins in RichFaces. We will show you how to use the built-in skins, how to create and use your own custom skins, and how to customize and overwrite skins-generated CSS. Finally, we will show you how to enable the skins feature for standard HTML and JSF tags.

Using Built-in Skins

RichFaces provides a number of built-in skins. You have to do very little to use them. The following are the out-of-the-box skins with color schema, which you will find in the `richfaces-core-impl-4.0.x` JAR file.

- DEFAULT (gray colors)

- plain (no predefined colors or background images)

- emeraldTown (green colors)

- blueSky (light blue colors)

- wine (dark green colors)

- japanCherry (pink colors)

- ruby (deep red colors)

- classic (blue colors)

- deepMarine (Cyan colors)

▪ **Note** Because the page you are looking at is black and white, we'll use two very different skins to demonstrate examples in the chapter. We'll use ruby, which is a dark skin, and blueSky, which is a lighter skin. You should be able to see the difference even on the black-and-white pages of this book. An even better option is to create a new project and follow the steps throughout this chapter; this way, you'll be able to see the results in actual color.

To start using skins in your application, you need to add the `org.richfaces.skin` context parameter to the `web.xml` file of the application and specify the name of the skin. Just take any application you have built and add the context parameter shown in Listing 13-1 (if the context parameter already exists in `web.xml`, just set it to the desired skin).

Listing 13-1. Adding the context parameter

```
<context-param>
    <param-name>org.richfaces.skin</param-name>
    <param-value>ruby</param-value>
</context-param>
```

That's it; you don't need to do anything else. Restart the server, and you should see the new look and feel.

Figure 13-1 shows an example using the ruby skin. The panel header (`<rich:panel>`) and tabs (`<rich:tab>`) have a dark red palette, and you didn't have to specify any CSS.

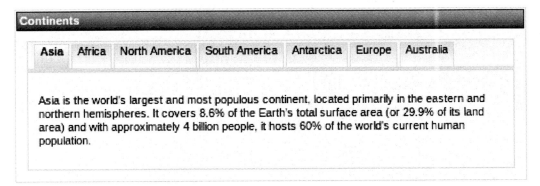

Figure 13-1. Rich panel and tabs in ruby skin

If you want to try another skin, just update the context parameter, restart the server, and see how it looks. Figure 13-2 is an example using the blueSky skin.

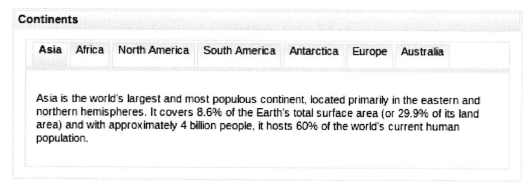

Figure 13-2. Rich panel and tabs in blueSky skin

Again, notice how the entire page has been updated according to the selected skin. Listing 13-2 shows the source (some text was omitted to save space).

Listing 13-2. The source

```
<rich:panel style="width:500px;">
    <f:facet name="header">
        Continents
    </f:facet>
    <rich:tabPanel switchType="client">
        <rich:tab header="Asia">
        ...
        </rich:tab>
        <rich:tab header="Africa">
        ...
        </rich:tab>
        <rich:tab header="North America">
        ...
        </rich:tab>
        <rich:tab header="South America">
        ...
        </rich:tab>
        <rich:tab header="Antarctica">
        ...
        </rich:tab>
        <rich:tab header="Europe">
        ...
        </rich:tab>
        <rich:tab header="Australia">
        ...
        </rich:tab>
    </rich:tabPanel>
</rich:panel>
```

■ **Note** As mentioned earlier, all the default skins are located in the `richfaces-core-impl-4.0.x.jar` file, which is in the `META-INF/skins` directory.

Listing 13-3 shows the code for the ruby skin (it's just property file). As you can see, the skin defines fonts, colors for various sections, and parts of the user interface. Later in the chapter you will see how you can easily build your own skin.

Listing 13-3. *Code for the ruby skin*

```
#Colors
headerBackgroundColor=#900000
headerGradientColor=#DF5858
headerTextColor=#FFFFFF
headerWeightFont=bold

generalBackgroundColor=#f1f1f1
generalTextColor=#000000
generalSizeFont=11px
generalFamilyFont=Arial, Verdana, sans-serif

controlTextColor=#000000
controlBackgroundColor=#ffffff
additionalBackgroundColor=#F9E4E4

shadowBackgroundColor=#000000
shadowOpacity=1

panelBorderColor=#C0C0C0
subBorderColor=#ffffff

tabBackgroundColor=#EDAEAE
tabDisabledTextColor=#C47979

trimColor=#F7C4C4

tipBackgroundColor=#FAE6B0
tipBorderColor=#E5973E

selectControlColor=#FF9409

generalLinkColor=#CF0000
hoverLinkColor=#FF0000
visitedLinkColor=#CF0000

# Fonts
headerSizeFont=11px
headerFamilyFont=Arial, Verdana, sans-serif

tabSizeFont=11
```

```
tabFamilyFont=Arial, Verdana, sans-serif

buttonSizeFont=11
buttonFamilyFont=Arial, Verdana, sans-serif

tableBackgroundColor=#FFFFFF
tableHeaderBackgroundColor=#EB9A99
tableSubHeaderBackgroundColor=#F7DBDB
tableFooterBackgroundColor=#cccccc
tableSubfooterBackgroundColor=#f1f1f1
tableBorderColor=#C0C0C0
tableBorderWidth=1px
tableHeaderTextColor=#980808

#Calendar colors
calendarWeekBackgroundColor=#f5f5f5
calendarHolidaysBackgroundColor=#FFF1F1
calendarHolidaysTextColor=#980808
calendarCurrentBackgroundColor=#808080
calendarCurrentTextColor=#ffffff
calendarSpecBackgroundColor=#f1f1f1
calendarSpecTextColor=#000000


warningColor=#FFE6E6
warningBackgroundColor=#FF0000

editorBackgroundColor=#F1F1F1
editBackgroundColor=#FEFFDA

#Gradients
gradientType=plain
```

▒ **Note** Two new properties were added in RichFaces 4: `tableHeaderBackgroundColor` and `tableSubHeader-BackgroundColor`. In RichFaces 3.3.x table headers used panel header colors.

How do the skins work? You now have the `org.richfaces.skin` context parameter in your *web.xml* file, so RichFaces will take the value of the parameter and parse bundled RichFaces ECSS stylesheets on the fly to fill corresponding properties with values from skin properties. Yes, it is still plain CSS behind the scenes.

▒ **Note** In addition to dynamic resources generation, RichFaces offers an option to generate all the skin resources during application compile time. That allows it to serve resources in a static manner through CDN (Content Delivery Network), for example. RichFaces provides a special resource plug-in that is responsible for static resources generation and makes it possible to deploy a RichFaces application in the cloud.

▪ **Note** In RichFaces 4 a new ECSS (EL CSS) format that uses standard CSS syntax is introduced, removing proprietary .xcss format. Later we'll show you how it looks and why a separate format rather than CSS parsing is used.

Creating Your Own Skins

As you can see, several skins are available for you to try, but you might want to create your own. That's easy enough to do. In fact, you can basically take an existing skin and make changes until you like how the page is rendered.

First you have to place a custom skin where RichFaces can find it. You can put it in one of the following classpath directories in your application: META-INF/skins/ or WEB-INF/classes.

▪ **Note** You could use skins packaged in application JAR files. Skin files should be placed in META-INF/skins/ folder inside the JAR file.

Take the ruby skin and copy it to the Java source directory in the application. When the application is built, it will be copied to WEB-INF/classes.

Let's say you want to change the skin name. Suppose you want to call your skin newyork. The naming convention is rather simple (name.skin.properties). Because you want to call your skin newyork, you will rename the file you just copied to

newyork.skin.properties

Next you have to register the skin in the web.xml file, as shown in Listing 13-4.

Listing 13-4. Register the skin in the web.xml file

```
<context-param>
    <param-name>org.richfaces.skin</param-name>
    <param-value>newyork</param-value>
</context-param>
```

If you keep it as it is, you simply have created a copy of the *ruby* skin with a different name. Your goal in this section is to create a custom skin that is different.

Make the changes to the following parameters in the skin, as shown in Listing 13-5.

Listing 13-5. Shows changes to the parameters in the skin

```
generalSizeFont=16px
headerSizeFont=16px
```

When using your custom skin, the rendered page should look like that shown in Figure 13-3. As you can see if you open the file, you have modified the font sizes. All RichFaces components will now inherit this look and feel throughout the application.

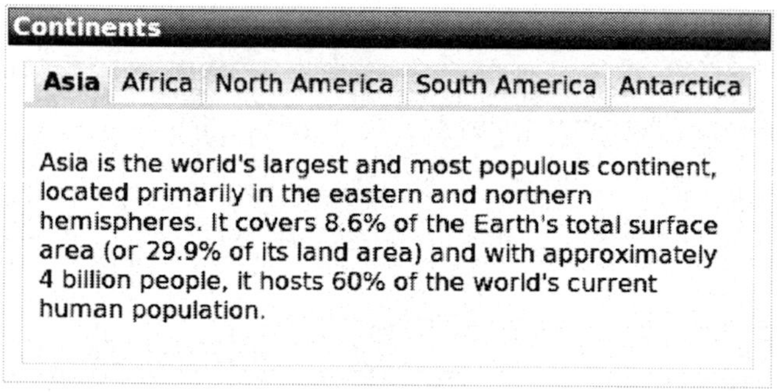

Figure 13-3. Rich panel and tabs in custom skin

Note We're changing only the font attributes to make it easier for you to see the difference on the black-and-white page.

In the previous example, you copied the whole skin and then modified skin parameters. An alternative way to create a custom skin (it's probably also simpler), is to create a new skin and base it on any of the existing skins, rather than copying the whole skin file. Overwrite only the parameter you need. For example, the newyork.skin.properties file will look like Listing 13-6.

Listing 13-6. The newyork.skin.properties file

```
baseSkin=ruby
generalSizeFont=16px
headerSizeFont=16px
```

The result would be identical to the previous image.

You are not only limited to redefining existing skin parameters, it's also possible to define custom skin parameters. The custom skin parameters will not be used in RichFaces components, but you will be able to apply them to some standard or third-party components. The way of applying skin parameters to any components on the view is described next. Skin parameters in the skin file could be defined with EL values.

Changing the Skin Parameter

You are probably asking, how do I know which skin parameter to change? In other words, how do the skin parameters correspond to the CSS properties of the components? To find this information, go to the RichFaces 4 Component Reference available at the JBoss Community RichFaces Documentation web site (*www.jboss.org/richfaces/docs*). The "Style classes and skin parameters" section is available for every component. There you'll find which skin parameters define which CSS properties.

You have used <rich:tabPanel> and <rich:tab>, so next you'll see how skin parameters for these components correspond to CSS properties.

\<rich:tabPanel\>

Table 13-1 shows how CSS properties correspond to skin parameters. From this table you can see that the border color of the \<div\> element, which wraps all the tab headers, is determined by the panelBorderColor skin property.

Table 13-1. CSS Properties and Skin Parameters for Tab Controls Containers*

CSS Property	Skin Parameter
border-color	panelBorderColor
background-color	additionalBackgroundColor

*Used in "rf-tb-hdr-tabline-vis" predefined CSS class

\<rich:tab\>

Determining how skin parameters correspond to CSS properties is the same for the \<rich:tab\> component. Tables 13-2, 13-3, 13-4, and 13-5 show how CSS properties correspond to skin parameters when using the \<rich:tab\> component.

Table 13-2. Skin Parameters for Header Sections*

CSS Property	Skin Parameter
color	generalTextColor
border-color	panelBorderColor
background-color	tabBackgroundColor

*Used in "rf-tb-hdr" predefined CSS class

Table 13-3. Skin Parameters for the Active Tab*

CSS Property	Skin Parameter
background-color	additionalBackgroundColor

*Used in "rf-tb-hdr-act" predefined CSS class

Table 13-4. Skin Parameters for Tab Labels*

CSS Property	Skin Parameter
font-family	generalFamilyFont
font-size	generalSizeFont

*Used in "rf-tb-lbl" predefined CSS class

Table 13-5. Skin Parameters for the Disabled Tab*

CSS property	Skin Parameter
color	tabDisabledTextColor

*Used in "rf-tb-hdr-dis" predefined class

To define the background color for the active tab, you would set the `additionalBackgroundColor` skin parameter, as shown in Table 13-3. To define the disabled tab text color, you would set the *tabDisabledTextColor* skin parameter, as shown in Table 13-5, which would result in the parameters in the skin file shown in Listing 13-7.

Listing 13-7. Parameters in the skin file

```
additionalBackgroundColor=blue
tabDisabledTextColor=green
```

Using Skins and CSS

Using skins gives you a lot of abstraction in defining CSS for the application. However, sometimes you might need more flexibility and control over the look and feel. In other words, you might want to define additional styles beyond what the skins permit.

There are three levels to defining the look and feel of your application. Each stage or level gives you a different degree of control. The three approaches are as follows:

- Skin-based CSS. Using ECSS (EL CSS) stylesheets with skin property values applied

- Redefining skin-inserted CSS classes

- Adding user-defined styles (via *style* or *styleClass*-like attributes; RichFaces components make available many other class-based attributes)

Skin-Based CSS

Using skins is basically a global way of describing the look and feel of the application. RichFaces will go through the ECSS files applying properties of the currently loaded skin. This is the first approach. You control the look and feel of an application entirely through skins.

What is ECSS?

In RichFaces 4, ECSS (EL CSS) files are used to generate component CSS according to skin on the fly when the page is rendered. It uses the familiar CSS format. Listing 13-8 shows how a portion of the `panel.ecss` file for `<rich:panel>` looks.

Listing 13-8. A portion of the panel.ecss file

```
.rf-p{
   background-color:'#{richSkin.generalBackgroundColor}';
   color:'#{richSkin.panelBorderColor}';
```

```
    border-width:1px;
    border-style:solid;
    padding:1px;
}
.rf-p-hdr{
    background-color:'#{richSkin.headerBackgroundColor}';
    border-color:'#{richSkin.headerBackgroundColor}';
    …
}
```

But why ECSS and not just simple CSS with EL inside? Yes, JSF 2 allows you to use EL expressions in CSS resources right out of the box. However, there are problems:

- JSF allows turning off EL usage in stylesheets if application CSS files have not used it. This is allowed in order to improve performance. But it is not acceptable for RichFaces components, where skins is the core feature and components styling could be completely broken.

- RichFaces parses the ECSS files to trim properties that are not defined by skin. This additional parsing should be done on RichFaces resources only and not applied to any third-party or standard stylesheets.

If you created your own ECSS stylesheet and need to add to the view, you should simply use JSF 2 facilities for that, for example

```
<h:outputStylesheet name="application.ecss"/>
```

or with a ResourceDependency annotation, such as

```
@ResourceDependency(name="application.ecss")
```

Redefining Skin-Based CSS Classes

We'll now demonstrate how to redefine or customize CSS styles generated by the skin.

To add new custom styles, simply append your custom style into any of the predefined CSS classes coming from the skin ECSS. Using the same approach, you can overwrite any of the default styles. Let's look at an example using the <rich:panel> component shown in Listing 13-9.

Listing 13-9. An example using the <rich:panel> component

```
<rich:panel id="panel" style="width:300px">
    <f:facet name="header">
        Using skins is so cool!
    </f:facet>
    I can easily change how my application looks
</rich:panel>
```

It produces the example using the *ruby* skin shown in Figure 13-4.

Using skins is so cool!

I can easily change how my application looks

Figure 13-4. Rich panel in ruby skin

Listing 13-10 shows part of the HTML generated for this component when the page is rendered.

Listing 13-10. Part of the HTML generated

```html
<div style="width: 300px;" id="panel" class="rf-p">
    <div id="panel_header" class="rf-p-hdr">
        Using skins is so cool!
    </div>
    <div id="panel_body" class="rf-p-b ">
        I can easily change how my application looks
    </div>
</div>
```

The <rich:panel> component consists of three <div> HTML tags: one for the header, one for the body, and one for a parent that wraps the header and body. If you look closely, you will see that special CSS classes have been inserted in Listing 13-11.

Listing 13-11. Inserted CSS classes

```html
<div style="width: 300px;" id="panel" class="rf-p">
<div id="panel_header" class="rf-p-hdr">
<div id="panel_body" class="rf-p-b ">
```

Those style classes are defined in the panel.ecss stylesheet and contain CSS properties based on current skin parameters. Listing 13-12 shows how the file looks.

Listing 13-12. Shows the file

```css
.rf-p{
    background-color:'#{richSkin.generalBackgroundColor}';
    color:'#{richSkin.panelBorderColor}';
    border-width:1px;
    border-style:solid;
    padding:1px;
}

.rf-p-hdr{
    background-color:'#{richSkin.headerBackgroundColor}';
    border-color:'#{richSkin.headerBackgroundColor}';
    font-size:'#{richSkin.headerSizeFont}';
    color:'#{richSkin.headerTextColor}';
    font-weight:'#{richSkin.headerWeightFont}';
    font-family:'#{richSkin.headerFamilyFont}';
    padding:2px;
    border-width:1px;
    border-style:solid;
    background-position:top left;
```

```
    background-repeat:repeat-x;
    background- ↵
      image:"url(#{resource['org.richfaces.renderkit.html.GradientA']})";
}

.rf-p-b{
    font-size:'#{richSkin.generalSizeFont}';
    color:'#{richSkin.generalTextColor}';
    font-family:'#{richSkin.generalFamilyFont}';
    padding:10px;
}
```

First let's redefine existing styles. Let's use the first CSS class *rf-p* for that. Well, you just take the defined CSS properties, create a CSS class in the page with the same name, and set them to values you want. Suppose we only want to overwrite color and border style properties, as shown in Listing 13-13.

Listing 13-13. Overwriting color and border style properties

```
<style>
.rf-p{

    color: red;
    border-style: dotted;
}

</style>
```

You can overwrite one, two, or all properties.

Adding new custom properties is just as simple. Using the rf-p-b skin-based CSS class, add any custom property not present in the skin-based CSS with a desired value, as shown in Listing 13-14.

Listing 13-14. Using the rf-p-b skin-based CSS class

```
<style>
.rf-p-b {
    font-style: italic;
    font-weight: bold;
}
</style>
```

The result is shown in Figure 13-5.

Figure 13-5. Overwriting skin-generated CSS

In general, to redefine styles for all <rich:panel> components on a page using CSS, it's enough to create classes with the same skin-based CSS class names and redefine necessary properties in them. You don't necessarily have to use the *style* tag; you can as easily define the styles in a separate CSS file and load it via <h:outputStylesheet> tag.

Keep in mind that redefining CSS properties in this way will affect all the tab panels on the same page. We will show you how to control that in a later section of this chapter.

Redefining the CSS Class Name

In Listing 13-5 you looked inside the generated HTML source, but that's not the best way to find the CSS class name. To find out which class names are generated, you again have to refer to the RichFaces 4 Component Reference at the JBoss Community web site. Go to www.jboss.org/richfaces/docs to open a reference. Find the <rich:panel> component section there and look through the "Style classes and skin parameters" section inside.

All components will display a table showing how various CSS class names correspond to components. Table 13-6 explains how each CSS class corresponds to the component's appearance.

Table 13-6. How Each CSS Style Affects the Components Shown in Figure 13-5

CSS Class	Class Description
rf-p	Defines styles for a wrapper <div> element of a component
rf-p-hdr	Defines styles for a header element
rf-p-b	Defines styles for a body element

The rest of components follow the same approach.

The last approach is to use fully user-defined classes just as you would normally.

User-Defined Style

The last approach is to use the attributes you have always used, such as style, styleClass, and any other component-defined style properties, such as bodyClass, headerClass, and so on, to define custom style classes. Using the same example, you add a user-defined class to the <rich:panel> component using the styleClass attribute, as shown in Listing 13-15.

Listing 13-15. Adding a user-defined class to the <rich:panel> component using the styleClass attribute

```
<rich:panel id="panel" style="width:300px" styleClass="myClass">
   <f:facet name="header">
      Using skins is so cool...
   </f:facet>
   I can easily change how my application looks
</rich:panel>
```

myClass is defined in Listing 13-16.

Listing 13-16. myClass

```
<style>

.myClass {
```

```
    font-style: italic
}
</style>
```

The generated HTML is shown in Listing 13-17.

Listing 13-17. *Generated HTML*

```
<div style="width: 300px;" id="panel" class="rf-p myClass">
    <div id="panel_header" class="rf-p-hdr">
        Using skins is so cool!
    </div>
    <div id="panel_body" class="rf-p-b">
        I can easily change how my application looks
    </div>
</div>
```

The final result shows how italics have been applied to the whole panel, as in Figure 13-6.

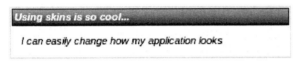

Figure 13-6. *Applying italics to the whole panel*

This approach allows you to control styling for a particular panel component. Even if you have multiple panels, only one will be affected.

To summarize, there are three different ways to work with the look and feel of your application. The first level is using the built-in skins feature. Keep in mind that skins are simply a higher-level abstraction to good old CSS. The next level is redefining the CSS classes automatically generated for each component. The last level is using attributes such as style and styleClass (and any other component that defines the style attribute) to gain even further control over the look and feel. This last method allows you to change the look and feel for just the component on the current page without affecting components on other pages.

Dynamically Changing Skins

We have shown you how to create and use custom skins. It's also possible to load any skin when the application is running, including your custom skin. To enable such functionality, the org.richfaces.skin parameter in web.xml has to point to an EL expression that resolves to the current skin, as shown in Listing 13-18.

Listing 13-18. *Using the* org.richfaces.skin *parameter*

```
<context-param>
    <param-name>org.richfaces.skin</param-name>
    <param-value>#{skinBean.currentSkin}</param-value>
</context-param>
```

The bean would look like Listing 13-19.

Listing 13-19. The managed bean

```
@ManagedBean(name="skinBean")
@SessionScoped
public class SkinBean implements Serializable {

    private String currentSkin = "newyork";

    public String getCurrentSkin() {
        return currentSkin;
    }

    public void setCurrentSkin(String skin) {
        this.currentSkin = skin;
    }
}
```

In this example, *skin* property inside the SkinBean managed bean will hold the currently selected skin. It should be initialized to some initial skin value, for example, through the managed bean's configuration or just initializing the property with initial skin name as done in Listing 13-13. The bean should also be placed in session scope so that the skin is not reset on each request.

Now you can easily change the look and feel of the application by dynamically setting the currentSkin property to one of the available skins in your application.

▓ **Note** If you are changing skins when the application is running, it makes sense to reload the full page. Without a full-page refresh, it's not possible to update all the ECSS loaded Update of resources via Ajax might result in unexpected results.

Standard Controls Skinning

Starting with RichFaces 3.2.1, the RichFaces team made standard controls skinning pretty simple. Nothing needs to be done in order for the skins to be applied to all standard controls.

In Listing 13-20, let's look at a very simple example of a JSF page without RichFaces.

Listing 13-20. Example of a JSF page without RichFaces

```
<h:panelGrid columns="1">
   <h:outputText value="Favorite city: "/>
   <h:inputText value="#{geography.city}"/>
</h:panelGrid>
<h:commandButton action="next" value="Submit"/>
```

The result is shown in Figure 13-7.

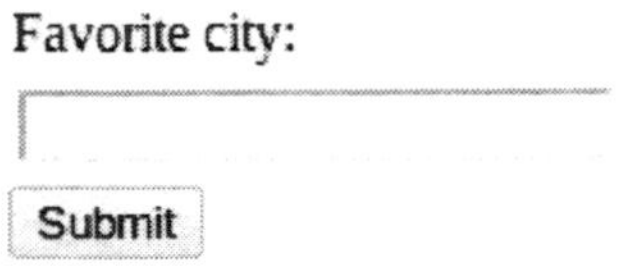

Favorite city:

Submit

Figure 13-7. *The resulted image*

So far, there is nothing interesting—just a plain JSF page.

In RichFaces 4, the context parameter shown in Listing 13-21 is available and set to *true* by default. This means that all standard controls on a page will be skinned.

Listing 13-21. *The context parameter*

```
<context-param>
    <param-name>org.richfaces.enableControlSkinning</param-name>
    <param-value>true</param-value>
</context-param>
```

This example will now look like Figure 13-8, with the RichFaces added and ruby skin defined.

Favorite city:

Submit

Figure 13-8. *Favorite City*

If you want to style controls on your own without influencing all the standard ones, define the context parameter with false value.

Another parameter that is set to false by default is org.richfaces.enableControlSkinningClasses. To enable it, add the code found in Listing 13-22 to your web.xml file.

Listing 13-22. *org.richfaces.enableControlSkinningClasses*

```
<context-param>
    <param-name>org.richfaces.enableControlSkinningClasses</param-name>
    <param-value>true</param-value>
</context-param>
```

When enabled, it offers a special predefined CSS class: rfs-ctn (the short name implies a RichFaces container, in case you are wondering). When this CSS class is used on a container-like component (<h:panelGrid>, <rich:panel>, or just <div>), any standard controls inside the container will be skinned using standard controls skinning classes.

The code examples in Listing 13-23 are basically equivalent. The only difference is that in the first one you apply the rfs-ctn style to a <div> tag, while in the second example you apply it to <h:panelGrid> instead.

Listing 13-23. Equivalent code samples

```
<div class="rfs-ctn">
    <h:panelGrid columns="1" >
        <h:outputText value="Favorite city: " />
        <h:inputText value="#{geography.city}" />
        <h:commandButton action="next" value="Submit" />
    </h:panelGrid>
</div>

<h:panelGrid columns="1" styleClass="rfs-ctn">
    <h:outputText value="Favorite city: " />
    <h:inputText value="#{geography.city}" />
    <h:commandButton action="next" value="Submit" />
</h:panelGrid>
```

When we enabled *org.richfaces.enableControlSkinningClasses,* we also turned off *org.richfaces.enableControlSkinning,* as only one approach should be used in application. The result is shown in Figure 13-9.

■ **Note** In general, you should use one of the standard control skinning approaches in your application. Either skin all the standard components and HTML tags automatically (setting org.richfaces.enableControlSkinning to true) or apply the special CSS class rfs-ctn (setting org.richfaces.enableControlSkinningClasses to true) on containers to skin standard components and HTML tags within that container only.

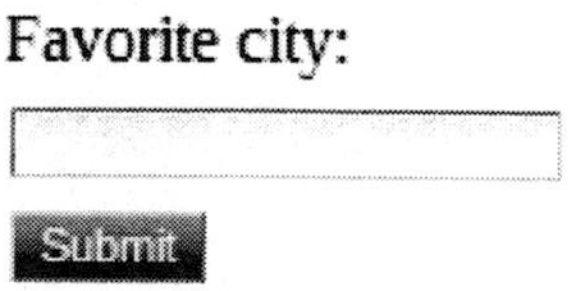

Favorite city:

Submit

Figure 13-9. Skinning standard JSF components

Standard Controls skinning applies not only to components but also to standard HTML controls (as simple CSS selectors for HTML elements used under the hood). The code in Listing 13-24 is an example.

Listing 13-24. Standard Controls skinning

```
<h:panelGrid columns="1" styleClass=" rfs-ctn">
    <h:outputText value="Favorite city: " />
    <h:inputText value="#{geography.city}" />
    <h:commandButton action="next" value="Submit" />
    <input type="button" value="HTML Button"/>
</h:panelGrid>
```

It will display Figure 13-10.

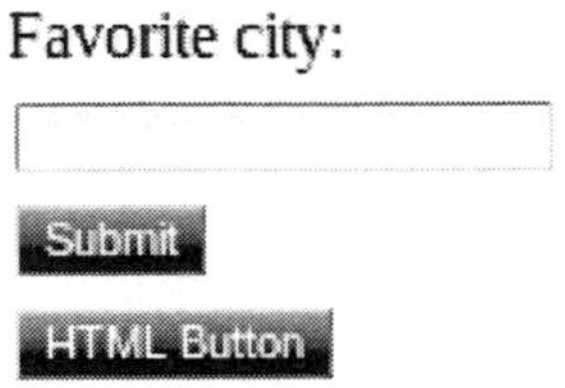

Favorite city:

[   ]

Submit

HTML Button

Figure 13-10. Applying the skins feature to standard HTML tags

More specific CSS classes representing various skin parameters are also available. To learn what's available, look inside the *richfaces-core-impl-4.0.x.jar* file in */META-INF/resources/skinning-classes.ecss*. This file will also show you the mapping between specially defined CSS class parameters and skin parameters. Listing 13-25 is an example entry.

Listing 13-25. Example entry

```
.rfs-txt-general{
    font-size: '#{richSkin.generalSizeFont}';
    font-family: '#{richSkin.generalFamilyFont}';
    color: '#{richSkin.generalTextColor}';

}
```

A specially defined *.rfs-txt-general* CSS class will be combined from the skin properties *generalSizeFont*, *generalFamilyFont*, and *generalTextColor*. In turn, these skin properties correspond to the *font-size*, *font-family*, and *color* CSS properties, respectively. Listing 13-26 is an example using *.rfs-txt-general* and another *.rfs-btn* (similar to *.rfs-txt-general*).

Listing 13-26. Example using .rfs-txt-general and another .rfs-btn

```
<h:panelGrid columns="1">
    <h:outputText value="Favorite city: " styleClass="rfs-txt-general"/>
    <h:inputText value="#{geography.city}" styleClass="rfs-txt-general"/>
    <h:commandButton action="next" value="Submit" styleClass="rfs-btn"/>
</h:panelGrid>
```

This will display Figure 13-11.

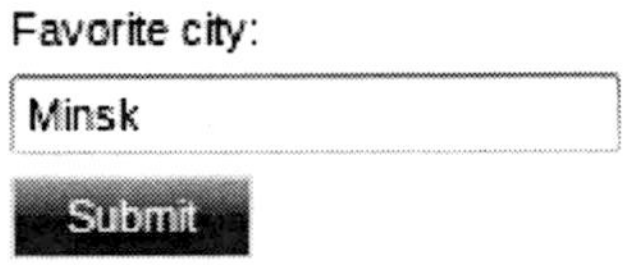

Favorite city:

[Minsk   ]

Submit

Figure 13-11. Using special RichFaces CSS classes to skin standard JSF components

Notice that "Favorite city" (<h:outputText>) has been skinned as well. It has a different style than the previous examples.

Using #{richSkin} Implicit Object

It's possible to turn off the "Standard Controls Skinning" feature and style a single component without loading the complete standard skinning ECSS. In such case you should use skin properties directly from the current skin, in particular components styles. This allows you to skin standard controls without having to update that particular style each time you change skin or skin parameters.

Suppose you add a button to your tabs example and turned the standard controls skinning feature off, as in the following code:

```
<h:commandButton action="next" value="Next page -
    I want to learn about world oceans!"/>
```

The result is shown in Figure 13-12.

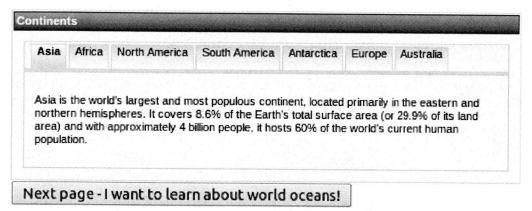

Figure 13-12. Using #{richSkin} to skin standard JSF components

As you can see, it's a standard JSF button (*h:commandButton*) and, of course, not skinnable. You can add a style via the style or styleClass attribute that matches the current skin (ruby), but then you would need to adjust it each time you change the skin. A better way is to use skin parameters to add style to the button. For example, you can use tabBackgroundColor as the color for the button, as shown in Listing 13-27. Of course, you can use any other skin parameter from the skin.

Listing 13-27. tabBackgroundColor

```
<h:commandButton action="next" value="Next page -
    I want to learn about world oceans!"
    style="background-color:#{richSkin.tabBackgroundColor}"/>
```

The result is shown in Figure 13-13.

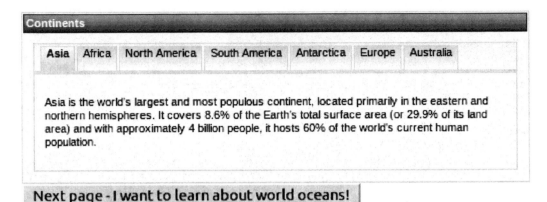

Figure 13-13. Standard JSF buttons styled with skin colors using #{richSkin}

Let's review #{richSkin.tabBackgroundColor}. #{richSkin} is an implicit object that points to the current skin and allows you to access any of the skin's parameters. It's no different from the #{view} and #{initParam} implicit objects. You can reference any skin parameter in this way. It's just the same as usage of the object in ECSS files.

You can pull styles from the skin without even using any RichFaces components, as shown in Listing 13-28.

Listing 13-28. Pulling styles from the skin without using RichFace components

```
<div style="color: #D01F3C;
    border: 2px solid #{richSkin.panelBorderColor};
    width: 300px">
    I can even use Skins without any RichFaces components
</div>
```

Listing 13-29 is an example of how to highlight a row in a table when the mouse cursor is over that row, and returns default color when the cursor moves out.

Listing 13-29. Highlighting a row in a table

```
<rich:dataTable value="#{carBean.allCars}" var="car" rows="10"
    onRowMouseOver="this.style.backgroundColor='#D5D2D1'"
    onRowMouseOut="this.style.backgroundColor='#{richSkin.tableBackgroundColor}'">

    <rich:column>
        <h:outputText value="#{car.make}" />
    </rich:column>
    <!--Other columns-->
</rich:dataTable>
```

Result from last example are shown in Figure 13-14.

Vendor	Model	Price	Mileage	VIN
Chevrolet	Corvette	46692	78899.0	XZIPVJLVNKEAVLLRN
Chevrolet	Corvette	26704	63097.0	YJWIBIUESUXJPIDFT
Chevrolet	Corvette	20028	46612.0	VDLBRIUMXGIKGJLFO
Chevrolet	Corvette	28815	19725.0	TDVPVAVWBLSZHXAUY
Chevrolet	Corvette	37034	40321.0	RGVOXGJRFPJYCMWLK
Chevrolet	Malibu	35056	70378.0	NKDAQUEWYMFJYAFVM
Chevrolet	Malibu	54435	67759.0	SXGSAGMJCAWANILQO
Chevrolet	Malibu	16415	6848.0	UBASZDJISCPVFFNMC
Chevrolet	Malibu	23698	61297.0	TNWJUHVEUTZMXUEPR
Chevrolet	Malibu	45401	40891.0	TBBTOLVPVKNBSKLGY

Figure 13-14. Highlighting currently selected row using #{richSkin}

Summary

This chapter demonstrated one of the major features in RichFaces: skins. Skins is simply a powerful extension to CSS. By using skins, you can easily change the look and feel of your entire application. The chapter also demonstrated various ways to create custom skins, as well as customizing, extending, and redefining existing skins. We also covered skinning non-RichFaces components, such as standard JSF tags and standard HTML tags.

Now that we are done with skins, the next chapter will cover RichFaces Component Development Kit (CDK). The CDK allows you to quickly and easily build your own custom rich components.

CHAPTER 14

RichFaces CDK: Building Custom Components

In this chapter we will cover one of the most interesting topics in RichFaces: building custom components with the Component Development Kit (CDK). As you can judge from this book and other resources on the Internet, RichFaces is more than just a component library for JSF. It extends JSF with advanced Ajax features and customization, client-side validation, skins, JavaScript component API, and much more. There is one great feature, however, to which we want to dedicate an entire chapter: building custom JSF components with RichFaces CDK. Note that we said JSF components and not RichFaces components. Yes, with CDK you can build custom JSF (not necessarily RichFaces) components. In our opinion, that's one of the strongest features of CDK.

Note This chapter requires slightly more advanced knowledge of JSF 2 features, such as life cycle, components building foundation, and behavior principles. If you feel you need to brush up your JSF skills, we recommend the following two books: *Core JavaServer Faces, Third Edition* by David Geary and Cay Horstmann (Prentice Hall, 2010) and *JavaServer Faces 2.0, The Complete Reference* by Ed Burns and Chris Schalk (McGraw-Hill, 2009).

We will start with a short overview of RichFaces CDK in order to understand how it will help us in our JSF component developer jobs.

JSF component development can be a rather tedious task. Components are usually easy to work with when you are placing them on pages, setting properties, or attaching actions or listeners. However, building the component is usually more challenging. Let's review the standard JSF component development process from the beginning.

First, you need to create a base component class and add all the component attributes as properties with accessor methods, which allows you to store and access property values by using the StateHelper object. Then, ideally, you will have to create a renderer-specific class, which will consist of all HTML-specific attributes, such as events, styles, and others that are defined in the same manner as the base component class. In addition, if a behavior support (such as Ajax) is present, behavior events should be declared separately, as well. Then you will need to perform another challenging task—writing a renderer that will process the changes made on the client and render the HTML code back. Even for simple components, rendering HTML code inside Java code is not simple. For example, it is challenging to review and debug such code by looking for missed end tags or missed attributes. Things usually get even more complicated when you need to extend your own component from these classes. Finally, in some cases we will need to write the Facelets TagHandler class for our component.

After we are done with these tasks, we will have to become good XML developers. Yes, even in the Java EE6 era, it's still an important part of the job in many instances. We need to add the JSF configuration file with all the component description information, such as component class, component family, renderkit definitions, and so on. After that, we will create a component.taglib.xml file, which will define a View Definition Language (VDL) tag for the component.

Similar work needs to be done to create client behavior.

How does RichFaces CDK help us? Almost at every step. Let's take a look at how the basic steps described earlier will be made easier.

1. *Component classes*. CDK allows you to generate a UI class with all the accessors for attributes just from an abstract class marked with a special annotation as a component and with set of abstract getter methods marked with the other annotations as attributes.

   In the best cases, when you have no complex component functionality that should be implemented in component classes, you will not need a base abstract class. If you prefer, you could just create faces-config.xml with a few CDK-specific extensions and all the component classes stuff will be generated.

2. *Renderer classes*. In the best case scenario, you will not need to write any line of Java code. CDK includes an XML template compiler that will generate renderer from the XML template (which is really just an HTML template under the hood and very similar to a JSF 2 composite component template). But, even if you need some Java utility methods for encoding, you will not need to write much code. Simply define the base class in the XML template and implement the base class with only the methods needed. Then the methods can be used directly in templates.

3. *XML configuration*. There is no longer any need for faces-config.xml and component.taglib.xml XML development. All the information will be extracted from abstract class annotations, and the template and the configuration files will be generated automatically. The only reason to write faces-config.xml on your own with CDK is if you prefer to generate a UI-component class instead of writing an abstract component class.

4. *Events, listeners, and behaviors*. CDK includes functionality for more easily defining events, listeners, behaviors, and so on.

Now that we have covered the basics of CDK, we are going to build a custom component together.

Before we start, there are two things we want to point out. First, RichFaces CDK is a separate feature in RichFaces. You don't need to know how to use the CDK to use any of the components we covered in this book. The topic of building custom components is extensive and could probably make up an entire book by itself. In this chapter we are going to introduce CDK and give you an idea of how it works. For anything more, please visit the JBoss Community RichFaces page at http://jboss.org/richfaces. Second, some CDK parts and functionality are still being finalized; so again, make sure to visit the RichFaces site often for any changes and updates.

Development Plan

Our plan is to create a simple spinner component that provides richer UI to simplify numerical input.

First, any component requires simple HTML prototyping work to create a future template to be rendered, and to define core attributes we will add to the component. This will help us prepare the

JavaScript part of the component, and if implement carefully, we can add it to the component without any additional changes.

Then we will create a Maven project and see how we will get component and renderer classes generated using an abstract component class and our HTML template moved to a special XML template file.

Next, we will create a project using the RichFaces project archetype and check the component in that application. We will also add a CSS stylesheet to the component, which is based on RichFaces skins, so it will be skinned as all the other RichFaces components.

Client-side Prototyping

Let's start with the HTML prototype. We won't be using any complicated markup because the goal is to show you how to use the CDK, not write complicated markup. We will start from the base markup and later you will be able to improve it with any customizations you want.

Listing 14-1 shows the code we will use.

Listing 14-1. Base markup

```
<!DOCTYPE html PUBLIC "-//W3C//DTD XHTML 1.0 Transitional//EN"
  "http://www.w3.org/TR/xhtml1/DTD/xhtml1-transitional.dtd">
<html>
  <head>
     <meta http-equiv="content-type" content="text/html; charset=UTF-8" />
  </head>
  <body>
     <span id="spinner" >
        <input type="text" value="100" id="spinnerInput"/>
        <button type="button" id="spinnerDec">&lt;</button>
        <button type="button" id="spinnerInc">&gt;</button>
     </span>
  </body>
</html>
```

Figure 14-1 shows the result.

Figure 14-1. Spinner HTML prototype

Let's create a jQuery plug-in that will add client functionality to the spinner. First we need to revise the options necessary for making it customizable. Later, we will convert these options to be attributes on the component.

Table 14-1 shows the final attribute list.

Table 14-1. Attribute List

Option	Default	Description
value	0	Current value of the spinner.
maxValue	100	Maximum value that can be entered
minValue	0	Minimum value that can be entered.
step	1	The value by which the current value will be decreased or increased during corresponding UI controls activation.

You would probably need more attributes if you were to use this component in production, but for the purpose of our example, these are sufficient. Listing 14-2 shows a simple jQuery plug-in that we created. It includes the following functionality:

- Binds the handlers to the buttons, which performs a value change on button click.

- Binds the handler to the keyup keyboard event and performs the same button click when up or down arrows are clicked.

- Binds the handler to the change event of the input, which verifies correctness of the current value and switches it to the last valid, in case the user entered some non-numerical value or a value that is outside of the min/max range.

Listing 14-2. spinner.js from meta-inf/resources/org.richfaces.book

```
(function($) {
   var defaultOptions = {
      step : 1,
      maxValue : 100,
      minValue : 0
   };
   $.fn.Spinner = function(opts) {
      var options = $.extend({}, defaultOptions, opts);
      return this.each(function() {
         var input = document.getElementById(this.id + "Input");
         var incControl = document.getElementById(this.id + 'Inc');
         var decControl = document.getElementById(this.id + 'Dec');
         var inc = function (event) {
            var newValue = Number(input.value) + (options.step);
            if (newValue < options.maxValue){
               input.value=currentValue=newValue;
            } else {
               input.value=currentValue=options.maxValue;
            }
         };
         var dec = function(event) {
            var newValue = Number(input.value) - (options.step);
            if (newValue > options.minValue){
               input.value=currentValue=newValue;
```

```
            } else {
                input.value=currentValue=options.minValue;
            }
        };
        var handleKey = function(event) {
            switch (event.keyCode) {
                case 38:
                    inc(event); break;
                case 40:
                    dec(event); break;
            }
        };
        var verify = function(event) {
            var valueToVerify = input.value;
            if (isNaN(valueToVerify)) {
                input.value = currentValue;
                return;
            }
            if (Number(valueToVerify) < options.minValue){
                input.value = currentValue = options.minValue;
                return ;
            }
            if (Number(valueToVerify) > options.maxValue) {
                input.value = currentValue = options.maxValue;
                return ;
            }
            currentValue = input.value;
        };
        $(incControl).click(inc);
        $(decControl).click(dec);
        $(input).keydown(handleKey);
        $(input).change(verify);
        if (!isNaN(options.value)) {
            input.value = options.value;
            verify();
        }
    });
};
})(jQuery);
```

The plug-in gets initialized with the options passed to constructor, and at the same time it provides defaults for them. This means that if some options are not passed, the component still works based on default values. In general, that's a very good practice because in many cases there are a set of parameters that often don't change. Performing such initialization will reduce the HTML size.

We then obtain DOM elements for the input and buttons because we need to bind handlers to their events. inc() and dec() functions are then defined to increase or decrease the current value from input to the number defined in the step option. The handleKey() function calls inc() or dec() functions depending on the keyCode we get from event. (We want the component to be able to change its value after keyboard events.) The verify() method will be called to verify the entered input when change event occurs. It will check the correctness of the new input (the user could change it manually by typing a non-numerical value in the input) and if it's incorrect, performs switching to the previous valid value or to some of the boundary values.

Finally, we perform binding on all methods to corresponding DOM element events and perform initialization of input with the initial value passed in options.

That's it. All we need now is add the script to our HTML template. As our client script is built as a jQuery plug-in, we should remember to add a base jQuery library there as well. We used jQuery 1.5.1, but you should also be able to use jQuery 1.6.x. Listing 14-3 shows what it looks like after the changes.

Listing 14-3. Adding script to the HTML template

```
<!DOCTYPE html PUBLIC "-//W3C//DTD XHTML 1.0 Transitional//EN"
  "http://www.w3.org/TR/xhtml1/DTD/xhtml1-transitional.dtd">
<html>
    <head>
        <meta http-equiv="content-type" content="text/html; charset=UTF-8" />
        <script src="jQuery.js" type="text/javascript"></script>
        <script src="spinner.js" type="text/javascript"></script>
    </head>
    <body>
        <span id="spinner" >
            <input type=text value="1" id="spinnerInput"/>
            <button type="button" id="spinnerDec">&lt;</button>
            <button type="button" id="spinnerInc">&gt;</button>
            <script>
                $('#spinner').Spinner({value:10});
            </script>
        </span>
</body>
</html>
```

When the page is rendered, we should be able to click on the buttons to increase or decrease value, and perform the same actions when pressing the key-up and key-down keyboard keys (when input has the focus). Figure 14-2 shows the result after rendering and increasing the value.

Figure 14-2. Interactive spinner HTML prototype

■ **Tip**   If you don't have much experience with jQuery, we recommend you spend some time learning it. Knowing jQuery is important when you build your own custom components or extend existing components.

Now we are ready to create the actual component. Let's start by creating a project for it.

Creating the Project

First, we are going to create a project in which we build the custom component.

▨ **Note** As of writing of this book, no special Maven archetype exists for creating a project where you would build a custom component with CDK. Thus, we are going to create a standard Maven project and add the required dependencies.

In our case, we are going to create a standard Maven project using the following command:

```
mvn archetype:generate
```

We choose the default `maven-archetype-quickstart` archetype of version 1.1 when prompted, and enter `org.richfaces.book` as our `groupId` and `spinner` as an `artifactId`. We leave the `1.0-SNAPSHOT` version prompted by default and define the package to be the same as the `groupId`.

Next, we need to add a set of dependencies that are required for dealing with JSF-based classes. But prior to adding the dependencies, you need to add the JBoss repository to your Maven `setting.xml`, as follows:

```
http://repository.jboss.org/nexus/content/groups/public-jboss/
```

▨ **Note** More information about additional settings can be found on the JBoss Community's Maven wiki at `http://community.jboss.org/wiki/MavenGettingStarted-Users`.

Now we are ready to obtain JBoss artifacts by using Maven. Listing 14-4 shows the list of dependencies.

Listing 14-4. List of dependencies

```xml
<properties>
  <org.richfaces.version>4.0.1-SNAPSHOT</org.richfaces.version>
  <project.build.sourceEncoding>UTF-8</project.build.sourceEncoding>
</properties>
<dependencies>
  <dependency>
    <groupId>org.richfaces.cdk</groupId>
    <artifactId>annotations</artifactId>
    <version>${org.richfaces.version}</version>
  </dependency>
  <dependency>
    <groupId>org.richfaces.ui</groupId>
    <artifactId>richfaces-components-ui</artifactId>
    <version>${org.richfaces.version}</version>
  </dependency>
  <dependency>
    <groupId>javax</groupId>
    <artifactId>javaee-web-api</artifactId>
    <version>6.0</version>
```

```
        <scope>provided</scope>
    </dependency>
    <!-- archetype generated dependencies-->
</dependencies>
```

You might want to ask why we added `richfaces-components-ui` to the list. Ideally, we should have neither impl nor RichFaces API as a dependency because CDK works separate from the main project. It's true but planning ahead we will use some utility classes from the `richfaces-ui.jar`. This is the only reason. You might not use it, and write your own code rather than be dependent on RichFaces classes.

Try to build the project at that point to check that things are fine and all the Maven settings are good so that the dependencies fetch successfully.

To add actual CDK processing to the project, we should add the plug-in to our POM. Listing 14-5 shows the plug-in definition.

Listing 14-5. The plug-in definition

```
<build>
    <plugins>
        <plugin>
            <groupId>org.richfaces.cdk</groupId>
            <artifactId>maven-cdk-plugin</artifactId>
            <version>${org.richfaces.version}</version>
            <executions>
                <execution>
                    <id>cdk-generate-sources</id>
                    <phase>generate-sources</phase>
                    <goals>
                        <goal>generate</goal>
                    </goals>
                </execution>
            </executions>
        </plugin>
    </plugins>
</build>
```

The added plug-in performs the generation of the classes and configurations from the base abstract component class and the renderer template is defined.

We need to create two folders in our project `src\main` folder. `resources` and `templates` folders should be manually added because the default archetype does not generate a `resources` folder and does not know that we need a `templates` folder for our renderer template.

■ **Note** So far in this book we have been IDE-neutral and only used Maven in our examples. We will continue using Maven, but will import the project into JBoss Tools and show you a number of screenshots throughout the chapter. Using JBoss Tools will make the development simpler. Having said that, you can still only use Maven and, of course, use any IDE that you choose.

JBoss Tools is a set of plug-ins for Eclipse to simply enterprise Java development. It provides source and visual tools for technologies such as JSF, RichFaces, Seam, Hibernate, and Portal, as well as others. To learn more about and install JBoss Tools, go to http://jboss.org/tools.

■ **Tip**   You can import the generated Maven project into Eclipse by either using the m2eclipse plugin or by generating Eclipse descriptors with Maven from running this command: `mvn eclipse:eclipse`

After importing the project, you should see the structure shown in Figure 14-3.

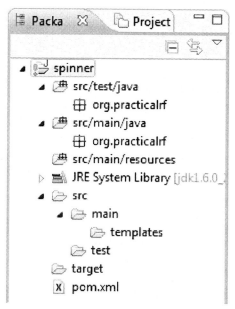

Figure 14-3. Project structure in Eclipse

■ **Note**   If you are getting "unavailable dependency" errors, most probably the Eclipse support to the project was added via a `mvn eclipse:eclipse` call and the "M2_REPO" environment variable was not set. Use Eclipse preferences and point it to your local repository, as shown in Figure 14-4.

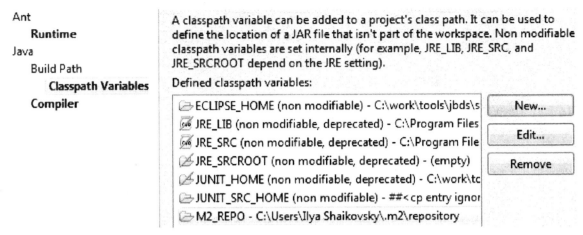

Figure 14-4. Setting Maven repository in Eclipse

Now that we are done with the setup, we can start building the component.

Creating a Components Library

Before creating the component classes and renderer templates, let's define our tag library from the beginning. Don't worry, it will not require any XML. Simply create a package-info.java class and put it in the org.richfaces.book package with the content shown in Listing 14-6.

Listing 14-6. Defining the tag library

```
@org.richfaces.cdk.annotations.TagLibrary(uri="http://org.richfaces.book/spinner",
shortName="in")
package org.richfaces.book;
```

■ **Note**   if you are working in Eclipse, use "Create File" instead of the "Create Class" wizard to create package-
info.java. Eclipse will not allow such a file name with a class wizard.

That's all. Using that annotation, CDK will add base information to the VDL (View Description Language) taglib when it is generated, as shown in Listing 14-7.

Listing 14-7. CDK adds base information to VDL taglib

```
<facelet-taglib xmlns="http://java.sun.com/xml/ns/javaee"
xmlns:xsi="http://www.w3.org/2001/XMLSchema-instance"
xsi:schemaLocation="http://java.sun.com/xml/ns/javaee http://java.sun.com/xml/ns/javaee/web-
facelettaglibrary_2_0.xsd" version="2.0" id="in">
    <namespace>http://org.richfaces.book/spinner</namespace>
```

```
    ...
</facelet-taglib>
```

Later it will be filled (also by the generator) with the tags and their attributes.

Creating an Abstract Component Class

In this section we describe the creation of the abstract component class for the spinner component. We will put it in the org.richfaces.book.component package. That class intention is to describe the generated component contract more easily than creating the UIComponent class manually. Our class will look as shown in Listing 14-8.

Listing 14-8. Abstract component class

```
@JsfComponent(type = "org.richfaces.book.Spinner", family = "javax.faces.Input", renderer =
@JsfRenderer(template = "spinner.template.xml"))
public abstract class AbstractSpinnerComponent extends UIInput {

    @Attribute
    public abstract boolean isDisabled();

    @Attribute(defaultValue = "1")
    public abstract String getStep();

    @Attribute(defaultValue = "0")
    public abstract String getMinValue();

    @Attribute(defaultValue = "100")
    public abstract String getMaxValue();
}
```

Looking through this class we see a set of CDK annotations. Annotating the class, there are @JsfComponent and @Attribute. The first marks the class as a base component class from which a UI class should be generated. The second one is used for specifying the attributes to be generated in that UI class. Each of the annotations has a set of attributes. We will review the most important attributes in Tables 14-2 and 14-3. Table 14-2 shows the @JsfComponent properties.

Table 14-2. @JsfComponent Properties

Property	Description
type	Specifies component type for the generated component.
family	Specifies component family for the generated component.
generate	Name of the UI class to be generated. By default is UI<Abstract class name> (without "abstract" prefix).
facets	Defines component facets. It's an array of @Facet annotations. The Facet#generate() attribute tells the CDK to generate a getter and setter for the facet.

fires	Array of @Event annotations that defines JSF events (and custom ones which inherited from FacesEvent) fired by component. For each event, CDK generates add/remove/get<Event>Listener methods, creates <event>Listener tag handler, and creates a listener class.
tag	Allows you to specify the tag name and handler class for the component. See @Tag for more details.
attributes	Contains array of strings, each contains the name of faces-config.xml fragment with attributes definitions, that lets CDK reuse the attributes definition in different components. CDK looks for these files in project classpath META-INF/cdk/attributes folder, and provides a set of such files for most HTML elements and standard components.
renderer	Associates component with Renderer implementation. There are two options to link the component with renderer: 1) by the renderer type or 2) by the template name. For the type, CDK doesn't check the existence of the target renderer because it would be defined in another module. For the template name, CDK enforces both the renderer and the component to share the same renderer type and family.
interfaces	Array of Java interface classes that should be implemented by generated component.

Table 14-3 shows the @Attribute properties.

Table 14-3. @Attribute Properties

Property	Description
aliases	Defines different names for the single attribute.
defaultValue	Valid Java expression evaluated to the default attribute value.
events	An array of ClientBehavior events definitions. The value of the @EventName annotation that should be used is the name itself, and the defaultEvent defined marks the event as a default behavior event.
literal	Disables EL expressions for the attribute.
passThrough	Defines the attribute to be rendered as an HTML attribute without conversion.
readOnly	Disables generation of the setter method.
required	Enforces the tag handler to check what the developer provided as an explicit value for that attribute.

■ **Note** These tables list only the most important attributes. For complete listings, please refer to RichFaces CDK documentation.

You could revise the simple code in Listing 14-8. All we are doing here is specifying the component type and component family, and also pointing the component to the renderer template that we will create later. In addition, we are marking all the abstract getter methods with the @Attribute annotation, and specifying the default value for the attributes where it applies. That's actually all there is to it!

Now let's build the project using mvn install.

Going to the target/generated sources folder, you find faces-config.xml in the "main/resources" folder. It contains standard component descriptor entries with some CDK extension tags inside. The more important part is in main/java/org/richfaces/book/component, where you see the UISpinner class.

You should also add the generated Java and resources folders to the source folders list of your IDE. After refreshing the project, the result in your IDE should look like Figure 14-5.

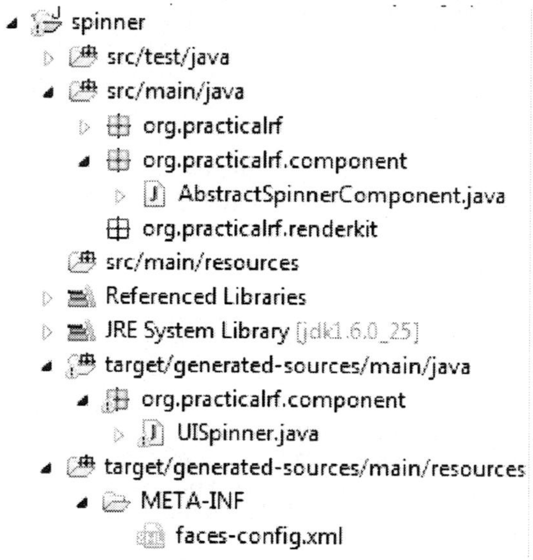

- ▲ 📂 spinner
  - ▷ 🗂 src/test/java
  - ▲ 🗂 src/main/java
    - ▷ ⊞ org.practicalrf
    - ▲ ⊞ org.practicalrf.component
      - ▷ 🗾 AbstractSpinnerComponent.java
      - ⊞ org.practicalrf.renderkit
    - 🗂 src/main/resources
  - ▷ 📚 Referenced Libraries
  - ▷ 📚 JRE System Library [jdk1.6.0_25]
  - ▲ 🗂 target/generated-sources/main/java
    - ▲ ⊞ org.practicalrf.component
      - ▷ 🗾 UISpinner.java
  - ▲ 🗂 target/generated-sources/main/resources
    - ▲ 📁 META-INF
      - 📄 faces-config.xml

Figure 14-5. Project structure with UISpinner and faces-config.xml generated

Listing 14-9 shows a snippet from the generated UISpinner class.

Listing 14-9. UISpinner class

```
public class UISpinner extends AbstractSpinnerComponent{
    public static final String COMPONENT_FAMILY="javax.faces.Input";
    public static final String COMPONENT_TYPE="org.richfaces.book.Spinner";
    @Override
    public String getFamily() {
        return COMPONENT_FAMILY;
    }
    protected enum Properties {
        disabled,
        maxValue,
        minValue,
        step
    }
    public boolean isDisabled() {
```

```
        Boolean value = (Boolean) getStateHelper().eval(Properties.disabled, false);
        return value;
    }
    // More component attributes accessor methods
}
```

Keep in mind that we got all this code by simply using @JsfComponent annotation as our abstract component class and only a couple of abstract getter methods annotated with @Attribute. This is all the time we are going to spend on UI-class generation. However, you can read RichFaces documentation to learn more advanced definitions. For instance, you learn that adding the fires=@Event(value=ValueChangeEvent.class,listener=ValueChangeListener.class to a @JsfComponent annotation as a parameter tells the CDK to generate additional methods for handling the ValueChangeListeners.

Creating a Component Renderer Template

Now it's time to return to the HTML template that we produced and create a renderer class that will encode the markup and script. It's also time to learn the basics of RichFaces CDK renderer templates. The template can be used for the following purposes:

- To define the markup of the component in a standard HTML format, this will be transformed to set or ResponseWriter methods in the generated renderer class.

- To allow common, renderer-specific attributes (for example, import common HTML attributes) to be added.

Now let's look at the first feature in action. The template file is a well-formed XML file that has the same structure as a JSF 2 composite component. Why not just HTML? Because similar to JSF 2 composite components, we also need an additional interface part where we can specify all renderer-related information, add imports, and so on. Also, it's already standardized by JSF and provides a convenient contract for definitions. The implementation contains an actual HTML template, which will be encoded.

Now let's go through Listing 14-10. We named the file spinner.template.xml according to CDK conventions and placed it in the src/main/resources/templates folder.

Listing 14-10. spinner.template.xml

```
<?xml version="1.0" encoding="UTF-8"?>
<cdk:root xmlns="http://jboss.org/schema/richfaces/cdk/xhtml-el"
    xmlns:cdk="http://jboss.org/schema/richfaces/cdk/core"
    xmlns:cc="http://jboss.org/schema/richfaces/cdk/jsf/composite"
    xmlns:c="http://jboss.org/schema/richfaces/cdk/jstl/core"
    xmlns:xi="http://www.w3.org/2001/XInclude">
    <cc:interface>
        <cdk:class>org.richfaces.book.renderkit.SpinnerRenderer</cdk:class>
        <cdk:superclass>org.richfaces.book.renderkit.SpinnerBaseRenderer</cdk:superclass>
        <cdk:component-family>javax.faces.Input</cdk:component-family>
        <cdk:renderer-type>org.richfaces.book.renderkit.SpinnerRenderer</cdk:renderer-type>
    </cc:interface>
    <cc:implementation>
        <span id="#{clientId}">
            <input type="text" name="#{clientId}" id="#{clientId}Input"
                value="#{getInputValue(facesContext, component)}" />
```

```
            <button type="button" id="#{clientId}Dec">&lt;</button>
            <button type="button" id="#{clientId}Inc">&gt;</button>
            <script>
               <cdk:scriptObject name="options">
                  <cdk:scriptOption attributes=" step maxValue minValue"/>
                  <cdk:scriptOption name="value" value="#{component.attributes['value']}"
defaultValue="0"/>
               </cdk:scriptObject>
               $(document.getElementById('#{clientId}')).Spinner(#{toScriptArgs(options)});
            </script>
         </span>
      </cc:implementation>
</cdk:root>
```

Let's start from the `<cc:interface>` section. The tag names explain what they do. We define the name for the generated renderer class. Then, defining that the renderer will extend the `SpinnerBaseRenderer` class (we will create it a little later), point it to the component family and specify the renderer type.

In the `<cc:implementation>` section, we copied the HTML template and added some references to component variables. As we already covered the markup during prototyping, let's move to EL definitions and the new special tags there. You should see `clientId`, `facesContext`, and `component` referenced there. The CDK template exposes these objects like implicit variables so that you can refer to them as needed in the template. You can easily reference any other object that you need in a similar manner. For that, you need to define it in the template using the `<cdk:object>` tag. (There and across the description we will point you to tags that are available in templates; later we will provide the table with detailed descriptions.)

■ **Caution** Before we continue with the description of tags, variables, and other CDK features, let us caution you about an important piece in the code that is not directly related to CDK or JSF. `name="#{clientId}"` should be used as an input element to make the value of the input passed request parameters properly. Don't forget that the simple requirement of HTML forms writing your components means that you don't spend much time debugging your decode() methods.

Input value gets encoded using `#{getInputValue(facesContext, component)}` method call. In fact, we are showing you a way to calling methods from superclass (we will define that method in `SpinnerBaseRenderer`). You might want to write any other utility methods and refer from the template as it is done for the value attribute.

Most interesting to us are the `<cdk:scriptObject>` and `<cdk:scriptOption>` tags. Considering that most rich components provides interactive UI using JavaScript, we will describe those tags used to initialize the JavaScript objects separately.

The `<cdk:scriptObject>` tag allows creating a hash map from the parameters defined using `<cdk:scriptOption>` tags for further referencing JavaScript statements in the template.

We have two script options. One of the options uses the `attributes` attribute to reference `step`, `maxValue`, and `minValue` component attributes. In this case they will be placed into a map with the same names, and the values will be retrieved from the component object. That's one way to insert a set of attributes into a JavaScript options map.

The second option shows you the way to output a single option. In fact, in our case we might output value using the first tag in the same way. We wanted to demonstrate an alternative and more flexible usage. We define any `name` using a corresponding attribute (and not use the same name that the attribute is using). We define defaultValue (in case it's not defined on a base component class using @Attribute or the class doesn't exist) and reference the value with any valid EL expression. In our case we are referencing the component using an implicit variable and getting value from the component attributes map.

That object is actually presented using LinkedHashMap in renderer Java code. In order to properly output it as a parameter to our client object initialization method, we should reference the toScriptArgs(hashMap) utility method. It's a method from org.richfaces.renderkit.RenderKitUtils class .

■ **Note** In our initialization script block, instead of using $('#id') as the prototype, we wrapped the #{clientId} with the getElementById() document JavaScript method. That is done in order to avoid escaping colons, which are added by naming containers (for example, the client id could be 'form:id' and jQuery will fail to process such a selector).

That's all for the template. But, we are not ready to build the project yet. We referenced, but did not implement, the base class for the renderer. Again, it's not required in simple cases. We wanted to show you how to add methods to the base class and reference from templates in case you need some utility staff defined in Java code. Listing 14-11 shows that class. It should be placed in the org.richfaces.book.renderkit package.

Listing 14-11. Shows the class

```
@ResourceDependencies({ @ResourceDependency(name = "jquery.js"),
@ResourceDependency(library = "org.richfaces.book", name = "spinner.js") })
public abstract class SpinnerBaseRenderer extends InputRendererBase {
    public void decode(FacesContext context, UIComponent component) {
        String clientId = component.getClientId(context);
        Map<String, String> requestParameterMap =
            context.getExternalContext().getRequestParameterMap();
        String newValue = (String) requestParameterMap.get(clientId);
            if (null != newValue) {
                AbstractSpinnerComponent input = (AbstractSpinnerComponent)
                    component;
                input.setSubmittedValue(newValue);
            }
    }
    public Object getConvertedValue(FacesContext context, UIComponent
        component, Object val) throws ConverterException {
        return InputUtils.getConvertedValue(context, component, val);
    }
    public String getInputValue(FacesContext context, UIComponent component)
        throws ConverterException {
        return InputUtils.getInputValue(context, component);
    }
}
```

We did two things in Listing 14-11. First, we declared two @ResourceDependency annotations to reference the scripts we are using. In fact, you do not need a base class for that. It could be done in the template using tags in the interface. But, now you know how to do it the other way as well. Also, note that we do not declare any library for jQuery dependency. That's because we plan to use the component in the RichFaces environment and the RichFaces resource handler automatically picks that resource from bundled ones (as jQuery is a base library used in RichFaces).

In case you're not using it, consider declaring library for spinner.js according to standard JSF 2 rules, and add it to component resources. According to our resource dependency annotation, spinner.js should be placed in the org.richfaces.book library. So let's draw our attention from server-side code for a moment to copy spinner.js, which we used as a prototype to the src\main\resources\META-INF\resources\org.richfaces.book\ folder in our project.

The second thing is the actual code that we implemented. We defined the decode() method for our component and added the utility method used in our renderer template. Now, let's look closer to the methods introduced.

The decode() method is used on any input JSF component to process all the changes and events from the client-side and maps them the server-side component instance and raises corresponding server-side events. The decode() method retrieves the value from request map and stores it in the UISpinner submitted value property. As UISpinner extends UIInput, the value will be validated and updated according to a standard JSF UIInput contract.

There are two more methods in the base class. getConvertedValue() overrides the UIInput method, which is called during process validation to convert it prior to validation. The getInputValue() method is referenced in the template to render value in the <input> tag. Both of them call utility methods in org.richfaces.component.util.InputUtils. These methods perform conversions according to the type of server-side properties used as value binding with default converters. So if we use the int or Integer property in the bean as our component value, the component will try to convert it using javax.faces.convert.IntegerConverter.

Now we are ready to build the project. We hope that you also get a "Build successful" message in your Maven log. The result after the build should look as shown in Figure 14-6.

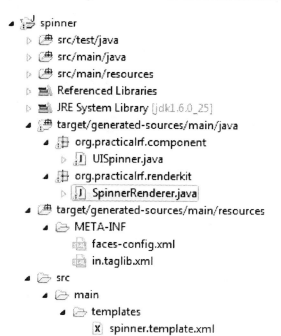

Figure 14-6. Project structure after renderer and taglib generated in Eclipse

---

■ **Note** Rebuilding the project using Maven is required every time changes occur in the Abstract component class or when the template or faces-config (if used instead of abstract class) is changed. This should be done in order to have a UI-component class and renderer re-generated correspondingly. When updating only utility methods code or resource files, it's usually sufficient to restart the server.

If we will look in the org/richfaces/book/renderkit package in the target/generated-sources/main/java folder, we can open a new SpinnerRenderer.java class. We will not provide a full listing of the generated renderer because it's large. Listing 14-12 is a snippet of encode.

Listing 14-12. Encode

```
@Override
public void encodeEnd(FacesContext facesContext, UIComponent component) throws IOException {
  ResponseWriter responseWriter = facesContext.getResponseWriter();
  String clientId = component.getClientId(facesContext);
  responseWriter.startElement("span", component);
  {
    String value = clientId;
    if (null != value && value.length() > 0) {
      responseWriter.writeAttribute("id", value, null);
    }
  }
  responseWriter.startElement("input", component);
  {
    String value = convertToString(clientId) + "Input";
    if (null != value && value.length() > 0) {
      responseWriter.writeAttribute("id", value, null);
    }
  }
  //More encode code for buttons and script including script object creation.
}
```

The encodeEnd method will contain all the necessary code, and some utility methods as well. You should now be able to tell how much easier it is to write (and much more important to maintain) your renderer encode portion in the XML template using just HTML code.

As you also see in the Figure 14-6, we also have a VDL configuration (in.taglib.xml) generated.

CDK Renderer Template Tags and Other Features

As promised, we will give you an overview of the available CDK template tags. Table 14-4 provides summary of the most important cdk: tags available for usage in a <cc:interface> section.

Table 14-4. Tags Available in the <cc:interface> Section

Tag	Description
`<cdk:class>`	Full-qualified Java class name for generated renderer.
`<cdk:superclass>`	Full-qualified Java class name for generated Renderer superclass. That class should extend `javax.faces.render.Renderer`, and can be used to put `decode()`, some logic and helper methods. By default if that tag is not used, the generated renderer extends `javax.faces.render.Renderer` class.
`<cdk:component-family>`	JSF component family id, used to associate renderer with component.
`<cdk:renderer-type>`	JSF Renderer type assigned to the generated renderer.
`<cdk:renders-children>`	Boolean value that will be returned from the `getRendersChildren()` method.
`<cdk:import>`	Defines additional Java import directives for the generated class. Has next attributes—`package`, `names` (comma separated names for imported classes) and `static` (allows you to generate an "import static" directive).
`<cdk:import-attributes>`	Allows CDK to import the attributes definition from the JSF configuration file fragment, the same as used by the `@JsfComponent#attributes`. The `src` attribute should contain a URL for that fragment.
`<cdk:resource-dependency>`	Defines JSF resource used by the component. Resource defined by that element added to `@ResourceDependencies` annotation for generated type. Attributes available are the same as for annotation.

▨ **Note** Table 14-4 lists the most important attributes as of writing of this book. For updates and new attributes in CDK, visit the JBoss Community RichFaces web site at `http://jboss.org/richfaces`.

Table 14-5 describes the tags that could be used in the <cc:implementation> section. (To save space and time, we will not mention tags already described in earlier Listings.)

Table 14-5. *Tags Available in <cc:implementation> Section*

Tag	Description
<cdk:body>	Allows you to separate the template into parts. All the content before the tag will be generated in the encodeBegin() method. All the content declared inside the <cdk:body> tag is compiled into statements of the encodeChildren() method. And all content declared after the <cdk:body> tag is compiled into statements of the encodeEnd() method. If that tag doesn't exist in template at all the content is rendered in the encodeEnd() method.
<cdk:call>	Arbitrary method invocation statement. Useful when you have some rendering method in abstract class and need to call it to encode some dynamical piece of component.
<cdk:switch> <cdk:case> <cdk:default>	Used to construct Java switch statement. All the expressions should be evaluated into valid code for switch statement. Switch tag uses key attribute, and case tag using values attribute.
<cdk:object>	Introduces new variable (The same as implicit facesContext and component). Variable's scope is limited to the context of the current method, i.e. variables defined before <cdk:body> are not available after it.

The last group of tags that should be mentioned are JSTL tags, which you are probably already familiar with. Currently CDK supports <c:forEach>, <c:choose>, <c:if>, <c:otherwise>, and <c:when> tags.

CDK templates tags also allow two special attributes to be used in any HTML tag. The first attribute is cdk:passThroughWithExclusions, which renders all attributes allowed for an HTML element except ones defined in attribute value (space separated list). CDK expects that component attribute name to be the same as in HTML. That's useful to render single-element components or for the root element. We added to our span as follows:

```
<span cdk:passThroughWithExclusions="id class">
```

This tells CDK to encode all <span> HTML attributes using the same named attributes at the component. That's why it's most useful only for the root element (style, dir, lang, and others should be applied to the root element of the component).

The second attribute is cdk:passThrough. As opposed to cdk:passThroughWithExclusions, it renders all attributes defined in its value (a space-separated list). If component and HTML attributes have the same name, it's typed as is. Otherwise, the developer can provide a component attribute name separated by a colon, for example:

```
<span cdk:passThrough=" style class:styleClass"/>
```

This means render component style attribute as HTML style, and component#styleClass as HTML class.

You should now be able to write templates of any complexity with options such as using special CDK tags, having implicit variables, the ability to define custom variables, and the facility to call the methods from your common classes. We will add a few enhancements a little later using some of these features.

Creating a Sample Application

We will add a number of enhancements to our custom component. Right now, it's not using any styles and has no client event handlers. But before we do that, let's create a RichFaces project in which we use the spinner component.

We will use the `richfaces-archetype-simpleapp` archetype, which is provided by RichFaces. Listing 14-13 creates a new RichFaces project.

Listing 14-13. Using the `richfaces-archetype-simpleapp` archetype

```
mvn archetype:generate
  -DarchetypeGroupId=org.richfaces.archetypes
  -DarchetypeArtifactId=richfaces-archetype-simpleapp
  -DarchetypeVersion=4.0.0.Final
  -DgroupId=org.richfaces.book
  -DartifactId=spinner-sample
  -Dversion=1.0-SNAPSHOT
```

In Listing 14-14 we add spinner dependency to the sample pom.xml.

Listing 14-14. Adding a spinner dependency

```
<dependency>
  <groupId>org.richfaces.book</groupId>
  <artifactId>spinner</artifactId>
  <version>1.0-SNAPSHOT</version>
</dependency>
```

Open the project you are using in IDE. Because we are not using the m2eclipse plug-in with JBoss Tools, we need to generate the Eclipse project descriptors using a simple Maven call, as follows:

```
mvn eclipse:eclipse –Dwtpversion=2.0
```

We can import our code into Eclipse as an existing project. The extra parameter that you see tells Maven to generate additional descriptors for the WTP web-project facet.

■ **Tip**   After a sample import, we removed the spinner JAR entry set to a Maven repository from library dependencies in project properties (Java build path) and pointed it to the spinner project from the workspace instead, as shown in Figure 14-7. We made the same change in the "Deployment assembly" list. This way, we won't need to refresh/rebuild the sample itself after changing the spinner; it will be done by the IDE.

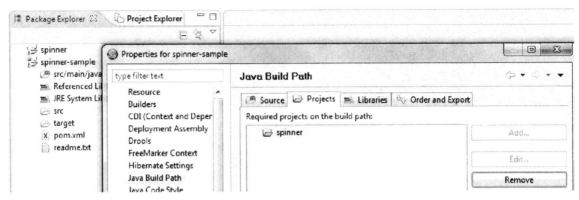

Figure 14-7. Using spinner project as a dependency in Eclipse

■ **Caution** Importing a project without m2eclipse while working in JBoss Tools 4.0.0.GA will cause you to get `src/main/java` listed twice in a deployment assembly list for projects generated by a RichFaces archetype. It will result in classes not properly deployed. To prevent this, you need to remove the occurrence targeted to the context root, shown highlighted in Figure 14-8.

Properties for spinner-sample

Web Deployment Assembly

Define packaging structure for this Java EE Web Application project.

Source	Deploy Path
src/main/webapp	/
src/main/java	/
src/main/java	/WEB-INF/classes

Resource
Builders
CDI (Context and Depender
Deployment Assembly
Drools
FreeMarker Context

Figure 14-8. Erroneous entry while using Eclipse WTP

We are now set and can deploy the project (we used Tomcat 7 as the default Maven project configuration generated by the archetype defined).

But before running it, we will add the spinner component to the index.xhtml page in the sample WebContent folder, as shown in Listing 14-15.

Listing 14-15. Add the spinner component to index.xhtml page

```
<!DOCTYPE html PUBLIC "-//W3C//DTD XHTML 1.0 Transitional//EN"
"http://www.w3.org/TR/xhtml1/DTD/xhtml1-transitional.dtd">
<html xmlns="http://www.w3.org/1999/xhtml" xmlns:h="http://java.sun.com/jsf/html"
xmlns:f="http://java.sun.com/jsf/core"  xmlns:ui="http://java.sun.com/jsf/facelets"
xmlns:a4j="http://richfaces.org/a4j" xmlns:prf="http://org.richfaces.book/spinner">
```

```
<body>
<ui:composition template="/templates/template.xhtml">
    <ui:define name="title">RichFaces Sample</ui:define>
    <ui:define name="body">
    <prf:spinner value="50"/>
    </ui:define>
</ui:composition>
</body>
</html>
```

Notice the namespace declared is one that we defined in `package-info.java` for the tag library. After deploying the project, running Tomcat, and pointing the browser to `http://localhost:8080/spinner-sample/` our spinner is rendered, and clicking on buttons will cause the value to be changed, as shown in Figure 14-9.

Figure 14-9. *Spinner component rendered*

Go ahead and try the component with different values, bind it to a bean property, and perform a submit. It should all work.

Adding Common Attributes

We would like to enhance our component to add encoding of styling, event, and other standard attributes. Turns out it's pretty simple to do. We won't even make changes to the `AbstractSpinner` class, defining all those standard attributes using getters marked with `@Attribute`. At first it's rather annoying to do that repetitive work for standard properties. And what is more important, it could be the cause of some mistakes and is hard to maintain. As all those attributes are renderer-specific, it would be more logical to group them somehow and, ideally, even add them at renderer-template level. We are able to do so using CDK.

Most of the standard HTML and JSF attributes are already available as common, reusable, JSF-configuration, XML fragments (faces-config CDK extensions) in CDK, so we will do it using the `<cdk:import-attributes>` tag in the template. And if you prefer this way, can still add them in abstract class using the `attributes` attribute of the `@JSFComponent` annotation. It also allows reusable config parts inclusions.

Let's look at one of the XML fragments from CDK (`core-props.xml`) in Listing 14-16.

Listing 14-16. *XML fragments from CDK*

```
<?xml version="1.0" encoding="UTF-8"?>
<cdk:properties xmlns:xi="http://www.w3.org/2001/XInclude"
    xmlns:cdk="http://jboss.org/schema/richfaces/cdk/extensions"
    xmlns:xsi="http://www.w3.org/2001/XMLSchema-instance"
    xmlns="http://java.sun.com/xml/ns/javaee">
    <property>
        <description>CSS style(s) to be applied when this component is rendered.</description>
        <display-name>CSS Styles</display-name>
        <icon />
```

```
      <property-name>style</property-name>
      <property-class>java.lang.String</property-class>
      <property-extension>
         <cdk:pass-through>true</cdk:pass-through>
      </property-extension>
   </property>
   <property>
      <description>Space-separated list of CSS style class(es) to be applied when this element
is rendered.
         This value must be passed through as the "class" attribute on generated
markup.</description>
      <display-name>CSS Style Classes</display-name>
      <icon />
      <property-name>styleClass</property-name>
      <property-class>java.lang.String</property-class>
      <property-extension>
         <cdk:pass-through>false</cdk:pass-through>
      </property-extension>
   </property>
   <!--more attributes definitions>
</cdk:properties>
```

■ **Note** We will not list all common fragment file names because the list is rather long. We just want to make sure that you are aware that they exist and know that using them will make development simpler. Refer to CDK documentation at `http://jboss.org/richfaces` to get a complete file list and listings.

When we include the XML in template or abstract class, corresponding attributes will be added to a generated component class. You're free to create your own XML fragments to reuse some attributes across similar components.

Let's see how it works. We need to add the next set of tags to our `spinner.template.xml` `<cc:interface>` section, as shown in Listing 14-17.

Listing 14-17. Adding tags to spinner.template.xml <cc:interface>

```
<cdk:import-attributes src="urn:attributes:events-props.xml"/>
<cdk:import-attributes src="urn:attributes:core-props.xml"/>
<cdk:import-attributes src="urn:attributes:i18n-props.xml"/>
<cdk:import-attributes src="urn:attributes:focus-props.xml"/>
<cdk:import-attributes src="urn:attributes:input-props.xml"/>
```

Now let's build the spinner and check the result in UISpinner.java generated class. Note that we are getting even more than expected, except for new attributes in the properties map, you can easily see that our class now implements ClientBehaviorHolder and provides the implementation of interface methods. So all the events like change, keyup, and so on are now available as behavior events.

Interested in how that was achieved? It's pretty simple; CDK makes the decision whether there are any client behavior events according to the events' definitions (doesn't matter if using the @Attribute annotation or a JSF configuration file fragment) and defines event name (using @EventName or `<cdk:event-name>`) property. If at least one such attribute is found, the component is marked as the client behaviors holder and corresponding attributes are added to a behavior events map.

So the only thing remaining for the attribute to be useful is to use them in an HTML template in the `<cc:implementation>` section in order for them to render on the page.

We will add most of the attributes to show you how it works. Let's change the beginning of our template implementation section, as shown in Listing 14-18

Listing 14-18. Changing the beginning of the template implementation section

```
<cc:implementation>
<span id="#{clientId}"  class="#{component.attributes['styleClass']}"
   cdk:passThroughWithExclusions="id class">
   <input type="text" name="#{clientId}" id="#{clientId}Input" cdk:passThrough="onchange"
      value="#{getInputValue(facesContext, component)}"/>
```

Note the `styleClass` encoded using a corresponding attribute at the `<span>` element and all the pass-through attributes except `id` and `class` are encoded there too. Also note that the component change event attribute will be encoded in the `<input>` element.

Now let's build the spinner in order for the renderer to be re-generated, and update the sample application code as shown in Listing 14-19.

Listing 14-19. Update sample application code

```
<h:form>
  <prf:spinner value="50" styleClass="fooClass">
    <a4j:ajax event="change" />
  </prf:spinner>
</h:form>
```

Let's examine the source HTML code generated in the result (visually the result will be the same). Listing 14-20 shows how our component code now looks on the client.

Listing 14-20. Component code

```
<span class="fooClass" id="j_idt7:j_idt8">
   <input id="j_idt7:j_idt8Input" name="j_idt7:j_idt8" type="text" value="50"

onchange="RichFaces.ajax(this,event,{"parameters":{"javax.faces.behavior.event":"change",
      "org.richfaces.ajax.component":"j_idt7:j_idt8"} ,"sourceId":this} )" />
   <button id="j_idt7:j_idt8Dec" type="button">&lt;</button>
   <button id="j_idt7:j_idt8Inc" type="button">&gt;</button>
   <script>
      $(document.getElementById('j_idt7:j_idt8')).Spinner({"value":"50"} );
   </script>
</span>
```

Notice the `fooClass` encoded at the `<span>` element, and the Ajax behavior for the change event encoded in our `<input>`.

Implementing the Disabled State

Implementing this feature is pretty simple. All we need to consider is the `disabled` attribute, which was added as one of the common inputs attributes from the `input-props.xml`.

We will implement it using JSTL tags support in the renderer template and rendering corresponding property to input and buttons using HTML attributes. See Listing 14-21 for `<cc:implementation>` section changes.

Listing 14-21. `<cc:implementation>` section changes

```
<cc:implementation>
<span id="#{clientId}" class="#{component.attributes['styleClass']}"
    cdk:passThroughWithExclusions="id class">
    <input type="text" name="#{clientId}" id="#{clientId}Input"
        cdk:passThrough="onchange" value="#{getInputValue(facesContext, component)}"
        disabled="#{component.attributes['disabled']?'disabled':''}" />
    <button type="button" id="#{clientId}Dec"
        disabled="#{component.attributes['disabled']?'disabled':''}">&lt;</button>
    <button type="button" id="#{clientId}Inc"
        disabled="#{component.attributes['disabled']?'disabled':''}">&gt;</button>
    <c:if test="#{not component.attributes['disabled']}">
        <script>
            <cdk:scriptObject name="options">
                <cdk:scriptOption attributes="step maxValue minValue" />
                <cdk:scriptOption name="value" value="#{component.attributes['value']}"
defaultValue="0" />
            </cdk:scriptObject>
            $(document.getElementById('#{clientId}')).Spinner(#{toScriptArgs(options)});
        </script>
    </c:if>
</span>
</cc:implementation>
```

As you can see, we added simple conditions for disabled attributes on elements. We wrapped the script declaration with `<c:if>`, which checks the disabled state because we do not want any scripts to be attached to our component in the disabled state. Now let's change the declaration of the spinner in the sample to have disabled="true" set (keeping the `<a4j:ajax>` behavior defined as in the previous sample) and check the HTML output, as shown in Listing 14-22.

Listing 14-22. HTML output

```
<span id="j_idt7:j_idt8" class="fooClass">
    <input type="text" value="50" name="j_idt7:j_idt8" id="j_idt7:j_idt8Input"
        disabled="disabled">
    <button type="button" id="j_idt7:j_idt8Dec" disabled="disabled">&lt;</button>
    <button type="button" id="j_idt7:j_idt8Inc" disabled="disabled">&gt;</button>
</span>
```

Except proper attributes encoded and script not being rendered, the client behaviors (our `<a4j:ajax>`) are also ignored. This looks absolutely correct as the disabled component is not supposed to fire any events.

Figure 14-10 shows the rendered component on the page when disabled.

Figure 14-10. Spinner component disabled

Skinning the Spinner Component

Finally, it would be a good idea to encode at least a few styles for the spinner to improve its look and feel, and make it consistent with the other RichFaces components, and again show RichFaces' skins in action.

As shown in Listing 14-23, let's add the stylesheet with the `spinner.ecss` name to our `\META-INF\resources\org.richfaces.book\` folder (the same where the script is placed).

Listing 14-23. Stylesheet with `spinner.ecss`

```
.practrf-sp {
    border-width: 1px;
    border-style: solid;
    border-color: '#{richSkin.panelBorderColor}';
    display: inline-block;
    font-size: 1px;
    white-space: nowrap;
}
input.practrf-sp-inp[type="text"] {
    background-color: '#{richSkin.controlBackgroundColor}';
    border: 0px;
    color: '#{richSkin.generalTextColor}';
    font-family : '#{richSkin.generalFamilyFont}';
    font-size : '#{richSkin.generalSizeFont}';
    margin: 0px;
    padding: 0px;
    vertical-align: top;
}
button.practrf-sp-dec, button.practrf-sp-inc{
    background-color:  '#{richSkin.headerBackgroundColor}';
    background-image:none;
}
```

> ■ **Note** We qualified our CSS selectors with `<input>` and `<button>` element names in order to overwrite the standard skinning classes, if standard elements skinning was enabled. By applying at the same time as the standard skinning classes, these selectors will have a higher priority.

Now, we need to encode this resource with the component by adding the following to the `SpinnerBaseRenderer` after the `spinner.js` dependency declaration:

```
@ResourceDependency(library = "org.richfaces.book", name = "spinner.ecss")
```

The class encoding should be added to our `spinner.template.xml` template, as shown in Listing 14-24.

Listing 14-24. Adding class encoding to template

```
<span id="#{clientId}" class="practrf-sp #{component.attributes['styleClass']}" ...>
    <input id="#{clientId}Input" class="practrf-sp-inp"... />
    <button id="#{clientId}Dec" class="practrf-sp-dec"...>&lt;</button>
    <button id="#{clientId}Inc" class="practrf-sp-inc"...>&gt;</button>
    ...
</span>
```

We now need to enable skinning in our test application (by default the RichFaces Maven archetype project doesn't generate any skin parameter in web.xml). Let's pick emeraldTown, as shown in Listing 14-25.

Listing 14-25. Enabling skinning

```
<context-param>
    <param-name>org.richfaces.skin</param-name>
    <param-value>emeraldTown</param-value>
</context-param>
 <context-param>
    <param-name>org.richfaces.enableControlSkinning</param-name>
    <param-value>false</param-value>
</context-param>
```

Note We disabled standard skinning, which is on by default, so that it would not interfere without skinning properties added (buttons and inputs could be affected by it). Now, we can check results in a "clean environment." Of course, as we continue working, we should turn it back on to check that all our styles are still applied and properly redefining standard skinning styles.

We now rebuild the spinner project, refresh the sample, and publish and check the result. It should render like Figure 14-11.

Figure 14-11. Skinned spinner component

By following this approach, you can add additional styling to the custom component.

Summary

As you can see from the results, RichFaces CDK makes is very easy to build rich, custom components. With CDK, we have a readable, HTML-based template that has about 30 lines of code, a small and simple basic renderer class, and a fairly basic abstract class. As a result, we have the UISpinner component class implementation, which has about 400 lines of code and performs all the basics, such as evaluating component attributes properly, storing with StateHelper, and implementing the ClientBehaviorHolder interface.

We now have a renderer class generated, which contains more than 250 lines of code and performs everything needed with component encoding, including the proper encode of behavior events.

Finally, we have large faces-config.xml and taglib.xml files generated without any significant effort.

The RichFaces Component Development Kit tool is one of the RichFaces development team's biggest achievements. It is worth being used by all JSF component developers—even if you are not using the components from rich:* tag library, but need to create your own custom component.

Index

CPSIA information can be obtained at www.ICGtesting.com
Printed in the USA
LVOW050125280911

248173LV00010B/6/P